# The Evolving Landscape of Ethical Digital Technology

# The Evolving Landscape of Ethical Digital Technology

## Simon Rogerson

CRC Press
Taylor & Francis Group
Boca Raton  London  New York

CRC Press is an imprint of the
Taylor & Francis Group, an **informa** business
AN AUERBACH BOOK

Dedicated to my post-millennial grandchildren,

Austin Charlie Haines, Faye Hilary Haines and Amber Anne Haines.

They are the future.

# Contents

## PART III   PRODUCT

## PART IV FUTURE

# PART V EDUCATION

# Foreword

## Chuck Huff

15 January 2021

In a world that is awash in ubiquitous technology, even the least tech-savvy know that we must take care of how the technology affects individuals and society; that governments and organizations around the world now focus on these issues; that universities and research institutes in many different languages dedicate significant resources to study the issues; and that international professional organizations having adopted standards and directed resources toward ethical issues in technology is in no small part the result of the work of Simon Rogerson. That we today have an international, interdisciplinary group of scholars to help us grapple with the complexity of not only the web but also the Internet of Things; the intricacies and reach of social networking apps; autonomous, artificially intelligent robots and weapons; and the myriad other issues technology raises is, again, in part the direct and indirect result of the tireless, idealistic, and open-hearted work of Simon Rogerson.

It is evident in this volume of collected essays that Prof. Rogerson has made groundbreaking contributions to the study and practice of digital ethics in his career. What is less evident in these pages is his role as a colleague, mentor, organizer and teacher, and the spreading ripples of influence of all those he has supported. If you look for it here, you can find traces in passages where the ETHICOMP conference is discussed and even in the organization of the book. But in the same spirit with which he hopes to institutionalize digital ethics in IT methods, Simon has institutionalized many welcoming and supportive forums for practitioners and researchers. This, too, is part of the change we need to integrate ethical vision into technology.

I hope this praise for Prof. Rogerson serves as an introduction to the personality behind the papers collected here and allows the reader to see a connecting thread of concern for not just the stakeholders of any technology but also his careful gardening of the community that is needed to illuminate the issues and implement solutions.

I would like to highlight three themes here that one can find stitching together Prof. Rogerson's career and these papers. First, that a particular, and unfortunately rare, kind of practical interdisciplinarity is needed to blend what we know with how we design and implement technology. Second, that this interdisciplinarity needs to extend to a multi-level system of influence that includes grassroots organizing and pressure, organizational culture building, and governmental guidance and regulation. And third, that the practical challenge of influencing the design and implementation of technology across its vast expanse is just at its beginning.

Work in digital ethics has almost always been interdisciplinary. The earliest founder of the field, Norbert Weiner, foresaw that the field would need to be massively interdisciplinary (Bynum, 2008). This proved right, of course, and the field(s) has seen significant contributions from anthropologists, computer scientists, economists, mathematicians, philosophers, psychologists and sociologists. Prof. Rogerson's background in practical software development, however, has led him to a peculiar kind of interdisciplinarity. He uses ideas from all the disciplines mentioned earlier, but applies them in the practical considerations of designing and implementing real computing artifacts. Much of the field is prone to fall back into its disciplinary silo, generating "generalizable knowledge" about abstract entities (organizations, work groups, social roles, virtues, justice, etc.). But in both his own authorship and his organizational work, Simon is fixedly focused on the practical, using abstract knowledge as it is helpful. This is not only driven in part by his professional proclivities but also by his evident empathy for users and other stakeholders of failed computer systems. You will find evidence for this practical and compassionate interdisciplinarity in every paper – even when it goes deep into the weeds of software design methodology, the people who might be helped or harmed are firmly in focus.

Because of this human-focused approach, Prof. Rogerson rightly sees that the interdisciplinarity needs to extend to all the levels of social influence that might help us grapple with the issues. For this reason, the guestlist for his signature ETHICOMP conference always includes, in addition to the usual academic suspects, people from government, corporate and grassroots backgrounds. You will find perspicacious comments on the necessary role of each of these levels throughout the book.

CODA:

"Falsehood flies, and the truth comes limping after it."

–Jonathan Swift

"The arc of the moral universe is long, but it bends toward justice."
–Dr. Martin Luther King Jr.

Finally, a word about where we are on this journey, and what success might look like. The two widely quoted aphorisms above are two sides of how we might think about progress in getting digital ethics broadly and successfully integrated into most actual software design.

In Chapter 21, Prof. Rogerson asks whether the work of the last 20 years had an effect on IT practice, and concludes: "Sadly, on balance the answer … seems to be no." His argument is compelling – in comparison to the vast scale of IT globally, the movement to integrate ethical concern into design is still quite small. There is still inattention or apathy toward ethical design and sometimes even resistance. IT surely flies ahead, while ethical design limps laboriously after it.

What might success look like? Prof. Rogerson's goal of widespread integration of digital ethics in design is surely the right one. But successes in any social change movement are always partial, incomplete, and require constant critique and amendment. For instance, what we today call "participatory design" has been stripped of most of its revolutionary, democratic fervor and goals (Bødker et al., 2000; Spinuzzi, 2002). As its methods have been both adopted and adapted over time, it lost its focus on strong critique of capitalist exploitation of labor and became a toolbox of methods for designing software that worked better because it took user's understandings into account. This falls short of the goal, but is still in progress.

The practical and visionary wisdom of MLK offers a horizon of hope. Any social change movement takes time, and impatience may even be a virtue for those pursuing justice. Grassroots, organizational, and governmental action can continue to bend the arc. The arc of the moral universe only bends when we urgently and persistently exert pressure on it. Digital ethics still has but a short history behind it and Prof. Rogerson documents some positive signs of how the arc is bending. That inclination is in no small part because of his work.

**Chuck Huff, PhD**, is a professor of social psychology at Saint Olaf College in Northfield, Minnesota. He received his PhD in social psychology from Princeton University in 1987 and was an NIH post-doctoral fellow with the Committee for Social Science Research in Computing at Carnegie Mellon University. His research includes moral psychology, the psychology of spirituality, gender and computing, the social and ethical issues of computing, and teaching computer ethics.

# References

Bødker, S., Ehn, P., Sjögren, D. & Sundblad, Y. (2000). Co-operative design—perspectives on 20 years with 'the Scandinavian IT Design Model'. *Proceedings of NordiCHI 2000: Oct 23-25*, pp. 22–24.

Bynum, T. W. (2008). Norbert Wiener and the rise of information ethics. In: van den Hoven, J. & Weckert, J. (eds.), *Information Technology and Moral Philosophy*. Cambridge Studies in Philosophy and Public Policy. Cambridge, Cambridge University Press, pp. 8–25. doi:10.1017/CBO9780511498725.002.

Spinuzzi, C. (2002). A Scandinavian challenge, a US response: methodological assumptions in Scandinavian and US prototyping approaches. *SIGDOC'02*.

# Chapter 1

# Introduction

1995 was the year when Apple launched its first WWW server, Quick Time On-line. It was the year Microsoft released Internet Explorer and sold 7 million copies of Windows 95 in just 2 months. On 28 March 1995, I opened the first ETHICOMP conference with these words:

> We live in a turbulent society where there is social, political, economic and techno-
> logical turbulence it is causing a vast amount of restructuring within all these orga-
> nisations which impacts on individuals, which impacts on the way departments are set
> up, organisational hierarchies, job content, span of control, social interaction and so
> on and so forth.... Information is very much the fuel of modern technological
> change. Almost anything now can be represented by the technology and transported
> to somewhere else. It's a situation where the more information a computer can process
> the more of the world it can actually turn into information. That may well be very
> exciting but it is also very concerning.

It could be describing today. Little did I realise that 25 years on, these issues would be still at the forefront of how ethical digital technology can be developed and utilised.

*The Evolving Landscape of Ethical Digital Technology* covers a 25-year period from 1995 to 2020 when the social and ethical issues surrounding digital technology have become increasingly important in a technologically dependent world. This anthology of my work, as illustrated by 25 papers, is interdisciplinary and links theory to practice. The aim is to demonstrate what has evolved over 25 years of technological advances. It is therefore essential that these papers have been included (wherever possible) in their original forms. In many respects, it is the natural follow-on to *Computer Ethics and Professional Responsibility* which I co-edited alongside Terry Bynum.

## Repeating Concepts, Observations and Insights

During this 25-year period, much has changed in terms of both the technology and attitudes towards the technology. However, this has been a challenging time (and continues to be so) because the societal ramifications of digital technological evolution are often unknown, misunderstood, ignored, or dismissed. In addressing this issue, ongoing research findings must be presented in a suitable form to audiences comprising those who can influence the manner in which digital technology is developed and deployed. This could lead to changing attitudes, which will increase the likelihood that ethical digital technology will prevail.

Kroenig, McAdam and Weber (2010) explain that the change of attitude occurs through effective communication which the recipient is persuaded by because of authorship credibility and content of the communicated message. They explain that repetition of a communication enhances comprehension and retention. Miller and Levine (2019) explain that persuasion involves an intentional communicative act that excludes force and achieves acceptance. For the academic researcher who desires to make a positive contribution to society, the successful act of persuasion of influential others is one of the hardest challenges to overcome.

Throughout civilised time, there have been many who have extolled the value of history in looking towards the future. Indeed, Polybius, who was a Greek historian of the Hellenistic period and died in c. 118 BC, expressed optimism that practical lessons concerning military technology and strategy could be successfully transmitted through studying history (Moore, 2020). Haddon et al. (2015) explain that history is a source of invaluable knowledge concerning context, concepts, infrastructure, paradigm shifts and different perspectives. In addition, accounts of historical disasters also provide invaluable knowledge. These sources of knowledge hold true for digital technology policy and development.

Within the 25 papers chosen for this anthology, the reader will discover some repetition of parts of previously published papers. This was done, at the time of original publication, for the reasons discussed previously. Thus, sections of papers were repeated to:

- enhance comprehension and retention as well as reach different audiences; and
- emphasise the lessons to be learnt from history and ensure historical contexts are understood.

Chapter 9 was written in 2001. It brought together many different strands of research and practical application to create a comprehensive landscape of ethical digital technology. In this landscape, the reader will find sections from previous chapters repeated as they legitimately create pieces of the whole jigsaw. This approach and indeed some of the materials can be found in later landscape papers such as *The Virtual World: A Tension between Global Reach and Local Sensitivity* (Chapter 20) written in 2004, and *Future Vision* (Chapter 21) written in 2015. Some of these repeated concepts, observations and insights suggest there is much work to be undertaken by the partnership of academics, developers and policy makers in addressing longstanding ethical challenges related to digital technology.

Chapter 6 is a clear demonstration of the value of history and how there is much to gain from reviewing the evolving technological landscape rather than restricting the review to only digital technology. Chapter 17 includes a historical thought experiment about the concentration camps. Part of this experiment is repeated in Chapter 26 to demonstrate the value of such thought experiments in digital technology education.

The anthology is structured into five themes: Journey, Process, Product, Future and Education. Each theme commences with an introductory explanation of the papers, their relevance and their interrelationship. The anthology finishes with a concluding chapter that summarises the key messages and suggests what might happen in the future. This chapter includes insights from some younger leading academics who are part of the community charged with ensuring that ethical digital technology is realised.

A synopsis of each chapter now follows. Each chapter heading includes the year of first publication. These synopses provide an overview of the anthology showing how, in total, a landscape has evolved, which has currency as well as historical integrity.

# Part I: Journey

The first part of the anthology groups together the papers which provide an overview of ethical digital technology over time. It provides a context for the remaining four parts.

## Chapter 2: Cyberspace: The Ethical Frontier [1995]

The information revolution has become a tidal wave that threatens to engulf and change all that humans value. Governments, organisations and individual citizens, therefore, would make a grave mistake if they view the computer revolution as "merely technological." It is fundamentally social and ethical. This chapter explores this problematic landscape.

## Chapter 3: But IS IT Ethical? [1995]

Society and its organisations have undergone, and are undergoing, restructuring through the widespread use of IS/IT. The technological and economic rates of change related to IT are still increasing. This restructuring affects department structures, organisation hierarchies, job contents, span of control, social interaction and so on. Each aspect of this impact has an ethical dimension which cannot and should not be ignored otherwise there will be an unacceptable penalty incurred in applying IS/IT in the wrong place, in the wrong way or at the wrong time. There is a need to develop goals, social objectives and a moral framework within which the technologies can be applied in an acceptable manner. This chapter provides some guidance on how to address such issues for those working in the industry.

## Chapter 4: Information Ethics: The Second Generation [1996]

Those responsible for the development and application of computer technology are faced with decisions of increasing complexity which are accompanied by many ethical dilemmas. Such issues have attracted the attention of researchers from many disciplines resulting in a broad body of knowledge albeit quite shallow in places. Given the vital role information systems (IS) professionals have in technology application, IS-focused research, which addresses the ethical dimension, must be undertaken. The pioneering work of the first generation of computer ethics is reviewed. This work has tended to be conceptual and more of a commentary on computer phenomena rather than an attempt to develop strategies to identify and address societal and ethical issues associated with IS and the underpinning information technology. The new era of information ethics is discussed in terms of its conceptual and application dimensions. Illustrations of ethical concerns within project management and systems development are used to demonstrate the dilemmas faced in IS practice due, in the main, to a lack of theoretical ethical underpinning. It is argued that information ethics research will have an impact on many of the ten sub-domains of IS as defined by the UK Academy of Information Systems as well as many of the Economic and Social Research Council's Thematic Priorities. Effective research is reliant upon the combined knowledge and expertise of disciplines that include IS, philosophy, sociology, law and computer science.

## Chapter 5: A Review of Information Ethics [2010]

This chapter focuses on the ethical perspective of information and communication technologies (ICTs) known as information ethics. It discusses the foundation of information ethics focusing on the work of Norbert Wiener which is then followed by an overview of the key definitions of information ethics. This in turn leads to a discussion on the practical relevance of information ethics for the strategists, developers and implementers of ICT. Three key issues of privacy, property and crime are considered from an ethical standpoint.

## Chapter 6: Towards a Chronological Taxonomy of Tourism Technology: An Ethical Perspective [2018]

As tourism has evolved, it has continued to utilise technological advances. There appear to be many ethical issues associated with technology usage in tourism evolution. Preliminary analysis of this evolution is undertaken using archival source materials and face-to-face interviews. An illustrative case study is used to investigate tourism links with technological advances and highlighting potential ethical issues related to such links. This initial study demonstrates the existence of a rich tourism technology history hitherto scarcely investigated. A method to structure the associated data is developed linking tourism, technology and ethics. This is an initial study which aims to generate interest in this new area. As such the data collected is limited and the new structure is embryonic. This is a new area of investigation, Tourism Technology Ethics. The outline Chronological Taxonomy is novel and potentially valuable across all empirical research disciplines.

# Part II: Process

This part considers the activities involved in delivering digital technology systems. It focuses on the ethical and social issues which surround such activity and how these issues need to be identified and addressed.

## Chapter 7: The Ethics of Software Development Project Management [1996]

It appears universally accepted that the most effective way to develop software is through the use of a project-based organisational structure which encourages individuals to participate in teams with the goal of achieving some common objectives. Much has been written about the management of software development projects and no doubt much will be written in the future. The purpose of this chapter is to examine whether project management practice effectively caters for the ethical issues surrounding the software development process. For the sake of clarity, only one project management approach is discussed. The aim is to tease out fundamental issues and not to dwell on the nuances of a particular approach.

## Chapter 8: An Ethical Review of Information Systems Development: The Australian Computer Society's Code of Ethics and SSADM [2000]

The rapid advance of computer-based technology has led to social policy vacuums. Most IS development tools concentrate upon technical issues, and offer few, if any, guidelines that address the moral issues inherent in new application possibilities. It is argued that the extension of such tools to include ethical and moral, human and environmental issues is possible. A good starting point is provided by mapping relevant clauses of professional codes of ethics upon each stage of the development methodology. The Australian Computer Society Code of Ethics and the Structured Systems Analysis and Design Method (SSADM) are used as examples.

## Chapter 9: A Practical Perspective of Information Ethics [2001]

Information is the new lifeblood of society and its organisations. Our dependence on information grows daily with the advance of ICT and its global application. The integrity of information relies upon the development and operation of computer-based IS. Those who undertake the planning, development and operation of these IS have obligations to assure information integrity and contribute to the public good. This chapter addresses these issues from three practical perspectives within the field of information ethics. First, the manner in which strategy is formulated and the dilemmas that might arise are considered. This is followed by a discussion as to how an ethical dimension might be added to the project management of computing applications. Finally, the methods used for IS development are reviewed from an ethical standpoint. These issues are important to information engineers and software engineers who are now playing a key role in the running of modern organisations.

## Chapter 10: Responsible Risk Assessment with Software Development: Creating the Software Development Impact Statement [2005]

Limiting the focus of risk analysis to quantifiable factors and using a narrow understanding of the scope of a software project are major contributors to significant software failures. A Software Development Impact Statement (SoDIS) process is presented which extends the concept of software risk in three ways: (1) it moves beyond the limited approach of schedule, budget and function; (2) it adds qualitative elements; and (3) it recognises project stakeholders beyond those considered in typical risk analysis. As the types of risks increase, the range of stakeholders that need to be considered also expands. Using this expanded view of risk analysis reduced or eliminated the impacts of many previously undetected risks of software development. The SoDIS process and its software associate development tasks with relevant stakeholders through the application of structured questions. This process was incorporated effectively into the software development life cycle and applied to software development projects in different domains on several continents. The successes of the SoDIS process provide strong evidence that a significant side-effect of narrowing project objectives is a root cause of ICT project failures.

## Chapter 11: Information Systems Ethics – Challenges and Opportunities [2019]

The purpose of this chapter is to explore the ethical issues surrounding IS practice with a view to encouraging greater involvement in this aspect of IS research. Information integrity relies upon the development and operation of computer-based IS. Those who undertake the planning, development and operation of these IS have obligations to assure information integrity and overall to contribute to the public good. This ethical dimension of IS has attracted mixed attention in the IS academic discipline. The authors of this chapter are a multidisciplinary team providing a rich, diverse experience which includes professional and information ethics, management IS, software engineering, data repositories and IS development. Each author has used this experience to review the IS ethics landscape, which provides four complementary perspectives. These are synthesised to tease out trends and future pointers. It is confirmed that there is a serious lack of research being undertaken relating to the ethical dimension of the IS field. There is a limited crossover between the well-established multidisciplinary community of Computer Ethics research and the traditional IS research community. An outline framework is offered which could provide an opportunity for rich and valuable dialogue across the two communities. This is proposed as the starting point for a proactive research and practice action plan for IS ethics.

# Part III: Product

This part includes examples of digital technology at different points of the digital technology timeline. Each example is subjected to some form of ethical review.

## Chapter 12: The Social Impact of Smart Card Technology [1998]

The application of information technology continues to expand in terms of diversity of use and the number of people using it. The impact is significant for individuals, organisations, nations and the world as a whole. This chapter focuses on smart card technology which is being applied in various ways to facilitate trade, gain access to services and products, verify identity and establish and influence relationships. The chapter starts with a review of the technology which includes typical applications from different countries. These cases are then analysed in terms of social costs and benefits. Illustrative guidelines are provided which might increase the chances of sensitive applications of smart cards. Examples of socially beneficial applications are given to illustrate how the technology might be used to good effect.

## Chapter 13: A Moral Approach to Electronic Patient Records [2001]

This chapter seeks to establish a morally appropriate balance between the various moral standards that are in tension in the field of Electronic Patient Records (EPRs). EPRs can facilitate doctor-patient relationships; however, at the same time, they can undermine trust and harm the doctor-patient relationship. Patients are becoming increasingly reluctant to tell their own doctor everything that is relevant. A number of moral principles and the question of consent to release of records are considered here. There is also explicit mention of the principles for the treatment of the EPRs of the deceased. A number of tensions between principles are explored, including that between privacy and promotion of welfare, both in an emergency and in more routine situations. The discussion also includes the tension between access and the right not to know about a condition that may undermine, for example, self-esteem; and the tensions between principles that arise when epidemiology, public health surveillance and healthcare evaluation are conducted. Suggestions are made about an appropriate balance between the principles. It is suggested that the patient's right to informed consent should be dominant.

## Chapter 14: Internet Voting – Well at least It's "Modern" [2003]

This was the first journal paper to give a systematic security analysis of vulnerabilities of Internet voting in public elections. It draws upon "… the laudably thorough Technical Options Report by

Ben Fairweather and Simon Rogerson at De Montfort" (www.vnunet.com/itweek/analysis/2086828/commentexperimental-voting-leaves-nasty-aftertaste). Disanalogies between voting and banking are described, and the 2002 electronic voting pilots were critiqued. The Electoral Commission heeded the advice for caution, suspending electronic voting pilots between 2003 and 2007, and has subsequently taken on board criticism in the paper that security analysis of pilots is needed.

## Chapter 15: Digital Existence – The Modern Way to Be [2018]

This is an interpretative viewpoint blending perspectives to form a composite view of digital existence. This chapter uses philosophy, sociology and linguistics within an ethnographic framework of contrasting cultural and cultural artefact views. Digital being and the relationship between physical and virtual are discussed. Evidence suggests acceptance of the virtual world as a location of coexistence. How technology has merged with humans so that humans have become more than their organic selves is examined. In a virtual world, digital existence is achieved through Daseinian avatars and so the concept of self is explored. There then follows a broader discussion about the online world which leads into how these new technologies become accepted by individuals and society. The influence of mass media is considered in this context. This is followed by a short analysis of the vocabulary used to describe the online world. The chapter ends with a call to rethink how to view and react to the online world. Existing positions are challenged as being inappropriate given the analysis undertaken.

## Chapter 16: Is Professional Practice at Risk Following the Volkswagen and Tesla Revelations? [2017]

With the world in economic crisis, the headlong drive for efficiency and effectiveness together with resulting profit is the watchword. Such pressure might have resulted in real gains but has also led to unscrupulous or reckless actions. The tempering of such drive with ethical consideration is often neglected until there is a detrimental event causing public outcry which in turn places pressure on the actors to account for the reasons the event had occurred. This cause and effect map is commonplace. The Volkswagen emissions scandal and Tesla Motors public beta testing of the Autopilot software in their cars illustrate the drive for efficiency and effectiveness without proper ethical consideration. This chapter focuses on the role of software engineers in such situations. An ethical analysis of the two cases is presented using the Software Engineering Code of Ethics and Professional Practice. The findings, together with previously published analyses, are used to draw general conclusions and recommendations about the efficacy of the software engineering profession.

## Chapter 17: The Dangers of Dual-Use Technology: A Thought Experiment Exposé [2019]

Dual-use technology can be used for both civilian and military purposes. As ICTs evolve so the scope for dual-use increases. This can often occur unheeded. Thought experiments are used to explore the possible dangers of dual-use technological advances that could occur in the absence of effective ethical scrutiny. Free and Open-Source Software (FOSS) is an ethical hotspot in this context. Therefore, two thought experiments are used to acquire new knowledge about the dangers of FOSS components which could have dual usage in the context of a fictitious system which is unethical and societally catastrophic. This exposé provides an argument to justify a new approach in education and awareness relating to all aspects of computing for the whole population.

### *Chapter 18: Grey Digital Outcasts and COVID-19 [2020]*

This chapter investigates the relationship between the COVID-19 pandemic and digital technology with specific focus on the elderly who are acknowledged as being the most vulnerable group in this global health emergency. Actions and inactions relating to grey digital outcasts are analysed through a snapshot study, using a heuristic approach, of ten countries, including China, the United Kingdom and United States. These analyses are used to tease out common global themes and issues. The chapter concludes with a set of guiding principles which lays the foundation for a global response to supporting grey digital outcasts, particularly in times of crisis.

## Part IV: Future

This part comprises three chapters written in 1998, 2004 and 2015, respectively. Together, they offer a vision of how ethical digital technology might be achieved and what challenges need to be addressed.

### *Chapter 19: E.Society – Panacea or Apocalypse? [1998]*

As society becomes more and more dependent on the ICTs inevitably there will be winners and losers, cost and benefits. It is unclear who will prosper and who might be at risk. What is clear, however, is that society will never be the same again. Popular opinion appears to be in favour of electronic everything – is this justified and do we have a choice? This chapter examines some of the trends of the so-called information age and suggests what society expects, gets and deserves can be very different.

### *Chapter 20: The Virtual World: A Tension between Global Reach and Local Sensitivity [2004]*

Society, its citizens and its organisations are becoming more dependent upon technology and its global application as the means of providing information and obtaining services in a virtual world. This chapter considers some of the issues surrounding a virtual world of global reach yet still having to be locally sensitive. It challenges current thinking and concepts on the basis that we have a new dimension to our person through our Internet existence. Strategic guidance is suggested in an attempt to realise the potential of the technology while supporting cultural tolerance.

### *Chapter 21: Future Vision [2015]*

This chapter reviews the world of ICT from its early days to the near future. The aim is to consider how successfully academia, industry and government have worked together in delivering ethically acceptable ICT which is accessible to those who might benefit from such advances. The chapter concludes with suggestions fof a fresh approach for the future. Evidence is drawn from the history of computers, funded research projects, professional bodies in the field, the ETHICOMP conference series and reported ICT disasters. The author uses his experience as both an ICT practitioner and an academic in the ICT ethics field to synthesise the evidence, so providing a foundation on which to build an outline global action plan. The chapter lays out the findings that there has been much detailed observation and analysis of the ethical challenges surrounding ICT but the transformation of this into widespread practical positive action remains elusive. It explores why progress has been difficult. This review of the interconnecting landscapes of practical ICT, funded research and the ICT ethics community is new. The attempt to demonstrate what progress has been made and to identify the underlying factors which influence progress are valuable to future generations working in this area. The concluding suggestions for action offer a starting point for entering the next phase of ICT ethics.

# Part V: Education

This final part focuses on how to provide effective digital ethics education and awareness. This includes provision for students, professionals and the public.

## Chapter 22: Preparing to Handle Dilemmas in the Computing Profession [1996]

Society in general and organisations in particular are becoming more dependent upon computer technology. Those responsible for the development and application of computer technology are faced with decisions of increasing complexity which are accompanied by many ethical dilemmas. This chapter explores how the combination of formal training through, for example, case study analysis and informal support through, for example, Ethics Circles, can help to ensure that computer professionals within organisations are equipped to handle the ethical dilemmas which they will inevitably face daily.

## Chapter 23: Preparing IT Professionals of the Future [2014]

The underlying aim that should be instilled in future IT professionals is to deliver fit-for-purpose systems which accommodate recipients' needs rather than recipients having to adapt to systems. Those entering the IT profession today are faced with a plethora of application areas using a vast array of technological armoury. The responsibilities of young IT professionals and their obligations to society are onerous. Yet it is uncertain how well they are prepared for such challenges and whether they have been educated to understand that they are the custodians of the most powerful and flexible technology mankind has invented. This chapter discusses the types of challenges to be faced; the practical tools that might be used in addressing such challenges and the style of educational preparation that could be used. The aim is to provide the stimulus to rethink the manner in which we should prepare IT professionals of the future.

## Chapter 24: Using Technology to Incorporate Students' Work-Based Experiences into a Blended Learning Environment [2008]

This chapter disseminates the experience in using a software-supported learning framework, called Experiential Learning Via Industrial Stories (ELVIS), which exists as part of a compulsory final-year undergraduate module for computer science and software engineering sandwich students. The module is designed to enhance the transformation of students from learners into mature and competent practitioners on graduation. ELVIS is a tool to help this transformation, by enabling students to share their experiences drawn from the world of work. The chapter discusses the

ELVIS framework, its current implementation, the software tools and procedures used and current levels of student engagement.

## Chapter 25: Poetical Potentials: The Value of Poems in Social Impact Education [2020]

For the technologist, it is easy to remain in safe technological enclaves with a bespoke language, a community of like minds and a familiar knowledge base. However, progress requires pushing the boundaries, thinking beyond the traditional and the ordinary, and questioning accepted norms. It requires the opening of minds. It may surprise the reader that poetry can offer the key to unlock the closed mind. This potential is explored through a variety of poems dealing, in a novel manner, with the social impact of technology.

## Chapter 26: Start a Revolution in Your Head! The Rebirth of ICT Ethics Education [2020]

This chapter is a viewpoint rather than grounded in research. It questions some of the established ICT norms and traditions which exist both in industry and academia. The aim is to review current ICT ethics educational strategy and suggest a repositioning which aligns with the concept of computing by everyone for everyone. Professional bodies, in their current role, have little influence on 97% of global software developers whose ethical code and attitude to social responsibility come from elsewhere. There needs to be a radical change in how the ethical and social responsibility dimension of ICT is included in education of the whole population rather than focusing on the elitist computing professional community. It is against this backdrop that this chapter explores new avenues for widening education, both formal and informal, to all those who may become involved in computing. The discussion concludes by laying out a new pathway for ICT ethics education which embraces people of all ages and all walks of life.

## Chapter 27: Landscape for the Future

The anthology concludes with this synthesis. Recurring themes across the 25 chapters are drawn upon. Lessons to be learnt from past generations of digital technology are discussed. Some suggestions are put forward as to what the future focus should be. This includes the views of five leading younger scholars involved in aspects of digital ethics research.

## References

Haddon, C., Devanny, J., Forsdick, C. & Thompson, A. (2015). *What is the Value of History in Policymaking*. Institute for Government, Arts and Humanities Research Council.

Kroenig, M., McAdam, M. & Weber, S. (2010). Taking soft power seriously. *Comparative Strategy*, 29(5), 412–431.

Miller, M. D. & Levine, T. R. (2019). Persuasion. In: Stacks, D. W., Salwen, M. B. & Eichhorn, K. C. (eds.), *An Integrated Approach to Communication Theory and Research*, 3rd Edition. Routledge, pp. 261–276.

Moore, D. W. (2020). Learning from history. In: *Polybius: Experience and the Lessons of History*. Brill, pp. 70–91.

# JOURNEY

*The information society continues to expand and those responsible for the policy, development and application of computer technology are faced with decisions of increasing complexity which are accompanied by many ethical and social dilemmas.*

(Simon Rogerson, 1998, p. 586)

The first part of the anthology groups together five papers which provide an overview of ethical digital technology over time. It provides a context for the remaining parts.

With a background in commercial systems development, I was, and remain, focused on the proper design and use of digital technology. By 1994, I had come to realise that proper meant not only efficient and effective but also ethical. It was at that time I first met Terry Bynum and together we embarked on a journey of research collaboration, which founded the acclaimed ETHICOMP international conference series following the highly successful ETHICOMP95. ETHICOMP95 was when the Centre for Computing and Social Responsibility was launched; Terry and I continued our collaboration as he became CCSR's first visiting professor. The first three chapters of Part 1 reflect that early collaboration.

The fourth chapter of Part 1 fast forwards to 2010. It is a review of the interdisciplinary field which, by that time, was being referred to as information ethics. It portrays a complex landscape of technologies, applications and ethical issues. The reader will sense that much has changed since 1995 and that the ethical dimension of digital technology has expanded with increasing utilisation and dependency.

One of the confusions, on this journey along ethics related to digital technology, is terminology. In the 1980s, this field was known as computer ethics. The combination of new research and new thinking together with evolving technology has led to the field, in part or as a whole, being termed: information ethics, IT ethics, software ethics and ICT ethics. These terms are often used by different people to mean different things. The term *digital ethics* is used in this book as a transdisciplinary field which includes all types of digital technology and all forms of related activity.

Digital ethics is not a new term. One of the first mentions, in the literature, of this term was by Mercedes (1996, p. 50) who wrote, "It is imperative that digital ethics be an important consideration in the development and refinement of emerging technologies. The computer can be an empowering tool when used intelligently and with much forethought." This paper is about the digital manipulation of photographs. The manipulation of photographs has occurred since the 1860s but technology has made it easier to undertake and conceal. A prime example of this was in 2004 when a potentially damaging, digitally manipulated picture was published in the news media showing the then Senator John Kerry and Jane Fonda sharing a stage at an anti-war rally emerged during the 2004 Presidential primaries as Senator Kerry was campaigning for the Democratic nomination. The picture was eventually identified as a fraud but had it not John Kerry's political stance might have been irreparably changed and his political involvement curtailed. At the time of writing, it has just been announced that US President-elect Joe Biden is to nominate John Kerry, who was one of the leading architects of the Paris climate agreement, as his climate envoy. This example illustrates how digital ethics spans many fields – in this case: technology, ethics, art, politics, history, journalism and climatology.

This leads to the final chapter of Part 1 which, at first, might seem out of place. It discusses the use of emerging technology in tourism which parallels Mercedes' paper, albeit in a different field. The historical technological journey arrives at a cutting-edge destination of, for example, the Internet of Things and Augmented Reality. Some of the ethical issues along this journey are discussed. The reason for inclusion of the paper in this part rather than elsewhere is that it illustrates how so many ethics lessons can be learnt from history for as Deborah Johnson once explained, digital technology simply creates new twists on existing ethical issues. For this reason, an important new tool on this journey is the Chronological Taxonomy which enables historical data to be systematically analysed, thus providing clues for how to deal with current new ethics twists.

# References

Mercedes, D. (1996) Digital ethics: computers, photographs, and the manipulation of pixels. *Art Education*, 49(3), 44–50.

Rogerson, S. (1998). Social values in the information society. In: *La Tecnologia dell'Informazione e della Comunicazione in Italia. Rapporto 1998* (Information and Communication Technology in Italy: 1998 Report), FTI (Italian Forum for Information Technology). Milan, Italy, Franco Angeli, pp. 586–594.

*Chapter 2*

# Cyberspace: The Ethical Frontier [1995]*

Computing technology is the most powerful and flexible technology ever devised. For this reason, it is changing everything – where and how we work, learn, shop, eat, vote, receive medical care, spend free time and make war, friends and love.

The information revolution has become a tidal wave that threatens to engulf and change all that humans value. Governments, organisations and individual citizens, therefore, would make a grave mistake if they view the computer revolution as "merely technological." It is fundamentally social and ethical.

As information technology accelerates, opportunities widen to satisfy the human thirst for knowledge, as well as the desire to be the dominant species on the globe and in the universe. But the newly-found powers of computing come at a price – dependence. Information is now the life-blood of society and its organisations, and our dependence, grows daily with the advance of the global information net and multimedia.

In the eyes of society, we exist and our needs are addressed through digital icons which represent us on the computer. National insurance numbers, driving licence numbers, bank account numbers and credit card numbers all are examples of these icons. We are reliant on such computerised icons, to be able to function successfully. Without them, we become invisible non-citizens with little hope of opportunities for success or of help in times of need.

Information, as the new life-blood of society, empowers those who have it; but it also disenfranchises those who do not. Wealth and power flow to the "information rich," those who create and use computing technologies successfully. They are primarily well-educated citizens of industrialised nations. The "information poor" – both in industrialised countries and in the third world – are falling further and further behind.

This yawning "information gap" grows steadily wider as employment opportunities, education, medical care, shopping, voting and other aspects of life move into cyberspace. The resulting inequality will lead to dissatisfaction and social turmoil.

---

* This chapter was first published as: Rogerson, S. & Bynum, T. W. (1995) Cyberspace: the ethical frontier. *The Times Higher Education Supplement.* No. 1179, 9 June. p iv. Copyright © Simon Rogerson and Terrell Ward Bynum.

**13**

The new research field of "computer ethics" examines the social and ethical impacts of information technology. In the United States, where the computer revolution is most advanced, it is already well established. There are academic journals, conferences, research centres, textbooks and university modules. In the United Kingdom, De Montfort University in Leicester recently established the Centre for Computing and Social Responsibility, which hosted ETHICOMP95 in late March of this year. This international conference on computer ethics attracted scholars from 14 nations and placed the United Kingdom at the cutting edge of computer ethics research.

Such research underpins action that must be taken not simply to harness, in a socially sensitive way, the power of the information technologies, but to survive its revolution. Action must take place on various fronts and must involve people from all walks of life.

They can focus on three topics: ethical development, ethical technology and ethical application. These three were the main themes of ETHICOMP95.

Ethical development considers the way information systems are developed. Ethical dilemmas surrounding any proposed system should be identified, debated and resolved. Professionals must be encouraged to involve their sponsoring clients and the users of the system in the development activities. In the past, the methods and practices used in developing systems were primarily oriented towards technological and economic issues. In the future, such practices should be enriched by including societal and ethical considerations. Computer professionals must act in an ethical manner that promotes socially sensitive applications.

Mary Prior of De Montfort University even suggested at ETHICOMP95 that all computer professionals should take a Hippocratic oath that commits them to work for the benefit, and not towards the destruction, of human society and the world it inhabits.

Ethical technology is concerned with the actual technologies that we use to build the systems which transfuse the information life-blood into organisations in the global community. The technologies must be scrutinised and each advance must be considered from an ethical standpoint before being applied to any business or societal problem.

Such action is not different from the safeguarding actions of many other industries such as the pharmaceutical industry, which is meticulous in considering the pros and cons of producing new drugs based on the latest medical advances. Why is this so? It is because an ill-conceived medical application can be very damaging and even life threatening to the recipient. With the advance of information technology, it is not difficult to see that it too has the potential to be very damaging and even life threatening. So, those involved must ensure that it becomes "ethical technology."

Ethical development and ethical technology are concerned with the building blocks of systems and the way those systems should be built. Ethical application is concerned with the game plan – with developing and implementing strategies that allow the technology to be applied in an ethically sensitive manner.

While small groups of individuals and organisations of all shapes and sizes can formulate strategies, it is probably the ones adopted by those responsible for public policy and legislation that will have the greatest impact on ethical application. Strategies must be in place which address a growing number of public policy questions resulting from advances and application of information technologies. Here are some of the questions that need to be addressed:

- How should society cope with resulting unemployment and underemployment?
- How should governments and businesses deal with possible exploitation of poor countries by wealthy countries and multinational conglomerates?
- How can society provide people with jobs that are interesting, fulfilling and challenging?
- How will education in cyberspace be planned, administered and financed?

- How can safeguards be introduced to ensure that the poor are not excluded from employment opportunities, education, shopping, medical care, entertainment and many more things on the global information net?

Information technology concerns especially computer professionals who design and create new information systems and devices. Recently, national and international organisations, such as the International Federation of Information Processing, the Association for Computing Machinery, the British Computer Society and the Institute of Data Processing Management, have recognised the need for new codes of ethics to inform and advise members about relevant social and ethical issues.

In the United States, the ACM has established a new committee on professional ethics; and national accrediting bodies, like the Computer Sciences Accreditation Board and the Accreditation Board for Engineering Technology, now require that accredited university curricula in the computing sciences include mandatory instruction in the social and ethical effects of information technology.

In Europe and other industrialised parts of the world, Jacques Berleur of the Facultes Universitaires Notre-Dame de la Paix, Belgium has been leading IFIP's efforts to establish a worldwide ethics code for computer professionals.

At the University of Kent in Canterbury, Duncan Langford has developed "a framework for the establishment of research ethics committees for computer science research and development." Such work is important in raising the profile of computer ethics among the professional community.

Computer ethics, however, should be the concern of everyone, not simply computer professionals. The future of society and the advancement of human values are too important to be left simply to technologists. Governments, public policy makers, organisations and private citizens must all take an interest and make their contributions. Current technology should be exploited in a socially and ethically sensitive way, and relevant strategies should be developed for future applications.

Perhaps the most radical view of the importance of computer ethics as a field of research is that of Krystyna Gorniak from the Research Center on Computing and Society at Southern Connecticut State University. She believes that computer ethics is the most important theoretical development in ethics since the Enlightenment 200 years ago.

Towering figures in ethics like Jeremy Bentham and Immanuel Kant, she says, developed their monumental ethical systems in response to a world revolutionised by printing and industrial technology. Their new and powerful ethical systems emerged from prior technological revolutions and were very appropriate to the world at the time. Now, however, in a world of teleworking and virtual-reality meetings, of telemedicine and cybersex, a powerful ethical theory must emerge to provide guidance and decision-making tools for the coming "cyber society."

Computer ethics, says Professor Gorniak, will likely be the birthplace of the next major advance in ethical theory.

If, as Professor Gorniak suggests, the ethical and social implications of information technology are so important, then why does the world at large seem to ignore them? One possible answer is that computing technology quietly seeps into our lives without being noticed. For example, in Vatican City, there is a library of magnificent, illuminated texts. But it is not the manuscripts themselves which make the greatest impression on visitors, it is the multimedia computers that allow visitors to browse digital copies of these tomes.

Paradoxically, the physical artefacts have given way to their computerised icons. This is a vivid illustration of how we have become dependent on the power and potential of information technology to provide whatever information we require in whatever format we desire without realising it. This throws a veil over the vitally important issues in computer ethics.

The brave new world of the information society – with its robots and global nets, telemedicine and teleworking, interactive multimedia and virtual reality – will inevitably generate a wide variety of social, political and ethical questions. What will happen to human relationships and the community when most human activities are carried on in cyberspace from one's home? Whose laws will apply in cyberspace when hundreds of countries are incorporated into the global network? Will the poor be disenfranchised – cut off from job opportunities, education, entertainment, medical care, shopping and voting – because they cannot afford a connection to the global information network? These and many more questions urgently need the attention of governments, businesses, educational institutions, public advocates and private individuals. We ignore ethics and computing at our peril.

*Chapter 3*

# But IS IT Ethical? [1995]*

## Introduction

Information systems and the underpinning information technologies have become very powerful change agents. At a macro level, they are capable of devastating industries, for example, the Swiss watch industry and creating new ones, for example, the video games industry. At the micro level, they are capable of creating new ways of working, for example, the automation of production lines through robotics and the integration of jobs in the office through the use of office automation systems. We now live in an information age where geographical distances have become irrelevant and where complex super corporations are being created and supported by an IS/IT life support system. Social, political, economic and technological turbulence in the sphere of operation has put organisations under a lot of pressure in responding effectively and efficiently to the needs of its clients.

Thus, society and its organisations have undergone and are undergoing restructuring through the widespread use of IS/IT. The technological and economic rates of change related to IT are still increasing. This restructuring affects department structures, organisation hierarchies, job contents, span of control, social interaction and so on. Each aspect of this impact has an ethical dimension which cannot and should not be ignored otherwise there will be an unacceptable penalty incurred in applying IS/IT in the wrong place, in the wrong way or at the wrong time. There is a need to develop goals, social objectives and a moral framework within which the technologies can be applied in an acceptable manner.

It is plain to see that the IS/IT professional through providing the information infrastructures wields great influential power over individuals within organisations. With that power goes responsibility and obligations to society, the employer, clients, colleagues and the profession. Actions founded on the ethical high ground are called for. For this to be achieved, it is important to understand the meaning of ethics so that actions can be kept under review regarding their ethical or unethical content.

---

* This chapter was first published as: Rogerson, S. (1995) But IS IT ethical? *IDPM Journal*, Vol 5, No 1, pp. 14–15. Copyright © Simon Rogerson.

## What is Ethics?

Ethics is the practice of making a principled choice between right and wrong. It is concerned with how people ought to act not how they do act. Ethics is value driven, action oriented and determined by the situation. In other words, ethics ensures that an action that is designed to achieve a certain objective will do so without violating a value. The only thing that is ever judged to be ethical or unethical is an action. The driving force in ethics is to do the right thing all the time and not to do the same thing all the time.

We need to understand that legality and ethical compliance are different. An action might be prudent and legal but may well be unethical. The development of a software system to improve the debt-collecting powers of a loan shark may be legal but is it ethical to help someone who feeds off the misery of others? Professional practice is more than simply acting to the letter of the law. This moral stance can be beneficial to organisations. The most significant input in instigating change is people and their attitudes to change. Success is more likely if influential players in the change process adopt the moral high ground rather than the legal baseline as this will promote a more favourable attitude from all those involved in the change process.

There are often situations where IS/IT activity promotes morally and ethically questionable practices, for example, the invasion of privacy, restricted practices, the unnecessary loss of jobs and the disregard for intellectual property rights. The existence of an organisational mission which links purpose, strategy, corporate values and standards provides a framework for ethical behaviour. The question is whether this behaviour is acceptable to individuals and society.

## Is Ethics an Issue?

There are numerous incidents of unethical practice occurring in IS-related/IT-related work. A recent survey of a weekly computer trade journal in the United Kingdom revealed some interesting facts on reported unethical incidents. During a 6-month period from mid-April, 1994 to mid-October, 1994, a total of 40 separate issues relating to ethics was reported. Of these, eight were general informative items, nine reported on multiple incidents of breaches and 23 reported on specific instances.

This is a serious problem which is getting some attention in the press but often when a system failure occurs or an organisation is detrimentally affected by an IS/IT event only, the technical aspects are debated. For example, in the debacle over the London Ambulance Service's new system implementation, many questions were asked concerning the technical issues but little attention was given to the ethical issues of a system which had a direct impact on the wellbeing of so many individuals.

George Edward Moore once wrote, "It appears to me that in ethics the difficulties are mainly due to the attempt to answer questions without first discovering precisely what question it is which you desire to answer." This would seem to be the case in IS/IT where reporting symptoms of unethical behaviour prevails and yet how people ought to act gains little attention. Indeed, the current focus tends to be one of outcome rather than process. A review of some of the recent literature revealed a list of issues, which includes invasion of privacy, computer viruses and hacking, computer crime, software theft and computerisation of the workplace. Discussion of how problematical are such unethical outcomes seems to preoccupy many and advice is often forthcoming on how to address these symptoms. What appears to be lacking is a discussion on the root causes and how they might be curtailed.

## An Ethical Focus for IS/IT

If we accept the need to consider the process and outcomes associated with IS/IT activity and that the current focus is heavily weighted towards symptom analysis, it would appear that to redress the balance we need to consider the process more carefully. In particular, there are three issues that warrant some attention: codes of conduct, project selection and systems development. Currently, codes of conduct are simply guidelines to which IS/IT professionals are politely asked to adhere. There are few, if any, instances where a breach of conduct has led to the rescinding of membership. When an unethical action comes to light a professional body should undertake an independent review to investigate whether any of its members are involved and what part they played in such action. For example, the recent police investigation of illegal software copying by Minstrel uncovered a large number of the software pirate's key customers in the United Kingdom. Professional bodies should now seek to ascertain whether these customers include any of their members and, if so, what was their part in these unethical transactions. In selecting projects to be funded, organisations tend to focus on economic and technical issues, little, if any, thought is given to the ethical issues raised through the commencement of a project. There are many available system development methodologies each pedalling its own particular strengths. However, the vast majority have one major weakness in that they do not have any moral dimension to them. It is totally unacceptable to assume such matters have been catered for through the established business values of the organisation in question.

The focus of ethics regarding IS/IT should comprise three dimensions. We should be concerned about how we develop systems. We should consider how advances in the technologies can be best used. Finally, we should develop strategies which promote ethical activity. This focus can be summarised by the following terms:

- Ethical Development – This is concerned with the use of development methodologies and the consideration of ethical dilemmas, user education and professionalism.
- Ethical Technology – This is concerned with the advances in technologies and the likely ethical issues they raise as they are applied to business and societal problems.
- Ethical Application – This is concerned with developing ethical strategies which allow technology to be exploited in an ethically acceptable way.

## Guiding the Individual

Barquin (1992) from the Computer Ethics Institute in the United States recently distributed a list of "dos and don'ts" entitled "The Computing Ten Commandments" as shown in Figure 3.1. It illustrates the type of action required of IS/IT professionals and demonstrates how difficult that can be at times.

The problem with this approach is that it is rule based and implies the need for legislation to regulate ethical behaviour. There are those who would argue that it is not possible to legislate ethical behaviour and therefore education must be relied upon to improve human behaviour. John McLeod cited in Parker, Swope and Baker (1990) drew up a list of generic questions to help determine the ethical nature of an action, as shown in Figure 3.2. Such a list provides practical help for IS/IT practitioners as they strive to serve society and its organisations.

Thou shalt not use a computer to harm other people.

Thou shalt not interfere with other people's computer work.

Thou shalt not snoop around in other people's computer files.

Thou shalt not use a computer to steal.

Thou shalt not use a computer to bear false witness.

Thou shalt not copy or use proprietary software for which you have not paid.

Thou shalt not use other people's computer resources without authorisation or proper compensation.

Thou shalt not appropriate other people's intellectual output.

Thou shalt think about the social consequences of the program you are writing or the systems you are designing.

Thou shalt always use a computer in ways that ensure consideration and respect for your fellow humans.

**Figure 3.1   The Computing Ten Commandments.**

To be ethical, an action should elicit a positive response to all applicable primary questions and a negative response to each clarification.

Is it honourable?

"Is there anyone from whom you would like to hide the action?"

Is it honest?

"Does it violate any agreement, actual or implied, or otherwise betray a trust?"

Does it avoid the possibility of a conflict of interest?

"Are there other considerations that might bias your judgement?"

Is it within your area of competence?

"Is it possible that your best effort will not be adequate?"

Is it fair?

"Is it detrimental to the legitimate interests of others?"

Is it considerate?

"Will it violate confidentiality or privacy, or otherwise harm anyone or anything?"

Is it conservative?

"Does it unnecessarily squander time or other valuable resources?"

**Figure 3.2   The ethical nature of an action.**

No longer can such issues be ignored; no longer can the profession seek absolution through focusing only on the technical agenda. Indeed, the first question any IS/IT professional should ask is "Is the action ethical?" and be able to answer based on reasoned thought. Geoff Walsham wrote, "If a more self-reflective and self-critical attitude on moral issues were adopted by considerable numbers of future IS analysts, the cumulative effect would be a significant and positive societal change." We all need to act and act now!

# References

Barquin, R. C. (1992) *In Pursuit of 'Ten Commandments' for Computer Ethics.* Computer Ethics Institute.
Parker, D. B., Swope, S. & Baker, B. N. (1990) *Ethical Conflicts in Information and Computer Science, Technology, and Business.* Wellesley, MA, QED Information Sciences.

## Chapter 4

# Information Ethics: The Second Generation [1996]*

## Introduction

Society in general and organisations in particular are becoming more dependent upon computer technology. Those responsible for the development and application of computer technology are faced with decisions of increasing complexity which are accompanied by many ethical dilemmas. Computer technology is a special and unique technology, and hence the associated ethical issues warrant special attention. Such issues have attracted the attention of researchers from many disciplines resulting in a broad body of knowledge albeit quite shallow in places. The growing interest in this area is due, primarily, to a lingering concern that computer professionals are unable, ill-prepared or simply ambivalent to consider ethical issues that occur in their work. There is increasing evidence that computer professionals do not recognise when and where ethical issues present themselves. Given the vital role information systems professionals have "in the gathering, processing, storing, distributing and use of information and its associated technologies, in society and organisations" (UKAIS, 1995), IS-focused research, which addresses the ethical dimension, must be undertaken.

The research to date has tended to be undertaken within single disciplines. There has been little multi-disciplinary work which has resulted in, for example, philosophical offerings being weak in the detailed knowledge of the technology while offerings from within IS and computer science have often lacked sufficient philosophical underpinnings. This may be the reason why according to Maner (1996), "Joseph Behar, a sociologist, finds computer ethics diffuse and unfocused." and why "Gary Chapman, when he spoke to the Computers and Quality of Life Conference in 1990, complained that no advances had been made in computer ethics." This situation is changing. The authors of this chapter represent a genuine partnership between IS and philosophy, and recent papers by the influential IS researchers Walsham (1996) and Wood-Harper et al. (1996) exhibit strong theoretical ethics foundations.

---

* This chapter was first published as: Rogerson, S. & Bynum, T. W. (1996) Information ethics: the second generation. *UK Academy for Information Systems Conference – The Future of Information Systems.* Copyright © Simon Rogerson and Terrell Ward Bynum.

This chapter samples the progress made in this area during the last 15–20 years. It is suggested that a change of emphasis has occurred resulting in the commencement of a second generation of research. This new information ethics era is focused on the global nature of information systems and requires multi-disciplinary research to address a growing number of associated ethical and sociological issues.

## Computer Ethics: The First Generation

According to Mitcham (1995), the evolution of computers has resulted in the emergence of at least eight ethics-related issues, which are as follows:

- the anthropological implications of artificial intelligence
- concerns about threats to individual privacy and corporate security
- the content and enforceability of ethics codes for computing
- software ownership and liability
- computer decision making
- fair public access and social power
- the character of an information society and culture
- the aesthetic-ontological interpretations of virtual realities

These issues have emerged as the result of work by computer scientists, philosophers and sociologists. Indicative work is included to provide an understanding of the breadth and depth of this area of study.

Weizenbaum (1976) suggested that there were areas of human endeavour that should be off-limits for computerisation. He stated that applications outside a pre-defined boundary ought not to be undertaken. In this way, technologists would be restricted so countering their ambivalence towards the social impact of their actions. This tendency to attempt to develop theoretical ethical rules before the identification of computer-related ethical issues had occurred led Parker to undertake empirical work using scenario analysis to ascertain the ethical and unethical practices in the computer field. The first study was undertaken in 1977 and repeated in 1990. The result of these studies was a set of ethical guidelines focused on the general public, professionals, employers and employees (Parker, Swope & Baker, 1990).

In the mid-1970s, Walter Maner coined the term "computer ethics" to refer to the application of ethics theories from philosophy to ethical problems "created, transformed or exacerbated by computing technology." He went on in the late 1970s and early 1980s to develop and present university courses, curriculum materials and faculty workshops in this new and important field of academic research (Maner, 1980). Now, 20 years later, Maner (1996) has examined and defended his original assumption that computer ethics is an academic field in its own right with unique ethical issues that would not have existed if computer technology had never been invented. He puts forward six levels of justification for the study of computer ethics, each level becoming a progressively stronger justification. These levels are as follows:

**Level 1:** The study of computer ethics will make us behave like responsible professionals.
**Level 2:** The study of computer ethics will teach us how to avoid computer abuse and catastrophes.
**Level 3:** The advance of computing technology will continue to create temporary policy vacuums.
**Level 4:** The use of computing permanently transforms certain ethical issues to the degree that their alterations require independent study.

**Level 5:** The use of computing technology creates, and will continue to create, novel ethical issues that require special study.
**Level 6:** The set of novel and transformed issues is large enough and coherent enough to define a new field.

Maner presents several examples to illustrate his argument, examples that appear to have no analogies in non-computing contexts. The failure to find satisfactory non-computer analogies, he says,

> testifies to the uniqueness of computer ethics. Lack of an effective analogy forces us to discover new moral values, formulate new moral principles, develop new policies and find new ways to think about the issues presented to us. For all of these reasons, the kind of issues presented deserve to be addressed separately from others that might at first appear similar. At the very least, they have been so transformed by computing technology that their altered form demands special attention.

It was Moor (1985) who asserted that computers are "logically malleable" in the sense that "they can be shaped and moulded to do any activity that can be characterised in terms of inputs, outputs and connecting logical operations." It was this that led Tucker (1991) to suggest that there is a need to understand the basic cultural, social, legal and ethical issues inherent in the discipline of computing. Furthermore, Moor's work influenced Gotterbarn (1992) who suggested that professionals must be aware of their professional responsibilities, have available methods for resolving non-technical ethics questions and develop proactive skills to reduce the likelihood of ethical problems occurring.

## The Scope of Computer Ethics

There is a growing body of knowledge in this area. In addition to that already mentioned, other valuable work has been undertaken, notably in the United States. The eminent philosopher Deborah Johnson (1994, 1995) is a leading authority in ethical issues. Her seminal book "Computer Ethics," now in its second edition, was the first philosophical textbook on computer ethics and was published in 1984. It was indicative, according to Mitcham (1995), "... of the shift in the philosophical community from metaphysical and epistemological discussions about computers to ethical and political ones ...." Johnson brings together philosophy, law and technology to provide an analysis of the ethical implications of widespread computer usage. She maintains that ethical issues surrounding computers are new species of traditional and recurrent moral issues. A similar stance is adopted by Spinello (1995). These types of perspectives are valuable in deriving ways to achieve IS ethical sensitivity.

Huff and Finholt (1994) have coordinated empirical research with a social science focus. They bring together research by sociologists, anthropologists, economists, political scientists and psychologists in order to inform the ethical and professional discussion related to computing. A number of useful commentaries exist on ethically charged issues. Forester and Morrison (1990) discuss major problems created in society through computer usage while Dejoie, Fowler and Paradice (1991) compiled a compendium of papers addressing the ethical and societal dilemmas of information technologies. Such commentaries while not providing guidance in resolving ethical dilemmas do provide valuable and detailed descriptions of the issues that need to be addressed.

It is interesting to note that much of the work has been concentrated in the philosophy and sociology disciplines with restricted input from the information systems and computer science disciplines. This may be the reason why Walsham (1996) has found that "... there is little published work which directly relates these [specific IS-related ethical] issues to more general ethical theory ...." The work has tended to be conceptual and more of a commentary on computer phenomena rather than an attempt to develop strategies to identify and address societal and ethical issues associated with information systems and the underpinning information technology. As a whole, this work has formed the first generation of computer ethics where conceptual foundations have been laid down. It has been a generation with a national focus on single technologies. Computer applications considered have tended to be quite restricted and mainly business oriented.

# The Dawning of a New Era

The mid-1990s has heralded the beginning of second-generation computer ethics. The time has come to build upon and elaborate the conceptual foundation while, in parallel, develop the frameworks within which practical action can occur, thus reducing the probability of unforeseen effects of information technology application.

## *The Conceptual Dimension*

Regarding the conceptual foundation, Gorniak (1996) expresses the view that computer ethics is the most important theoretical development in ethics since the enlightenment 200 years ago. Towering figures in ethics like Jeremy Bentham and Immanuel Kant, she says, developed their monumental ethical systems in response to a world revolutionised by printing and industrial technology. Their new and powerful ethical systems emerged from prior technological revolutions and were very appropriate to the world at that time. Now, however, in a world of teleworking and virtual reality, of telemedicine and cybersex, a new powerful ethical theory must emerge to provide guidance and decision-making tools for the coming "cybersociety." Computer ethics, says Gorniak, will likely be the birthplace of the next major advance in ethical theory.

This is an interesting contrast to the view expressed by Walsham (1996) who states that "... the use of ethical theory is that it provides a basis for a cumulative tradition of research and writing ..." and that "... those writing on ethical issues related to computer-based IS ... incorporate an explicit connection between their work and mainstream ethical theory." Thus, on the one hand, Gorniak postulates that considering ethical issues related to IS will change the very nature of ethical theory while, on the other hand, Walsham postulates that ethical theory simply underpins the study of ethical issues related to IS. Time will tell who is nearer the truth but both arguments do illustrate the need for a partnership between philosophy and IS in order to research the ethical dimension of IS.

## *The Application Dimension*

Turning from the conceptual dimension to the application dimension, it is clear that a comprehensive set of ethical instruments needs to be identified and developed which will promote good practice. Within computing, there are numerous activities and decisions to be made and most of these will have an ethical dimension. It is impractical to consider each minute issue in great detail and still hope to achieve the overall goal. The focus must be on the key issues which are likely to influence the success of the particular IS activity as well as promoting ethical sensitivity in a broader context. Rogerson and Bynum (1995a) define these ethical hotspots as points where activities and decision making are likely to include a *relatively* high ethical dimension.

An example ethical hotspot can be found in project management of an information system development activity. Investigating O'Connell's (1994) Structured Project Management (SPM) approach, Rogerson (1996) suggested that it is the planning element of project management which lays down the foundations on which the project ethos is built. Here, the *scope of consideration* is established, albeit implicitly or explicitly, which in turn locates the horizon beyond which issues are deemed not to influence the project or be influenced by the project. The scope of consideration is an ethical hotspot. It is a common problem with information systems development projects that decisions concerned with, for example, feasibility, functionality and implementation do not take into account the requirements of all those affected by the system once it becomes operational. This is illustrated by the cost-benefit analysis activity undertaken at the beginning of most projects. This only takes into account the interests of those involved in the analysis and does not usually consider the rights and interests of *all* parties affected by the proposed system. This view appears primarily "techno-economic" rather than "techno-socio-economic" that is often claimed.

The scope of consideration is influenced by the identification and involvement of stakeholders. Investigating 16 organisational IS-related projects led Farbey, Land and Targett (1993) to conclude that regarding the evaluation of IT investment, "… the perception of what needed to be considered was disappointingly narrow, whether it concerned the possible scope and level of use of the system, [or] the range of people who could or should have been involved …." They discovered, with the exception of vendors, all stakeholders involved in the evaluation were internal to the organisations. The implications of such restricted stakeholder involvement on achieving a socially and ethically sensitive evaluation are obvious.

The potential well-being of many individuals is likely to be at risk unless an ethically sensitive horizon is established for the scope of consideration. This horizon is more likely to occur if the principles of due care, fairness and social cost are prevalent during this activity. In this way, the project management process will embrace, at the onset, the views and concerns of all parties affected by the project. Concerns over, for example, deskilling of jobs, redundancy, the breakup of social groupings can be aired at the earliest opportunity, and the project goals adjusted if necessary.

Turning to the overall development process, there are numerous methodological approaches to information systems development. Few deal adequately with the ethical dimensions of the development process. Avison (1995) criticises the development methodologies, such as SSADM, Merise and Yourdon, that are adopted by most organisations today because they tend to stress formal and technical aspects. He argues that, "The emphasis … must move away from technical systems which have behavioural and social problems to social systems which rely to an increasing extent on information technology." He suggests that the human, social and organisational aspects are often overlooked. The consideration of this broader perspective only seems to occur in the event of systems failure or under-performance. This issue is addressed by Wood-Harper et al. (1996) who identify a number of dilemmas which a systems analyst might face when undertaking a systems development activity using a methodological approach. These dilemmas are summarised as:

- Whose ethical perspective will dominate the study of the situation and the development of the IS?
- Will ethical viewpoints be included in the study?
- What methodology should be used for the study?
- What approach should the analyst use if there is an obvious conflict of interests?

It seems clear that research is required in the generalised manner in which ethical issues can be accounted for together with the enhancement of specific methodologies. Some work has already been undertaken by Rogerson and Bynum (1995b) in developing a four perspectives model, based on Aristotle's model of ethical decision making, for the preliminary analysis and decision making at the beginning of any systems development project.

It is important to recognise that there are a few methodological approaches, notably ETHICS from Mumford (1983), Soft Systems Methodology from Checkland (1981) and Multiview from Avison and Wood-Harper (1990) that attempt to include consideration of ethical and societal issues. In evaluating ETHICS, Jayaratna (1994) suggests that, "[it] offers many design guidelines useful for the understanding and the design of human-centred systems, but ... does not offer models or ways for performing ... the steps. Nor does it offer any models for handling inter-personal and political conflicts." He concludes that, "ETHICS is committed to a particular ethical stance [and] does not offer any means of discussing or resolving many of the ethical dilemmas ... in systems development." This appears to be a recurrent criticism of such methodologies. While it is laudable that ethical sensitivity is raised as an issue worthy of investigation, the manner in which investigation is undertaken and, ultimately, an ethically defensible position derived is vague. Methodologies need to be enhanced to address these criticisms.

While methodologies provide frameworks for action, it is people who undertake the work and therefore it is people who directly influence the level of ethical sensitivity within the process and outcome of information systems development. Therefore, professional conduct is a key element of computer ethics. There are eight ethical principles regarding how computer professionals should conduct themselves (Rogerson, 1996). These principles can be found embedded in professional codes of conduct such as that of the ACM. Given the global nature of computing, it is interesting to note that the International Federation for Information Processing (IFIP) has decided to establish an "Ethics Task Group" to analyse the codes of ethics of a wide variety of its member organisations and then offer member societies non-binding advice and guidelines for the development of good codes of ethics (Berleur, 1996). Connolly (1996) argues that a kind of global ethics is necessary to the success of the information superhighway. Since national and regional laws differ widely around the world, and since laws provide only minimum standards for behaviour anyway, users of the information superhighway cannot depend only on laws to govern the behaviour of all users. The adoption of a global set of ethical rules seems to be the only way to make the information superhighway fully functional.

It is very concerning that there are numerous occurrences of unethical practice in IS-related work. A recent survey of a weekly computer trade journal in the United Kingdom revealed a total of 40 separate issues relating to ethics was reported in a 6-month period. Of these, eight were general informative items, nine reported on multiple incidents of violations and 23 reported on specific instances (Rogerson, 1995). The well-publicised failures of information systems projects at the London Ambulance Service (LASCAD), the Stock Exchange (Taurus) and Wessex Health Authority (RISP) together with the recent catalogue of software problems in "fly-by-wire" systems for aircraft are indicative of the detrimental social and ethical impact of systems improperly developed and implemented.

## *The Scope of Research*

From this range of illustrations, it appears that there is much more research to be undertaken in this area. Perhaps research to date has focused too much on causal effects and issues/phenomena identification at the expense of research resulting in usable instruments which promote ethical sensitivity within the information systems domain. Maybe this is the reason why poor IS practice appears prevalent and why methodologies such as ETHICS are relatively unpopular. This new research thrust is not simply restricted to the sub-domain defined by UKAIS (1995) as the social and cultural effects of technology-based information systems. It can be argued that this research will have an impact upon many of the ten sub-domains of information systems as defined by UKAIS. Similarly, it will impact upon the ESRC's Thematic Priorities of Globalisation, Regions and Emerging Markets; Governance and Regulation; Social Integration and Exclusion; and Human Communication and the Social Shaping of Technology. This research must embrace professional practice, user and potential user concerns, policy and strategy formulation and technological impact. Such work is multi-disciplinary. It needs the combined knowledge and expertise of disciplines that include information systems, philosophy, sociology, law and computer science. Badaracco (1992) puts forward the four questions evaluation model for decision making and action in the world of work. It comprised the following four questions:

- Which course of action will do the most good and the least harm?
- Which alternative best serves other's rights including shareholders' rights?
- What plan is personally acceptable which is consistent with the basic values and commitments of the organisation?
- Which course of action is feasible in the world as it is?

The first question deals with the morality of consequences, the second with the morality of rights, the third with integrity and the fourth with practicality. There is a correspondence between these questions and the description of the roles of an IS analyst put forward by Walsham (1993), particularly the role of moral agent which focuses on "… power and political action, social differentiation and the bias and limitations of particular language usage." Addressing Badaracco's four questions in the context of IS is the foundation for a research agenda which aims to make IS intuitively ethical and to make *ethical sensitivity* the motto of IS practitioners. To succeed locally, the research must be multi-disciplinary. To succeed globally, the research must be multi-disciplinary and multinational.

# Information Ethics not Computer Ethics

The second generation of computer ethics is better termed *information ethics*. At its heart, there is a rich, broad and rigorous conceptual platform. There is a global focus on multiple technologies that are integrated to create powerful information systems. These powerful information systems have applications in all aspects of human activity and endeavour. The social impact of information technology is growing exponentially. Computers are changing where and how we work, where and how we learn, shop, eat, vote, receive medical care, spend free time, make war, make friends and even make love. The computer revolution, therefore, is not merely technological and financial; it is fundamentally social and ethical. It is clear, therefore, that activity related to the development and the use of information systems and the underpinning information technologies must include explicit action which addresses the ethical issues surrounding the development and the use of such systems. The rise of computer ethics over the past two decades brought much-needed ethical and social perspectives to information technology. However, more and more of the world is becoming "wired." We are entering a generation marked by globalisation and ubiquitous computing. The second generation of computer ethics, therefore, must be an era of global information ethics. The stakes are much higher, and consequently considerations and applications of information ethics must be broader, more profound and above all effective in helping to realise a democratic and empowering technology rather than an enslaving or debilitating one.

# References

Avison, D. E. (1995). *What is IS?*. An inaugural lecture delivered at the University of Southampton, 3 November 1994.

Avison, D. E. & Wood-Harper, A. T. (1990). *Multiview: An Exploration in Information Systems Development*. Alfred Waller Ltd.

Badaracco, J. L. (1992). Business ethics: four spheres of executive responsibility. *California Management Review*, 34(3), 64–79.

Berleur, J. (1996). The IFIP framework for computer ethics. *Science and Engineering Ethics*, 2(2), 155–165.

Checkland, P. B. (1981). *Systems Thinking, Systems Practice*. Wiley.

Connolly, F. W. (1996). A call for a statement of expectations for the global information infrastructure. *Science and Engineering Ethics*, 2(2), 167–176.

Dejoie, R., Fowler, G. & Paradice, D. (1991). *Ethical Issues in Information Systems*. Boston, Boyd & Fraser Publishing Company.

Farbey, B., Land, F. & Targett, D. (1993). *How to Assess Your IT Investment*. Butterworth Heinemann.

Forester, T. & Morrison, P. (1990). *Computer Ethics: Cautionary Tales and Ethical Dilemmas in Computing*. Basil Blackwell.

Gorniak, K. (1996). The computer revolution and the problem of global ethics. *Science and Engineering Ethics*, 2(2), 177–190.

Gotterbarn, D. (1992). The use and abuse of computer ethics. In: Bynum, T. W., Maner, W. & Fodor, J. L. (eds.), *Teaching Computer Ethics*. Research Center on Computing and Society, Southern Connecticut State University, pp. 73–83.

Huff, C. & Finholt, T. (eds.) (1994). *Social Issues in Computing: Putting Computing in its Place*. McGraw-Hill.

Jayaratna, N. (1994). *Understanding and Evaluating Methodologies*. McGraw-Hill.

Johnson, D. G. (1994). *Computer Ethics*, 2nd Edition. Englewood Cliffs, NJ, Prentice-Hall.

Johnson, D. G., & Nissenbaum, H. F. (eds.) (1995). *Computers, Ethics, and Social Values*. Englewood Cliffs, NJ, Prentice-Hall.

Maner, W. (1980). *Starter Kit on Teaching Computer Ethics*. Helvetia Press.

Maner, W. (1996). Unique ethical problems in information technology. *Science and Engineering Ethics*, 2(2), 137–154.

Mitcham, C. (1995). Computers, information and ethics: a review of issues and literature. *Science and Engineering Ethics*, 1(2), 113–132.

Moor, J. H. (1985). What is computer ethics?. *Metaphilosophy*, 16(4), 266–279.

Mumford, E. (1983). *Designing Participatively*. Manchester Business School.

O'Connell, F. (1994). *How to Run Successful Projects*. Prentice-Hall.

Parker, D. B., Swope, S. & Baker, B. N. (1990). *Ethical Conflicts in Information and Computer Science, Technology, and Business*. Wellesley, MA, QED Information Sciences.

Rogerson, S. (1995). But IS IT ethical?. *IDPM Journal*, 5(1), 14–15.

Rogerson, S. (1996). The ethics of software development project management. *PASE'96 Conference*. University of Westminster, UK, 1–2 February.

Rogerson, S. & Bynum, T. W. (1995a) Identifying the ethical dimension of decision making in the complex domain of IS/IT. *ETHICOMP95 Conference*, UK.

Rogerson, S. & Bynum, T. W. (1995b) Towards ethically sensitive IS/IT projected related decision making. Submitted to: *COOCS'95*, Milpitas, California.

Spinello, R. A. (1995). *Ethical Aspects of Information Technology*. Prentice-Hall.

Tucker, A. (ed.) (1991). *Computing Curricula 1991: Report of the ACM/IEEE-CS Joint Curriculum Task Force*. New York, ACM Press.

UKAIS (1995). Information systems – subject definition and scope. *UK Academy for Information Systems Newsletter*, 1(3), 3.

Walsham, G. (1993). *Interpreting Information Systems in Organisations*. John Wiley.

Walsham, G. (1996). Ethical theory, codes of ethics and IS practice. *Information Systems Journal*, 6(1), 69–81.

Weizenbaum, J. (1976). *Computer Power and Human Reason: From Judgement to Calculation*. W H Freeman.

Wood-Harper, A. T., Corder, S., Wood, J. R. G. & Watson, H. (1996). How we profess: the ethical systems analyst. *Communications of the ACM*, 39(3), 69–77.

# Chapter 5

# A Review of Information Ethics [2010]<sup>*</sup>

## Introduction

Information has increasingly become the new lifeblood of society, its organisations and its peoples. The veins of data communications along which this blood circulates are the new utility of the information age. Our dependence on information grows daily with the advance of information and communication technologies (ICTs) and its global application. ICT now influences the way we live, work, socialise, learn, interact and relax. We expect the information on which we rely to be correct. The integrity of such information relies upon the development and operation of computer-based information systems. Those who undertake the planning, development and operation of these information systems have obligations to assure information integrity and overall contribute to the public good (Rogerson, 2001). This presents new challenges to the business community at large.

Johnson (1997) explains that the potential benefit of the information society is being devalued by antisocial behaviour such as unauthorised access, theft of electronic property, launching of viruses, racism and harassment. Add to that list identity theft, spam, electronic snooping and aggressive electronic marketing, and it is clear that this new society is not problem-free. Such issues raise new ethical, cultural, economic and legal questions. It is questionable whether legal or technological counter measures are and ever will be very effective in combating the ever-changing antisocial behaviour in the information society. The absence of effective formal legal or technological controls presents grave dangers for all of us (Rogerson, 2004b). Even when controls are implemented, ICT has moved on with new ethical issues often arising. In the absence of effective controls, we must rely upon ethics coupled with education and awareness. The added advantage of this approach is that it not only addresses problematic issues within the information society but also promotes its positive attributes. Such moral guidance has been called computer ethics but in this chapter it will be termed information ethics.

* This chapter was first published as: Rogerson, S. (2010) A review of information ethics. *Journal of Information and Management*, Vol. 30, No. 3, pp. 6-18. Copyright © Japan Society for Information and Management. Reprinted by permission. DOI 10.20627/jsim.30.3_6.

This chapter focuses on the ethical perspective of ICT known as *information ethics.* The discussion starts with a brief look at the roots of information ethics focusing on the work of Norbert Wiener. This is followed by an overview of the definitions of information ethics which leads to a discussion on its practical relevance. This chapter finishes by considering some of the common current information ethics issues.

## The Beginning of Information Ethics

The foundation of information ethics is to be found in the mid-1940s. This foundation lay un-appreciated for many decades and has only recently become widely accepted primarily through the scholarship of Terrell Ward Bynum (2004, 2008) who has undertaken a detailed analysis of the writings of Norbert Wiener. Through his work in cybernetics, Wiener became aware of the huge social and ethical impacts this fledgling ICT would have. Bynum (2008) explains that Wiener "predicted that after the [Second World] War, the world would undergo a second industrial re-volution – an *automatic age* with enormous potential for good and for evil that would generate a staggering number of new ethical challenges and opportunities." Bynum's analysis shows that Wiener discussed a range of information ethics-related topics which are still very relevant today. These include computers and security, computers and unemployment, responsibilities of computer professionals, computers for persons with disabilities, computers and religion, information networks and globalisation, virtual communities, teleworking, merging of human bodies with machines, robot ethics and artificial intelligence. Wiener (1950) had the insight to see ICT in the context of fundamental human values such as access, freedom, happiness, health, knowledge, life and op-portunity. This concept of core human values has been developed further by Moor (1998) where he suggests this is the essential grounding for ethical judgement related to ICT.

Wiener's enlightened view had little impact for many years perhaps because the societal in-fluence of ICT was still in its infancy. The start of a growing consciousness is illustrated by two important events. In 1976, Joseph Weizenbaum, the eminent MIT computer scientist, published his influential book *Computer Power and Human Reason* in which he examines the dangers of ICT and suggests that computers should never be allowed to make important decisions because com-puters will always lack human qualities such as wisdom and compassion. In October 1981 a group of concerned computer professionals from Xerox/PARC and Stanford University started to have meetings articulating concerns over the increasing role of computers in nuclear war and how the misuse of computers would increase the risk of nuclear war. They adopted the name "Computer Professionals for Social Responsibility" (CPSR) which is now an international organisation with chapters in over 30 countries. Its practical perspective aligns with business practice.

## Definitions of Information Ethics

According to van Luijk (1994), ethics comprises both practice and reflection. Ethical practice is the conscious appeal to norms and values to which individuals are obliged to conform, while reflection on practice is the elaboration of norms and values that colour daily activity. Norms are collective expectations regarding a certain type of behaviour whilst values are collective re-presentations of what constitutes a good society. The information ethics field considers both practice and reflection related to the development and application of ICT within society. As such it offers rich guidance to those involved in organisational ICT. It is a field of contrasting views which reflect differences in both discipline and experience of those working in the field.

Bynum and Rogerson (2004, pp. 17–20) discuss five different definitions which have credibility and together have helped shape the field.

## Maner's Definition

The name "computer ethics" was not commonly used until the mid-1970s when Walter Maner (1980) began to use it. He defined this field of study as one that examines "ethical problems aggravated, transformed or created by computer technology." Some old ethical problems, he said, were made worse by computers, while others came into existence because of computer technology. Maner (1996) showed how the key characteristics of computers have led to a series of significant ethical challenges. He suggested that we should use traditional ethical theories of philosophers, such as the *utilitarian* ethics of the English philosophers Jeremy Bentham and John Stuart Mill, or the *rationalist* ethics of the German philosopher Immanuel Kant.

## Johnson's Definition

In her book, *Computer Ethics*, Deborah Johnson (1985) claims that computer ethics studies the way in which computers "pose new versions of standard moral problems and moral dilemmas, exacerbating the old problems, and forcing us to apply ordinary moral norms in uncharted realms." Like Maner before her, Johnson adopted the "applied philosophy" approach of using procedures and concepts from utilitarianism and Kantianism. But, unlike Maner, she did not believe that computers create wholly new moral problems. Rather, she thought that computers gave a "new twist" to ethical questions that were already well known. Johnson (2004) later argues that as ICT evolves it will become increasingly integrated into the human and natural world, and consequently new profound ethical issues will arise. Johnson (2004, p. 74) claims that "as we become more and more accustomed to acting with and through [ICT], the difference between ethics and computer ethics may well disappear."

## Moor's Definition

In his seminal paper "What Is Computer Ethics?", James Moor (1985) provided a definition of computer ethics that is much broader and more wide-ranging than that of Maner or Johnson. It is independent of any specific philosopher's theory, and it is compatible with a wide variety of approaches to ethical problem-solving. Since 1985, Moor's definition has been the most influential one. He defined computer ethics as a field concerned with "policy vacuums" and "conceptual muddles" regarding the social and ethical use of information technology. Moor (1985, p. 266) wrote,

> A typical problem in Computer Ethics arises because there is a policy vacuum about how computer technology should be used. Computers provide us with new capabilities and these in turn give us new choices for action. Often, either no policies for conduct in these situations exist or existing policies seem inadequate. A central task of Computer Ethics is to determine what we should do in such cases, that is, formulate policies to guide our actions … . A difficulty is that along with a policy vacuum there is often a conceptual vacuum. Although a problem in Computer Ethics may seem clear initially, a little reflection reveals a conceptual muddle. What is needed in such cases is an analysis that provides a coherent conceptual framework within which to formulate a policy for action.

Moor (1985, p. 269) explained that computer technology is genuinely revolutionary because it is "logically malleable",

> Computers are logically malleable in that they can be shaped and moulded to do any activity that can be characterised in terms of inputs, outputs and connecting logical operations … . Because logic applies everywhere, the potential applications of computer technology appear limitless. The computer is the nearest thing we have to a universal tool. Indeed, the limits of computers are largely the limits of our own creativity.

## Bynum's Definition

In 1989, Terrell Ward Bynum developed another broad definition of computer ethics following a suggestion in Moor's (1985) paper. According to this view, computer ethics identifies and analyses the impacts of information technology on social and human values such as health, wealth, work, opportunity, freedom, democracy, knowledge, privacy, security and self-fulfilment. Solution generation is not covered by this definition. This very broad view of computer ethics employs applied ethics, sociology of computing, technology assessment, computer law and related fields. It employs concepts, theories and methodologies from these and other relevant disciplines. This conception of computer ethics is motivated by the belief that, eventually, information technology will profoundly affect everything that human beings hold dear.

## Gotterbarn's Definition

In the 1990s, Donald Gotterbarn became a strong advocate for a different approach to computer ethics. From his perspective, computer ethics should be viewed as a branch of *professional ethics,* concerned primarily with standards of good practice and codes of conduct for computing professionals. Gotterbarn (1991) wrote,

> There is little attention paid to the domain of professional ethics – the values that guide the day-to-day activities of computing professionals in their role as professionals. By computing professional I mean anyone involved in the design and development of computer artefacts … The ethical decisions made during the development of these artefacts have a direct relationship to many of the issues discussed under the broader concept of computer ethics.

With this "professional ethics" approach to computer ethics, Gotterbarn co-authored the 1992 version of the ACM Code of Ethics and Professional Conduct and led a team of scholars in the development of the 1999 ACM/IEEE Software Engineering Code of Ethics and Professional Practice.

## A Definition for Organisational ICT

Given these differing definitions, it would be useful to derive a common definition which might be useful in a business context. Therefore, information ethics is defined as integrating ICT and human values in such a way that ICT advances and protects human values, rather than doing damage to them which therefore must include the formulation and justification of policies for the ethical use of ICT and carefully considered, transparent and justified actions leading to ICT products and services.

This definition provides a foundation on which to build some clear guidance. ICT is a practical pursuit whose participants are significantly affected by ethically volatile situations (Rogerson, Weckert, & Simpson, 2000). The practice element of ethics manifests itself in methods and procedures adopted in the development of, for example, information systems. However, the reflection element of ethics manifests itself in, for example, professional codes of conduct which are concerned with establishing what are the generalised ways of working that are acceptable to a wider community. These two elements are now considered in more detail.

## ICT Practice

The ethical dimension of the ICT practice has two distinct elements: process and product. Process concerns the activities of ICT professionals when undertaking research, development and service/product delivery. The ethical focus is professional conduct. It is the focus which is typically addressed by professional bodies in their codes of conduct. The aim for professionals is to be virtuous in Aristotelian terms. In other words, a professional knows that an action is the right thing to do in the circumstances and does it for the right motive. For example, cutting profit so that more development time can be spent on making systems more accessible to those with limited ability, such as dexterity, is a virtuous action if it helps to overcome social exclusion. From a business perspective, such action is likely to improve reputation and trust which in turn increases repeat business. Process is considered in the "Professionalism" section later.

Product concerns the outcome of professional ICT endeavour. One of the issues of ICT is to avoid systems being used for inappropriate secondary reasons, for example, a security system which has been implemented to reduce the risk of property theft being used additionally to monitor employee movement. Another issue is the thirst of the ICT industry to add more and more facilities in future system releases. Both issues are illustrations of unwarranted function creep. The emphasis should be on accessibility and transparency of information systems so people can use them more easily and can understand, where necessary, how such systems work internally. One final issue regarding product is to do with the increasing use of non-human agents based on complex systems. Such agents might interact with humans, for example, those used on the Internet to enable e-trading, or they might interact with each other, for example, agents which monitor the environment and order other agents to take remedial action if necessary.

The ethics focus of the product element is technological integrity from, for example, a Kantian or utilitarian perspective. This can be addressed by embedding ethics within ICT products themselves. This might be as simple as building in "opt-in" facilities in service provision via the Internet whereby a person must ask to be informed of future service offerings rather than having to request explicitly not to receive such information by default. They might be more complex, for example, whereby a non-human agent in telecare is programmed with defined ethical principles so that it will only instigate actions which are deemed to be societally acceptable. From a business perspective, "good" products are likely to be profitable over an extended period with high volumes of sales made to a trusting customer base. Product is considered in "ICT Development" section.

## ICT Development

ICT applications are about satisfying a particular requirement or need so that people can realise, for example, some economic and/or social and/or leisure objective. Consideration of stakeholders should not be limited to those who are financing the development project or politically influential or using the developed information system but broadened to be consistent with models of ethical analysis. Stakeholder must include individuals or groups who may be directly or indirectly affected by the information system and thus have a stake in the development activities. For example, the unelected political candidate due to a poor voting machine interface is a stakeholder in the development of an electronic voting system. Similarly, anyone who suffers identity theft through a security flaw in an information system is a stakeholder, albeit indirect, of that system (Gotterbarn, Clear, & Kwan, 2008, p. 435). Those stakeholders who are negatively affected are particularly important regarding ethical sensitivity because they are often the ones overlooked.

Information systems developers must guard against the design principles where users must adapt to ICT rather than ICT being moulded to users. The Design for All (DfA) approach is a way forward. This is because DfA's perspective is one of individualism and acceptability (Stary, 2001). Roe (2007) explains that DfA is not a one-off effort but an ongoing and permanent commitment over the longer term so that throughout the design cycle of products and services the focus is always on ensuring use by the broadest possible section of the population. DfA principles must focus on understanding the potential impact on people. These people include those whose behaviour/work process will be affected by the development or delivery of ICT systems or whose circumstance/job will be affected by the development or delivery of ICT systems or whose experiences will be affected by the development or delivery of ICT systems (Gotterbarn & Rogerson, 2005, p. 741). However, it is important to recognise that identified needs are often difficult to turn into feasible and realistic design requirements and subsequent specifications. However, designers are predisposed to ignore these issues, due frequently to the lack of knowledge and supporting methodologies, guidelines and tools. Therefore, Roe (2007, p. 200) argues that in order to prevent undesired ethical impacts, it is necessary to provide designers with ethical or moral guidelines. This is not a new call. For example, Gotterbarn (1992) suggests that professionals must be aware of their professional responsibilities, have available methods for resolving non-technical ethics questions, and develop proactive skills to reduce the likelihood of ethical problems occurring.

One such approach is the Software Development Impact Statement (SoDIS) process which belongs to the family of issues-oriented approaches used in information systems development. SoDIS takes a comprehensive stakeholder perspective of the whole development cycle through considering each development task within the structured/defined plan of the information system project (Gotterbarn & Rogerson, 2005, p. 738). It expands existing information systems development quantitative risk analysis methods by explicitly addressing a range of qualitative and ethically grounded questions about the impacts of the information system from a stakeholder perspective. "The use of qualitative best practice questions associates a full range of stakeholders with the [information system] project tasks providing a comprehensive risk analysis which helps identify social, professional and ethical risks for a project. SoDIS is the first fully-developed approach of this kind. It points the way to achieving successful [information system] development ..." (Gotterbarn & Rogerson, 2005, p. 746). As Gotterbarn, Clear and Kwan (2008, p. 442) explain, "The process of developing a SoDIS requires the consideration of ethical development and the ethical impacts of [an information system] product. The SoDIS analysis process also facilitates the identification of new requirements or tasks that can be used as a means to address the ethical issues." It is this type of explicit ethical consideration from a stakeholder perspective which will reduce the risk of information system failure during implementation and/or operation. It will increase the chance of fit for purpose systems which are acceptable and adopted.

## Professionalism

ICT professionals have specialised knowledge and often have positions with authority and respect in the community. Their professional activity spans the management, development and operation of all kinds of applications. For this reason, they are able to have a significant impact upon the world, including many of the things that people value. Along with such power to change the world comes the duty to exercise that power in a socially responsible manner. Six social responsibility principles (Rogerson, 2004a) establish an ethos of professionalism within ICT. These principles are as follows:

- Develop a socially responsible culture within work which nurtures moral individual action
- Consider and support the well-being of all stakeholders
- Account for global common values and local cultural differences
- Recognise social responsibility is beyond legal compliance and effective fiscal management
- Ensure all business processes are considered from a social responsibility perspective
- Be proactive rather than reactive

Adherence to such principles can be problematic because of ICT professional relationships with other people (Johnson, 1994), including employer-to-employee, client-to-professional, professional-to-professional and society-to-professional. These relationships involve a diversity of interests, and sometimes these interests can come into conflict with each other. Socially responsible ICT professionals, therefore, have to be aware of possible conflicts of interest and try to avoid them thereby adhering to the six principles. In line with the six social responsibility general principles, specific guidance has been provided in the codes of conduct of professional bodies such as the British Computer Society (BCS), the Institute for the Management of Information Systems (IMIS) and the influential Software Engineering Code of Ethics and Professional Practice (Gotterbarn, Miller & Rogerson, 1999). In addition to such codes, professional bodies have established curriculum guidelines and accreditation requirements to help ICT professionals understand and manage ethical responsibilities.

This is because there are many ethical issues surrounding the decisions and actions within the information systems field and there are limitations on professional time to respond to such issues. An ICT professional educated in ethical responsibilities will be better placed to respond in a socially responsible manner. It is important to prioritise these issues on the basis of impact on the public good and so focus effort on the ethical hotspots (Rogerson, 1997). If businesses were to adopt this approach in their ICT activity, they would ensure they were in harmony with the society within which they exist. Three issues illustrate the typical issues faced by modern businesses.

## ICT and Privacy

Privacy is one of the earliest information ethics issues to capture public interest both across Europe and in the United States from the mid-1960s onwards. It continues to be a hot topic because privacy is a fundamental right of individuals and is an essential condition for the exercise in self-determination and the advances in technology have facilitated more incursions into privacy. Much has been written about privacy as it relates to ICT. Before ICT, privacy primarily referred to non-intrusion and non-interference but that has now changed. There are those who propose that privacy is about control over personal information (Elgesem, 1996; Fried, 1984; Miller, 1971). This is countered by an argument that control of personal information is insufficient to establish or protect privacy and that privacy is best defined in terms of restricted access rather than control (Tavani & Moor, 2001). Privacy even extends to our presence in public spaces or circumstances (Nissenbaum, 1998) with the advent of, for example, CCTV, electronic voting and government-operated data matching. The ability to restrict access to or control personal information is certainly an important factor in sustaining privacy. Collste (2008) argues that the right to privacy exists, albeit in varying degrees, across cultures as it is seen as an instrument for sustaining autonomy, freedom and personal relationships.

Organisations are increasingly computerising the processing of personal information. This may be without the consent or knowledge of the individuals concerned. There has been a growth in databases holding personal and other sensitive information in multiple formats of text, pictures and sound. The scale and type of data collected and the scale and speed of data exchange have changed with the advent of computers. The potential to breach people's privacy at less cost and to greater advantage continues to increase. It is situations like this that have led to a growing unwillingness to submit personal data to information systems. Furthermore, there is growing public discernment and demand for evaluation of ICT trustworthiness (Camp, McGrath & Nissenbaum, 2001).

Balancing the rights and interests of different parties in a free society is difficult. The acceptable balance will be specific to the context of a particular relationship and will be dependent upon trust between concerned parties and subscription to the principle of informed consent. This balance might incur the problem of protecting individual privacy while satisfying government and business needs. For example, a social services department might hold sensitive information about individuals that provides an accurate profile of individual tendencies, convictions and so on. The sharing of this data with, for example, the local education authority in cases of child sex offenders living in the area might be considered morally justified even though it might breach individual privacy. Furthermore, once personal information is digitised and entered into a computer on a network the information becomes *greased data* that can easily slip across networks and into many different computers (Moor, 1997). It leaves data shadows across the whole network. As a result, personal information may no longer be controlled and people may have unauthorised access to it. Unlike ordinary shadows, our data shadows remain long after (and often permanently) we have passed through the network of conduits in the information society. Such problems are indicative of the information society where it is the norm to hold electronic personal information about health, lifestyle, finance, buying habits, relationships, ethnicity, gender, religion, genetic makeup and much more.

## Intellectual Property

Ownership is having control of one's property with the right to use it and the right to decide whether and how others can use it. Ownership extends to intellectual property which includes, for example, stories, poems, drawings, watercolour paintings, musical recordings, paintings, photographs, computer programs, films and television programmes. Most forms of intellectual property can now have digital forms. Thus, intellectual property ownership is an important information ethics topic. At least four theories can be used when considering intellectual property rights. Locke's theory of labour argues that a person who mixes his/her labour with resources that are not owned by others, and thereby creates a product, has gained the right to own and control the resulting product. Hegel's theory of personality argues that intellectual property is an expression or extension of the creator's personality and therefore the creator has the right to control it. The utilitarian theory of ownership argues that property rights should be recognised, promoted and protected as they provide incentives for creative people to generate a continuous flow of new creations, which in turn will contribute to the greatest happiness for the greatest number of people. Finally, social contract theory views ownership as a social agreement whereby the community agrees to pass laws and create conditions that are conducive to property ownership and in return owners agree to use their property in ways that society considers appropriate.

Software ownership continues to be controversial. Johnson (1994) argues that a utilitarian framework is best for analysing software intellectual property rights because it puts the focus on deciding ownership in terms of affecting continued creativity and development of software. She argues that software developers would not invest the necessary time and significant funds if they could not get the investment back in the form of license fees or sales of software. In contrast, Stallman (1992) claims that current forms of software ownership are unjust and immoral, inflict many kinds of harm on society, and should be eliminated. Using the utilitarian theory of ownership, he concludes that current laws restrict and discourage creativity and invention and therefore should be abandoned in favour of free software. Stallman's position led to the open-source movement. These two opposing positions are described by de Laat (2005) as the private regime and public regime. The private regime is based on exclusion of outsiders. Organisations use secrecy, copyright and patents to protect their intellectual properties from imitation and theft by others. The public regime is based upon property rights being used to include others through open-source licences and regulated commons where intellectual property is freely exchanged and discussed.

Copies of digital intellectual property are identical to the originals. Owners of intellectual property can easily find they are unable to sell, lease or rent their property, thereby making a profit, because of the ease and trivial cost of creating digital copies which can be then be easily distributed and sold cheaply or even disseminated for free as was the case with Napster music file swapping and Morpheus movie swapping. This latter case of peer-to-peer software has been ethically scrutinised by Spinello (2005). He argues that those who provide peer-to-peer software are accomplices in wrongdoing if they deliberately design their software to enable illicit copying of copyrighted music and movie files.

Overall, where software contains ideas and knowledge that can benefit society as a whole, clashes can occur between the owner, who has the right to exploit the product commercially, and society which has a general right to access and benefit from it. An equitable balance must be found that takes into account these competing rights. From an ethical perspective, there are two fundamental questions that summarise this debate and that need to be answered regarding software. Who owns the software? Who has the right to modify, distribute or use it?

## Computer Crime

As ICT becomes more widely used and is used in more domains, the risk of misuse increases and the detrimental impacts of such acts are likely to be greater for society, organisations and individuals. The laws around the world have struggled to address these new forms of criminal activity. It is a classic Moorian policy vacuum which is slowly being addressed. The Convention on Cybercrime is the first international treaty seeking to address ICT-related crime. It was drawn up by the Council of Europe (2001) in co-operation with Canada, Japan and the United States, and adopted on 8 November 2001. The Convention lays out a framework within which ICT-related crime can be addressed. This framework is summarised as:

- Offences against the confidentiality, integrity and availability of computer data and information systems
  - Illegal access
  - Illegal interception
  - Data interference
  - System interference
  - Misuse of devices
- Computer-related offences
  - Computer-related forgery
  - Computer-related fraud
- Content-related offences
  - Offences related to child pornography
- Offences related to infringements of property ownership
  - Offences related to infringements of copyright and related rights

The framework provides good coverage but there are some omissions. For example, under content-related offences, it is unclear why all pornography or content which insights hatred are not included. Nevertheless, it is possible to categorise most of the incidents of ICT misuse. Parliamentary Office of Science and Technology (2006) suggests there are two types of incidents: old crimes conducted using computers as a tool and new types of crime made possible by specific types of ICT. Examples of old crimes are storage of illegal images on a hard disk instead of in print, harassment using mobile telephones, illegal downloads of music and confidence tricks involving spoof emails and fraudulent websites to acquire sensitive information known as phishing. Examples of new crimes are denial of service attacks which prevent ICT resources being available to intended users, gaining unauthorised access to an ICT system through hacking and releasing a virus to delete stored data.

While ICT-related crime is a legal consideration, it is also an ethical consideration. In creating law account must be taken of civil liberties. This is particularly important within the information society. There are civil liberties concerns about the Convention on Cybercrime. For example, the treaty allows information to be exchanged between all the national governments signing up to treaty, thus creating seamless monitoring of activities using electronic networks across Europe. The treaty's common approach fails to take into account cultural differences. An act deemed criminal in the country of the target of the crime may not be considered so in the country from which the offending act was launched. For example, the attitude towards nudity is different across cultures which have led to different legal positions on the availability of images of nudes over the Internet.

Spinello (1995) argues that organisations and individuals are ethically obliged to protect the systems and information entrusted to their care and must strive to prevent or minimise the impact of computer misuse incidents. He suggests that those stakeholders at greatest risk from a computer misuse incident might be party to decisions made concerning security arrangements. He argues that computer misuse offences should not be treated lightly, even if the detrimental outcome is negligible, because, at the very least, valuable resources will have been squandered and property rights violated. Spinello also points out that a balance has to be struck regarding stringent security measures and respect for civil liberties. Threats to business and personal computers and information assets are an everyday menace. It is essential that organisations and individual users identify the vulnerabilities and plan for corrective action to thwart these threats. Indeed, there is a dual responsibility regarding computer misuse. Organisations have a duty to minimise the temptation of perpetrating computer misuse, while individuals have a responsibility to resist such temptations. ICT professionals have a responsibility not to facilitate computer crime. For example, it is unacceptable to use programming languages which easily allow buffer overloading because this is the most common way to break into computer systems and commit offenses against confidentiality and integrity.

## Concluding Remarks

In the information society, individuals are subjected to e.junkmail, e.money, e.commerce, e.library, e.identity and e.education to mention but a few. Whether these are beneficial depends on a number of factors some of which have been discussed here. An information society that empowers everyone including those with disabilities and less fortunate members of society and sustains equality of opportunity regardless of race, colour, or creed is achievable. Governments, policy makers, developers and service providers of the information society have the wherewithal to balance global common values and local cultural differences. Businesses across the globe have an important role to play in realising an inclusive information society.

## References

Bynum, T. W. (2004) Ethical challenges to citizens of 'the automatic age': Norbert Wiener on the information society. *Journal of Information, Communication and Ethics in Society*, 2(2), 65–74.

Bynum, T. W. (2008) Computer and information ethics. In: Zalta, E. N. (ed.), *The Stanford Encyclopedia of Philosophy*, Winter 2008 Edition. Available from http://plato.stanford.edu/archives/win2008/entries/ethics-computer/ (Accessed 05 April 2009).

Bynum, T. W. & Rogerson, S. (eds.) (2004) *Computer Ethics and Professional Responsibility*. Blackwell Publishing.

Camp, J., McGrath, C. & Nissenbaum, H. (2001) Trust: a collision of paradigms. *Faculty Research Working Papers Series*. John F. Kennedy School of Government, Harvard University.

Collste, G. (2008) Global ICT-ethics: the case of privacy. *Journal of Information, Communication and Ethics in Society*, 6(1), 76–87.

Council of Europe (2001) *ETS No. 185 - Convention on Cybercrime*. Available from http://conventions.coe.int/Treaty/EN/Treaties/Html/185.htm (Accessed 26 April 2009).

de Laat, P. B. (2005) Copyright or copyleft? An analysis of property regimes for software development. *Research Policy*, 34(10), 1511–1532.

Elgesem, D. (1996) Privacy, respect for persons, and risk. In: Ess, C. (ed.), *Philosophical Perspectives on Computer-Mediated Communication*. Albany, SUNY Press, pp. 45–66.

Fried, C. (1984) Privacy. In: Schoeman, F. D. (ed.), *Philosophical Dimensions of Privacy*. Cambridge University Press, pp. 203–222.

Gotterbarn, D. (1991) Computer ethics: responsibility regained. *National Forum: The Phi Beta Kappa Journal*, 71(3), 26–31.

Gotterbarn, D. (1992) The use and abuse of computer ethics. *Journal of Systems and Software*, 17(1), 75–80.

Gotterbarn, D., Clear, T. & Kwan, C. (2008) A practical mechanism for ethical risk assessment – a SoDIS inspection. In: Himma, K. E. & Tavani, H. T. (eds.), *The Handbook of Information and Computer Ethics*. John Wiley and Son.

Gotterbarn, D., Miller, K. & Rogerson, S. (1999) Software engineering code of ethics is approved. *Communications of the ACM*, 42(10), 102–107.

Gotterbarn, D. & Rogerson, S. (2005) Next generation software development: responsible risk analysis using SoDIS. *Communications of the Association for Information Systems*, 15(article 40), 730–750. Available from http://aisel.aisnet.org/cgi/viewcontent.cgi?article=3162&context=cais.

Johnson, D. G. (1985) *Computer ethics*. Prentice Hall.

Johnson D. G. (1994) *Computer ethics*, 2nd Edition. New Jersey, Prentice Hall (3rd Edition 2000, 4th edition 2009).

Johnson, D. G. (1997) Ethics online. *Communications of the ACM*, 40(1), 60–65.

Johnson, D. G. (2004) Computer ethics. In: Floridi, L. (ed.), *Philosophy of Computing and Information*. Blackwell Publishing, pp. 65–75.

Maner, W. (1980) *Starter Kit in Computer Ethics*. Helvetia Press (published in cooperation with the National Information and Resource Center for Teaching Philosophy). [Originally self-published by Maner in 1978.]

Maner, W. (1996) Unique ethical problems in information technology. *Science and Engineering Ethics*, 2(2), 137–154.

Miller, A. (1971) *The Assault on Privacy: Computers, Data Banks, and Dossiers*. University of Michigan Press.

Moor, J. H. (1985) What Is computer ethics?. *Metaphilosophy*, 16(4), 266–275.

Moor, J. H. (1997) Towards a theory of privacy in the information age. *Computers and Society*, 27(3), 27–32.

Moor, J. H. (1998) Reason, relativity, and responsibility in computer ethics. *Computers and Society*, 28(1), 14–21.

Nissenbaum, H. 1998 . Protecting privacy in an information age: The problem of privacy in public. *Law and Philosophy*, 559–596.

Parliamentary Office of Science and Technology (2006) Computer crime. *Postnote*, 271(October), 1–4.

Roe, P. R. (ed.) (2007) *Towards an Inclusive Future: Impact and Wider Potential of Information and Communication Technologies*. COST 219 report, COST, Brussels.

Rogerson S. (1997) Software project management ethics. In: Myers, C., Hall, T. & Pitt, D. (eds.), *The Responsible Software Engineer*. Springer-Verlag, pp. 100–106.

Rogerson, S. (2001) A practical perspective of information ethics. In Goujon, P. & Dubreuil, B. H. (eds.), *Technology and Ethics: A European Quest for Responsible Engineering*. Leuven, Belgium, Peeters, pp. 305–325.

Rogerson, S. (2004a) Aspects of social responsibility in the information society. In: Doukidis, G. I., Mylonopoulos, N. A. & Pouloudi, N. (eds.), *Social and Economic Transformation in the Digital Era*. IDEA Group Publishing, pp. 31–46.

Rogerson, S. (2004b) The virtual world: a tension between global reach and local sensitivity. *International Journal of Information Ethics*, 2(2-1). Available from http://www.i-r-i-e.net/inhalt/002/ijie_002_22_rogerson.pdf (Accessed 05 April 2009).

Rogerson, S., Weckert, J. & Simpson, C. (2000) An ethical review of information systems development: the Australian Computer Society's code of ethics and SSADM. *Information Technology and People*, 13(2), 121–136.

Spinello R. A. (1995) *Ethical Aspects of Information Technology*. New York, Prentice Hall.

Spinello, R. A. (2005) Secondary liability in the post Napster era: ethical observations on MGM v. Grokster. *Journal of Information, Communication and Ethics in Society*, 3(3), 121–130.

Stallman R. (1992) Why software should be free. In: Bynum, T. W., Maner, W. & Fodor, J. L. (eds.), *Software Ownership and Intellectual Property Rights*. Research Center on Computing and Society, Southern Connecticut State University, pp. 35–52.

Stary, C. (2001) User diversity and design representation: towards increased effectiveness in Design for All. *Universal Access in the Information Society*, 1(1), 16–30.

Tavani, H. T. & Moor, J. H. (2001) Privacy protection, control of information, and privacy-enhancing technologies. In: Spinello, R. A. & Tavani, H. T. (eds.), *Readings in CyberEthics*. Jones and Bartlett, pp. 378–391.

van Luijk, H. (1994) Business ethics: the field and its importance. In: Harvey, B. (ed.), *Business Ethics: A European Approach*. Prentice Hall.

Wiener, N. (1950, 1954) *The Human Use of Human Beings: Cybernetics and Society*. Houghton Mifflin (Second Edition Revised, Doubleday Anchor, 1954).

## Chapter 6

# Towards a Chronological Taxonomy of Tourism Technology: An Ethical Perspective [2018]*

## Introduction

Thomas Cook is the acknowledged founder of modern tourism. In 1841, he organised a one-day rail excursion at a shilling-a-head from Leicester to Loughborough in England for temperance supporters. As reported at the time, "About half-past eleven they arrived, the train consisting of one second class carriage and nine third class carriages, each crowded with respectably-dressed, and, apparently, happy teetotallers. We understand that there were about five hundred in all" (Correspondent, 1841). This was one of the earliest times that such a large group of people had been transported for a social occasion of their choice.

It was the birth of his international travel company which still operates today. Without an advanced technology of the time, the railway, Cook could not have embarked upon his visionary scheme. From this small, yet significant, beginning mass tourism evolved. The United Nations World Tourism Organisation (UNWTO) estimates that by 1950 internationally there were 25 million tourist arrivals. In 2016, 66 years later, this number had increased to 1.2 billion international arrivals per year, a 49-fold increase (Roser, 2018).

As tourism has evolved, it has continued to utilise technological advances in, for example, transport, booking systems, sales and marketing and now actual tourist experiences. There seem to be many ethical issues, such as access, privacy, security, digital divide and job loss, associated with technology usage in tourism evolution.

---

* This chapter was first published as: Rogerson, S. (2019) Towards a Chronological Taxonomy of Tourism Technology: an ethical perspective. *ETHICOMP 2018*. Copyright © Simon Rogerson. DOI 10.13140/RG.2 .2.20245.88809.

This chapter undertakes a preliminary analysis of this evolution, linking aspects of tourism with technological advances and highlighting potential ethical issues related to such links. Thomas Cook is used as an illustrative case study. The eventual outcome of this project will be a rich chronological taxonomy of tourism technology, providing a novel insight which places modern advances into historical context.

## Tourism Technology

Tourism technology is defined as the application of IT or Information and Communication Technology (ICT) in the travel, tourism and hospitality industry (see, for example, https://en.wikipedia.org/wiki/Travel_technology). Such a definition appears very limited as it fails to take into account the rich technological continuum over time that tourism has depended upon and continues to depend upon. Thus, tourism technology is redefined as *the application of any advanced or emerging technology in the travel, tourism and hospitality industry.* Furthermore, this chapter adopts the Consensus Definition of Technology as discussed by Dusek (2006) where the technological system is the complex of hardware, knowledge, inventors, operators, repair people, consumers, marketeers, advertisers, government administrators and others involved in a technology (ibid, p. 35). This avoids the misnomer of technology being ethically neutral because involved humans lie within the technology system boundary. Thus, ethical behaviour of humans contributes to the ethical profile of the associated technology. This enables a taxonomy to be developed which includes a rich ethical perspective.

It is unclear how much emphasis has been placed on the ethical dimension of technology usage in the tourist industry. Today, the need to understand and address the ethical issues surrounding technology is paramount given the use of, for example, virtual and augmented reality and social networks to embellish the tourist experience, as well as new experiences, such as space tourism, becoming viable possibilities. The 21st century tourists are of generation Y and beyond (Sziva & Zoltay, 2016). They are neither beach nor culture tourists; they are creative tourists (Fernández, 2010) demanding and expecting before, during and after experiences. Creative tourists have a perspective of educational, emotional, social and participative interaction with the place, its living culture and the people who live there (ibid). Technology, and ICT in particular, provides the key to satisfying this demand. It is technology on which the next evolutionary step, smart tourism is founded. Such advancing technologies are powerful and adaptive but also potentially ethically dangerous. This risk must be recognised, analysed and addressed.

## Thomas Cook and Technology

Thomas Cook is used as an illustrative case study to explore the redefined tourism technology. A series of visits to the Thomas Cook Archives together with interviews with two store managers provided access to a rich information source. This coupled with information in the public domain has enabled a large range of material to be collected. It is an ongoing process. For the purposes of this chapter, some examples of technology through the ages have been chosen commencing with horse and carriage and finishing with virtual reality (VR). The aim is to illustrate the rich relationship between tourism and technology over time.

## Horse and Carriage

According to Turner and Stone (2006), livery stables were the garages and service stations of the 19th century providing public transportation. There are many references to Cook using this early and well-established technology when other forms of transport were unavailable. Here is just one example.

Smith (1998) provides a detailed account of Thomas Cook & Son's link with Vesuvius. In 1887, John Mason Cook bought the funicular railway on Mount Vesuvius with Thomas Cook & Son becoming the general agent. An inclusive tourist ticket included a horse-drawn carriage from Naples, ascent of the funicular railway and guide services at the crater. The potential for the business was hampered by the slow, steep and expensive ascent by horse-drawn carriage with tourists being pestered by beggars, musicians and vendors *en route*. In the mid-1890s, Cook decided to improve the tourist offer and thus the business by replacing horse with rail – a line from Naples to the lower funicular station. Although completed after his death this was an engineering masterpiece, and electric railway using self-generation electricity which reduced the ascent to less than 1 hour. In 1906, Vesuvius erupted destroying the funicular railway but the electric link railway survived and was back in service within days. A zigzag bridle path was built to the summit and so the horse once again became part of the Vesuvius tourist experience.

## Railway

The railway, an advanced technology of the time, was fundamental to Cook's visionary scheme of transporting a large group of people *en masse* to an organised event in a distant location, all within the duration of one day. Excursion tickets cost one shilling or £3.02 (National Archives currency convertor) when the weekly wage of a common labourer was 3s 9d and bricklayers, carpenters, masons, smiths was 6s 6d (Porter, 1998) or £11.33 and £19.22, respectively, in today's money. This raises the question of affordability for anyone who wanted to go, given the trip was aimed at the working classes. From an ethical perspective, there is an equality-of-access issue associated with this venture involving leisure use of technology. Cook followed up his first success with a three-year series of temperance excursion trains between Leicester, Nottingham, Derby and Birmingham (Simmons, 1973).

From at least 1840 onwards, train excursions with reduced fares became popular and were increasingly organised by railway companies in partnership with private organisations located at destinations (ibid). However, there were many reports of mismanagement and gross incompetence. The Board of Trade issued a warning on 17 October 1844 that a major disaster was likely unless better systems were in place when conveying large numbers of people (ibid). This is a clear ethical statement that public wellbeing is paramount.

## Telegraph

An early example of tourism technology, as redefined earlier, is the telegraph which was co-developed by Sir William Fothergill Cooke and Charles Wheatstone. The Cooke and Wheatstone system came into commercial use in 1837. As well as the rapid expansion of the use of the telegraphs along the railways, they soon spread into the field of mass communication with the instruments being installed in post offices across the country. The era of mass personal communication had begun. By the 1890s, most of the British Empire was connected by telegraph. However, there were some concerns about interception which is probably one of the first occurrences of awareness of communication hacking.

This new form of communication was quickly adopted by Thomas Cook. On 21 December 1872, he sent a telegram from the Post Office and Submarine Telegraph in Penang to his wife in England. Cook was on the first world tour he had organised and sent Christmas greetings to his wife, telling her that he expected to arrive back in England in January (Cook, 1872). The Company used the telegraph extensively for business communications. Cook was aware of the insecurity of the technology when sending commercially sensitive telegrams. A locked cipher book was created; a copy of which was held at each Thomas Cook office worldwide. The book, cryptically entitled "Abbreviated Address Book," contained random words representing key business-related phrases, for example, "nasal" meant "can I conclude contract on following terms with …" and "nymph" meant "the matter is now under consideration" (Cook, 1880).

## Space Technology

In December 1926, a cartoon appeared in The Globe Trotter, the staff magazine of the time. It depicted Donald White, a Thomas Cook Uniformed Man, standing on the moon about to welcome passengers on a rocket from Moscow. It had been prompted by news that Russia was developing lunar travel. In 1950, to coincide with the release of the film Destination Moon, a leaflet stating that reservations for future holidays on the moon and elsewhere in the solar system were now being taken (One, 2008, p. 14). By 1996, following a number of press stories, the Lunar Tours database had grown to 10,000 (Insight, 1996, p. 5) when it was eventually withdrawn.

It appears the idea of space tourism at times was taken seriously by the public which is possibly why the register was withdrawn. While lunar travel was an amusing aside, it does demonstrate a visionary culture which seems to have always existed within the Thomas Cook organisation. However, the 1926 cartoon is remarkably similar to today's reality. In the near future, the SpaceX Dragon 2 capsule powered by a Falcon Heavy rocket is planned to transport the first paying passengers to the moon as part of the Nasa Commercial Crew Program (Woollaston, 2017).

## Early Computational and Computer Technology

Records show that Thomas Cook was using tabulators for accounts in 1932. They remained in use, albeit updated models, until the introduction of an IBM 1401 computer in March 1963 when the first application system was payroll, then accounts. It was not until 1974 that CICERO, a real-time reservation system, was implemented (Ref X, 1990).

The accounts of 1981 mention that Holidaymaker, the private Viewdata system, was being piloted and was planned to be in all stores within 18 months. This was a ground breaking system as, for the first time, it linked the customer-facing system directly to the customer reservation system. One recollection shared during the store interviews was that while Viewdata systems improved administration, their dull black and white display could act as a barrier, so the agent had to "paint pictures with words" about the holiday to keep the customer interested. Both stores visited commented on how the latest version of OneWeb, Thomas Cook's international web platform, was a much-improved aid to establishing customer relationships. From the 1980s, various Point of Sales projects undertaken and resulting in RIO being finally implemented in December 2000 across all stores. RIO still runs today as a back-office system holding complete customer records. There were mixed reactions to the usability of RIO. The issue of embedded legacy systems is a difficult challenge for organisations and has ethical ramifications for the customer.

## Electronic Cash

Thomas Cook has often been a leader in offering travel money, which is safe, secure, easy to access and widely accepted. This dates from 1867 with the introduction of hotel coupons and a few years later the introduction of the circular note which was an early form of travellers cheque. In 1995, Thomas Cook participated in the Mondex card trial in Swindon. The smart card held money downloaded from a bank account allowing the card to be used as a direct alternative to cash. There were some serious technological weaknesses such as there was no audit trail, so customers were not protected from theft or fraud (Rodgers, 1995). Only 14,000 people took a Mondex card when it was estimated the take up would be 40,000. A range of ethical and social issues surrounded Mondex which included lax security, unfit for purpose, technology aversion and resistance to change. The trial finished and Mondex was never implemented in the United Kingdom. However, it was acquired by MasterCard and its technology was used in the company's smart card products (Leighton, 2014). MasterCard by coincidence provides Lyk which is Thomas Cook's, latest prepaid travel card launched early in 2018. It holds up to ten different currencies with five different ways to load the money including online banking and the Lyk App for smartphones. Liability for unauthorised transactions is with MasterCard. Advanced smart card technology provides the highest level of security. The Lyk App provides a usable interface for the customer. The contributory ethical factors which led to the demise of Mondex 20 years earlier seem to have been addressed with Lyk.

## World Wide Web

Thomas Cook was the first UK travel company to develop a website in 1995 when WWW was in its infancy. In July 1998, 53,000 people visited the site per week. By August 2000, the traffic had risen to 1 m hits per month. During stores interviews, it was mentioned that there had been huge reliance on guides one known as "The Truth Guide" to help agents provide accurate and impartial travel information. In December 2000, the well-respected paper-based official aviation guide (OAG) including the "Truth Guide" were transformed into online Web pages heralded as a major step forward (Insight, 2000). That same month thomascook.com was top of the travel league table operated by independent research agency Nielson Netratings, ahead of ebookers.com and expedia.uk. Today, OneWeb (mentioned earlier) is the umbrella which offers an impressive online facility across the customer journey.

## Smart App

The Holiday Report (2018) reports that smartphones continue to dominate the growth in links with customers. It states (p. 14), "One trend which shows no sign of slowing down is the growth of mobile in the looking and booking. In the last 12 months, mobile searches on thomascook.com have increased by 27% year-on-year and mobile bookings by 24%. 1 in 5 bookings made on thomascookairlines.com come from a mobile."

The Thomas Cook App, My Holiday, is a very successful tool incorporating augmented reality which probably uses gathered data from sensors and other sources, using machine learning algorithms and predictive analytics to provide the location and customer-related information to improve experiences and customer service, before, during and after. Staff were very positive about the app and reported a good take up but some age-related aversion at times. Technology aversion, security, location tracking and privacy are just some of the ethical issues related to this type of smart app. Ayeh (2018) has found that overuse of mobile devices and smart apps takes something away from individual and group travel experiences through loss of social interactions and consumption of sights and sounds.

## Virtual Reality

Thomas Cook has always been innovative in its store facilities from the moment it opened its travel agency in London in 1861 to the present day. The venture in 1861 was vilified by the establishment for it offered guided tours to working-class and lower middle-class people in Victorian Britain steeped in class structure (Hampel & Tracey, 2017). Such reaction today would be judged wholly unethical. In 1994, 133 years later, *One* reported the launch of the travel kiosk where customers could browse holidays and complete booking using interactive technology. This was the first time the industry had used such customer-facing applications and Thomas Cook received many accolades in the press. Expert systems, in many ways the forerunner and foundation for Virtual and Augmented reality, were also trialled back in 1986 in an attempt to provide relevant information to ensure customers service according to John Birkle. In the first edition of Holiday Report (2017), it was reported eight Thomas Cook stores in the United Kingdom were piloting the use of VR headsets to assist customers in choosing holidays. It saw significant increases in sales which had the VR experiences available. VR has become part of the hi-tech offer in the new Discovery stores which are being opened in large retail areas. Customers can use the latest self-service technology, a concept pioneered by the travel kiosk in 1994. Staff use tablets to help them assist customers as they move around the store rather than having an anchor point within the store. This type of facility is ideal for the technology savvy but might be a barrier for those who are technology resistant. Will lasting relationships be established, the basis of repeat business, when the customer is being wooed by technology and the virtual world? It raises a range of ethical issues.

# One Further Ethical Concern

Concerns about hacking have existed as long as mass tourism has existed as explained earlier. In 2017, Morris reported that as many as 42,000 holidaymakers were at risk of fraud after having their personal details (including email addresses, passwords and contact information) stolen in a cyber-attack on association of British travel agent (ABTA), Britain's leading travel association. This is only one type of risk. As technological dependency increases, societal vulnerability can increase. Tourism is no exception. Three other recent calamities in 2017 are testimony to this: the collapse of Monarch Airlines leading to UK's biggest peacetime repatriation of 110,000 customers (Topham, 2017), the inadequacy of Ryanair's pilot roster system resulting in 400,000 passengers having their flights cancelled (Collinson, 2017) and British Airways cancelling all flights from London Heathrow and London Gatwick airports following a massive global IT failure (Telegraph Reporters, 2017).

The preliminary analysis undertaken and reported in this chapter demonstrates there is a plethora of technologies and many ethical issues which should be investigated so that lessons can be learnt. Thus, a method needs to be established whereby technology utilisation within tourism together with associated incidents worthy of ethical analysis can be captured and classified. This would enable a rich data set to be created which would be invaluable to all those involved in developing tourism. A method is now proposed in outline.

| Date | Technology | Tourism perspective | Possible ethical perspective |
|---|---|---|---|
| 1841 | Train | Start of modern tourism | equality of access |
| 1875 | Automobile | Customised tours | safety |
| 1914 | Passenger planes | Package holidays abroad | safety, access, social impact |
| 1946 | Computer reservation system | Travel agency | privacy, security |
| 1989 | World Wide Web | Travelogues, marketing, bricks & clicks | subliminal issues, privacy |
| 1996 | Public internet booking | Customised tourism | digital divide, job loss |
| 1999 | Virtual and augmented reality – forerunner was Second Life | Smart tourism maturity | digital divide |
| 2000 | GPS | Location tracking | privacy, surveillance |
| 2004 | Social Media e.g. Trip Advisor, Booking.com | Tourist information and reservation | privacy, security, trustworthiness |
| 2008 | iPhone | Anywhere anytime anything | digital divide |
| 2023 | Space travel | Space tourist | safety |

**Figure 6.1   An example timeline showing the impact of technology on tourism.**

## Chronological Taxonomy

A timeline (Figure 6.1) displays a list of important events in chronological order. Timelines can be linear where one subject area is considered, for example, IT, or they can be comparative where two or more subject areas, for example, tourism and technology, are displayed. There are several timelines related to this current chapter in the literature. Hjalager (2015) provides a timeline of innovations which have changed tourism. Joyce (2013) provides a history of travel technology from its evolution through to the future but fails to acknowledge the wider definition of technology used in this chapter. Such timelines tend to be one-dimensional which suggests there is a dimensional gap in the body of knowledge which, if filled, would provide greater insight into the range of impact that technology has had on tourism.

Taxonomy is a scheme of classification of things or concepts. Manktelow (2010) explains that taxonomies are known to have existed in China in 3000 BC but the founder of modern taxonomies is recognised as the 18th-century Swedish scientist Carolus Linnaeus. Well-known taxonomies include Bloom's Taxonomy of Learning Domains, the Dewey Decimal System for library classification and the Linnaean classification of animals.

By using a literature search, the term chronological taxonomy was found to have been used in a few other areas; some examples are included here. Reynolds (2008) uses it to explore the prehistory of the Crusades. However, his is simply a time-based classification. This type of approach is discussed by Löblová (2016) regarding health technology assessment. Kohn (1992) uses the term to describe an analysis of the changes in the classification of *Conus* over time. It appears that the common thread of other works is that time is the classification. This chapter proposes a new two-dimensional method of ordering: the first dimension is Chronology and the second dimension is Taxonomy, hence Chronological Taxonomy.

An example of the Chronology dimension is shown in Figure 6.1. Possible ethical perspectives are shown for each entry. The dates on this linear timeline relate to when a technology had an impact on tourism rather than when the technology was invented. There can be a long lag between invention and impact. A comparative timeline showing impact and invention dates would provide additional value.

In the Thomas Cook Group plc Annual Report and Accounts of 2017, a significant empahsis was placed on the customer journey, which is shown in Figure 6.2. The report (p. 7) states, "Our customers' journey doesn't start in the airport. It begins with the first holiday inspiration online or in a store, through to planning and booking their time away, to the experience on holiday with us and then the memories they carry with them afterwards." Thomas Cook emphasises that technology underpins every process they undertake in the support of the customer journey. Discussions in store confirm this. Therefore, it is reasonable to use this empirical data to construct a suitable taxonomy for tourism.

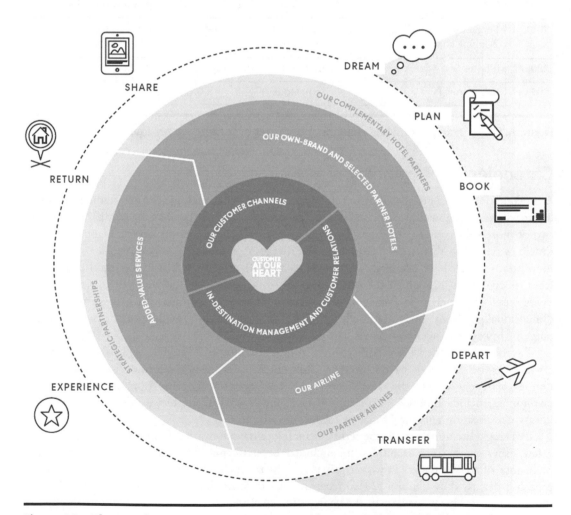

**Figure 6.2   The travel customer journey. (Source: Thomas Cook Annual Report, 2017, p. 6)**

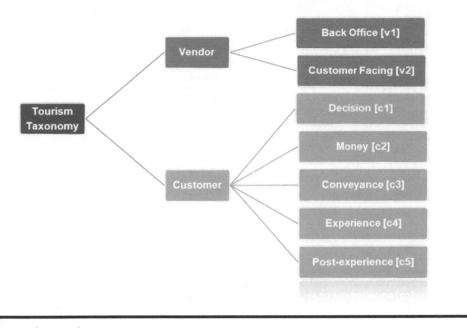

**Figure 6.3   The tourism taxonomy.**

The first level reflects the very strong relation between Thomas Cook and its customers. Therefore, there are just two categories: Vendor and Customer. There is a clear demarcation of technology that is used to help customers and technology which is used to operate the company. Therefore, the Vendor second level comprises Back Office and Customer Facing. The customer journey provides the foundation for constructing the Customer second-level classifications and comprises Decision, Money, Conveyance, Experience and Post-experience. This initial taxonomy, as shown in Figure 6.3, could be expanded, if necessary, through creating lower levels but it is thought that this level of granularity is not required.

The timeline and the taxonomy are now merged to form the Chronological Taxonomy. Any duplication, redundancy or inconsistencies need to be addressed in the merger. The outcome is shown in Figure 6.4. The Chronology dimension is the column headed Year and the Taxonomy dimension is the column headed Category in which an item is coded according to the scheme in Figure 6.3. An item could relate to more than one category, so there might be multiple entries. An item's underpinning technology and any associated ethical issues complete the entry.

The Chronological Taxonomy is a powerful tool to structure and analyse tourism technology through using concatenated keys to sort the data, thus making issues, trends and patterns more visible. As the data set expands and perhaps automatic feeds are established to harvest advances and issues, the use of Big Data analytics might be needed. Providing analysed data can aid the tourist industry in many ways. For example, given the May 2018 General Data Protection Regulation, it would be interesting to highlight where the greatest impact of this change might be. If the data were sorted by Ethical Issue then Category then Year, it would be possible to see the major areas in the most recent past where privacy was an issue. The technologies and applications could then be looked into further. A second example is where a new experience offer is going to be implemented. Sort by Category then Year would result in a checklist of ethical issues to ensure the new offer did not suffer from ethical setbacks. An investigation of the impact of a particular technology could be supported by

| Category | Year | Item Description | Underpinning Technology | Ethical Issues |
|---|---|---|---|---|
| c4 | 1855 | First package tour commemorated in 2005 | railway | equality of oportunity |
| v1 | 1880 | Abbreviated Address Book | cryptography | security, confidential |
| c4 | 1950 | Moon travel register: summer 1950 -Nov 1996 | space technology | safety |
| v1 | 1974 | CICERO | 3GL | Personal data |
| v2 | 1981 | Holidaymaker | prestel | personal data |
| v2 | 1995 | First website | web | access |
| c1 c2 c3 c4 c5 | 2017 | My Holiday travel app | augmented reality | surveillance, privacy |
| c1 | 2017 | Discovery VR headsets | virtual reality | distraction, sublimation |
| c2 | 2018 | Lyk money card | smart card | privacy, fraud |

**Figure 6.4 The Chronological Taxonomy with example entries taken from the Thomas Cook case.**

sorting the data by Underlying technology then Year then Category. This acknowledges the speed of technological change by setting time as the second sort. Trends in impact and reach could be then investigated as well as lessons to be learnt from similar technologies. It is hard to see how the data could not be presented in a meaningful way to assist in any research question in this field.

## Conclusion

This chapter has briefly explored tourism technology from an ethical standpoint. It has redefined the term so it fits more appropriately over time. It has created a new structure for collected data which offers great potential in developing greater understanding within this hitherto poorly investigated area. A case study has been used to illustrate these advances with just a small sample of the data collected so far. The data will be used in further publications to analyse Thomas Cook more deeply. The current frontier is smart tourism, so it is appropriate to conclude in that area.

With vision and careful application, smart technology can be used to enrich the tourist experience. The Buxton Museum and Art Gallery has recently embraced smart technology to modernise its offer to the public. The Museum's collections can now be accessed within the museum and outside where the archaeological and geological artefacts were found and where the artists sat to paint their pictures. The Wonders of the Peak web app was launched in September 2017, alongside a new interactive museum gallery entitled *Wonders of the Peak: A Journey through Time and Place*. The app contains a very detailed map of the Peak District using Pinterest to mark cultural and heritage *Wonders* which, when clicked, provides details of the Wonder, sometimes including oral accounts of the item. Linked to this are two mobile apps Museum Wonders and Pocket Wonders which enables one to get more information and generate and download a tour to follow in the landscape, based on the Wonders. This is a great example of smart tourism which satisfies the needs of generation Y and beyond, culture tourists demanding and expecting before, during and after experiences.

A gap exists in the research literature concerning the ethical dimension of ICT usage in tourism. In this context, ICT is viewed as a modern subset of tourism technology. This gap should be filled to help inform those rolling out tourism technology to grow the tourist economy and offer as wide a range as possible of experiences to the prospective customer. Quality offers such as the Buxton Museum's Wonders project should become the norm supporting ethically sound access. The multidisciplinary ICT ethics research community can help in addressing this gap. This chapter acts as a catalyst for this initiative, the chronological taxonomy being the first step in this process.

## Addendum (17 December 2020)

On 23 September 2019, Thomas Cook filed for compulsory liquidation and ceased trading with immediate effect. The company had £1.7bn of debt. Over 150,000 stranded holidaymakers had to be brought home. Hernandez (2020) suggested that the collapse was due to, "Failure to adapt and stay competitive with a new generation of more flexible travel companies, travel-related online services and low-cost airlines … [coupled with] … potential customers becoming increasingly accustomed to devising their own holidays rather than using travel agents." Subsequently, the Fosun Tourism Group acquired the Thomas Cook trademarks, websites and social media accounts. On 16 September 2020, Thomas Cook was relaunched as a travel website and so the name and the company live on, albeit in a different guise.

At the time of the collapse, there was much concern among historians and scholars in general regarding the protection of the Thomas Cook Archive. Large numbers of people raised this issue in many quarters. I alerted the executive of my university, De Montfort University, which is located in Leicester which is the birthplace of the Thomas Cook travel company and as such the University had a potential role to play in saving the archive. Indeed, the University leant its support to the Record Office for Leicestershire, Leicester and Rutland in its successful bid to house the archive which was moved to Leicester in December 2019.

### *Thomas Cook Archive Preservation – Statement to the Business Archives Council by Professor Simon Rogerson (29 September 2019)*

I am Professor Emeritus in Computer Ethics, founding director of the Centre for Computing & Social Responsibility, creator of the international ETHICOMP conference series and founder and editor of the *Journal of Information, Communication and Ethics in Society*.

With a background in practical computing, my research has inevitably focused on the acceptable use of ICT in a wide range of application areas. During the past three years, I have been focusing on the use of ICT in tourism given the increasing advances in, for example, smart technology and artificial intelligence.

In order to undertake this type of research in any application area, it is vital to understand the nature, culture and history of the area in question. Those working or having worked in the area are an important primary source but the need to go beyond that as well as developing triangulation is vital. An archive is unquestionably one of the most important primary sources available. It was this which led to my discovery of the Thomas Cook Archive and subsequent use of this unique resource.

Thomas Cook is acknowledged as the founder of modern tourism taking his first tentative steps in 1841. Today tourism is probably the world's largest industry and touches every corner of the globe and soon to move even beyond that into space. The Thomas Cook archive, a national UK treasure, is a unique record of this evolution through the history of the only company to exist (until 23 September 2019) throughout the age of modern tourism.

Through a series of visits to the archive, I was able to construct an account of the use of technological advances by Thomas Cook in his (and the company's) drive to expand tourism. This led me to conclude that the current accepted definition of Tourism Technology was flawed as it was ground in the present and specifically in ICT. There is so much to learn from the historical accounts in the archive of technological advances such as the railway and the telegraph in the 1800s. I found resonance between the challenges of these historical technological advances and those of today's ICT advances.

Without the archive, my research would not have been possible. It is important to recognise the key elements of this archive, these being the artefacts, the index and the archivist. To handle the artefacts was so special and inspirational. Finding historical gems to illustrate and confirm my thinking was so exciting. This could only happen with the expert advice of the archivist, Paul Smith. In my view, the archivist is a mandatory requirement for an archive for it is this person who acts as custodian and guide. In many ways, the archive is only as good as the archivist in charge. The Thomas Cook archive was excellent as was the archivist Paul Smith.

This statement is from an established researcher who is not from the tourism discipline but from computer science. It illustrates the immense value of the archive as it offers priceless resources across the disciplines. Indeed, it has the potential to promote interdisciplinarity and transdisciplinarity.

It is unthinkable that this archive should be destroyed and possibly distributed through auction. It must remain as an important element of our national heritage and as the definitive historical resource of modern tourism. It must be freely accessible to all those interested in tourism regardless of status, discipline, or reason.

## Acknowledgements

The author would like to thank Paul Smith, Archivist at Thomas Cook; Kelly Middleton, Store Manager at Thomas Cook Macclesfield; Leah Cavoto, Acting Assistant Manager, Thomas Cook Buxton; and Joe Perry, Buxton Museum and Art Gallery. Without their help, the collection of empirical data would have not been possible.

## References

Ayeh, J. K. (2018). Distracted gaze: problematic use of mobile technologies in vacation contexts. *Tourism management perspectives*, 26, 31–38.

Birkle, J. (1986). Quoted in technology first! *Internationally Speaking with Thomas Cook*, 4(February), 10.

Collinson, P. (2017). Ryanair to tell 400,000 passengers of cancelled flights after roster 'mess-up'. *The Guardian*, 19 September. Available from https://www.theguardian.com/business/2017/sep/18/ryanair-flight-cancellation-passengers-holiday (Accessed 9 January 2018).

Cook, T. (1872). *Telegram*. Peterborough, Thomas Cook Archives. Accessed November 2016.

Cook, T. (1880). *Abbreviated Address Book*. Peterborough, Thomas Cook Archives. Accessed November 2017.

Correspondent (1841). Teetotal festival at Loughborough. *The Leicester Mercury*, 10 July, p. 2.

Dusek, V. (2006). *Philosophy of Technology: An Introduction*. Malden, Oxford, Carlston, Blackwell.

Fernández, T. (2010). More than sun, beach and heritage: innovating Mediterranean tourism through creative tourism. *2010 RESER Conference papers*. Gothenburg, Sweden, Vol. 30.

Hampel, C. E. & Tracey, P. (2017). How organizations move from stigma to legitimacy: the case of cook's travel agency in Victorian Britain. *Academy of Management Journal*, 60(6), 2175–2207.

Hernandez, V. (2020). The collapse of Thomas Cook: what happened and why. *International Bank*, 16 January. Available from https://internationalbanker.com/brokerage/the-collapse-of-thomas-cook-what-happened-and-why/ (Accessed 15 December 2020).

Hjalager, A. M. (2015). 100 innovations that transformed tourism. *Journal of Travel Research*, 54(1), 3–21.

Holiday Report (2017). Gogglebooks. *Thomas Cook Holiday Report 2017*. Available from https://www.thomascookgroup.com/wp-content/uploads/2017/06/Thomas-Cook-Holiday-Report-2017.pdf (Accessed January 2018).

Holiday Report (2018). Clicks vs bricks. *Thomas Cook Holiday Report 2018*. Available from https://scdn.thomascook.com/images/wcms/dam/tcuk/campaigns/campaigns2018/holidayreport2018/TCookHolidayReport2018.pdf?_ga=2.65835438.1232217731.1526050402-619595162.1508258628 (Accessed February 2018).

Insight (1996). *The Newspaper for All Staff in Thomas Cook UK and Ireland*. Peterborough, Thomas Cook Archives. Accessed April 2018.

Insight (2000). OAG: At the Touch of a Button. The Newspaper for All Staff in Thomas Cook UK and Ireland. Peterborough, Thomas Cook Archives. Accessed April 2018.

Joyce, S. (2013). A brief history of travel technology–from its evolution to looking at the future. *Tnooz* [referred 20 September 2013]. Available from https://www.phocuswire.com/A-brief-history-of-travel-technology-from-its-evolution-to-looking-at-the-future

Kohn, A. J. (1992). *A Chronological Taxonomy of Conus, 1758-1840*. Smithsonian Inst Pr.

Leighton, B. (2014). How smart was that? *Swindon Advertiser*, 21 May. Available from https://www.swindonadvertiser.co.uk/news/11225462.how-smart-was-that/No volume for this newspaper

Löblová, O. (2016). Three worlds of health technology assessment: explaining patterns of diffusion of HTA agencies in Europe. *Health Economics, Policy and Law*. 11(3), 253–273.

Manktelow, M. (2010). *History of Taxonomy*. Lecture from Department of Systematic Biology, Uppsala University.

Morris, H. (2017). ABTA cyber attack: what holidaymakers should do if they're affected. *The Telegraph*, 16 March. Available from http://www.telegraph.co.uk/travel/news/abta-customers-members-hacked-cyber-attack/?WT.mc_id=tmg_share_em (Accessed 9 January 2018).

National Archives. Historical currency convertor. Available from https://www.nationalarchives.gov.uk/currency-convertor (Accessed 9 May 2018).

One (1994). Travel kiosk to transform holiday booking. *The Magazine for Thomas Cook People*. Peterborough, Thomas Cook Archives. Accessed April 2018.

One (2008). *The Magazine for Thomas Cook People*. Peterborough, Thomas Cook Archives. Accessed April 2018.

Porter, D. H. (1998). *The Thames Embankment: Environment, Technology, and Society in Victorian London*. Akron, Ohio, University of Akron Press.

Ref X (1990). *An Unpublished History of Thomas Cook in the Twentieth Century*. Written by a former head of IT Strategy at Thomas Cook. Peterborough, Thomas Cook Archives. Accessed November 2017 [author details embargoed].

Reynolds, B. W. (2008). The prehistory of the Crusades: toward a developmental taxonomy. *History Compass*, 6(3), 884–897.

Rodgers, P. (1995). Not-so-smart card will flop, says City. *The Independent*, 26 March.

Roser, M. (2018). Tourism. Published online at *OurWorldInData.org*. Available from https://ourworldindata.org/tourism/ (Accessed 9 January 2018).

Simmons, J. (1973). Thomas Cook of Leicester. *Transactions of the Leicestershire Archæological and Historical Society*, 49, 18–32.

Smith, P. (1998). Thomas Cook & Son's Vesuvius Railway. *Japan Railway & Transport Review*, EJRCF, 15(March), 10–15.

Sziva I. & Zoltay R. A. (2016). How attractive can cultural landscapes be for generation Y?. *Journal of Tourism, Culture and Territorial Development*, 7(14), 1–16.

Telegraph Reporters (2017). British Airways chaos: all flights cancelled at Heathrow and Gatwick after global computer failure. *The Telegraph*, 28 May. Available from http://www.telegraph.co.uk/news/2017/05/2 7/british-airways-chaos-computer-systems-crash-across-world-causing/ (Accessed 9 January 2018).

Topham, G. (2017). Monarch Airlines collapse: UK's biggest peacetime repatriation under way. *The Guardian*, 2 October. Available from https://www.theguardian.com/world/2017/oct/02/monarch-airlines-flights-cancelled-as-airline-goes-into-administration (Accessed 9 January 2018).

Turner, W. T. & Stone D. K. (2006). *Hopkinsville*. Arcadia Publishing.

Woollaston, V. (2017). Elon Musk is sending two space tourists to the Moon in 2018. *Wired*. Available at http://www.wired.co.uk/article/space-x-tourists-moon (Accessed 9 January 2018).

# PROCESS

**II**

*... IT often presents new ways of working that have not previously been subject to ethical scrutiny ...*

(Simon Rogerson, 1998, p. 13)

As a young Fortran programmer in the 1970s, I was once told to incorporate a covert time bomb into a design system that was to be rolled out to a subsidiary company. At the time, I saw nothing wrong in building these functions; the ethics of the decision did not cross my mind. After all, I was a junior programmer and had been told to do it by the most senior member of staff in the department. Furthermore, it was a fascinating technological challenge as the subsidiary company was supplied with the source code rather than the executable program. You might say I was an uneducated technologist.

Today, I believe that professional practice is unprofessional without ethics, and yet it seems that huge ethical issues still remain in the industry. In January 2017, for example, car giant VW pleaded guilty to using a defeat device to cheat on mandatory emissions tests, as well as to lying and obstructing justice to further the scheme. At the centre of this scandal was misinformation, in fact, disinformation, generated by onboard software. That system was developed and implemented by computer professionals, who must have been party to the illegal and unethical purpose behind it. This case study is analysed in Chapter 16.

Nearly half a century passed between these two events, which suggests that the software industry has learnt little about the importance of ethics in system design. However, as digital technology becomes more and more central to our lives, the ethical dimension ought to become more central too. Consequently, Part 2 focuses on the process element of the *process-product model* discussed in Chapter 5. As explained, process concerns the activities undertaken in planning, research, development and service/product delivery of digital technology. The five chapters in Part 2 consider the process from different perspectives. However, all focus on the ethical and social issues which surround such activity and how these issues need to be identified and addressed in order to deliver acceptable digital technology systems. The aim is to ensure that those involved in the delivery of digital technology perform their duties with virtue.

## Reference

Rogerson, S. (1998) *Ethical Aspects of Information Technology: Issues for Senior Executives*. London, Institute of Business Ethics.

# Chapter 7

# The Ethics of Software Development Project Management [1996]*

## Introduction

It appears universally accepted that the most effective way to develop software is through the use of a project-based organisational structure which encourages individuals to participate in teams with the goal of achieving some common objective. Much has been written about the management of software development projects and no doubt much will be written in the future. The purpose of this chapter is to examine whether project management practice effectively caters for the ethical issues surrounding the software development process. For the sake of clarity, only one project management approach is discussed. The aim is to tease out the fundamental issues and not to dwell on the nuances of a particular approach.

"The Target Project Management Approach" section briefly considers the chosen project management methodology, Structured Project Management (SPM); "Principles of Ethics" section establishes a set of guiding ethical principles for computer professionals; "Ethical Project Management" section analyses SPM using the guiding principles; "The Primary Ethical Hotspots of Project Management" section considers the critical ethical issues of project management; and, finally, "Conclusions" section provides some concluding remarks.

## The Target Project Management Approach

In his book, *How to Run Successful Projects*, in the British Computer Society Practitioner Series, O'Connell (1994) provides details of the SPM approach. He explains that SPM is a practical methodology that, as DeMarco and Lister (1987) state, is a "basic approach one takes to getting a

---

\* This chapter was first published as: Rogerson, S. (1996) The ethics of software development project management. PASE'96, University of Westminster, 1–2 February, pp. 145–152. Copyright © Simon Rogerson.

**Table 7.1   The Ten Steps of Structured Project Management**

| Step 1 | Visualise what the goal is |
|---|---|
| Step 2 | Make a list of the jobs that need to be done |
| Step 3 | Ensure there is one leader |
| Step 4 | Assign people to jobs |
| Step 5 | Manage expectations, allow a margin of error and have a fallback position |
| Step 6 | Use an appropriate leadership style |
| Step 7 | Know what is going on |
| Step 8 | Tell people what is going on |
| Step 9 | Repeat Step 1 through 8 until Step 10 is achievable |
| Step 10 | Realise the project goal |

job done." SPM has been chosen for discussion as it is practical rather than conceptual and provides practitioners with realistic guidance in undertaking the vastly complex activity of project management.

SPM comprises ten steps as shown in Table 7.1. The first five steps are concerned with planning and the remaining five deal with implementing the plan and achieving the goal. O'Connell states that most projects succeed or fail because of decisions made during the planning stage thereby justifying the fact that half of the effort expended in the SPM approach is on preparation.

It is this planning element of project management which lays down the foundations on which the project ethos is built. Here the scope of consideration is established, albeit implicitly or explicitly, which in turn locates the horizon beyond which issues are deemed not to influence the project or be influenced by the project. How the project is conducted will depend heavily upon the perceived goal. The visualisation of this goal takes place in Step 1. The first two points in the visualisation checklist given by O'Connell are:

1. What will the goal of the project mean to all the people involved in the project when the project completes?
2. What are the things the project will actually produce? Where will these things go? What will happen to them? Who will use them? How will they be affected by them?

These are important because through answering these questions an acceptable project ethos and scope of consideration should be achieved. The problem is that in practice these fundamental questions are often overlooked. It is more likely that a narrower perspective is adopted with only the obvious issues in close proximity to the project being considered. The holistic view promoted by the two checklist points requires greater vision, analysis and reflection. The project manager is under pressure to deliver and so the tendency is to reduce the horizon and establish an artificial boundary around the project.

Steps 2–5 are concerned with adding detail and refinements, thus arriving at a workable and acceptable plan. Steps 6–8 are concerned with implementing the plan, monitoring performance and keeping those associated with the project informed of progress. Step 9 defines the control feedback loops which ensure that the plan remains focused, current and realistic. Finally, Step 10 is the delivery of the project output to the client and an opportunity to reflect upon what has and has not been achieved.

## Principles of Ethics

Relevant ethical principles must now be established in order to identify the ethical issues associated with software development project management in general and SPM in particular.

Ethics comprises both practice and reflection (van Luijk, 1994). Practice is the conscious appeal to norms and values to which individuals are obliged to conform, while reflection on practice is the elaboration of norms and values that colour daily activity. Norms are collective expectations regarding a certain type of behaviour while values are collective representations of what constitutes a good society. The existence of a plan and a controlling mechanism is the accepted norm in project management which itself is an accepted value in software development. For the purpose of this chapter, it is sufficient to consider only ethics practice because project management is concerned with action rather than conceptual reflection. Conceptual reflection might manifest itself in, for example, codes of conduct which are concerned with establishing what are the generalised ways of working that are acceptable to a wider community. This community would include all potential stakeholders of software development projects. In other words, project management is concerned with how to use and when to apply norms and values rather than establishing what these norms and values are.

An interesting list of generic questions was devised by John McLeod (Parker et al., 1990) to help determine the ethical nature of actions within the computing profession. The list is shown in Table 7.2. Within these questions, there are embedded norms which will impact upon the process of project management.

Software development is about the delivery of a product by a supplier to a client under some agreement. It is irrelevant whether this is an in-house arrangement or whether it is between two independent organisations. According to Velasquez (1992), such an agreement is concerned with product quality and moral product liability. Two parties enter into an agreement to develop a piece of software. Such agreements are often unbalanced with the client being disadvantaged. Velasquez argues that the principles of due care and social cost must take effect in these situations. There must be due care from the developer over and above what has been accepted in the contract so that adequate steps are taken to prevent any foreseen detrimental effects occurring through the use of the software. Social cost is based upon utilitarian ideas. Even after the software developer has given all reasonable due care to the software produced he/she still remains responsible for every damaging effect, be it caused by negligence, stupidity or recklessness.

By combining the ideas of McLeod and Velasquez, a set of ethical principles can be derived, as shown in Table 7.3. The principle of honour is to ensure that actions are beyond reproach which in turn demands honesty from the professional. The principle of bias focuses on ensuring decisions and actions are objective rather than subjective. Professional adequacy is concerned with the ability of individuals to undertake allocated tasks. The principle of due care is linked with the concept of software quality assurance. Fairness focuses on ensuring all affected parties are considered in project deliberations. This leads to social cost which recognises that it is not possible to abdicate from professional responsibility and accountability. Finally, the principle of effective and efficient action is concerned with completing tasks and realising goals with the least possible expenditure of resources.

**Table 7.2   Questioning the Ethical Nature of an Action**

| |
|---|
| To be ethical, an action should elicit a positive response to all applicable primary questions (*) and a negative response to each clarification (~). |
| * Is it honourable? |
| ~ Is there anyone from whom you would like to hide the action? |
| * Is it honest? |
| ~ Does it violate any agreement, actual or implied, or otherwise betray a trust? |
| * Does it avoid the possibility of a conflict of interest? |
| ~ Are there other considerations that might bias your judgement? |
| * Is it within your area of confidence? |
| ~ Is it possible that your best effort will not be adequate? |
| * Is it fair? |
| ~ Is it detrimental to the legitimate interests of others? |
| * Is it considerate? |
| ~ Will it violate confidentiality or privacy, or otherwise harm anyone or anything? |
| * Is it conservative? |
| ~ Does it unnecessarily squander time or other valuable resources? |

**Table 7.3   Ethical Principles for a Computer Professional**

| |
|---|
| Honour |
| Honesty |
| Bias |
| Professional adequacy |
| Due care |
| Fairness |
| Consideration of social cost |
| Effective and efficient action |

# Ethical Project Management

These guiding principles, which are based on ethical concepts, can be easily applied in practical situations and are now used to consider how to undertake ethical project management. The activities within each of the ten steps of SPM have been analysed in order to identify the

**Table 7.4   The Dominant Ethical Principles in the Steps of SPM**

| Principle | Steps | | | | | | | | | |
|---|---|---|---|---|---|---|---|---|---|---|
| | 1 | 2 | 3 | 4 | 5 | 6 | 7 | 8 | 9 | 10 |
| 1. Honour | yes | | | yes | | yes | | yes | | yes |
| 2. Honesty | yes | | | yes | yes | | | yes | | |
| 3. Bias | yes | yes | yes | yes | | | | yes | | yes |
| 4. Adequacy | | | yes | yes | | yes | | | | |
| 5. Due care | yes | | yes | | yes | | | yes | yes | |
| 6. Fairness | yes | | | | yes | | | yes | | |
| 7. Social | yes | | | | yes | yes | | | | yes |
| 8. Action | | yes | yes | yes | | yes | yes | | yes | yes |

dominant ethical issues of each step. The results of this analysis are shown in Table 7.4. It is recognised that most of the eight principles will have some impact on each step but it is important to identify those which will have a *significant* impact. The mapping in Table 7.4 shows those relationships which are considered significant. Steps 1 and 8 are now considered in further detail to illustrate the implication of the mapping.

## Step 1: Visualise What the Goal Is

As mentioned previously, this step establishes the project ethos and consequently there are several ethical issues that need to be borne in mind. This is the start of the project and it is vitally important to be above board at the onset so that a good working relationship is established with client. The principles of honour and honesty address this point. As shown in Table 7.4, bias in decision making and the undertaking of actions is a major concern throughout the project including Step 1. It is important to take a balanced viewpoint based on economic, technological and sociological information. The view often portrayed is skewed towards technology and economics which can have disastrous results leading to major system failure or rejection, as was the case, for example, at the London Ambulance Service and the London Stock Exchange. This leads to the remaining three dominant principles of due care, fairness and social cost. Computer systems impact directly and indirectly on many people and it is important to include all parties in decisions that affect the way in which the project is conducted. Software development projects involve many stakeholders and each is worthy of fair treatment. The principles of due care and social cost will ensure that a longer term and broader perspective is adopted.

## Step 8: Tell People What Is Going On

The project is dynamic and exists in a dynamic environment. Step 8 is essential so that everyone is aware of occurring change and so that their assignments can be adjusted accordingly. Being over-optimistic, ultra-pessimistic or simply untruthful about progress can be damaging not only to the project but also to both the client and supplier organisations. Those involved in this communication would be the project team, the computer department line management and the client. An honest, objective account of progress which takes into account the requirements and feelings of all concerned is the best way to operate. Drawing upon the principles of honour, honesty, bias, due care and fairness will assist in achieving this.

### The Ethical Verdict

While SPM provides practical guidance on the management of projects, it does not explicitly include an ethical dimension, though it is accepted there are implicit ethical issues in some parts of the methodology. There is a need for a stronger and more obvious emphasis on ethical issues. The derived mapping provides the framework for this additional ethical perspective within the project management process.

## The Primary Ethical Hotspots of Project Management

The mapping of ethical principles onto the steps of the methodology provides overall guidance on how to approach the project management process throughout the life of the project. However, within the project, there are numerous activities and decisions to be made and most of these will have an ethical dimension. It is impractical to consider each minute issue in great detail and still hope to achieve the overall project goal. The focus must be on the key issues which are likely to influence the success of the project. These are the primary ethical hotspots of project management. In Rogerson and Bynum (1995), ethical hotspots are defined as points where activities and decision making are likely to include a *relatively* high ethical dimension. There are two primary ethical hotspots in project management, namely, the defining of the scope of consideration (in Step 1 of SPM) and the information dissemination to the client (primarily in Step 8 of SPM).

### Scope of Consideration

It is a common problem with software development projects that decisions concerned with, for example, feasibility, functionality and implementation do not take into account the requirements of all those affected by the system once it becomes operational. This is illustrated by the cost benefit analysis activity undertaken at the beginning of most projects. This only takes into account the interests of those involved in the analysis and does not usually considered the rights and interests of *all* parties affected by the proposed system. The view is primarily techno-economic rather than techno-socio-economic. Potential well-being of many individuals is likely to be at risk unless an ethically sensitive horizon is established for the scope of consideration. This is more likely to happen if the principles of due care, fairness and social cost are prevalent during this activity. In this way, the project management process will embrace, at the onset, the views and concerns of all parties affected by the project. Concerns over, for example, deskilling of jobs, redundancy, the break-up of social groupings can be aired at the earliest opportunity and the project goals adjusted if necessary.

### Information Dissemination to the Client

The second ethical hotspot is to do with informing the client. No one likes to get shocking news, and so early warning of a problem and an indication of the scale of the problem are important.

Project managers must not see information dissemination to the client as information dissemination to the enemy which can be the stance in some organisations. The key is to provide factual information in non-emotive words, so the client and project manager can discuss any necessary changes in a calm and professional manner. Confrontational progress meetings achieve nothing. The adoption of the principles of honesty, bias, due care and fairness would help to ensure a good working relationship with the client.

## Conclusions

Without any doubt, the project management process for software development is capable of accommodating an ethical perspective. This has been demonstrated by mapping the derived eight ethical principles onto the SPM methodology. The major criticism of current practice is that any ethical consideration tends to be implicit rather than explicit which has a tendency to devalue the importance of the ethical dimension. By using ethical principles and the identification of ethical hotspots, it is possible to ensure that the key ethical issues are properly addressed. Quite simply, project management should be guided by a sense of justice, a sense of equal distributions of benefits and burdens and a sense of equal opportunity. In this way, software development project management will become ethically aligned.

## References

DeMarco, T. & Lister, T. (1987). *Peopleware.* Dorset House.

O'Connell, F. (1994) *How to Run Successful Projects.* Prentice Hall.

Parker, D. B., Swope, S. & Baker, B. N. (1990). *Ethical Conflicts in Information and Computer Science, Technology, and Business.* Wellesley, MA, QED Information Sciences.

Rogerson, S. & Bynum, T. W. (1995). Identifying the ethical dimension of decision making in the complex domain of IS/IT. *ETHICOMP95 Conference,* De Montfort University, UK, 28–30 March 1995.

van Luijk, H. (1994). Business ethics: the field and its importance. In: Harvey, B. (ed.), *Business Ethics: A European Approach.* Prentice Hall.

Velasquez, M. G. (1992). *Business Ethics – Concepts and Cases,* 3rd Edition. Prentice Hall.

# Chapter 8

# An Ethical Review of Information Systems Development: The Australian Computer Society's Code of Ethics and SSADM [2000]*

## Introduction

Moor (1985) asserted that computers are "logically malleable" in the sense that "they can be shaped and moulded to do any activity that can be characterised in terms of inputs, outputs and connecting logical operations." This might lead to policy vacuums caused by possibilities that did not exist before computers. In these situations, there are often no useful analogies to draw upon for help. Maner (1996) states that, "Lack of an effective analogy forces us to discover new moral values, formulate new moral principles, develop new policies and find new ways to think about the issues presented to us."

While this may be a little strong – it is not altogether clear just what a new moral principle or value might be – we must certainly apply principles in new situations. In such situations, Gotterbarn (1992) suggests that professionals must be aware of their professional responsibilities, have available methods for resolving non-technical ethics questions, and develop proactive skills to reduce the likelihood of ethical problems occurring. Those involved in information systems (IS) development are one group significantly affected by this ethically volatile situation.

Much of the work in computer ethics has been concentrated in the philosophy and sociology disciplines with restricted input from the IS and computer science disciplines. This may be the reason why Walsham (1996) claims that, "... there is little published work which directly relates

---

* This chapter was developed from an earlier paper: Rogerson, S. (1996) An ethical review of information systems development and the SSADM approach. *ETHICOMP96 proceedings*, Vol. 1, Spain, pp. 384–393.

these [specific IS-related ethical] issues to more general ethical theory ….” The work has tended to be conceptual and more of a commentary on computer phenomena than an attempt to develop strategies to identify and address societal and ethical issues associated with IS and the underpinning information technology (IT; Rogerson & Bynum, 1996). There are some notable exceptions, however, including Laudon (1995), Mason (1995), Anderson et al. (1993), Mason, Mason and Culnan (1995), de Raadt (1997), Harris, Prichard and Rabin (1997) and Martin and Schinzinger (1996).

The purpose of this chapter is to address some of the ethical challenges associated with IS development. Specifically, various principles from the Code of Ethics of the Australian Computer Society (ACS) will be applied to a particular methodology. The structured systems analysis and design method (SSADM) will be used as an illustrative example because it is felt that if ethical enrichment can be achieved in a “hard” systems approach then it is likely to be achievable in most approaches. The ethical enhancement of SSADM is a considerable task that is beyond the scope of the present study. This discussion is confined to making some suggestions regarding how that task might be achieved employing the aforementioned code of ethics. Several important assumptions underlie the chapter. One is that both deontological and consequential theories of ethics are important here. For practical purposes, we must often follow rules, but consequences are important in the formulation of rules, and for making decisions when rules clash. A second assumption is that ethical principles are, in an important sense, objective. Both of these assumptions are contentious, but detailed examination of them would allow no time for the issue at hand.

## IS Development

Turning to the overall development process, there are numerous methodological approaches to IS development. Few deal adequately with the ethical dimensions of systems development. Avison (1995) criticises the development methodologies, such as SSADM, Merise and Yourdon, that are adopted by most organisations today because they tend to stress formal and technical aspects. He argues that, “The emphasis … must move away from technical systems which have behavioural and social problems to social systems, which rely to an increasing extent on information technology.”

He suggests that the human, social and organisational aspects are often overlooked. The consideration of this broader perspective only seems to occur in the event of systems failure or under-performance. This issue is addressed by Wood-Harper et al. (1996) who identify a number of dilemmas which a systems analyst might face when undertaking a systems development activity using a methodological approach. These dilemmas are summarised as:

- whose ethical perspective will dominate the study of the situation and the development of the IS?
- will ethical viewpoints be included in the study?
- what methodology should be used for the study?
- what approach should the analyst use if there is an obvious conflict of interests?

It is important to recognise that there are a few methodological approaches, notably ETHICS from Mumford (1983), Soft Systems Methodology from Checkland (1981) and Multiview from Avison and Wood-Harper (1990) that attempt to include consideration of ethical and societal issues. In evaluating ETHICS, Jayaratna (1994) suggests that it, "offers many design guidelines useful for the understanding and the design of human-centred systems, but … does not offer models or ways for performing … the steps. Nor does it offer any models for handling interpersonal and political conflicts." He concludes that, "ETHICS is committed to a particular ethical stance [and] does not offer any means of discussing or resolving many of the ethical dilemmas … in systems development."

This appears to be a recurrent criticism of such methodologies. While it is laudable that ethical sensitivity is raised as an issue worthy of investigation, the manner in which investigation is undertaken and an ethically defensible position derived is vague.

Methodologies need to be enhanced to address these criticisms. It seems clear that research is required into the generalised manner in which ethical issues can be accounted for together with enhancement of specific methodologies. This chapter specifically addresses the question, "Will ethical viewpoints be included in the study?" The approach explored here is to use the relevant elements of a code of conduct to create an analytical tool that can be used to identify where and how to ethically enrich an IS development approach. The code of the ACS has been chosen for this purpose (see the Appendix 8.A).

## The ACS Code as an Analytical Tool

IS practitioners will readily acknowledge that they are professionals who use computers to resolve organisational problems. As professionals, they should be willing to adhere to a professional code of conduct that embeds ethical principles (Rogerson, 1997). The ACS has developed a code of ethics which constitutes a comprehensive and appropriate tool to provide guidance in computing practice.

The ACS Code of Ethics and Standard of Conduct is largely reproduced in the Appendix 8.A of this chapter. It is segmented into six areas of concern (priorities, competence, honesty, social implications, professional development and IT profession). Although this contrasts with the British Computer Society (BCS) code, which focuses upon the public interest, duty to the employer and clients, duty to the profession and professional competence and integrity, in fact the detail when viewed overall is quite similar. Still fewer headings are used in the Association for Computing Machinery (ACM), namely, general moral imperatives, more specific professional responsibilities, organizational leadership imperatives and compliance with the code.

In reality, it could be argued that the headings used in the ACS code lend themselves better to the "hard" checklist approach of SSADM than the other codes, for example, to achieve a review of proper priorities and likewise for social implications. The introduction to the code states the following.

> *A Requirement*
> *an essential characteristic of a profession is the need for its members to abide by a code of ethics. The society requires its members to subscribe to a set of values and ideals which uphold and advance the honour, dignity, and effectiveness of the profession of IT. The member is required at all times to be honest, forthright, and impartial, to loyally serve employers, clients and the public, to strive to increase the competence and prestige of the profession and to use special knowledge and skill for the advancement of human welfare.*

The guidelines clearly imply that the future of the computing profession depends on both technical and ethical excellence and consequently any violation has to be considered as unprofessional practice. It is worth noting here that, in certain circumstances, some violations may be impossible to avoid. It is not too difficult to imagine a situation in which it is not possible to "loyally serve employers, clients and the public" simultaneously. This is recognised, at least minimally, in 1.5. of the code: "I will advise my client or employer of any potential conflicts of interest between my assignment and legal or other accepted community requirements." No clear guidelines are given, however, on the best methods of resolving these conflicts.

Particular areas of the code exist that should be considered during an IS development project. These can be identified and used to measure how methodologies attend to ethical considerations. They become tools for deciding how methodologies might have to be modified. This chapter indicates how this may be done.

Compared with other codes, the architecture of the ACS code is categorised into areas of concern that make it relatively easy to create pragmatic checklists for adding to the SSADM procedures, particularly when considering "priorities" and "social implications."

Clearly, there are still gaps in the code when it comes to detailed considerations of, for example, flow-on effects of one's product and services to clients and further into the community. No imperative is stated to consider far-reaching secondary effects or the desirability of resulting cultural changes. The closest we get to this is in the ACM code: "1.1 Contribute to society and human wellbeing," "2.5. Give comprehensive and thorough evaluations of computer systems and their impacts, including analysis of possible risks," and "2.7. Improve public understanding of computing and its consequences." These are rather vague. "Public health and safety" and "environment" are mentioned in both BCS (1.) and ACS (4.1) codes. BCS (4.) mentions "basic human rights" and ACS refers to "people's privacy affected by my work" in (4.2). ACS section (4.5) is even less specific: "increase the feelings of personal satisfaction, competence and control of those affected by my work." We return to the issue of far-reaching secondary effects further on in this chapter.

In producing an extension to the SSADM checklist, the essential ethical questions can be explicitly detailed and revised periodically as professional wisdom and sensitivity grows.


# An Overview of SSADM Version 4

SSADM is now used as an illustrative method to further discussion of the ethics of IS development. SSADM is a set of procedural, technical, and documentation standards for IS development (Skidmore, Farmer & Mills, 1994). SSADM comprises five core modules: feasibility study, requirements analysis, requirements specification, logical systems specification and physical design module. The position of these modules in the development life cycle is shown in Figure 8.1 (Skidmore, Farmer & Mills, 1994). SSADM adopts a product-oriented approach where each element, be it a module, stage or step, produces predictable outputs from given inputs.


## *Core Modules*

Each of the five self-contained modules has a set of objectives:

1. Feasibility study:
   - to determine whether systems can be developed to meet defined business and technical objectives within specified financial and operational constraints

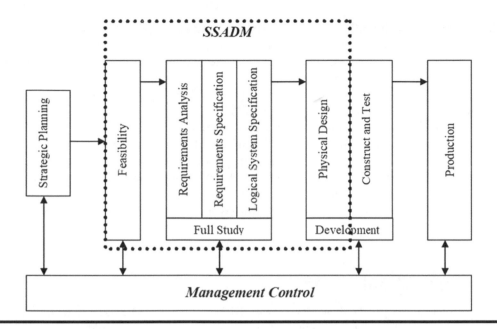

**Figure 8.1 Position of SSADM in the systems development life cycle. (Source: Skidmore, Farmer & Mills, 1994)**

2. Requirements analysis:
   - to determine the application scope
   - to establish how to integrate IT with other needs
   - to form an overall view of system costs and benefits
   - to confirm the viability of continuing further
   - to achieve user buy-in of the requirement

3. Requirements specification:
   - to produce a complete specification that informs the subsequent logical systems specification

4. Logical systems specification:
   - to enable management to select the technical environment that offers the best value for the money
   - to provide an independent non-procedural specification of system functionality

5. Physical design module:
   - to develop a physical design that defines data, processes, inputs and outputs while incorporating installation standards
   - to form the basis for system construction

## Modelling Perspectives

There are three modelling perspectives within SSADM, which are as follows:

1. Functions: this is an attempt to capture the user's view of system processing. Techniques used include data flow modelling.

2. Events: these are business activities that trigger processes to update system data. Techniques involved include entity life histories and affect correspondence diagrams.
3. Data: this is a description of the data used in the system utilising a logical data model.

## Products

Products are defined within a product breakdown structure hierarchy, the top level of which has three elements: management products, technical products and quality products. These three categories are designed to be complementary to ensure that a high-quality solution is provided in a managed and controlled way (CCTA, 1990). Management products are used in planning and controlling the project, technical products document how the project proposes to realise the project objectives and quality projects demonstrate how quality has been built into the system.

# Reviewing SSADM

Winter, Brown and Checkland (1995) explain that computer-based IS are systems that serve purposeful human actions. They argue that there is a very heavy emphasis on the serving IS in the systems development life cycle with, in the main, only limited and implicit account taken of the purposeful human action or the so-called served system. This is particularly the case in the "hard" systems thinking approaches of structured methods that are highly technical and rational. In examining SSADM, Winter, Brown and Checkland (1995) found no explicit organisational activity model. There also appeared to be an acceptance without question of the image, activities and performance aspects of the organisation in question. Furthermore, they were critical of the information requirements of SSADM's concept, which concerned the information required for the system to function rather than the information needed by the people undertaking organisational activities. Upon analysis of the ACS code, several of the articles detailed in its Standards of Conduct align with the areas of criticism within SSADM. It is argued that a method needs to address effectively these areas before it can be considered to be a professional approach. Clearly, the authors have reservations about SSADM. If it is to be a professional approach, it must be modified in some way, or used in conjunction with a complementary method, in order to overcome its deficiencies.

The approach adopted by Winter, Brown and Checkland (1995) is organisationally oriented. It does not appear to go beyond the environs of the organisation. Potential well-being of many individuals is likely to be at risk unless an ethically sensitive horizon is established for the scope of consideration. Issues beyond the horizon are deemed not to influence the project or be influenced by the project. The scope of consideration is an ethical hotspot that is influenced by the identification and involvement of all stakeholders including those beyond the organisational boundary (Rogerson, 1997). It is this that is particularly addressed in articles (1.5), (4.1), (4.2) and (4.5) of the ACS code. This is an area not effectively covered by SSADM and it is unclear whether distant stakeholders will be identified let alone involved. The implications of such restricted stakeholder involvement on achieving a socially and ethically sensitive approach are obvious.

The ACS code, in the last three articles just mentioned, talks of "those affected by my work." The "ethically sensitive horizon" is clearly relevant here. In order to make clearer some of the issues regarding stakeholders, it will be useful to identify the main groups, following

Collins et al. (1994). They identify four principal groups: developers who develop and sell the system; buyers who purchase and own the system; users who use the system; and the penumbra, comprising anyone affected by the use of the system. These groups are not mutually exclusive of course. The developers and buyers could be the same people, and might also be users of the system. Any of the first three groups could also overlap with the penumbra. This identification assists in the clarification responsibilities and tensions in the software development enterprise. Developers want to make profits, but products need to be affordable by potential buyers. Buyers want products to be as inexpensive as possible, but they also want reliable products. Users also want the products to be reliable but they also desire them to be "friendly." The penumbra in general just wants software which is not going to harm them or make their lives less pleasant. The basic tension is clearly between cost, on the one hand, and reliability and ease of use on the other. The more time spent developing a product, the better it can be, but the more expensive it will be. Typically there will be some trade-off between these two. The important question then is what criteria should be used to determine where the line will be drawn. Collins et al. suggest three criteria:

1. Do not increase harm to the least advantaged.
2. Do not risk increasing harm in an already risky environment.
3. Use the publicity test for difficult trade-offs.

The first criterion in most cases would refer to members of the penumbra, that is, those who are affected by the system but who may derive little or no benefit from it. The second criterion is unlikely to help much in identifying who will be harmed, but it does emphasise that more care needs to be taken in some situations than in others. The third criterion is explained thus: "trade-offs between financial benefits to the one party and personal (i.e. non-financial) harm to another party should be made on the basis of a cost-benefit ratio that, if made public, would not outrage most members of the public" (Collins et al., 1994, p. 86).

This does something to help set the horizon. It seems intuitively plausible to assume that there would normally be more public disquiet, if not outrage, if financial benefits took precedence over direct and fairly immediate harm than over more vague harm in the future, or further removed from the system's direct effects. While these three criteria have some plausibility and usefulness, there are problems. Public outrage, for example, can be partly a result of the level of information given, so might not always identify the unethical, and the majority might not be outraged at some injustice done to a small minority, when it ought to be. A rights-based alternative will sometimes be more appropriate than the consequentialism of Collins et al. (1994).

Identifying the stakeholders in the manner above certainly assists in making some of the issues clearer. There is, however, still some problem with the ideas of "distant stakeholders" and the "ethically sensitive horizon." The problem is not new, and any consequentialist theory of ethics must face it. Mill (1859) in On Liberty, arguing that individuals should be free to do as they like with respect to actions which affect only themselves, acknowledged that most actions affect others as well. This is the same problem of scope as that which must be faced by software developers. Which effects should be taken into account and which need not? Mill required an answer in order to set limits to the state's legitimate coercion of individuals. Software developers require it to make decisions regarding their work, where their own legitimate interests must be considered alongside the interests of those affected by their work. Mill's suggested solution was to say that people should be allowed to do as they want with respect to actions which affect themselves "directly and in the first instance," or primarily only affect themselves. Applying this to the software development environment, perhaps the horizon should be set so that all those affected by the software "directly and in the first instance," or who are primarily affected, have their interests taken into account. This would indicate that the interests of those using, say, an unfriendly ATM should be taken into account, but not the interests of their families on whom they vent their spleen. This is still vague, and it may not always draw the line in the right place, but it does give some guidance. It must be noted too that, in practice, there may be different stakeholders and horizons at each phase of the development process. The ethical guidelines must take account of this. For example, at the feasibility study phase, there will be a host of social and environment concerns involving many groups in society, while at the logical system phase the focus will be more on management, technical staff, users and company shareholders.

de Raadt (1997), in a series of papers about multi-modal systems thinking, proposes a number of modes of action, analysed into a high to low sequence from wholly inspirational to wholly foundational. In order, these are credal, ethical, juridical, aesthetic, economic, operational, social, epistemic, informatory, historical, psychic, biotic, physical, kinematic, spatial, numeric, logical. The professional codes of ethics seem to be concerned about the modes from logical up to and including economic, sometimes embracing aesthetic, often juridical (rules) but seldom venturing into the so-defined ethical (love) mode, which is of a higher order than the common view of ethics, and never into the credal (faith) mode. This "multi-modal systems approach" inherently embraces the "ethically sensitive horizon" and therefore promises to be a useful tool for future extensions to SSADM. At the same time, it invites us to rethink higher order professional standards.

## Ethics and SSADM

As noted earlier, the ethical enhancement of SSADM is no small task, and hence this discussion is limited to outlining some methods for its achievement. It seems obvious that prescriptive rules for action are required, together with consideration of consequences. Such rules are needed if for no other reason than that in practice we cannot always consider all of an action's likely outcomes. Consequences must be taken into account because sometimes rules clash, and sometimes they need to be overridden for a greater good.

These comments partly mirror more fundamental discussions in ethics. Is something morally right or wrong because of its consequences, or because it follows or breaks some rule or violates some right? This is not the place to argue about whether ethics is essentially consequentialist, deontological, rights or virtue based, or something else, important as these positions are for ethics in general. For everyday, practical purposes, we must frequently follow rules, albeit, defeasible ones; hence our reliance on a code of ethics in this chapter. In everyday life, if we are to get anything done, we cannot examine in detail the consequences of all of our actions to see whether they cause, or are likely to cause, more or less harm than alternative actions. Nor can we in every case decide whether someone's rights have been violated. In important instances, and whenever possible, and particularly when rules clash, such thought should be given, but many decisions are made "on the run," with little time for reflection. This is not to suggest that ethical theory is not important in everyday life, it certainly is important, and it plays a central role in the formulation of codes of ethics such as the one used here.

Another basic issue in ethics is whether ethical principles are objective or relative. Our assumption, also noted earlier, is that they are objective in an important sense, and are not just matters of opinion. Nor is ethics merely relative to a culture. While many ethical practices are certainly related to cultures, it is much less clear that basic ethical principles are (see Weckert and Adeney (1997) for discussion).

With this in mind, it is important to address both the process and the product of SSADM. The product breakdown structure provides the impetus to address issues in a certain way. The completeness of these products needs to be considered given their powerful influence in the development. Consideration must also be given to how the systems developers should think when undertaking the various development tasks. The SSADM culture explicitly promotes technological and economic thinking, but not ethical thinking. The new version 4+ appears to be moving to a more balanced view with more emphasis on business orientation and the inclusion of user culture in the systems development template (Hall, 1995).

## Changing the Structure

It is now recognised that quality should permeate the whole of the IS development process and not simply be considered at discrete points within the process. This is reflected in SSADM by the inclusion of a quality product set comprising a number of files that demonstrate that quality has been built into the system (CCTA, 1990). Product descriptions are part of this set. There are product descriptions for all the products specified in SSADM. The details include quality criteria against which the product can be checked. Product descriptions are used to monitor progress and success of the project. Including quality in each description ensures that it permeates the whole process and promotes a quality culture throughout the development team. Similarly, ethical and societal consideration should permeate the whole process, and in many cases quality issues overlap with ethical ones, for example, in safety critical systems. It follows that each product description should include ethical and social criteria to promote this awareness and consideration. This might be systematically addressed by using the ACS articles to form the ethical criteria for products within each of the core modules. This is illustrated in Table 8.1 which shows which articles apply to each of the modules.

The clauses below are selected from the ACS code of ethics as the most relevant to ethical issues in systems development and hence to extending a methodology such as SSADM. During the construction of Table 8.1, there emerged a number of grey areas that depend upon point of view. The purpose here is not definitive accuracy, but a possible approach to adding checkpoint questions where they would be most effective. Future developments of the table could well differ.

As an example, consider the application style guide, which is one of the products from stage 4, "technical environment" options within "logical systems specification." This sets the standards for the user environment within the particular project and includes ergonomic details and system-based requirements. The ethical criteria for this product based on the appropriate ACS articles might be:

- Does the system protect and promote the health and safety of those affected by it? (4.1)
- Is the application style such that integrity and security of individuals is not compromised? (1.2)
- Am I happy that this product is suitable? (3.1)
- Has a walk-through of the application style taken place? (4.5)
- Is the working environment enhanced? (4.1, 4.5).

**Table 8.1  Mapping Acs Articles onto the Core Modules**

| | SSADM Core Modules | | | | |
|---|---|---|---|---|---|
| ACS Clauses | Feasibility Study | Requirements Analysis | Requirements Specification | Logical Systems Specification | Physical Design |
| 1.2 | X | X | X | X | X |
| 1.3 | X | X | X | X | X |
| 1.5 | X | X | X | | |
| 2.1 | | X | X | | |
| 2.4 | | | X | X | |
| 2.6 | X | X | | | |
| 3.1 | X | X | X | X | |
| 3.4 | X | | | | |
| 3.5 | X | X | X | X | X |
| 4.1 | X | X | X | X | X |
| 4.2 | X | X | | | |
| 4.4 | X | | | | |
| 4.5 | X | X | X | X | X |
| 6.1 | X | X | X | X | X |

It is suggested that the top level of the product breakdown structure be extended to include ethics products. In this way, ethical issues would be explicitly considered within the SSADM method. These would comprise enhanced product descriptions, described earlier, plus appropriate outputs from the ethical instruments within SSADM. Three examples of these instruments are now briefly outlined.

## Example Instruments

The move from the current data flow diagram to the required logical data model is a demanding process from requirements analysis through requirements specification to logical systems specification. The process logically reduces the requirements definition by removing data redundancy and irrelevance. This is done from an economic and technological standpoint (and possibly legal). The question of whether items are redundant from ethical and societal standpoints needs also to be addressed. There is also the issue of ethical and societal verification of data item inclusion. Both might be addressed by developing a criterion reference model that enables the ethically and socially charged items to be systematically identified. A course of action can then be chosen based on balanced and comprehensive information.

An approach that could be incorporated both in the feasibility study and requirements analysis modules of SSADM is suggested by Rogerson and Bynum (1995). They developed a four-perspectives model, based on Aristotle's model of ethical decision making, for the preliminary analysis and decision making at the beginning of any systems development project. This entails the integration of ethics, based upon the concepts and guidelines already outlined, in two different ways. A comprehensive analysis is undertaken from four perspectives: technical, economic, legal and ethical. The four-perspective analysis is the major input to the decision-making process which in turn results in a tentative action plan. It is essential that an ethical control loop exists providing the opportunity to review the decision made.

A feedback loop based on the outcome of the action is inappropriate as it will then be too late to influence that outcome. For this reason, a feed-forward loop is included which evaluates the tentative decision before the action takes place. This ethical evaluation provides a prediction of the likely outcome should action be undertaken. A predicted unethical outcome will result in a reconsideration of the project definition or the four-perspectives analysis or both. A series of analytical iterations could take place until the ethical feed forward analysis predicts an ethically acceptable outcome of the proposed practical action.

Given the scientific nature of SSADM that encourages rational logic, it is worth considering how ethical modelling might be incorporated. The SSADM process is based on logical decomposition that identifies the "best" way of satisfying a user requirement. It is oriented to the end product with the analytical journey simply being the means to that end result. A consequentialist approach is attractive in this context. Indeed, it might be possible to develop an ethical modelling approach based on Bentham's hedonistic calculus. The seven aspects in the calculus used to compare relative outcomes can be reinterpreted in six terms more appropriate for IS development which are as follows:

1. The value of the benefit
2. The duration of the benefit
3. The degree of certainty in benefit realisation
4. When the benefit will be realised
5. Whether the system will lead to secondary or indirect benefits
6. The individuals, businesses and communities affected

Note that the last two items require consideration of all stakeholders, alterations to community ethos, and effects upon environment. A significant reduction in complexity of these avenues could be achieved through the use of checklists (which as suggested, could be quite extensive, yet dynamic, being revised as professional wisdom grows).

This consequentialist approach has merit in that it links the ethical character of actions to their practical outcome. However, this can be extremely difficult. As White (1993) points out, "a full account of an action's results means not only careful analysis of the immediate consequences to all involved and astute discernment of the quality and comparative value of the sensations experienced, but also an uncovering of the subtle, indirect, far-reaching and long-term results as well."

This is particularly relevant for IS where it is usually the case that systems interact resulting in long-term synergistic effects that are difficult to predict and measure. Yet we have to try.

# Conclusion

This chapter has discussed the ethical problems associated with IS development. Little research has been undertaken in this area to date. It has been demonstrated that approaches like SSADM do not encompass ethical considerations effectively. The ACS code has been used to identify where and how SSADM could be modified and some examples were used to illustrate this approach. This is only the beginning. Ethical enrichment of development methods must be carefully undertaken and validated through fieldwork. Only then there will be an increase in ethically sensitive IS.

# References

Anderson, R. E., Johnson, D. G., Gotterbarn D. & Perrolle, J. (1993). Using the new ACM Code of Ethics in decision making. *Communications of the ACM*, 36(2), 98–107.

Avison, D. E. (1995). *What is IS*: an inaugural lecture delivered at the University of Southampton. 3 November 1994.

Avison, D. E. & Wood-Harper, A. T. (1990). *Multiview: An Exploration in Information Systems Development*. Alfred Waller.

CCTA (1990). *SSADM Version 4, Reference Manual: Volume 4, Dictionary*. NCC Blackwell.

Checkland, P. B. (1981). *Systems Thinking, Systems Practice*. Wiley.

Collins, W. R., Miller, K. W., Speilman, B. J. & Wherry, P. (1994). How good is good enough? An ethical analysis of software construction and use. *Communications of the ACM*, 37(1), 81–91.

de Raadt J. D. R. (1997). Faith and the normative foundation of systems science. *Systems Practice*, 10(1), 13–35.

Gotterbarn, D. (1992). The use and abuse of computer ethics. In: Bynum, T. W., Maner, W. & Fodor, J. L. (eds.), *Teaching Computer Ethics, Research Center on Computing and Society*. Southern Connecticut State University, pp. 73–83.

Hall, J. (1995). How is SSADM4.2 different from SSADMV4?. *SSADM4+ for Academics*. CCTA & International SSADM User Group Workshop. Leeds Metropolitan University.

Harris, C. E. Jr., Prichard, M. S. & Rabin, M. J. (1997). *Practicing Engineering Ethics*. New York, Institute of Electrical and Electronics Engineers.

Jayaratna, N. (1994). *Understanding and Evaluating Methodologies*. McGraw-Hill.

Laudon, K. C. (1995). Ethical concepts and information technology. *Communications of the ACM*, 38(12),33–39.

Maner, W. (1996). Unique ethical problems in information technology. *Science and Engineering Ethics*, 2(2), 137–155.

Martin, M. W. & Schinzinger, R. (1996). *Ethics in Engineering*. McGraw-Hill.

Mason, R. O. (1995). Applying ethics to information technology issue. *Communications of the ACM*, 38(12), 55–57.

Mason, R. O., Mason, F. M. & Culnan, M. J. (1995). *Ethics of Information Management*. Sage Publications.

Mill, J. S. (1859). On liberty. In: Spitz, D. (ed.), *John Stuart Mill, On Liberty: Annotated Text Sources and Background Criticism*. WW Norton.

Moor, J. H. (1985). What is computer ethics?. *Metaphilosophy*, 16(4), 266–279.

Mumford, E. (1983). *Designing Participatively*. Manchester Business School.

Rogerson, S. (1997). Software project management ethics. In: Myers, C., Hall, T. & Pitt, D. (eds.), *The Responsible Software Engineer*. Springer-Verlag, pp. 100–106.

Rogerson, S. & Bynum, T. W. (1995). *Towards Ethically Sensitive IS/IT Projected Related Decision Making*. Submitted to COOCS'95, Milpitas, California, August 13–16, 1995.

Rogerson, S. & Bynum, T. W. (1996). Information ethics: the second generation. *UK Academy for Information Systems Conference*, UK.

Skidmore, S., Farmer, R. & Mills, G. (1994). *SSADM Version 4 Models and Methods*, 2nd Edition. NCC Blackwell.

Walsham, G. (1996). Ethical theory, codes of ethics and IS practice. *Information Systems Journal*, 6(1), 69–81.

Weckert, J. & Adeney, D. (1997). *Computer and Information Ethics*. Greenwood Press.

White, J. (1993). *Money isn't God. So Why is the Church Worshipping It?* Downers Grove, IL, Inter-Varsity Press.

Winter, M. C., Brown, D. H. & Checkland, P. B. (1995). A role for soft systems methodology in information systems development. *European Journal of Information Systems*, 4(3), 130–142.

Wood-Harper, A. T., Corder, S., Wood, J. R. G. & Watson, H. (1996). How we profess: the ethical systems analyst. *Communications of the ACM*, 39(3), 69–77.

## Appendix 8.A: The Australian Computer Society Code of Ethics

Following is the Australian Computer Society (ACS) Code of Ethics, extracted from the ACS WWW site http://www.acs.org.au/ as it existed in January 1998. Apart from the omission of the initial introduction and the introductory paragraph to the Standard of Conduct section, the Code is reproduced in full. The bracketed words have been added.

### Code of Ethics

I will act with professional responsibility and integrity in my dealing with clients, employers, employees, students and the community generally. By this I mean:

1. [Priorities] I will serve the interests of my clients and employers, my employees and students and the community generally, as matters of no less priority than the interests of myself or my colleagues.
2. [Competence] I will work competently and diligently for my clients and employers.
3. [Honesty] I will be honest in my representations of skills, knowledge, services and products.
4. [Social implications] I will strive to enhance the quality of life of those affected by my work.
5. [Professional development] I will enhance my own professional development, and that of my colleagues, employees and students.
6. [Computing profession] I will enhance the integrity of the Computing Profession and the respect of its members for each other.

### Standard of Conduct

1. *Priorities*: I will serve the interests of my clients and employers, my employees and students and the community generally, as matters of no less priority than the interests of myself or my colleagues.

    1.1. I will endeavour to preserve continuity of computing services and information flow in my care.
    1.2. I will endeavour to preserve the integrity and security of others' information.
    1.3. I will respect the proprietary nature of others' information.
    1.4. (missing in original).
    1.5. I will advise my client or employer of any potential conflicts of interest between my assignment and legal or other accepted community requirements.

1.6. I will advise my clients and employers as soon as possible of any conflicts of interest or conscientious objections which face me in connection with my work.

2. *Competence*: I will work competently and diligently for my clients and employers.

   2.1. I will endeavour to provide products and services which match the operational and financial needs of my clients and employers.
   2.2. I will give value for money in the services and products I supply.
   2.3. I will make myself aware of relevant standards, and act accordingly.
   2.4. I will respect and protect my clients' and employers' proprietary interests.
   2.5. I will accept responsibility for my work.
   2.6. I will advise my clients and employers when I believe a proposed project is not in their best interests.
   2.7. I will go beyond my brief, if necessary, in order to act professionally.

3. *Honesty*: I will be honest in my representation of skills, knowledge, services and products.

   3.1. I will not knowingly mislead a client or potential client as to the suitability of a product or service.
   3.2. I will not misrepresent my skills or knowledge.
   3.3. I will give opinions which are as far as possible unbiased and objective.
   3.4. I will give realistic estimates for projects under my control.
   3.5. I will qualify professional opinions which I know are based on limited knowledge experience.
   3.6. I will give credit for work done by others where credit is due.

4. *Social implications*: I will strive to enhance the quality of life of those affected by my work.

   4.1. I will protect and promote the health and safety of those affected by my work.
   4.2. I will consider and respect people's privacy which might be affected by my work.
   4.3. I will respect my employees and refrain from treating them unfairly.
   4.4. I will endeavour to understand, and give due regard to, the perceptions of those affected by my work, whether or not I agree with those perceptions.
   4.5. I will attempt to increase the feelings of personal satisfaction, competence and control of those affected by my work.
   4.6. I will not require, or attempt to influence, any person to take any action which would involve a breach of this Code.

5. *Professional development*: I will enhance my own professional development, and that of my colleagues, employees and students.

   5.1. I will continue to upgrade my knowledge and skills.
   5.2. I will increase my awareness of issues affecting the computing profession and its relationship with the community.
   5.3. I will encourage my colleagues, employees and students to continue their own professional development.

6. *Computing profession*: I will enhance the integrity of the Computing Profession and the respect of its members for each other.

   6.1. I will respect, and seek when necessary, the professional opinions of colleagues in areas of competence.

6.2. I will not knowingly engage in, or be associated with, dishonest or fraudulent practices.

6.3. I will not attempt to enhance my own reputation at the expense of another's reputation.

6.4. I will co-operate in advancing information processing by communication with other professionals, students, and the public, and by contributing to the efforts of professional and scientific societies and schools.

6.5. I will distance myself professionally from someone whose membership of the ACS has been terminated because of unethical behaviour or unsatisfactory conduct.

6.6. I will take appropriate action if I discover a member, or a person who could potentially be a member, of the ACS engaging in unethical behaviour.

6.7. I will seek advice from the ACS when faced with an ethical dilemma I am unable to resolve by myself.

6.8. I will do what I can to ensure that the corporate actions of the ACS are in accordance with this Code.

6.9. I acknowledge my debt to the Computing Profession and in return will protect and promote profession.

# Chapter 9

# A Practical Perspective of Information Ethics [2001]*

## Introduction

Information is the new lifeblood of society and its organisations. Our dependence on information grows daily with the advance of information and communication technology and its global application. The integrity of information relies upon the development and operation of computer-based information systems. Those who undertake the planning, development and operation of these information systems have obligations to assure information integrity and contribute to the public good. This is the field of information ethics, a brief discussion of which is included after this introduction.

It is interesting to note that much of the work in this area has been concentrated in the philosophy and sociology disciplines with restricted input from the information systems and computer science disciplines. This may be the reason why Walsham (1996) found that "… there is little published work which directly relates these [specific information systems related ethical] issues to more general ethical theory …." The work has tended to be conceptual and more of a commentary on computer phenomena rather than an attempt to develop strategies to identify and address societal and ethical issues associated with information systems and the underpinning information and communication technology (Rogerson & Bynum, 1996). Given the overall focus of this book, it has been decided to adopt an organisational view of information ethics in this chapter rather than considering specific ethical issues such as privacy, access and privacy which are dealt with extensively in other publications in this field.

This chapter addresses these issues from three practical perspectives within the field of information ethics. In "Information Strategy" section, the manner in which strategy is formulated and the dilemmas that might arise are considered. This is followed by a discussion in "Project Management" section as to how an ethical dimension might be added to the project management of software development. Finally, in "Information Systems Development" section, the methods

---

* This chapter was first published as: Rogerson (1997) A practical perspective of information ethics. In: Goujon, P. & Dubreuil, B. H. (eds.), Technology and Ethics: A European Quest for Responsible Engineering. Chapter 2.2.3. pp. 305–325. ISBN 9042909501. Copyright © Peeters Publishers. Reprinted by permission.

used for information systems development are reviewed from an ethical standpoint. These issues are important to information engineers and software engineers who are now playing a key role in the running of modern organisations.

## Information Ethics

According to van Luijk (1994) ethics comprises both practice and reflection. Practice is the conscious appeal to norms and values to which individuals are obliged to conform, while reflection on practice is the elaboration of norms and values that colour daily activity. Norms are collective expectations regarding a certain type of behaviour while values are collective representations of what constitutes a good society. The existence of a plan and a controlling mechanism is the accepted norm in project management which itself is an accepted value in software development. For the purpose of this chapter, it is sufficient to consider only ethics practice because it is concerned with professional action rather than conceptual reflection. Conceptual reflection might manifest itself in, for example, codes of conduct which are concerned with establishing what are the generalised ways of working that are acceptable to a wider community. In other words, the chapter is concerned with how to use and when to apply norms and values rather than establishing what these norms and values are.

Bynum (1999) maintains that information ethics is the most important field of applied philosophy since "the world is transforming exponentially … under the influence of the most powerful and the most flexible technology ever devised." The main thrust of information ethics must be to integrate computing and human values in such a way that computing advances and protects human values rather than harms them (Bynum, 1992). There are however complex problems to overcome if such a goal is to be realised. It was Moor (1985) who asserted that computers are "logically malleable" in the sense that "they can be shaped and moulded to do any activity that can be characterised in terms of inputs, outputs and connecting logical operations." This might lead to policy vacuums caused by possibilities that did not exist before computers. In these situations, there are often no useful analogies to draw upon for help and as Maner (1996) explains we are therefore forced, "to formulate new moral principles, develop new policies and find new ways to think about the issues presented to us." In such situations, Gotterbarn (1992) suggests that professionals must be aware of their professional responsibilities, have available methods for resolving non-technical ethics questions, and develop proactive skills to reduce the likelihood of ethical problems occurring. Given the global nature of computing, it is important to base professional responses on Moor's (1998) suggestion of common core values and a respect for others. Those involved in computer-based information provision are one group significantly affected by such ethically volatile situations.

An ethical framework for computer professionals has been developed comprising a list of eight ethical principles that professionals need to be aware of, and a method by which these ethical principles can be applied to a particular application domain (Rogerson, 1997). The eight ethical principles are:

- *Honour* – is the action considered beyond reproach?
- *Honesty* – will the action violate any explicit or implicit agreement or trust?
- *Bias* – are there any external considerations that may bias the action to be taken?
- *Professional adequacy* – is the action within the limits of capability?

- *Due care* – is the action to be exposed to the best possible quality assurance standards?
- *Fairness* – are all stakeholders' views considered with regard to the action?
- *Consideration of social cost* – is the appropriate accountability and responsibility accepted with respect to this action?
- *Effective and efficient action* – is the action suitable, given the objectives set, and is it to be completed using the least expenditure of resources?

Looking at some of the principles in more detail, the principle of honour can be considered as the "umbrella" principle, to which all other principles contribute. It is concerned with the verification that all actions are beyond reproach. The principle of bias focuses on due consideration of any factors that may influence the action to be taken. The principle of due care is concerned with putting into place the measures by which any undesirable effects can be prevented, which may require additional attention beyond that agreed formally within a contract. The principle of social cost recognises that those involved in an action should take responsibility and be held accountable for the action. Such principles are enshrined in the codes of conduct of professional bodies such as the British Computer Society, the Australian Computer Society, the ACM and the influential Software Engineering Code of Ethics and Professional Practice (Gotterbarn, Miller & Rogerson, 1997).

These ethical principles are not mutually exclusive. They were developed to establish a checklist of ethical aspects to be applied whenever an action associated with computer systems takes place. The term action is used to represent any process or task undertaken, which normally includes a human element as the performer of the task or as the beneficiary, or as both performer and beneficiary. Within the information and communication technology domain, actions may be associated with the development, management or use of information and communication technology.

These principles can be used to analyse, inform and colour practice within the whole of computing. They are useful in identifying areas of high ethical sensitivity known as the ethical hotspots (Rogerson, 1997). There are many ethical issues surrounding the decisions and actions within the information systems field and there are limitations on professional time to respond to such issues. It is important to prioritise these issues on the basis of impact on the public good and so focus effort on the ethical hotspots.

## Information Strategy

The alignment of corporate strategy and information systems strategy continues to be of critical concern to organisations. This is one of the key directions identified as being fundamental to corporate wellbeing into the next century (Business Intelligence, 1995). Such alignment can be achieved through Strategic Information Systems Planning (SISP) which is the means of identifying applications systems that support and enhance organisational strategy and provides for the effective implementation of these systems (Fidler & Rogerson, 1996). For SISP to be effective, both the SISP process and the products identified as a result of SISP need to be accepted by the organisation and its wider community. Acceptance is multi-faceted and requires the examination of technical, social, legal and economic aspects. More recently, acceptance has been coloured by greater attention being paid to ethical issues associated with information and communication technology (Forcht & Thomas, 1994; Forester, 1992; Hawk, 1994; Langford & Wusteman, 1994; Oz, 1993). This is particularly given the advent of technologies with the potential to re-shape dramatically many aspects of our current lifestyles (Rogerson & Bynum, 1995; Widdifield

& Grover, 1995). Therefore, it is important to identify those key areas of SISP activity that warrant particular attention to ethical issues.

A good approach to SISP, within a particular organisation setting, depends on several factors, including:

- The environment of the organisation and the external pressures constraining IS/IT application (Flynn & Hepburn, 1994)
- The relative maturity of the organisation with respect to IS/IT use (Burn, 1993)
- The size and stability of the organisation (Bergeron & Raymond, 1992)
- Whether a SISP methodology and its supportive techniques are already determined

Despite the variability of approach between organisations (Earl, 1993), a list of six generic activities typically encountered within SISP can be identified:

1. Defining the scope of the SISP exercise
2. Understanding and interpreting the business requirements
3. Defining the organisational information needs and the underpinning Systems Architecture
4. Formulating the information, information systems and information technology strategies
5. Presenting the final output to the client
6. Reviewing the SISP experience

The first activity, defining the scope of the SISP exercise, is concerned with obtaining the authorisation to proceed, establishing the SISP team participants, setting out an agenda and creating a timetable for activities and allocating responsibilities. Essentially, this is the planning phase of SISP. Understanding and interpreting the business requirements involves establishing the corporate strategy and corporate Critical Success Factors, reviewing the current state of IS/IT within the organisation, and identifying potential IS/IT applications by taking both an internal and an external perspective to the organisation. Defining the organisational information needs and the underpinning systems architecture involves the mapping of systems to needs. This may provide some initial insight into the priority of subsequent systems developments or enhancements. From this, the strategies concerning the provision of information, the applications to support the provision of information and the underlying technologies to support the applications can be derived. These strategies are presented to the client. Finally, the experiences of the overall SISP exercise are reflected upon. This may lead to proposals for changes to be incorporated into future SISP activity.

Although the activities appear to follow a natural sequence, in practice many iterations to previous activities may occur, due to changes in requirements or in the operational environment. Furthermore, several activities may occur in parallel. SISP activity may also lead to changes in strategy, which leads subsequently to changes in the defined scope for the SISP exercise.

Undertaking an analysis using the eight ethical principles suggests that there are two ethical hotspots in SISP, namely, the first and fifth activities.

## Activity 1: Defining the Scope of the SISP Exercise

As previously mentioned, this activity is concerned with the planning of subsequent SISP activities. Setting out the scope of the exercise, deciding on the team membership and their respective tasks, and obtaining authorisation to proceed based on the plan, involves many decisions regarding the requirements and involvement of others. Ethical issues are therefore highly significant within this activity. For example, it is vitally important at this initial stage to be above board so that a good working relationship is established with the client. The principle of honesty addresses this point. It is also important to ensure that decisions concerning the team membership, for example, are not biased by previous stereotypical situations, but are for the good of the organisation in hand and are as fair as possible for all. The principles of bias and fairness are significant here. Any shortfalls in the team's experience in performing SISP should be made explicit at the outset of the project, and measures taken to make good this shortfall. This relates to the principle of adequacy. Appropriate quality control procedures should be considered as part of the planning process to ensure due care is given to the quality of each ensuing activity. Thus, the principle of due care is invoked. Attention to the social cost principle is also warranted to ensure that the plan incorporates issues of broader significance and that the accountability of the project team is appropriately defined. Actions on the part of those team members involved in the planning of the SISP exercise should always be considered beyond reproach, which directly relates to the principle of honour.

## Activity 5: Presenting the Final Output to the Client

This activity involves significant client liaison, and many of the ethical principles are dominant within this activity. The output must be presented efficiently and effectively so that deliberations are focused on the principal aspects of importance to the organisation and so that costly management time is not wasted. This relates to the principle of action. The presentation of results should paint an accurate and fair picture of the situation. This relates to the principles of bias, fairness and honesty. All stakeholders' views should be taken into account within the plan, although diplomacy concerning stakeholders' views is required at all times. Overall, the SISP team's approach to this activity must be professional and beyond reproach. This relates directly to the principle of honour.

SISP provides general guidance on the activities to be undertaken in order to achieve strategically aligned information systems and the ICT infrastructure. Any ethical consideration tends to be implicit rather than explicit which has a tendency to devalue the importance of the ethical dimension. Therefore, a stronger more explicit emphasis on ethical issues is needed. The mapping of ethical principles to SISP activities provides a general framework for explicitly including an ethical perspective within the SISP process.

## Project Management

It appears universally accepted that the most effective way to develop information systems software is through the use of a project-based organisational structure which encourages individuals to participate in teams with the goal of achieving some common objective. Much has been written about the management of software development projects and no doubt much will be written in the future.

In his book, *How to Run Successful Projects*, in the British Computer Society Practitioner Series, O'Connell (1994) provides details of the Structured Project Management (SPM) approach. He explains that SPM is a practical methodology that, as DeMarco and Lister (1987) state, is a "basic approach one takes to getting a job done." SPM has been chosen for discussion as it is practical rather than conceptual, generalist rather than specific and provides practitioners with realistic guidance in undertaking the vastly complex activity of project management. SPM comprises the following ten steps:

1. Visualise what the goal is.
2. Make a list of the jobs that need to be done.
3. Ensure there is one leader.
4. Assign people to jobs.
5. Manage expectations, allow a margin of error and have a fallback position.
6. Use an appropriate leadership style.
7. Know what is going on.
8. Tell people what is going on.
9. Repeat Step 1 through 8 until Step 10 is achievable.
10. Realise the project goal.

The first five steps are concerned with planning and the remaining five deal with implementing the plan and achieving the goal. O'Connell states that most projects succeed or fail because of decisions made during the planning stage thereby justifying the fact that half of the effort expended in the SPM approach is on preparation. It is this planning element of project management which lays down the foundations on which the project ethos is built. Here the scope of consideration is established, albeit implicitly or explicitly, which in turn locates the horizon beyond which issues are deemed not to influence the project or be influenced by the project. How the project is conducted will depend heavily upon the perceived goal. The visualisation of this goal takes place in Step 1. The first two points in the visualisation checklist given by O'Connell are:

- What will the goal of the project mean to all the people involved in the project when the project completes?
- What are the things the project will actually produce? Where will these things go? What will happen to them? Who will use them? How will they be affected by them?

These are important because through answering these questions an acceptable project ethos and scope of consideration should be achieved. The problem is that in practice these fundamental questions are often overlooked. It is more likely that a narrower perspective is adopted with only the obvious issues in close proximity to the project being considered. The holistic view promoted by the two checklist points requires greater vision, analysis and reflection. The project manager is under pressure to deliver and so the tendency is to reduce the horizon and establish an artificial boundary around the project. Steps 2–5 are concerned with adding detail and refinements thus arriving at a workable and acceptable plan. Steps 6–8 are concerned with implementing the plan, monitoring performance and keeping those associated with the project informed of progress. Step 9 defines the control feedback loops which ensure that the plan remains focused, current and realistic. Finally, Step 10 is the delivery of the project output to the client and an opportunity to reflect upon what has and has not been achieved.

Once again undertaking an analysis suggests that the ethical hotspots are the first and eighth step and that probably the most important ethical issues lie within the first step. This first step, visualising what the goal is, as previously mentioned establishes the project ethos and consequently there are several ethical issues that need to be borne in mind. This is the start of the project and it is vitally important to be above board at the onset so that a good working relationship is established with client. The principles of honour and honesty address this point. Bias in decision making and the undertaking of actions is a major concern throughout the project including Step 1. It is important to take a balanced viewpoint based on economic, technological and sociological information. The view often portrayed is skewed towards technology and economics which can have disastrous results leading to major system failure or rejection, as was the case, for example, at the London Ambulance Service regarding LASCAD its computer-aided despatch system and at the London Stock Exchange regarding TAURUS its computerised trading system (Rahanu, Davies & Rogerson, 1999). This leads to three further dominant principles of due care, fairness and social cost. Computer systems impact directly and indirectly on many people and it is important to include all parties in decisions that affect the way in which the project is conducted. Software development projects involve many stakeholders and each is worthy of fair treatment. The principles of due care and social cost will ensure that a longer term and broader perspective is adopted.

## Stakeholders

Establishing the right scope of consideration is essential in defining acceptable project goals. The scope of consideration is influenced by the identification and involvement of stakeholders. In traditional software project management, the stated needs of the customer are the primary items of concern in defining the project objectives. There has been some recognition that in defining how software will address those needs the customer is also presented with a predefined set of constraints which limit the customer's freedom of expression (McCarthy, 1996). There is a mutual incompatibility between some customer needs, for example, the amount of code required to make a system easy to use makes a system difficult to modify. The balancing of these items is an ethical dimension in the development of a software product. Such considerations have been limited in scope to the customer. Investigating 16 organisational IS-related projects led (Farbey, Land & Targett, 1993) to conclude that regarding evaluation of IT investment, "… the perception of what needed to be considered was disappointingly narrow, whether it concerned the possible scope and level of use of the system, [or] the range of people who could or should have been involved …." They discovered, with the exception of vendors, all stakeholders involved in evaluation were internal to the organisations. The reason for this restricted involvement is that these are the only stakeholders originally identified in the traditional project goals. However, consideration of stakeholders should not be limited to those who are financing the project or politically influential but broaden it to be consistent with models of ethical analysis. Stakeholders must include individuals or groups who may be directly or indirectly affected by the project and thus have a stake in the development activities. Those stakeholders who are negatively affected are particularly important regarding ethical sensitivity because they are often the ones overlooked.

## The Software Development Impact Statement

One way of addressing the need to modify project goals in a formal way is to use a modification of a social impact statement. A social impact statement is modelled on an environmental impact statement which is required before major construction is undertaken. The environmental impact statement is supposed to specify the potential negative impacts on the environment of the proposed construction and specify what actions will be taken to minimise those impacts. Proposed social impact statements have been described for identifying the impact of information systems on direct and indirect system users (Shneiderman & Rose, 1995). The limitations of these proposals are addressed by the Software Development Impact Statement (SoDIS) which is intended to reflect the software development process as well as the more general ethical obligations to various stakeholders (Rogerson & Gotterbarn, 1998).

There are two types of SoDIS. The first is a Generic SoDIS which has as its primary function the identification of stakeholders and related ethical issues. In the light of the identified issues, a preliminary project management plan is developed. A second more detailed SoDIS is then employed. This is the Specific SoDIS. There will be a number of Specific SoDIS within a particular methodology. Each SoDIS is tied to a particular development methodology and to each step in that methodology. Even though each Specific SoDIS is tied to a development methodology, they all include the means of revisiting and re-evaluating ethical issues in the light of the unfolding development process. This organic nature of the SoDIS is very different from the environmental impact statement model.

Just as producing software of high quality should be second nature to the software engineer so should producing software that is ethically sensitive. Indeed, there is clearly an overlap in these two requirements. The project management process for software development must accommodate an ethical perspective. The major criticism of current practice is that any ethical consideration tends to be implicit rather than explicit which has a tendency to devalue the importance of the ethical dimension. By using ethical principles, identifying of ethical hotspots and using SoDIS, it is possible to ensure that the key ethical issues are properly addressed as an integral part of the software development process. Quite simply, project management should be guided by a sense of justice, a sense of equal distributions of benefits and burdens and a sense of equal opportunity.

## Information Systems Development

There are numerous methodological approaches to information systems development. Few deal adequately with the ethical dimensions of the development process. Avison (1995) criticises the development methodologies, such as Structured Systems Analysis and Design Method (SSADM), Merise and Yourdon, that are adopted by most organisations because they tend to stress formal and technical aspects. He argues that, "The emphasis ... must move away from technical systems which have behavioural and social problems to social systems which rely to an increasing extent on information technology." He suggests that the human, social and organisational aspects are often overlooked. The consideration of this broader perspective only seems to occur in the event of systems failure or under-performance. This issue is addressed by Wood-Harper et al. (1996) who identify a number of dilemmas which a systems analyst might face when undertaking a systems development activity using a methodological approach. These dilemmas are summarised as:

- Whose ethical perspective will dominate the study of the situation and development of IS?
- Will ethical viewpoints be included in the study?
- What methodology should be used for the study?
- What approach should the analyst use if there is an obvious conflict of interests?

Wood-Harper et al. (1999) have further articulated these concerns by suggesting four principles that can be used to identify issues related to ethically sensitised information systems development. These are:

- Ethical reasoning should be conducted throughout the life of an information system, including inception, testing, distribution, modification and termination.
- Every information systems should improve the ethical actions of its users.
- The benefits of an information system should be distributed to all people who have an ethical need for its use.
- The design of every information system should include the design of its ethical use, the design of its ethical distribution, the design of its ethical risk and the methods of justifying ethical criteria.

It is important to recognise that there are a few methodological approaches, notably ETHICS from Mumford (1983), Soft Systems Methodology from Checkland (1981) and Multiview from Avison and Wood-Harper (1990) that attempt to include consideration of ethical and societal issues. In evaluating ETHICS, Jayaratna (1994) suggests that, "[it] offers many design guidelines useful for the understanding and the design of human-centred systems, but ... does not offer models or ways for performing ... the steps. Nor does it offer any models for handling interpersonal and political conflicts." He concludes that, "ETHICS is committed to a particular ethical stance [and] does not offer any means of discussing or resolving many of the ethical dilemmas ... in systems development." This appears to be a recurrent criticism of such methodologies. While it is laudable that ethical sensitivity is raised as an issue worthy of investigation, the manner in which investigation is undertaken and, ultimately, an ethically defensible position derived is vague. Methodologies need to be enhanced to address these criticisms.

SSADM is now used as an illustrative method to further discussion of the ethics of information systems development because it is felt that if ethical enrichment can be achieved in a "hard" systems approach then it is likely to be achievable in most approaches. SSADM is a set of procedural, technical and documentation standards for information systems development (Skidmore, Farmer & Mills, 1994). SSADM comprises five core modules: feasibility study, requirements analysis, requirements specification, logical systems specification and physical design module. SSADM adopts a product-oriented approach where each element, be it a module, stage or step produces predictable outputs from given inputs.

Winter, Brown and Checkland (1995) explain that computer-based information systems are systems that serve purposeful human actions. They argue that there is a very heavy emphasis on the serving information system in the systems development life cycle with, in the main, only limited and implicit account taken of the purposeful human action or the so-called served system. This is particularly the case in the "hard" systems thinking approaches of structured methods that are highly technical and rational. In examining SSADM, Winter, Brown and Checkland found no explicit organisational activity model and that it appeared to accept without question the image, activities and performance aspects of the organisation in question. Furthermore, they were critical of SSADM's concept of information requirements was concerned with that required for the system to function rather than the information needed by the people undertaking organisational activities. The approach adopted by Winter, Brown and Checkland is organisationally oriented. It does not appear to go beyond the environs of the organisation where one finds a greater range of system stakeholders. This lack of stakeholder involvement is a further shortcoming of SSADM and it is unclear whether distant stakeholders will be identified let alone involved. The implications of such restricted stakeholder involvement on achieving a socially and ethically sensitive approach are obvious (Rogerson, Weckert & Simpson, 2000).

The ethical enhancement of SSADM is a considerable task that is beyond the scope of this chapter. The discussion is confined to making some suggestions as to how that task might be achieved. It is clear that a combination of teleology and deontology should be used. This is because teleological approaches focus on outcomes whilst deontological approaches focus on actions. White (1993) explains that together, "they reveal a wide array of internal and external factors of human actions that have moral consequences. Although these two outlooks conflict in theory, they complement one another in practice … each acts as a check on the limitations of the other."

With this in mind, it is important to address both the process and product of SSADM. The Product Breakdown Structure provides the impetus to address issues in a certain way. The completeness of these products needs to be considered given their powerful influence in the development process. Consideration must also be given to how the systems developers should think when undertaking the various development tasks. The SSADM culture promotes technological and economic thinking but not ethical thinking explicitly. The later enhanced version 4+ appears to be moving to a more balanced view with more emphasis on business orientation and the inclusion of user culture in the systems development template (Hall, 1995). This albeit minor change in emphasis towards people offers more scope to include ethical sensitivity.

It is now recognised that quality should permeate the whole the information systems development process and not simply be considered at discrete points within the process. This is reflected in SSADM by the inclusion of a quality products set comprising a number of files that demonstrate quality has been built into the system (CCTA, 1990). Product descriptions are part of this set. There are product descriptions for all the products specified in SSADM. The details include quality criteria against which the product can be checked. Product descriptions are used to monitor progress and success of the project.

Including quality in each description ensures it permeates the whole process and promotes a quality culture throughout the development team. Similarly, ethical and societal consideration should permeate the whole process. It follows that each product description should include ethical and social criteria to promote this awareness and consideration. This might be systematically addressed by using clauses from a code of conduct to form the ethical criteria for products within each of the core modules. A suitable code to use would be the Software Engineering Code of Ethics and Professional Practice which has its clauses in eight groups relating to the public, the client and employer, the software product, professional judgement, management, the profession, colleagues and oneself (Gotterbarn, Miller & Rogerson, 1997).

# Conclusion

The provision of information is a complex activity involving many decisions, many people and much time. This chapter has highlighted the major elements of this activity and considered the level of ethical sensitivity of each element. It appears that current practice is deficient in addressing the broader social implication of information provision through the use of information and communication technology. Suggestions have been made in using information ethics to address such shortcomings through the modification and enhancement of current processes and procedures. Failure by information engineers and software engineers to consider the broader social and ethical issues is at best unprofessional and at worst societally disastrous.

# References

Avison, D. E. (1995) *What is IS?* An inaugural lecture delivered at the University of Southampton, 3 November 1994.

Avison, D. E. & Wood-Harper, A. T. (1990) *Multiview: An Exploration in Information Systems Development*. Alfred Waller.

Bergeron, F. & Raymond, L. (1992) Planning of information systems to gain a competitive edge. *Journal of Small Business Management*, 30(1), 21–26.

Burn, J. M., (1993) Information systems strategies and the management of organisational change – a strategic alignment model. *Journal of Information Technology*, 8, 205–216.

Business Intelligence (1995) *IT and Corporate Transformation*. Business Intelligence.

Bynum, T. W. (1992) Computer ethics in the computer science curriculum. In: Bynum, T. W., Maner, W. & Fodor, J. L. (eds.), *Teaching Computer Ethics*. Research Center on Computing & Society.

Bynum, T. W. (1999) The development of computer ethics as a philosophical field of study. *Australian Journal of Professional and Applied Ethics*, 1(1), 1–29.

CCTA (1990) *SSADM Version 4, Reference Manual: Volume 4, Dictionary*. NCC Blackwell.

Checkland, P. B. (1981) *Systems Thinking, Systems Practice*. Wiley.

DeMarco, T. & Lister, T. (1987) *Peopleware*. Dorset House Publishing.

Earl, M. J. (1993) Experiences in strategic information systems planning. *MIS Quarterly*, 17(1), 1–24.

Farbey, B., Land, F. & Targett, D. (1993) *How to Assess Your IT Investment*. Butterworth Heinemann.

Fidler, C. S. & Rogerson, S. (1996) *Strategic Management Support Systems*. Pitman Publishing.

Flynn, D. J., & Hepburn, P. A. (1994) Strategic planning for information systems – a case study of a metropolitan council. *European Journal of Information Systems*, 3(3), 207–217.

Forcht, K. A. & Thomas, D. S. (1994) Information compilation and disbursement: moral, legal and ethical considerations. *Information management and computer security*, 12(2), 23–28.

Forester, T. (1992) Megatrends or megamistakes? What ever happened to the information society?. *The Information Society*, 8(3), 133–146.

Gotterbarn, D. (1992) The use and abuse of computer ethics. In: Bynum, T. W., Maner, W. & Fodor, J. L. (eds.), *Teaching Computer Ethics*. Research Center on Computing and Society, Southern Connecticut State University, pp. 73–83.

Gotterbarn, D., Miller, K. & Rogerson, S. (1997) Software engineering code of ethics. *Communications of the ACM*, 40(11), 110–118.

Hall, J. (1995) How is SSADM4.2 different from SSADMV4?. *SSADM4+ for Academics*. CCTA & International SSADM User Group Workshop, Leeds Metropolitan University.

Hawk, S. R. (1994) The effects of computerised performance monitoring: an ethical perspective. *Journal of Business Ethics*, 13(12), 949–957.

Jayaratna, N. (1994) *Understanding and Evaluating Methodologies*. McGraw-Hill.

Langford, D. & Wusteman, J. (1994) The increasing importance of ethics in computer science. *Business Ethics – A European Review*, 3(4), 219–222.

Maner, W. (1996) Unique ethical problems in information technology. *Science and Engineering Ethics*, 2(2), 137–155.

McCarthy J. (1996) *Dynamics of Software Development*. Microsoft Press.

Moor, J. H. (1985) What is computer ethics?. *Metaphilosophy*, 16(4), 266–275.

Moor, J. H. (1998) Reason, relativity, and responsibility in computer ethics. *Computers and Society*, 28(1), 14–21.

Mumford, E. (1983) *Designing Participatively*. Manchester Business School.

O'Connell, F. (1994) *How to Run Successful Projects*. Prentice Hall.

Oz, E. (1993) Ethical standards for computer professionals: a comparative analysis of four major codes. *Journal of Business Ethics*, 12(9), 709–728.

Rahanu, R., Davies, J. & Rogerson, S. (1999) Ethical analysis of software failure cases. *Failure & Lessons Learned in Information Technology Management*, 3(1), 1–22.

Rogerson, S. (1997) Software project management ethics. In: Myers, C., Hall, T. & Pitt, D. (eds.), *The Responsible Software Engineer*. Springer-Verlag, pp. 100–106.

Rogerson, S. & Bynum, T. W. (1995) Cyberspace the ethical frontier. *Multimedia, the Times Higher Education Supplement* (1179), iv.

Rogerson, S. & Bynum, T. W. (1996) Information ethics: the second generation. *UK Academy for Information Systems Conference*, Cranfield University, UK, 10–12 April 1996.

Rogerson, S. & Gotterbarn, D. (1998) The ethics of software project management. In: Collste, G. (ed.), *Ethics and Information Technology*. Delhi, India, New Academic Publishers, pp. 137–154.

Rogerson, S., Weckert, J. & Simpson, C. (2000) An ethical review of information systems development: the Australian Computer Society's code of ethics and SSADM. *Information Technology and People*, 13(2), 121–136.

Shneiderman, B. & Rose, A. (1995) Social impact statements: engaging public participation in information technology design. *Technical Report of the Human Computer Interaction Laboratory* (September), 1–13.

Skidmore, S., Farmer, R. & Mills, G. (1994) *SSADM Version 4 Models and Methods*, 2nd Edition. NCC Blackwell.

van Luijk, H. (1994) Business ethics: the field and its importance. In: Harvey, B. (ed.), *Business Ethics: A European Approach*. Prentice Hall.

Walsham, G. (1996) Ethical theory, codes of ethics and IS practice. *Information Systems Journal*, 6(1), 69–81.

White, T. I. (1993) *Business Ethics: A Philosophical Reader*. Macmillan.

Widdifield, R. & Grover, V. (1995) Internet and the implications of the Information Superhighway for business. *Journal of Systems Management* (May/June), 46, 16–21.

Winter, M. C., Brown, D. H. & Checkland, P. B. (1995) A role for soft systems methodology in information systems development. *European Journal of Information Systems*, 4(3), 130–142.

Wood-Harper, A. T., Corder, S. & Byrne, B. (1999) Ethically situated information systems development. In: Simpson, C. R. (ed.), *AICE99 Conference Proceedings*. Australian Institute of Computer Ethics, pp. 449–460.

Wood-Harper, A. T., Corder, S., Wood, J. R. G. & Watson, H. (1996) How we profess: the ethical systems analyst. *Communications of the ACM*, 39(3), 69–77.

*Chapter 10*

# Responsible Risk Assessment with Software Development: Creating the Software Development Impact Statement [2005]*

## Introduction

Software developers continually evolve and refine techniques to mediate the risk of failure in software development projects. They pay significant attention to risks which contribute to impeding a project; risks which contribute to missed schedule, budget overrun and failure to meet the system's specified requirements. In risk analysis and mitigation literature, the primary focus is on the project development vision defined in terms of budget and schedule overruns and not on satisfying the customer by meeting technical requirements. Henry (2004) defines project risk as

> an event, development, or state in a software project that causes damage, loss, or delay.

Schwalbe (2004) also defines "project risk" as

> ... problems that might occur on the project and how they might impede project success.

* This chapter was first published as: Gotterbarn, D. & Rogerson, S. (2005) Responsible Risk Assessment with Software Development: Creating the Software Development Impact Statement. *Communications of the Association for Information Systems (CAIS)*, Vol. 15, May, Article 40. Copyright © the Association for Information Systems. Reprinted by permission. DOI: 10.17705/1CAIS.01540.

These common risks internal to the software development process, "intra-project risks" are managed and evaluated using quantifiable values. In a major KPMG study of runaway projects, failing to follow this risk analysis model was identified as the primary causes of project failure (Cole, 1995). Reliance on a high-level generic risk analysis is inadequate or incomplete as a methodology. For example, software may be produced on schedule, within budget and meet all the owner's specified software requirements, but nevertheless fail due to other adverse impacts of the delivered project.

Why do we still have the number of IT failures even when risk analysis is applied during development? We argue that these failures are due in part to an institutionalised narrowing of the scope of a project's objectives and vision to development objectives. For example, consider the development of traffic control software to direct traffic approaching a multi-lane bridge into the least congested lanes facilitating a maximum and continuous traffic flow across the bridge, especially in rush hours. From this description, we would identify stakeholders in this software as including vehicle drivers traversing the bridge, bridge maintenance people and the city traffic authority. It is also straightforward to define success criteria for this software. They might include the following: the system works well in its context; it does not promote vehicle accidents; the project was delivered on time; the project was within budget; and the cost/benefit analysis was accurate showing that those developing the system could expect a reasonable return on investment. The system met all of these conditions and yet it was judged a failure. Why?

The system needs to manage large amounts of traffic moving through 20 lanes. The bridge had two levels. The computer had to do some continuous interactive rapid and accurate processing making decisions about lane capacity, average speed of the lane, stopped lanes, taking lanes out of use, changing directions of lanes to account for rush-hour flows and so on. The system was installed and worked well until there was a mass exodus from the city and the system had to manage constant heavy traffic loads for 8 hours during an emergency nuclear disaster evacuation exercise. In the eighth hour, the software changed lane directions for lanes already filled with cars and the misdirection and accidents clogged the bridge for almost 20 hours. The crystal clock used for the timing of these decisions would gradually go out of synchronisation with 7 or more hours of continuous use. The developer was fully aware of this problem and to meet the problem wrote in the User Manual that the software should be briefly stopped and restarted after 6 hours of continuous heavy traffic loads. This action would reset the clock and no problem would be encountered.

The vision, objectives and stakeholders were all considerably narrowed when the project became a software project. The order of the success conditions listed above was also reversed. The primary goals were to deliver the system on time, within budget and satisfying the customer. The focus of the risk analysis and mitigation narrowed to those many issues which impact these goals negatively and risks that would derail the project's development. This narrowing of focus to development risks is canonised in many information systems and software development textbooks and risk management articles (Henry, 2004; Schach, 2003; Schwalbe, 2004) and documented in official development standards (CMM, PMBOK, ISO929). To meet schedule and budget constraints, the bridge software developers opted merely to place a warning in the user manual rather than provide a software solution. This choice to focus on high-level intra-project risks and stakeholders related directly to the software development.

One of the typical ways to address risks is to focus on the quantifiable risks related only to those directly involved in the development of the software and overlook identifiable qualitative risks. For example, Watts Humphrey, a fellow of Carnegie Mellon's Software Engineering Institute, defines good software as "usable, reliable, defect free, cost effective and maintainable"

(Humphrey, 1989). Humphrey's focus is on software characteristics: how many remaining defects; how long the software will continue to run; and the simplicity of the design which is a way to quantify maintainability. He does not consider the potential negative impacts of the software.

Extended action research and Delphi studies by Lyytinen and Hirschheim (1987), Keil et al. (1998) and Schmidt et al. (2001) categorising and extending traditional software risk confirmed the failure and consequences of this narrow focus on risk. This kind of limited quantitative approach contributed to numerous software failures, some of which received very public notice. For example, the Aegis radar system was a success in terms of budget, schedule and requirements satisfaction. Even so, the user interface to the system was a primary factor in the USN Vincennes shooting down a commercial airliner killing 263 innocent people. The narrow focus on function and budget to the exclusion of others, led to developing an interface that was inadequate for use by the sailors (stakeholders in this software) in a combat situation. Fortunately, not all software failure impacts are of this magnitude, nevertheless the problem is significant. Mackenzie (2001) confirms the view that a narrow focus frequently leads to software "that works brilliantly but doesn't fulfil the need."

Research results indicate restricting the scope of types of risk factors considered is inadequate for effective risk management. Boehm (1989) and others argue that risks must be identified before they can be addressed. Schmidt et al. (2001) catalogued and categorised 53 risk factors. A mechanism is needed to identify additional potential risks that, Schmidt et al. (2001) did not identify in the 53 project risk factors they catalogued.

The generic quantifiable approaches to risk focus on "complexity" in terms of the number of lines of code or the number of function points. Often systems are evaluated in terms of the number of faults per 1,000 lines of code rather than the side-effects these faults may have on system users or those affected by the system. These are interesting numbers but they mislead developers in their specificity. This numerical approach is now canonical in the software engineering methodology literature in approaches like the Personal Software Process (Humphrey, 1996), the Team Software Process (Humphrey, 1999) and the earlier Capability Maturity Model (SEI Software Engineering Institute, Carnegie Mellon University, 1995).

This emphasis on quantitative measures is seen in a process improvement presentation, by Gabriel Hoffman (2003) of Northrup Grumman who described the quality of their software development process. He included measures of quality: the number of hours saved in production, the number of defects per thousand lines of code, low schedule variance, an improved design code *ratio*, defect density, code *size* and cost variance.

Software development's shift of project vision contributed to the narrowing of focus on specific types of risks, an emphasis on quantifiable risk almost to the exclusion of qualitative risk. This emphasis on quantitative risk contributes to underestimating or ignoring the need to consider risks to extra-project stakeholders in the development of the software. Schmidt points out that the "[f]ailure to identify all stakeholders: Tunnel vision leads project management to ignore some of the key stakeholders in the project, effecting requirements and implementation, etc." (Schmidt et al., 2001 p. 15). Project risk analysis must be expanded beyond the traditional risk analysis to include a broader scope of risks and stakeholders. The need for a formal mechanism to do this is evidenced by the discovery of the additional difficulty

> that managers are biased in their attention to particular risk factors [schedule, budget, function] at the expense of other factors. (Schmidt et al., 2001, p. 26)

Those responsible for software development need to be fully informed about all aspects of risk if they are to increase the likelihood of success rather than failure. Indeed, Keil et al. (2000) found that,

> risk perception appears to have a much more significant influence on decision-making than does risk propensity. This result is significant because it implies that decision-making can be modified through manipulation of risk perception, in spite of any individual differences that may exist in terms of risk propensity. Thus, it may be possible to design risk assessment instruments and other interventions that reduce the incidence of project failure by altering managers' risk perceptions.

We describe how the SoDIS process improves and expands risk perception. Enhanced risk perception should reduce the dangers of a narrow focus on quantitative risks.

## Addressing the Risk Analysis Problems

The problems of risk analysis can be addressed in several ways including:

- Expanding the list of generic risks
- Maintaining focus on the broader project goals
- Extending the list of considered project stakeholders

### *Research by Project Type*

Generic risk analysis also limits the developer's perceptions. Failure to identify, understand and address the risks associated with different types of software projects is a key contributory factor to project failure by constraining the developer's perceptions of the real project risks. It is commonplace to define project types by the nature of the software being developed. For example, Jones (2000) classifies software development project types as systems software, commercial software, internal information systems, outsourced software, military software and end-user software. Software development projects differ in a number of significant ways. For example, real-time military applications are different from commercial batch applications in their technical risks. Software development risks differ by types of software projects. The systems delivered. also have different types of stakeholders and risks. Recent research documents the need to extend standard project risk analysis to include analysis of the risks created by the delivered system. For example, Schmidt et al. (2001) studied and correlated types of common software project risk factors and the attention given to them. After looking at the business-related stakeholder and theories which limit the extension of stakeholders considered to users of the software, Schmidt concludes that these extended risk factors remain "largely unexplored areas in software project risk management."

For a project development to succeed, risk resolution should consider:

- The delivered project type, consisting of sector and application
- All stakeholders' opinions
- The different stakeholder expectations regarding how to judge a project as a success or a failure

Even for the simplest of projects, with a small development team working on software with low complexity and limited functionality, responsible risk analysis requires categorisation and description of the delivered project and the associated direct and latent stakeholders.

For example, in a recent case in New Zealand, a software developer was asked to develop an Internet filter which would only allow a browser to access websites which were on an approved list. Based on this description a developer addresses the generic risks of schedule delay, incomplete functionality and cost estimation. Software was developed which allowed one administrator to enter and remove websites from the list. The list filtered all Internet access. It was delivered on time and under budget. At installation, the developer learned that the filter was to be installed in a school that was going to network all of its computers. If we merely consider the functionality then one set of risks in development would be addressed. The contextualisation of the school setting identifies delivered project risks and changes the way in which the software should be developed to mitigate these newly identified risks. The project is now constrained by needs of administrators, teachers and students who will be using the network and the Internet, and those who may have access to their sites prohibited.

These are extra-project risks which involve stakeholders beyond the project team and the customer. It is the failure to consider these "extra-project" risks and "extra-project" stakeholders which make this a failed project. The inattention to these risks and stakeholders contributes to estimates from the Product Development and Management Association that the failure rate of newly launched software products is approximately 59% (Cooper, 2001).

## Categorising Projects to Aid Risk Identification

How can we best categorise a project to promote this better perception of risk? Among the various answers offered to this question are:

- The size and complexity of the software and thus the project will impact the types of control and monitoring tools used by the project manager. Current thinking using the nature of the project appears limited to aspects of the development process and development environment.
- Simply categorise projects by the size of the code or duration in order to guide their risk management approach. For example, the Prestwood Software Development Process (Prestwood Software, 2002) defines software, using a look-up table, as "small," "medium," or "large" and this designation is used to determine the number of iterations of the development cycle.
- Categorise by the technological aspects. For example, Shenhar, Renier and Wideman (1996) use four levels of technological uncertainty to ascertain the way to develop software.

These approaches do not shed much light on the risks of the delivered Internet filter discussed earlier. The problem we identify with these approaches is that they are inward looking, focusing simply on the obvious within the narrowly confined boundaries of the development of the software. The inattention to potential side-effects – extra-project impacts – leaves the system development vulnerable to unforeseen problems and risks which can radically hamper progress, cause flawed implementation and lead to eventual total failure of the development or failure of the delivered system. Such situations are easy to imagine in the Internet example. The risk of limiting a teacher's Internet research by applying student access constraints to the networked filter would have been missed if the teacher stakeholders were not considered. The system could be delivered on time, within budget and meeting the filtering functionality but would be a failure. It would be one of those projects that are delivered but never used. This project failure was caused by the same narrow focus on stakeholders directly related to development that contributed to the Aegis disaster (see *Introduction*).

Risk analysis should also be outward looking and take into account the overall environment within which the software will be used and the target application area. This contextualisation directs the focus to relevant stakeholders and colours the way in which more traditional aspects such as size and technological complexity are considered. In this way, everyone involved in the software development or affected by its delivery are catered for and, by implication, the process of development as well as the outcome (the software) is properly reviewed. The lack of a good risk perspective by contextualisation of the product is a widespread deficiency in software development. For example, Aladwani (2002) found that it was essential to understand the context of the project in order to increase the likelihood of project success in developing countries yet such consideration was usually missing (cf. Gotterbarn, Clear & Kwan 2004). Given a project's development process is simply a means to an end and not the end itself then the contextualisation of a project deliverable should focus on the impact space of the software rather than just an introspective focus on the development process. Therefore, in this sense, contextualisation involves three main dimensions:

- The sector within which the software will be used
- The type of application that is to be addressed
- The application's surrounding circumstances

These dimensions are important in adequate risk and stakeholder identification. In the Internet filter project, the context of a school changes the types of risk that need to be addressed in this software development. Moving from the context of a single classroom to the installation of one filter on a network for the entire school involves new risks including technical issues, privacy issues and restrictions on illegitimate access. In the bridge example, the failure to modify the system to avoid the errors caused by multiple hours of use during emergency nuclear disaster evacuation exercises led to not being able to use the system in its time of greatest need. Clearly, all of the elements of a product's context – sector, application type and circumstance – are required for an adequate project categorisation and for effective risk analysis. The results of this analysis of product risk by product contextualisation must be added to development risk analysis for a complete risk analysis for system development.

## Identifying Stakeholders

In addition to inadequate project categorisation, misidentified or unidentified stakeholders are a major contributory factor to the ineffectiveness of current risk analysis methods. Some researchers try to develop generic methods of stakeholder identification that they believe can be domain-independent. For example, Sharp, Finkelstein and Galal (1999) and Henry (2004) identify methods based on either direct stakeholder interaction with the system or financial involvement with the system. Stakeholders are "people with a direct internal involvement or investment in a software project" (Henry, 2004). This common approach ignores the special circumstances generated by the nature of the product delivered. A patient waiting to be identified by software as a heart transplant recipient would not be considered a stakeholder during development.

Other even more limited views are that the only critical stakeholders are the project team members (Spafford, 2002). Such views of who are the relevant stakeholders are clearly too limited. The need to expand the stakeholder group is supported by Keil, Amrit and Bush (2002).

> Incorporation of the user perspective on risk is significant because focusing solely on project managers' perceptions may result in some risk factors receiving a lower level of attention than they might deserve. To mitigate project risk, it is necessary to consider all risk factors judged to be important by both groups and then reconcile differences through dialogue, deliberation and communication. (Keil, Amrit & Bush, 2002)

As we have seen, a fully responsible risk analysis needs to go beyond even Keil et al.'s inclusion of a user as an extra-project stakeholder.

The concept of "stakeholder" is used in many different ways. One extreme talks of "stakeholder" as "participants in corporate affairs" (Ackoff, 1974). The stakeholder should have some financial stake in the corporation. Lyytinen and Hirschheim (1987) extend the realm of "stakeholder" further to include those whose expectations go beyond the requirements since only a fraction of a stakeholder's concerns are usually formulated in the requirements. Lyytinen and Hirschheim use this definition of "stakeholder" to argue that many IS failures actually met the requirements, but were considered failures because some other vital concerns were not met. Our use of "stakeholder" is closest to Willcocks and Mason (1987) who define the stakeholders of a computer system as the

> people who will be affected in a significant way by, or have material interests in the nature and running of the new computerised system. (p. 79)

These various concepts of "stakeholder" each provide associated techniques, some purely quantitative, to aid in identifying project-relevant stakeholders. A qualitative approach to stakeholder identification is suggested in *The SoDIS Summary* which opts for the more general concept of stakeholder. Successful project management needs to consider the people impacted by the system.

In the Internet filter example, the stakeholders initially consisted of the teacher requesting the filter and the developer; then when the filter was placed on classroom computers the stakeholders expanded to the students in the class. Then, because the computer was networked, the stakeholders changed again. The stakeholders for the Internet application changed as it was placed in the education sector and changed again with the changes in circumstance. In part, these changes are related to the contextualisation of the product. Developing and using an expanded standard checklist methodology facilitates identifying stakeholders directly and indirectly associated with the project deliverables. A preliminary default list of stakeholders associated with and affected by particular project types ensures their consideration during the risk analysis. The complete contextualisation of a system and identification of relevant stakeholders is only part of a satisfactory risk analysis. The risk analysis problems of narrowing the risk focus to generic risks are compounded by limiting the way such risks are analysed.

## Quantitative versus Qualitative Approaches to Risk

Quantifiable risk analysis is critical for good judgement in software development. A quantitative approach to risk relies on developing metrics that can be used to describe the risks in terms of money lost, days over schedule, numbers of functionalities not met. These quantities can be measured periodically to ascertain the existence and severity of risk in terms of Risk Exposure and Risk Leverage (Boehm, 1989). The two problems with this emphasis on quantification are:

1. The emphasis on quantifiable risk to the exclusion of qualitative risk
2. How this emphasis changes the risk perception of the developer by only admitting those quantitative risks which result in quantifiable intra-project impacts

This approach impacts risk perception because it limits the concept of "software failure." "Software failure" is not simply an issue of schedule, budget and reliability. As Kuruppuarachchi, Mandal and Smith (2002) point out,

> the effective management of changes in a sociological context, not only in economic and technological terms, is a prime requirement for success. The project's success is determined by customer acceptance of the project rather than the factors such as budget, timeliness or technological sophistication. Software has been developed which, although meeting stated requirements, has significant negative impacts on the circumstances, experiences, behaviour, livelihood, or daily routine of others.

In the Internet filter project, the system promotes censorship by omission. The system requires constant monitoring by the school's designated Internet censor. The system limits student preparation for later courses. In general, these types of qualitative issues with software are recognised but treated inadequately by information systems professionals.

This problem of addressing both quantitative and qualitative risk is a global issue. For example, based on empirical research, Dey (2002) recommends that best practice for Caribbean organisations must rely upon balanced risk analysis based upon

- "Aligning the project goals with the strategic intentions of the organisation"
- "Appropriate requirement analysis with the involvement of project stakeholders"
- "Equal emphasis on all aspects of analysis (market and demand analysis, technical analysis, financial analysis, economic analysis and impact assessment)"

This clear inclusion of qualitative risk analysis helps to address the Caribbean governments'

> need to strengthen the planning and development framework in the public sector, as the basis for improving the delivery capacity and economic performance of development projects.

In the Internet filter project, risks like over-constraining Internet access and security of the "approved web sites list" are not quantifiable but can be categorised by their impact on the project. Sometimes these qualitative risks are converted into financial impact on the project. However, this limited approach to qualitative risk is based on the narrow views of stakeholders and the type of project challenged above. When a project's deliverable is properly contextualised and the relevant stakeholders identified, then the set of qualitative risks is extended. In most cases, these risks cannot reasonably be quantified but only categorized by their side-effects on extra-project stakeholders as "critical," "significant," and "minor." This categorisation provides an understanding of unique types of risks, thus facilitating the discovery of appropriate solutions for heretofore unidentified risks.

Information systems professionals frequently fail to give appropriate weight to one of the approaches to risk analysis. Because of the focus on ROI and quantifiable issues, even when they do qualitative analysis, they limit it with quantitative constraints. It must be recognised that qualitative risk analysis and quantitative risk analysis are complementary, and both are necessary.

Some of the risks missed by quantifiable risk analysis were documented in a detailed empirical analysis of two failed systems cases by Dalcher and Tully (2002). They confirm that software failure is the result of "multiple, complex and interrelated" causes. Two of the failure causes they identify are:

- "Deafness to alerts" which concerns the lack of interest by senior management, project management and technical developers making project-related decisions to warnings given by a variety of sources often beyond the traditional stakeholders
- "Groupthink" which is an active resistance to any outside influences that might threaten the accepted norm mindset

Together these causes justify a new approach to how risk analysis is undertaken and by whom.

> It is essential that ... stakeholder groups are integrated into the system process, with each having an effective voice so as to be able to express both their needs and their knowledge. (Dalcher and Tully, 2002)

It is recognised that stakeholder involvement, particularly by indirect stakeholders, can be difficult to realise but this must not deter developers from striving to ensure all stakeholders' interests are properly represented during risk analysis. Unfortunately, at times, some stakeholder's interests can only be included by developer's speculating about external stakeholder needs. Pouloudi and Whitley (1997) provide mechanisms to facilitate the identification of stakeholder needs.

## Towards Expanded Risk Analysis

We developed a risk identification process to complement existing quantitative risk analysis methods and reduce the number of software failures. The risk analysis method is called a "Software Development Impact Statement" (SoDIS) (Gotterbarn, 2004). The SoDIS process expands existing software development risk analysis methods by developers explicitly addressing a range of qualitative questions about the impacts of their development from a stakeholder perspective. SoDIS overcomes the limitations described in *Quantitative Versus Qualitative Approaches to Risk*.

The SoDIS process was tested on software development in organisations with different location, size, function, scope, development methodology and technology level; from small projects in consulting companies to projects as large as the United Kingdom's scheme for Electronic Voting. In one case, using blind tests, risks were identified which could save the company $250,000 USD. Applying the SoDIS method to system development documents from known software failures, novices were able to anticipate the potential risks that were realised in the actual project. Just as quantitative risk analysis can be applied at every stage of software development, SoDIS was tested successfully against every phase of development (Gotterbarn, Clear & Kwan, 2004).

The SoDIS process belongs to the family of issues-oriented approaches used in software systems development. Early approaches like Hirsheim and Klein (1989) proposed to expand the scope of consideration within a system development project and add "quality of the work life" (which encompasses, for example, working conditions and progression opportunities) and ethical concerns. This inclusion of "quality of the work life" does not fully address the complete set of impacted stakeholders in information systems development. This family of approaches also includes Soft Systems Methodology (SSM) which can address "improvements to problem situations and lessons that can be learned in the problem solving process" (Checkland & Howell, 1998; Jayaratna, 1994). One approach to SSM takes a holistic perspective of analysis. Another member is ETHICS which is concerned with "the design process and in encouraging the participation of those organisational members whose lives may be affected by the design" (Mumford, 1996; Jayaratna, 1994). ETHICS takes a restricted stakeholder perspective of design.

Keil, Amrit and Bush (2002) argue that stakeholders, in particular developers and users, harbour different perceptions regarding potential project risks. They showed empirically that, by understanding and taking these differences into account, the chances of successful software delivery increases. SoDIS is different from the Keil et al.'s approach in that it takes a comprehensive stakeholder perspective of the whole development cycle because it considers each task within the structured plan of the project. A SoDIS risk analysis can be applied to any work product such as a work breakdown structure in a system's development. It can function as a review or preliminary audit of any development milestone. In this way, it can seamlessly fit within a software engineering approach to development (Gotterbarn, 2004), whereas both SSM and ETHICS cannot inasmuch as their roots are in interpretative analysis.

## The SoDIS Summary

The SoDIS process is a modification of the environmental impact statement process. A SoDIS, like an engineering environmental impact statement, is used to identify potential negative impacts of a proposed project and specify actions that will mediate these anticipated impacts.

A SoDIS risk inspection process (Gotterbarn, Clear & Kwan, 2004) includes steps to complete the project contextualisation and maintain the view of the project scope. Inspection is followed by a detailed SoDIS audit process which can be applied at various points in information systems development. The SoDIS audit process expands existing software development risk analysis methods by helping developers identify the appropriate set of project stakeholders or entities and by examining the impact of the tasks of software development on each of the stakeholders.

Although similar on an abstract level, in practice software development projects vary on several axes such as size, the context, circumstances of the project, complexity/uncertainty and application type.

Variations on these orthogonal axes need to be acknowledged because they change the stakeholders who need to be considered in a complete risk analysis. For example, imagine how a simple change of context in the Internet filter project from a school to a penal institution would significantly alter the risk analysis or how a change of context from directing bridge traffic at fee lanes to directing Patriot missiles would alter the risk analysis.

The goal of the SoDIS audit process is to identify significant ways in which the completion of individual tasks, that collectively constitute the project, may negatively affect intra-project and extra-project stakeholders. It identifies additional project tasks that may be needed to prevent any anticipated problems and identifies changes that may be needed in some tasks to prevent any problems anticipated.

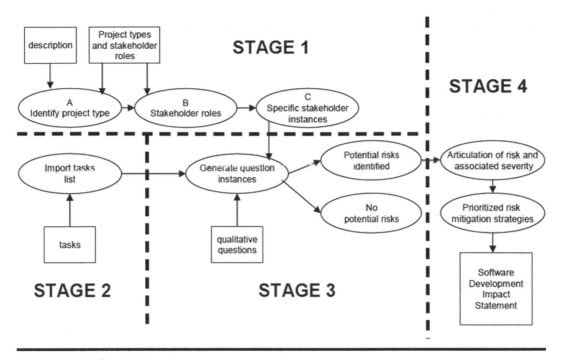

**Figure 10.1   The SoDIS process.**

As shown in Figure 10.1, the SoDIS process consists of four stages:

1. The identification of the project type together with immediate and extended stakeholders in a project
2. The identification of the tasks in a particular phase of a software development project
3. The association of every task with every stakeholder using structured questions to determine the possibility of specific project risks generated by that particular association
4. Completing the analysis by stating the concern and the severity of the risk to the project and the stakeholder, and recording a possible risk mitigation or risk avoidance strategy

The resulting document, which complements a quantitative analysis, is a SoDIS which identifies all types of potential qualitative risks for all tasks and project stakeholders.

This process can be done both bottom up and top down. The SoDIS process can be applied at any level of a hierarchy of tasks. As new risks are identified, any stage of the SoDIS process can be revisited for any task level. This flexibility is significantly different from the environmental impact model which makes a single pass at the project concept at a very high level and leaves risks that can only be discovered with more information later in the process unaddressed.

The SoDIS is the missing element in current risk analysis which primarily focuses on some of the quantitative intra-project relationships between selected tasks and selected stakeholders that constitute a software development project. A responsible professional risk analysis examines both the quantitative and qualitative associations between tasks and project internal and extended stakeholders. To leave out either the quantitative or the qualitative analysis results in unidentified and, worse yet, unaddressed risks and project failures is problematic. We will illustrate this claim with the Internet filter project discussed earlier.

## Stage 1: Define Project and Identify Stakeholders

The first stage of the SoDIS process involves:

- Categorising the project type
- Identifying its default project stakeholders
- Expanding the default stakeholder list based on the unique attributes of the particular instance of the project type

The specific project information is first developed in the early stages of the SoDIS inspection process.

### Project Type Identification (1A)

To organise project types in a way that helps to identify their unique risks, we chose two of the three orthogonal models: sector and application.

*Sector*: Given the diversity of software development projects, it is reasonable to ask, "Exactly what sectors should be identified?" Many detailed socioeconomic classification systems are in use, for example, the Standard Industrial Classification (SIC) in the United Kingdom, the North American Industry Classification System (NAICS) and the World Bank groupings. The software development risks to address differ in each of the socioeconomic groups but also include some common risks. Using this idea of classification, several sectors appear to incur unique types of associated software development risks. These sectors are government, education, medicine and military, together with those systems developed for key internal use across other sectors. The risks and standards of quality of Internet filtering in the education sector are different from those of a military project. Given the evolving nature of the contexts of Information and Communication Technologies, new sectors will be identified.

*Application*: The application area is a second form of classification which helps to identify system development risk. For example, Turban et al. (1996) suggest system classification can be done according to organisational level (e.g. departmental), major functional area (e.g. manu-facturing), support provided (transaction processing) or system architecture (e.g. distributed system). These types of classification can be used to identify types of applications that might exhibit unique risks. These applications include real-time systems, scientific systems and system software. The Internet filtering project would exhibit one set of characteristics when used by one teacher in one classroom and a very different set of characteristics when it is being networked to every computer in the school, including computers used by all the other teachers.

*Circumstance*: The third element of delivered project's contextualisation is identification of circumstance. Project circumstance cannot be specified because of its diversity. The circumstance of the project is used as a key to adequate stakeholder identification. Therefore, the SoDIS does not come at the circumstance question directly. In addition to identifying unique project circumstances during the SoDIS inspection, the SoDIS audit portion of the inspection uses three questions which force an analyst to understand the context to answer these three questions:

1. Whose behaviour/work process will be affected by the development and delivery of this system or project?
2. Whose circumstance/job will be affected by the development and delivery of this system or project?

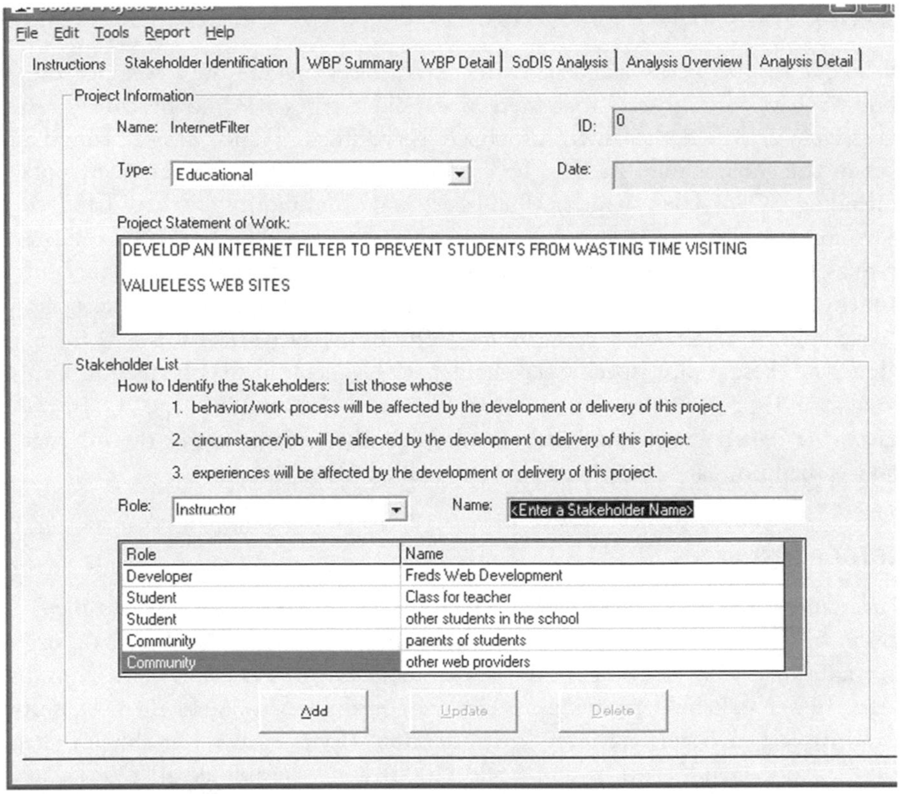

**Figure 10.2   Contextualisation of the project.**

3. Whose experiences will be affected by the development and delivery of this system or project?

Answering these questions requires stories or scenarios about the software's various contexts. Answering these questions identifies the stakeholders related to the project in a given circumstance.

The three elements of sector, application and circumstance complete the contextualisation of the project. The relations among these elements can be seen in Figure 10.2 from a prototype software tool which implements the SoDIS process.

The *Type* drop-down menu lists applications and sectors from which to choose. Once chosen Type determines the list in the *Role* drop-down menu for the stakeholder list. By answering the three circumstances questions the stakeholders can be added in the *Name* field for each *Role*.

In addressing software development impact the intention is to select the dominant project type for the sector group or application area. The aim is to focus risk analysis on the prevailing types to extend the project manager's risk perspective beyond intra-project stakeholders to several extra-project stakeholder groups. Thus, those involved in the risk analysis must choose the dominant project type from a shortlist of Government, Education, Medicine and Military, Internal, Real Time, Scientific and System.

## Stakeholder Roles (1B)

The stakeholder roles typically associated with any project include the developer and the customer, but we have already seen that more stakeholder types need to be considered even in projects as simple as the Internet filter. A survey of successful and failed projects found a minimal generic set of stakeholder roles need to be examined including: Customer, Developer, Project Team (including SQA), User, Vendor (Publisher) and Community (Farbey, Land & Targett, 1993). The contextualisation of a project means that there are slightly different clusters of stakeholder roles for each project type. For example, the development of educational software includes students and educators as stakeholders; researchers are stakeholders in scientific projects, and the development of aerospace navigational software involves astronauts and pilots as stakeholders. Ignoring these project-specific stakeholders yields incomplete risk analysis. During Stage 1B the generic and specific stakeholder roles are identified and used in Stage 1C. In the Internet filter project, the stakeholders would include all the teachers whose use of the Internet for class preparation is inappropriately restricted by the specified filter.

## Stakeholder Instances (1C)

The circumstances identify a particular instance of this project type. To complete the contextualisation of the delivered project requires that specific relevant stakeholders must be identified. In traditional risk assessment, the focus remains on those who are considered key stakeholders. Other stakeholders and the ethical responsibilities owed to them by software developers and project managers are given little attention. Lyytinen and Hirschheim (1987), Keil et al. (1998), Ropponen, Lyytinen and Kalle (2000) and Schmidt et al. (2001), also found Boehm's (1989) ten risk factors incomplete and assembled a fuller lists of software project risks. But even in these studies, the User is the only stakeholder considered outside of the original development team and business stakeholders.

Many project failures are caused by limiting the range of possible system stakeholders to just the software developer and the customer, thereby limiting the understanding of the scope of the project. In their research on failed projects, Farbey, Land and Targett (1993) found that, with the exception of vendors, all stakeholders involved in the evaluation were internal to the organisations involved in the development. These people tend to be the only stakeholders originally identified among traditional project goals. A limited scope of consideration leads to the development of systems that have surprisingly negative effects because the needs of relevant system stakeholders are not considered.

Those development models that address risks typically do so in this narrow sense. For example, even Boehm's (1998) "spiral lifecycle," which specifically addresses risk, limits stakeholder consideration to those people that impact the project. He also limits the risk to the three major traditional risks: budget, function and schedule. Similarly, cost-benefit analysis undertaken at the beginning of most projects only takes into account the interests of those involved in the analysis. The SoDIS process is different from other stakeholder analysis methods which do not consider stakeholders beyond the organisation or beyond those with a financial obligation. For example, stakeholders in the Internet filter project include: "other teachers in the school," "the network administrator," "the person who maintained the list of acceptable websites." and "the owners of unlisted web sites." If any one of these stakeholders was not considered, then the software would be inadequate and would require a significant change after installation.

## Stage 2: Generate the Task List

In Stage 2 of the SoDIS process, a list of tasks is generated. This list could simply be a work breakdown structure from a standard project management package. "Tasks" is used as a generic term to identify the elements requiring our attention in each phase. These elements might be activities in a project plan or lists of functions from a requirements specification. SoDIS has been used to analyse different phases of software development. For example, in New Zealand, it was used on a "task list" consisting of site maps and story-boards during the development of an e-commerce system.

The close relation to the task structure provides a link to a standard engineering approach to software development, emphasising modularity and decomposition of the work into a hierarchy of tasks. The examination of the task list sometimes generates the awareness of new stakeholders and at that point they should be added to the stakeholder list.

## Stage 3: Identifying Risks

In Stage 3 of the SoDIS process, potential qualitative risks are identified by associating tasks with stakeholders through pre-defined structured questions. A set of permanent questions for the process was derived from international codes of practice and conduct. These questions articulate qualitative issues common to all software development projects, such as

> Might <task> cause loss of information, loss of property, property damage … that impacts the <stakeholder>?

These questions (the qualitative glue holding the task and stakeholder together) ought to be addressed in any software project. As new tasks or stakeholders are added iteratively the risks can be analysed similarly. New project-specific questions can be added to the set of permanent questions. Answering these questions identifies potential qualitative risk. The prototype screen in Figure 10.3 shows a generated question about the Internet filter project.

The SoDIS analyst is asked to answer the question formed at the bottom of the screen about the potential impacts of the task on the stakeholder. Decision-making and problem solving in software development go far beyond the structured realms of traditional software engineering. Failure is likely to be caused by a lack of recognition of and/or an ineffective approach to risks which are non-routine and unfamiliar or novel. Some of these risks require a qualitative approach to risks demanding intuition and judgement in their resolution. Concerns are initially recorded without pausing to assign a specific quantitative probability to the potential occurrence of the risk. In many cases, the types of risk identified are not amenable to a precise probability assignment.

To address qualitative issues such as "deafness to alerts" and "groupthink" (mentioned earlier) a group decision approach is required which brings to bear a rich variety of values and beliefs of its diverse members. Group decisions promote collaborative creativity which facilitates successful implementation.

It is these concepts of extended qualitative risk analysis and group decision-making on which the SoDIS process is founded. The SoDIS process uses active decision support in that it provides "mechanisms for the analysis and manipulation of information to provide greater insight into the decision situation and the associated options" (Fidler & Rogerson, 1996). The SoDIS process

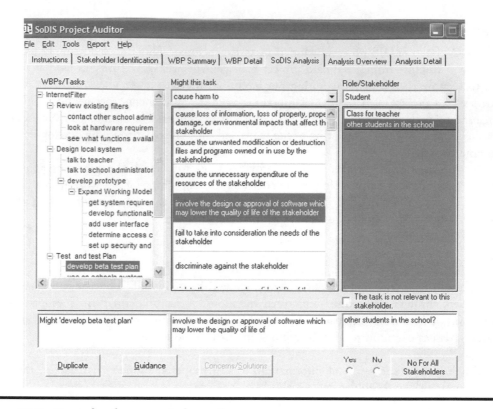

**Figure 10.3    Example of a generated question.**

supports standard group decision-making, problem identification and problem resolution techniques such as the Nominal Group Techniques, Delphi Techniques and Brainstorming.

Group decision-making in SoDIS works (Gotterbarn, Clear & Kwan, 2004). For example, with minimal instruction, a group of Australian Defence Department personnel, a group of New Zealand software engineers, a group of Polish university computer science tutors and a group of UK computer science postgraduates were all able to use the SoDIS process to identify potential risks in real-world projects which were not identified by other means.

Risk analysis is often unsystematic, composed of recently noticed hotspots. This lack of a systems approach leaves open the possibility that later in the process a developer does not know if a particular risk was checked. The SoDIS process is different because it uses software engineering procedures for testing to maintain an accurate record of all elements considered. Thus, explicit statements of risk-assessed situations can be issued. Those potential risks that are identified explicitly are passed on to Stage 4 for further analysis.

## Stage 4: Identification and Articulation of Solution and Generation of the SoDIS

At Stage 4, the analysts address the potential risks to stakeholders and to the project. The input to this stage is the concerns developed in Stage 3.

A group of analysts, which may consist of software developers, domain and application specialists, formalise their risk concerns. This formalisation consists of a specification of the

**Table 10.1  The SoDIS Process Decision Model**

| SoDIS Stage | Granularity | Action |
|---|---|---|
| 1 | Coarse – ill-defined | Informing |
| 2 | Fine | Informing |
| 3 | Fine – detailed | Identifying |
| 4 | Coarse – well-defined | Resolving |

concern and an estimation of the severity of the impact of the risk. A particular identified risk may impact elements of the project at one level and may impact extended stakeholders at another. The analysts record the worst-case severity for each particular risk.

SoDIS uses three broad levels of severity: critical, significant and minor. Instead of making difficult and debatable quantitative judgements, the analyst uses one of these qualitative categories. These categories are used later to prioritise the risks into an order in which they need to be addressed and further analysed. This procedure meets a management need sometimes addressed by quantified rankings.

If the analysts notice that the risk may also be true for other task-stakeholder relations, they can revisit Stage 3 and apply that concern to the other relationships. In a standard group decision process, the articulation of an issue may bring to mind a heretofore unidentified or misidentified stakeholder. The analyst can return to Stage 1 and add the new stakeholder and then work through Stages 3 and 4 for the new stakeholder.

The relation between Stages 3 and 4 is not a forced linear relation. While in Stage 3 recording a concern, the analyst can also record a possible solution to the problem. If they have no immediate suggested solution, they can proceed with the analysis.

The potential solutions can be reordered and tracked similar to the quantitative monitoring and management approach. The process also requires a declaration as to whether the risk mitigation requires new tasks, deleting tasks, or modifying tasks. The resulting SoDIS consists of a set of qualitative risks ordered by a degree of severity. Some of these risks can have a probability assigned and others cannot. The project manager can use this information to structure an approach to risk mitigation.

The SoDIS decision-making process moves from a coarse granularity to a fine granularity as it iterates through the stages, as shown in Table 10.1. Stage 1 is a coarse high level and often sparse or ill-defined project description which simply sets the scene and informs succeeding stages. Stage 2 provides a detailed or fine description of the project work which informs the succeeding stages. Stage 3 is a detailed low-level analysis which identifies potential risks. Finally, Stage 4 goes back to the higher level to resolve risks in a systematic manner providing a well-defined account of the risks. At any stage, the introduction of new elements – tasks or stakeholders – generates new questions and their impact on the project is ill-defined until an analysis is performed.

This process of moving from the traditional superficial description of a project to analyse risk in a detailed qualitative manner for each component and then to restate the project based on this new perspective is a new approach. It provides those responsible for the project with a comprehensive perception of associated risks and addresses the limited risk perspective which focuses on high-level generic intra-project risks and intra-project stakeholders.

## Conclusion

Careful application of traditional risk analysis has limited success in mitigating project failures. In traditional risk analysis, the categorisation of software projects is limited to inter-project characteristics such as project size and complexity. Furthermore, it is narrowly focused on internal project stakeholders and emphasised quantifiable risk factors to the exclusion of qualitative ones. Thus, traditional risk analysis is either inadequate or incomplete. The SoDIS process complements and completes traditional risk analysis by specifically addressing these problems of traditional risk analysis. The resulting SoDIS provides a snapshot of the risk potential of the planned tasks before undertaking system implementation. This pre-audit provides an opportunity to address the risks by mitigation or avoidance. Its use provides checkpoints in the project that enable the software developer to stop or modify a project before disaster strikes. The use of qualitative best practice questions associates a full range of stakeholders with the project tasks providing a comprehensive risk analysis which helps identify social, professional and ethical risks for a project. SoDIS is the first fully developed approach of this kind. It points the way to achieving successful software development by design rather than by accident.

## Acknowledgements

The Software Development Research Foundation (sdreasearch.org) promotes the use of the SoDIS process and makes a SoDIS software tool available for free. Research on this process and software development was partially funded by National Science Foundation Grant NSF 9874684 and the work in New Zealand has been supported by grants from NACCQ, AUT Faculty of Business, AUT School of Computer and Information Sciences and Kansas State University. East Tennessee State University also supported Professor Gotterbarn's work in New Zealand. The SoDIS research for the Deputy Prime Minister "The Implementation of Electronic Voting" was funded by the UK Government (LGR 65/12/72).

## References

Ackoff, R. L. (1974). *Redesigning the Future*. New York, Wiley.

Aladwani, A. M. (2002). IT project uncertainty, planning and success: an empirical investigation from Kuwait. *Information Technology*, 15(3), 210–226.

Boehm, B. (1989). *Risk Management*. Los Alamitos, CA, IEEE Computer Society Press.

Boehm, B., Egyed, A., Kwan, J., Port, D., Shah, A. & Madachy, R. (1998). Using the WinWin spiral model: a case study. *Computer*, 31(7), 33–44.

Checkland, P. & Howell, S. (1998). *Information, Systems and Information Systems*. Brisbane, Wiley.

Cole, A. (1995). Runaway projects: cause and effects. *Software World*, 26(3), 3–5, Andy Cole of KPMG.

Cooper R. (2001). *Winning at New Products: Accelerating the Process from Ideas to Launch*, 3rd Edition. Cambridge, MA, Perseus Publishing.

Dalcher, D. & Tully, C. (2002). Learning from failures. *Software Process Improvement and Practice*, 7(2), 71–89.

DeMarco, T. & Lister, T. (2003). *Waltzing with Bears: Managing Risk on Software Projects*. New York, Dorsett House.

Dey, P. K. (2002). Benchmarking project management practices of Caribbean organizations using analytic hierarchy process. *Benchmarking: An International Journal*, 9(4), 326–356.

Farbey, B., Land, F. & Targett, D. (1993). *How to Assess Your IT Investment.* Butterworth Heinemann.

Fidler, C. & Rogerson, S. (1996). *Strategic Management Support Systems.* London, Pitman Publishing.

Goodpaster, K. E. (1993). Business ethics and stakeholder analysis. In: Beauchamp, T. L. & Bowie N. E. (eds.), *Ethical Theory and Business.* New Jersey: Prentice Hall, pp. 85–93.

Gotterbarn, D. (2004). Reducing software failures using software development impact statements. In: Spinello, R. & Tavani, H. (eds.), *Readings in Cyber Ethics*, 2nd Edition. Jones & Bartlett Learning, pp. 674–689.

Gotterbarn D., Clear, T. & Kwan, C. (2004). An inspection process for managing requirements risks: software development impact statements. *Proceeding of NACCQ Conference*, Christchurch, New Zealand, 6–9th July 2004

Henry, J. (2004). *Software Project Management: A Real-World Guide to Success.* Boston, MA, Addison Wesley.

Highsmith, J. (2004). *Agile Project Management.* Boston, MA, Addison Wesley.

Hirsheim, R. & Klein, H. (1989). Four paradigms of information systems development. *Communications of the ACM*, 32(10), 1199–1216.

Hoffman, G. (2003). Integrating PSP and CMMI Level 5. Available from http://www.stc-online.org/stc2003proceedings/PDFFiles/pres1001.pdf (Accessed 2 February 2005).

Humphrey, W. (1989). *Managing the Software Process.* Boston, MA, Addison-Wesley.

Humphrey, W. (1996). *Introduction to the Personal Software Process.* Boston, MA, Addison-Wesley.

Humphrey, W. (1999). *Introduction to the Team Software Process.* Boston, MA, Addison-Wesley.

Jayaratna, N. (1994). *Understanding and Evaluating Methodologies.* Maidenhead, UK, McGraw-Hill.

Jones, C. (2000). *Software Assessments, Benchmarks, and Best Practices.* Boston, MA, Addison-Wesley.

Keil, M., Amrit, T. & Bush, A. (2002). Reconciling user and project manager perceptions of IT project risk: a Delphi study. *Information Systems Journal*, 12(2), 103–119.

Keil, M., Cule, P. E., Lyytinen, K. & Schmidt, R. C. (1998). A framework for identifying software project risks. *Communications of the ACM*, 41(11), 76–83.

Keil, M., Wallace, L., Turk, D., Dixon-Randall, G. & Nulden, U. (2000). An investigation of risk perception and risk propensity on the decision to continue a software development project. *Journal of Systems and Software*, 53(2), 145–157.

Kuruppuarachchi, P. R., Mandal, P. & Smith, R. (2002). IT project implementation strategies for effective changes: a critical review. *Logistics Information Management*, 15(2), 126–137.

Lyytinen K. &. Hirschheim, R. (1987). Information systems failures: a survey and classification of empirical literature. *Oxford surveys in Information Technology*, 4, 257–309.

Mackenzie, K. (2001). IT a necessary evil: survey. *The Australian*, 21 August.

Mitchell K. R., Agle, R. B. & Wood, J. D. (1997). Toward a theory of stakeholder identification and salience: defining the principle of who or what really counts. *Academy of Management Review*, 22(4), 853–886.

Mumford, E. (1996). *Systems Design: Ethical Tools for Ethical Change.* Basingstoke, UK, Macmillan Ltd.

PMI (2000). *Member Ethical Standards and Member Code of Ethics.* Project Management Institute. Available from http://www.pmi.org/membership/standards (Accessed May 2005).

Pouloudi, A., Papazafeiropoulou, A., & Poulymenakou, A. (1999). Use of stakeholder analysis for electronic commerce applications in the public sector: different development scenarios. In: Pries-Heje, J., Ciborra, C. U., Kautz, K., Valor, J., Christiaanse, E., Avison, D. E. & Heje, C. (eds.), Proceedings of the Seventh European Conference on Information Systems, ECIS 1999, Denmark, Copenhagen Business School.

Pouloudi, A. & Whitley, E. A. (1997). Stakeholder identification in inter-organizational systems: gaining insights for drug use management systems. *European Journal of Information Systems*, 6(1), 1–14.

Prestwood Software (2002). *Prestwood Software Development Process, Overview.* Version 3.0 R1, July 2002. Available from www.prestwood.com/standards/psdp/downloads/PSDP%20Overview.pdf (Accessed May 2005).

Rogerson, S. & Gotterbarn, D. (1998). The Ethics of Software Project Management. In: Collste, G. (ed.) *Ethics and information technology.* Delhi, India, New Academic Publishers, pp. 137–154.

Ropponen J., Lyytinen, N. & Kalle, N. (2000). Components of software development risk: how to address them? A project manager survey. *IEEE Transactions on Software Engineering*, 26(2), 98–112.

Schach, S.R. (2003). *Introduction to Object-Oriented Systems Analysis and Design with UML and the Unified Process.* McGraw-Hill.

Schmidt, R., Lyytinen, K., Keil, M. & Cule, P. (2001). Identifying software project risks: an international Delphi study. *Journal of Management Information Systems*, 17(4), 5–36.

Schwalbe, C. (2004). *Information Technology Project Management*, 3rd Edition. Boston, MA, Thomson Publishing.

SEI (Software Engineering Institute, Carnegie Mellon University) (1995). *The Capability Maturity Model: Guidelines for Improving the Software Process.* Boston, MA, Addison Wesley Professional.

Sharp, H., Finkelstein, A. & Galal, G., (1999). Stakeholder identification in the requirements engineering process. In: *Proceedings. Tenth International Workshop on Database and Expert Systems Applications. DEXA 99*, pp. 387–391.

Shenhar, A. L., Renier, J. J. & Wideman, R. M. (1996). Improving PM: linking success criteria to project type. In: *Creating Canadian Advantage through Project Management.* Calgary, Project Management Institute Symposium.

Shneiderman, B. & Rose, A. (1995). Social impact statements: engaging public participation in information technology design. *Technical Report of the Human Computer Interaction Laboratory*, September, 1–13.

Simon, H. A. (1960). *The New Science of Management Decision.* New Jersey, Prentice Hall.

Simon, H. A. (1984). Decision making and organisational design. In: Pugh, D. S. (ed.), *Organization Theory*. Penguin Books Ltd, pp. 202–223.

Smith, H. J. & Keil, M. (2003). The reluctance to report bad news on troubled software projects: a theoretical model. *Information Systems Journal*, 13(1), 69–95.

Spafford, G. (2002). Staking out the Stakeholders. *Gantthead.com.* Available from https://www.projectmanagement.com/articles/145600/Staking-Out-the-Stakeholders, October (Accessed 15 May 2003).

Turban, E., Mclean, E. & Wetherbe, J. (1996). *Information Technology for Management.* New York, John Wiley.

Willcocks, L., & Mason, D. (1987). *Computerising Work: People, Systems Design and Workplace Relations.* London, Paradigm.

## Chapter 11

# Information Systems Ethics – Challenges and Opportunities [2019]*

## Introduction

Each day society becomes more and more reliant upon information created and communicated using technology. Everybody expects such information to be correct. Central to this evolution is the increasingly disparate array of application information systems (IS). It seems that individuals, organisations and society as a whole have an insatiable appetite for information.

Some argue that as a consequence society becomes more and more vulnerable to catastrophe. The ransomware attack of May 2017, which caused the closure of many of the accident and emergency units in hospitals in the United Kingdom, is evidence of this. With the world in current economic crisis, the headlong drive for efficiency and effectiveness (and resulting profit) is the watchword. Such pressure might have resulted in real gains but has also led to unscrupulous or reckless actions. The tempering of such drive with ethical consideration is often neglected until there is a detrimental event causing public outcry. Such an event will usually attract both media interest and social media postings, which in turn places more and more pressure on the actors to account for the reasons why the event had occurred. This cause and effect map is commonplace.

---

* This paper has been developed from a panel session "The ethics of Information Systems – challenges andopportunities: a panel discussion by the authors at the Midwest Association for Information Systems conference – MWAIS 2017 in May 2017. This chapter was first published as: Rogerson, S., Miller, K., Winter, J. S. & Larson, D. (2019) Information Systems Ethics – challenges and opportunities. *Journal of Information, Communication and Ethics in Society*, Vol. 17, No. 1, pp. 87–97. Copyright © Emerald Publishing Limited. Reprinted by permission. DOI 10.1108/JICES-07-2017-0041.

## Indicative Examples

On such example is the Volkswagen emissions scandal. On 11 January 2017, the US Department of Justice (2017) announced that,

> Volkswagen had agreed to plead guilty to three criminal felony counts, and pay a $2.8 billion criminal penalty, as a result of the company's long-running scheme to sell approximately 590,000 diesel vehicles in the United States by using a defeat device to cheat on emissions tests mandated by the Environmental Protection Agency (EPA) and the California Air Resources Board (CARB), and lying and obstructing justice to further the scheme.

At the centre of the scandal is misinformation generated by onboard software – an IS. This IS was developed and implemented by professionals who must have been party to this illegal and unethical act.

In general, the integrity of information relies upon the development and operation of computer-based IS. Those who undertake the planning, development and operation of these IS have obligations to assure information integrity and overall to contribute to the public good (Rogerson, 2011). The ethical practice of the IS practitioner is paramount. Practice comprises two distinct facets: process and product. Process concerns the activities of IS practitioners and whether their conduct is deemed virtuous, which is a deontological perspective. Whereas product concerns the outcome of professional IS endeavour and whether systems are deemed to be ethically viable, which is a teleological perspective. The Volkswagen case appears to have failed on both counts.

By contrast, in a more traditional setting, an example of poor IS practice is the UK Child Support Agency's system, which overpaid 1.9 million people and underpaid around 700,000 in 2004. Inadequate systems analysis resulted in the introduction of a large and complex IS at the same time as restructuring the agency, leading to enormous operational difficulties (Essendal & Rogerson, 2011). In terms of IS practice, it appears this was a process failing which could be deemed to be unethical.

IS professionals have specialised knowledge and often have positions with authority and respect in the community. Their professional activity spans management, development and operations. Thus, they can have a significant impact upon the world, including many of the things that people value. Alongside this power to change the world comes the duty to exercise such power in a socially responsible manner. Six social responsibility principles (Rogerson, 2004) establish an ethos of professionalism within IS. These principles are as follows:

- Develop a socially responsible culture within work which nurtures moral individual action
- Consider and support the wellbeing of all stakeholders
- Account for global common values and local cultural differences
- Recognise social responsibility that is beyond legal compliance and effective fiscal management
- Ensure all business processes are considered from a social responsibility perspective
- Be proactive rather than reactive

Overall, professional IS practice must exhibit a balance between rights and justice, and care and empathy. Such ethical responsibilities of IS professionals have been discussed at length in several well-cited works (Mason, 1986; Mingers & Walsham, 2010; Oz, 1992). This section considers four important aspects of these responsibilities, which are both challenges to the professionals and opportunities to do the right thing. Each is identified using a *bumper sticker slogan* which is a few words that describe the challenge.

## 1. Avoid Obvious Evils

When people think of professional ethics, they often think of the "thou shalt not" aspects: don't cheat, don't lie, and don't steal. These prohibitions are important, and can be found in many professional ethics codes, including the code for software engineers approved by the IEEE Computer Society and the ACM (Gotterbarn, Miller & Rogerson, 1999). In that code, some of those prohibitions are straightforward: "Reject bribery." Others are more circumspect, as in this passage about conflicts of interest: "Accept no outside work detrimental to the work they perform for their primary employer." Either way, the message is clear: avoid doing bad things.

## 2. Accomplish Good Deeds

Although avoiding evil is important, the story of an ethical professional does not end there. Another crucial aspect is that IS professionals should embrace opportunities to do good. Many such opportunities for positive professional action are available to volunteers as well as to professional organisations; the people who organised the Midwest Association for Information Systems conference, MWAIS 2017, are doing a good deed for IS academics. Recently, organisations such as CodeMontage (https://www.codemontage.com/) and Code for America (https://www.codeforamerica.org/) have encouraged IT professionals (and others) to donate pro bono information processing work to improve the world. Many who volunteer their services to open source and free software projects do so with altruistic intent (Hars & Ou, 2001).

## 3. Pay Attention to Subtle Nuances

Some ethically significant actions are neither obviously evil nor obviously good deeds. Instead, these actions require careful thought and analysis before an alert professional can decide what the most ethical action is. For example, statistics show that in many countries – although not all countries (Varma, 2010) – women are under-represented in IS. But why? If this imbalance is a free choice, perhaps there is no ethical problem; but if there is overt, covert or subtle pressure, and unfair practices that keep women out, then there is clearly an ethical issue that should be addressed (Johnson & Miller, 2002). IS professionals have a responsibility to be sensitive to these kinds of issues, and willing to study, discuss, and then act appropriately after such an issue has been identified.

## 4. Plan for a Complex IS Future

The last slogan is related to the previous slogan because slogan 3 encourages IS professionals to look beyond the obvious. But "pay attention to subtle nuances" refers to current events; slogan 4 encourages IS professionals to think about the future with imagination and resolve to do the right thing. A prominent example of a future area in which IS professionals are likely to encounter a plethora of ethical challenges is artificial intelligence (Russell et al., 2015). Weapons that kill without a human in the decision loop, AI employees causing broad unemployment for humans, and sophisticated machines that mimic human bigotry are just three examples that are already under discussion, and are likely to rapidly gain importance. Since IS professionals have special knowledge about these newly powerful machines, and because they are part of the socio-technical system that brings such machines to society, they have special responsibilities for educating the public about these machines, and for ensuring that the machine benefit, more than harm, humanity.

These four slogans do not trivialise ethical responsibilities in IS but help people to stay focused on these issues in their professional lives. In many ways, IS professionals are on the ethical front line. The public depends on them to be vigilant.

There are many ethical issues which the IS professional faces in the modern, technologically dependent world. The complexities of data governance illustrate the types of challenges to be faced, addressed and resolved.

As business processes are increasingly digitised, and as everyday objects are redesigned to include digital sensors, computing power, and communication capabilities, people are experiencing dramatic changes in the scope and volume of data that are generated. The Internet of Things, and associated machine-to-machine communication, machine learning/artificial intelligence – collectively called the *Embedded Infosphere* (Taylor, 2016) – pose many new ethical challenges. In addition to enhanced magnitude of data, the *Embedded Infosphere* introduces many new data types, as tens of billions of everyday objects become equipped with networked sensors (e.g. location-based data or biometric data). Data are increasingly being aggregated and mined, and data analytics has become embedded at the core of business and operational functions (Davenport, Barth & Bean, 2012). The Economist argues that "data are to this century what oil was to the last one: a driver of growth and change" (Economist, 2017, para. 4). The value of user-generated data is growing, and even where data have been anonymised in order to ensure privacy or anonymity, they may be "re-personalised" via data mining techniques (Schwartz & Solove, 2011; Winter, 2015).

These developments have led to a renewed focus in IS on data governance issues, that is, how to create, aggregate, and manage data and the conflicting values that surround data use. This has revitalised the discourse about responsibilities for security, privacy protections, and data integrity (Rosenbaum, 2010), and scholars and policy makers are also beginning to grapple with the ethics of algorithms.

There are two emerging areas related to the ethics of data that are of particular relevance to IS researchers.

First, should big data repositories such as medical claims databases be treated as a public good or "private garden"? For example, in the health domain, big data sets and analytics are seen by management as a "fruitful foundation for innovation, competition and productivity" (Lycett, 2013, p. 381). Electronic health records (EHRs) have enabled massive medical data sets, and big data analytics may "greatly expand the capacity to generate new knowledge" (Murdoch & Detsky, 2013, p. 1351). Where these data are seen as a public good, then such a medical repository can support policy research related to healthcare costs, quality, service gaps, and disparities, improving health outcomes for various populations, reducing costs, and fostering basic medical research. How can multiple value claims about these data resources be navigated in order to lower the barrier between public and private goods? If big data health repositories are in fact a public good, should access to reasonably secure medical claims data be provided without profit to researchers or citizen scientists? Should they be governed as a Commons – a resource affecting the entire community – rather than held as a "private garden"? (Winter & Davidson, 2017a, 2017b). In the private garden model prevalent today, data are often siloed and treated as private goods by the aggregator. This occurs even when the data collected represent individuals, who may not have access to the data about themselves or the ability to control its use.

The second area of concern is unjust discrimination based on big data analytics (Boyd, Levy & Marwick, 2014; Custers, 2013; Winter, 2015). Data about individuals and groups are being increasingly aggregated in order to make data profiles that can be used to categorise people and even forecast behaviours. Everyday interactions with technologies – Internet browsing, traveling in a car, using a "smart" refrigerator, washing machines, or television, or moving through a public space where cloud-based facial recognition is employed – has led to increasing aggregation and analysis of trace data by corporations. Decisions made based on these analyses pose potential harms. Highly sensitive personal information related to politics, religion, or health is collected and may be used to discriminate against individuals seeking housing, immigration eligibility, or employment (Winter, 2013). In the United States, for example, a major credit reporting agency/data broker, sells "a 'data enrichment' service that provides 'hundreds of attributes' such as age, profession and 'wealth indicators' tied to a particular IP address" (Angwin, 2015, para. 5–6). Data brokers such as idiCORE have collected detailed profiles for every American citizen, including personal information such as addresses, property and mortgage records, voter registration, and names/contact information of neighbours. "The reports also include photos of cars taken by private companies using automated license plate readers – billions of snapshots tagged with GPS coordinates and time stamps to help PIs [private investigators] surveil people or bust alibis" (Herbert, 2016, para. 3). These data can be used to forecast heath, for example. In a recent case, Microsoft researchers demonstrated that they could predict upcoming diagnoses of pancreatic cancer by analysing web searches (McFarland, 2016, para. 3). These "health surveillance systems" are problematic not only due to privacy and security issues, but there is also great potential, and even incentive, to abuse these data (e.g. sharing with insurance underwriters). The financial incentives for collection and analysis are growing, and big data analytics can enable non-protected "proxy" fields that are highly correlated to any protected by law to be used instead (Barocas & Selbst, 2016).

## Addressing the Ethical Dimension

The ethical dimension of IS has attracted mixed attention in the IS academic discipline. Given issues such as data governance, as discussed earlier, this is becoming increasingly problematic. This situation has existed for a considerable period. Walsham who is an eminent IS professor (1996), found little published work which directly related IS-related ethical issues to more general ethical theory. Wood-Harper et al. (1996) identified four categories of dilemmas which a systems analyst might face when undertaking IS development. Two were explicitly ethical: *Whose ethical perspective will dominate the study of the situation and the development of the IS?*; and *Will ethical viewpoints be included in the study?* Rogerson, Weckert and Simpson (2000) addressed both questions in a review of the popular methodology, SSADM. However, the general lack of interest continued (Bell & Adam, 2004; Bull, 2009). Indeed, there has been limited crossover between the Computer Ethics and Information Systems disciplines. Warren and Lucas (2016) found that there are very few researchers who are active in both fields and that there are very few papers from the computer ethics journals which are cited in the journals of the Association of Information Systems. Weiss (2017) found that there were few papers relating to ethics or corporate social responsibility in top-ranked IS journals although there was some evidence of an increase (Abbasi, Sarker & Chiang, 2016; White & Ariyachandra, 2016). Furthermore, there is a tendency for these few papers to adopt a positivist approach, which is contrary to the computer ethics body of knowledge. Hassan and Mathiassen (2017) address the growing interest in creating an

Information Systems Development Body of Knowledge. Their proposals focus on traditional techniques cited in the IS literature and so the ethical dimension is side-lined. Overall, it seems there has been little progress in the 20 years that have passed since Walsham's paper. This is confirmed by an ethical review of current IS practice which follows.

## An Ethical Review of Current IS Practice

To illustrate the importance of addressing ethical behaviour within the IS community, examples are discussed which provide potential evidence of the need to include ethical thinking and ethical analysis processes with the design of IS and technology in general. Three examples are chosen where technology played a part in some ethical violations. These are Volkswagen emissions cheat, Wells Fargo fake accounts, and smart TVs.

The Volkswagen emissions scandal (mentioned previously) is most like the most widely known and expensive of the three. So far, the costs of the emissions cheat have approached nearly $30 billion in fines, criminal penalties and restitution (Eisenstein, 2017). Additionally, employees face criminal charges. The VW reputation damage is hard to gauge but is huge and may take a long time to repair. Even loyal supporters of Volkswagen are no longer supportive (Willems, 2016). In the VW case, someone wrote the software to misrepresent emissions. It would seem, ethically speaking, that someone throughout the process of creating the software would have asked, "Why are we doing this?" The focus of the VW scandal is on someone writing code to circumvent accurate emissions readings. It can reasonably be assumed that this was done from a specification which was developed during a requirements analysis process, was approved by a project manager, and was requested by a stakeholder. The software worked so was successfully tested and implemented, which most likely assumes more IS/IT employees were involved as well as engineering staff.

The Wells Fargo scandal, which has resulted in nearly $300 million in penalties, fines, settlements and damaged reputation (Egan, 2017), might not be as apparent of an ethics problem as the VW scandal. However, the violators who set up the fake accounts did so through an IS. The system most likely did exactly what it was designed to do, but, ethically, should the system have had safeguards to not allow the fake accounts? As reported (Levine, 2016), in setting up the accounts, employees used simple codes to fake information such as a *1234@wellsfargo.com* email address and a *0000* PIN. If ethical processes were incorporated within the system design and project management processes, perhaps additional risk considerations would focus on or address the question, "How can this system be used unethically?" and then build in the safeguards to help eliminate unethical use of the system.

The Internet of Things has brought about the emergence of smart devices that are becoming ubiquitous. According to various authors (Barrett, 2017; Schneier, 2015; Vaughan-Nichols, 2017) smart TVs, for example, while looking benign on the surface, and unless users take measures not commonly known or necessarily easy to do, are actively sending information about viewing habits to databases owned by the various television vendors. Many smart TVs also have the ability to listen to and watch viewers via built-in microphones and cameras. Many television manufacturers, such as Samsung, Vizio, LG, and Sony, have been known to have tracking software and can hear and/or view owners. Trying to apply ethical concepts to the Internet of Things is not a simple right versus wrong consideration. It is convenient and beneficial for smart TVs to have the ability to listen to commands such as changing a channel, suggesting a program (based on viewing habits) or searching for a particular show or movie. Perhaps the ethical questions that should be asked by the developers of this technology are, "Should we do more to make the user aware of what is being done with their commands?" and/or "Should we be more open about the capabilities of our smart devices and build in easy-to-use features to disable unwanted smart features?"

Given these background examples, is enough being done in terms of ethics education and research as it relates to IS? If popular information-systems-focused conferences and textbooks are indicators of whether or not there is sufficient emphasis on this topic, the news is not good. In reviewing topics covered by several international, national and regional IS conferences, the topic of ethics is totally missing or minimally represented. A review of popular IS textbooks reveals again, the topic of ethics is inadequately addressed. However, there is some positive movement. The *MSIS 2016 Global Competency Model for Graduate Degree Programs in Information Systems* developed jointly by AIS and ACM does include ethics within the curriculum's core competencies.

Does more need to be done to integrate ethics methodologies with IS methodologies? Given the impact of the three examples previously explored, the answer is "Yes." System failures are often discussed in IS courses and research but are mostly focused on inadequate requirements definition, uncontrolled scope, lack of stakeholder involvement, lack of management commitment and many other non-ethical issues. While such failures indeed can be costly and damage the reputation of an organisation they are not the only factors to consider. Ethical failures should be covered as well. Ethics in the real world of IS is a crucial issue which cannot and should not be ignored. It follows that IS education programmes should be fit-for-purpose, addressing the ethical dimension in a timely and appropriate manner. It seems that a global audit of IS education offerings would worthwhile, as it would provide evidence of how serious and widespread is the lack of ethics content and education.

## Conclusions

From the arguments laid out earlier, it follows that there is a need to increase awareness, interest and action concerning the ethical dimension of IS both as a discipline and as a practice. There is an opportunity for multidisciplinary dialogue which will promote greater attention to these issues. The overall aim is to act as a catalyst for action within the IS community. As such there are four objectives:

1. To encourage wider debate concerning the ethics of IS
2. To explore current application areas and technological infrastructures in order to tease out some of the key ethical challenges
3. To consider how current management practices allow or hinder the addressing of such challenges
4. To suggest ways forward for practitioners which will increase the chance of ethically acceptable application systems

It is possible to develop an agenda of ethical issues surrounding the development and use of IS. The agenda could be subdivided into three parts:

- **Application areas**: examples, Internet of Things, Cloud Computing, Social Media, Big Data
- **Techniques**: examples, Ethics Algorithms, Sentiment Analysis, Public Beta Testing

- **Holistic concerns**: examples, Privacy, Cybersecurity, Equality of Access, Data and Discrimination

The success of such an initiative requires all those involved in IS research, education, and practice to contribute to the detailed planning of the initiative and to be proactive in its implementation.

# References

Abbasi, A., Sarker, S. & Chiang, R. H. L. (2016). Big data research in information systems: toward an inclusive research agenda. *Journal of the Association for Information Systems*, 17(2), Article 3.

Angwin, J. (2015). Own a Vizio Smart TV? It's watching you. *ProPublica*. Available from https://www.propublica.org/article/own-a-vizio-smart-tv-its-watching-you (Accessed 30 May 2017).

Barocas, S. & Selbst, A. D. (2016). Big data's disparate impact. *California Law Review*, 104(3), 671–732.

Barrett, B. (2017). How to stop your smart TV from spying on you. *Wired*. Available from https://www.wired.com/2017/02/smart-tv-spying-vizio-settlement/ (Accessed 2 June 2017).

Bell, F. & Adam, A. (2004). Whatever happened to information systems ethics? Caught between the devil and the deep blue sea. In: Kaplan, B., Truex, D. P., Wastell, D., Wood-Harper, A. T. & De Gross, J. (eds.), *Information Systems Research: Relevant Theory and Information Practice*. Boston, Kluwer Academic, pp. 159–174.

Boyd, d., Levy, K. & Marwick, A. (2014). The networked nature of algorithmic discrimination. In: Gangadharan, S. (ed.), *Data and Discrimination: Collected Essays*. Washington, DC, Open Technology Institute – New America Foundation, pp. 53–57.

Bull, C. M., (2009). A review of ethical theory in the 'upper echelons' of information systems research. Presented at *17th European Conference on Information Systems*. Available from https://e-space.mmu.ac.uk/70673/1/ecis2009-0070.pdf (Accessed 8 May 2017).

Cisco (2014). The Zettabyte era: trends and analysis. *Cisco White Paper*, 10 June. San Jose, CA, Cisco Systems. Available from http://www.netmode.ntua.gr/courses/postgraduate/video_communications/2014/VNI_Hyperconnectivity_WP.pdf (Accessed 30 May 2017).

Custers, B. (2013). Data dilemmas in the information society: introduction and overview. In: Custers, B., Calders, T., Schermer, T. & Zarsky, T. (eds.), *Discrimination and Privacy in the Information Society: Data Mining and Profiling in Large Databases*. New York, Springer, pp. 3–26.

Davenport, T. H., Barth, P. & Bean, R. (2012). How 'big data' is different. *MIT Sloan Management Review*, 54(1), 43.

Economist (2017). Fuel of the future: data is giving rise to a new economy. *The Economist*, 6 May. Available from http://www.economist.com/news/briefing/21721634-how-it-shaping-up-data-giving-rise-new-economy (Accessed 8 May 2017).

Egan, M. (2017). Wells Fargo still faces over a dozen probes tied to fake account scandal. *CNN Money*, 31 March. Available from http://money.cnn.com/2017/03/31/investing/wells-fargo-investigations-fake-account-scandal/ (Accessed 2 June 2017).

Eisenstein, P. A. (2017). Volkswagen slapped with largest ever fine for automakers. *NBCNews*, 21 April. Available from http://www.nbcnews.com/business/autos/judge-approves-largest-fine-u-s-history-volkswagen-n749406 (Accessed 2 June 2017).

Essendal, T. & Rogerson, S. (2011). A holistic approach to software engineering education. In: Hussey, M., Wu, B. & Xu, X. (eds.), *Software Industry Oriented Education Practice and Curriculum Development: Experiences and Lessons*. IGI Global, pp. 83–97.

Gotterbarn, D., Miller, K. & Rogerson, S. (1999). Computer society and ACM approve software engineering code of ethics. *Computer*, 32(10), 84–88.

Hars, A. & Ou, S. (2001). Working for free? Motivations of participating in open source projects. In: *System Sciences, Proceedings of the 34th Annual Hawaii International Conference on System Sciences*, Vol. 7, 7014.

Hassan, N.R. & Mathiassen, L. (2017). Distilling a body of knowledge for information systems development. *Information Systems Journal*, 28(1), 175–226. doi: 10.1111/isj.12126.

Herbert, D.G. (2016). This company has built a profile on every American adult. *Bloomberg Businessweek*. Available from https://www.bloomberg.com/news/articles/2016-08-05/this-company-has-built-a-profile-on-every-american-adult (Accessed 30 May 2017).

Johnson, D. G. & Miller, K. W. (2002). Is diversity in computing a moral matter?. *ACM SIGCSE Bulletin*, 34(2), 9–10.

Levine, M. (2016). Wells Fargo opened a couple million fake accounts. *Bloomberg*. Available from https://www.bloomberg.com/view/articles/2016-09-09/wells-fargo-opened-a-couple-million-fake-accounts (Accessed 2 June 2017).

Lycett, M. (2013). 'Datafication': making sense of (big) data in a complex world. *European Journal of Information Systems*, 22(4), 381–386.

Mason, R. O. (1986). Four ethical issues of information age. *MIS Quarterly*, 10(1), 5–11.

McFarland, M. (2016). What happens when your search engine is first to know you have cancer?. *The Washington Post*, 10 June. Available from https://www.washingtonpost.com/ news/innovations/ wp/2016/06/10/what-happens-when-your-search-engine-is-first-to-know-you-have-cancer/ (Accessed 30 May 2017).

Mingers, J. & Walsham, G. (2010). Toward ethical information systems: the contribution of discourse ethics. *MIS Quarterly*, 34(4), 833–854.

Murdoch, T. B. & Detsky, A. S. (2013). The inevitable application of big data to health care. *JAMA*, 309(13), 1351–1352.

Oz, E. (1992). Ethical standards for information systems professionals: a case for a unified code. *MIS Quarterly*, 16(4), 423–433.

Rogerson, S. (2004). Aspects of social responsibility in the information society. In: Doukidis, G., Mylonopoulos, N. & Pouloudi, N. (eds.), *Social and Economic Transformation in the Digital Era*. IGI Global, pp. 31–46.

Rogerson, S. (2011). Ethics and ICT. In: Galliers, R. & Currie, W. (eds.), *The Oxford Handbook on Management Information Systems: Critical Perspectives and New Directions*. Oxford University Press, pp. 601–622.

Rogerson, S., Weckert, J. & Simpson, C. (2000). An ethical review of information systems development: the Australian Computer Society's code of ethics and SSADM. *Information Technology and People*, 13(2), 121–136.

Rosenbaum, S. (2010). Data governance and stewardship: designing data stewardship entities and advancing data access. *Health Services Research*, 45(5p2), 1442–1455.

Russell, S., Hauert, S., Altman, R. & Veloso, M. (2015). Ethics of artificial intelligence. *Nature*, 521(7553), 415–418.

Schneier, B. (2015). You TV may be watching you. *CNN*, 12 February. Available from http://www.cnn.com/2015/02/11/opinion/schneier-samsung-tv-listening/ (Accessed 2 June 2017).

Schwartz, P. M. & Solove, D. (2011). The PII problem: privacy and a new concept of personally identifiable information. *New York University Law Review*, 86, 1814–1894.

Taylor, R. D. (2016). The next stage of U.S. communications policy: the emerging Embedded Infosphere. *Telecommunications Policy*. Available from http://dx.doi.org/10.1016/j.telpol.2016.11.007 (Accessed 30 May 2017).

US Department of Justice (2017). Volkswagen AG agrees to plead guilty and pay $4.3 billion in criminal and civil penalties and six Volkswagen executives and employees are indicted in connection with conspiracy to cheat U.S. Emissions Tests. *Justice News*, 11 January. Available from https://www.justice.gov/opa/pr/volkswagen-ag-agrees-plead-guilty-and-pay-43-billion-criminal-and-civil-penalties-six (Accessed 15 January 2017).

Varma, R. (2010). Computing self-efficacy among women in India. *Journal of Women and Minorities in Science and Engineering*, 16(3), 257–274.

Vaughan-Nichols, S. J. (2017). How to keep your smart TV from spying on you. *ZDNet*, 8 March. Available from http://www.zdnet.com/article/how-to-keep-your-smart-tv-from-spying-on-you/ (Accessed 2 June 2017).

Walsham, G. (1996). Ethical theory, codes of ethics and IS practice. *Information Systems Journal*, 6(1), 69–81.

Wang, J., Hong, H., Ravitz, J. & Ivory, M. (2015). Gender differences in factors influencing pursuit of computer science and related fields. In: *Proceedings of the 2015 ACM Conference on Innovation and Technology in Computer Science Education*, pp. 117–122.

Warren, M. & Lucas, R. (2016). Ethics and ICT: why all the fuss?. *Journal of InformationCommunication and Ethics in Society*, 14(2), 167–169.

Weiss, J. (2017). Ethics and CSR research in top ranked IS Journals, 1980-2013: a developing trend or anomaly?, In: *Proceedings of the 50th Hawaii International Conference on System Sciences*, 4–7 January, Hilton Waikoloa Village, Hawaii, pp. 5758–5762.

White, G. & Ariyachandra, T. (2016). Big data and ethics: examining the grey areas of big data analytics. *Issues in Information Systems*, 17(4), 1–7.

Willems, S. (2016). Rebuilding Volkswagen's reputation – hard or downright impossible? An Expert Weighs In, the truth about cars, 17 May. Available from http://www.thetruthaboutcars.com/2016/05/rebuilding-volkswagens-reputation/ (Accessed 2 June 2017).

Winter, J. S. (2013). Surveillance in ubiquitous network societies: normative conflicts related to the consumer in-store supermarket experience in the context of the Internet of Things. *Ethics and Information Technology*, 16(1), 27–41.

Winter, J. S. (2015). Algorithmic discrimination: big data analytics and the future of the Internet. In: Winter, J. S. & Ono, R. (eds.), *The Future Internet: Alternative Visions*. New York, Springer, pp. 125–140.

Winter, J. S. & Davidson, E. J. (2017a). Investigating values in personal health data governance models. *The 23rd Americas Conference on Information Systems*, August 2017, Boston, MA.

Winter, J. S. & Davidson, E. J. (2017b). Values-driven data governance: is personal health data a public good or a private garden? *The Social Movements and IT Symposium of the Hawaii International Conference on System Sciences*, January 2017. Waikoloa, HI.

Wood-Harper, A. T., Corder, S., Wood, J. R. G. & Watson, H. (1996). How we profess: the ethical systems analyst. *Communications of the ACM*, 39(3), 69–77.

# PRODUCT

> *... embedded social norms lead to technological integrity of the ICT [digital technology] product.*
>
> (Simon Rogerson, 2013, p. 131)

Part 3 focuses on the product element of the *process-product model* as discussed in Chapter 5. As explained, product concerns the outcome of professional endeavour and the potential impact of these products on people, society and the environment. The ethics focus of the product perspective is technological integrity from, for example, a Kantian or utilitarian perspective. The relationship between this and the Aristotelian virtue of process is discussed in Chapter 27.

Integrity can be achieved by embedding ethics within digital technology products themselves. Sadly, this aspect of design and development is often overlooked or ignored. This is explored in detail in Part 3, which includes seven examples of digital technology at different points of the 25-year timeline. Each example is subjected to some form of ethical review. These examples represent significant impacts on the global society and provide a clear message that digital ethics must not be overlooked at any time.

## Reference

Rogerson, S. (2013). The integrity of creating, communicating and consuming information online in the context of higher education institutions. In: Engwall, L. & Scott, P. (eds.), *Trust in Universities*. Wenner-Gren International Series, 86. London: Portland Press Ltd, 125–136.

*Chapter 12*

# The Social Impact of Smart Card Technology [1998]*

## Introduction

The application of information technology continues to expand in terms of diversity of use and the number of people using it. The impact is significant for individuals, organisations, nations, and the world as a whole. This chapter focuses on smart card technology which is being applied in various ways to facilitate trade, gain access to services and products, verify identity, and establish and influence relationships. In the United Kingdom, there have been many applications of this technology, for example, the electronic purse – Mondex, the Shell loyalty card, and the Social Security Benefits Card. Similar examples can be found in different parts of the world. In Spain, a smart card has been introduced for benefit payments and access to government databases (Honeywood, 1997). Security measures to combat fraudulent use of this card include biometric fingerprinting.

As we become more dependent on information technology, there is a tendency for society's citizens to exist and their needs addressed through digital icons which represent us in the computer (Rogerson & Bynum, 1995). The smart card has become one such icon. One can envisage a time when the lack of ownership of a multi-functional smart card will result in a dramatic loss of opportunity and of help in times of need for the "non-citizen." The aim of this chapter is to consider the social impact of the smart card and how such technological take-up might be managed sensitively.

## The Nature of Smart Cards

A smart card is a credit-sized plastic card containing one (usually) or more embedded semi-conductor chips and so has all the capabilities of a computer. It can store large amounts of data, process and update that data, and restrict access to that data. Contact smart cards make physical

* This chapter was first published as: Rogerson, S. (1998) The social impact of smart card technology. In: Banerjee, P., Hackney, R., Dhillon, G. & Jain, R. (eds.), Business Information Technology Management: Closing the International Divide. New Delhi, India, Har-Anand Publications Pvt. Chapter 45. pp. 712–723. Copyright © Simon Rogerson.

contact with the reader/writer device, while contactless cards rely on electronic induction principles to link up. There are several sophisticated development platforms using, for example, Java, that enable complex application programs to be written for use on smart cards.

Smart cards can facilitate a high level of security which makes it much harder to access data fraudulently or impersonate the card holder compared the magnetic stripe card. There are two types of security measures: data encryption and biometric identification.

## Data Encryption

Data encryption relies on converting data into a form that is meaningless to all those attempting unauthorised access. This is done using a key to encode the data and another to decrypt it. How effective encryption is depends directly on the size of the keys used. Public key encryption and private key decryption is the common and effective approach to smart card data encryption. Private decryption key escrow is a system for the management of strong cryptography whereby trusted third parties act as confidential registries for decryption keys and law enforcement agencies require a warrant to gain access to a key to access in some legal investigation (Perri 6, 1996). This management system is gaining significant acceptance regarding smart card applications.

## Biometric Identification

Biometric identification relies on storing physical attributes to authenticate the card holder. This might include digital photographs, fingerprint scans, hand geometry, retina scans, voice prints and dynamic signatures. Currently, fingerprint scanning is the most advanced of these techniques (Violino, 1997). The fingerprint is reconstructed into digital form and the matched against a sample given earlier and held on the smart card. Facial recognition systems such as FaceIt SDK are capable of accurately comparing facial features stored on a smart card with real-time features using techniques that ensure unvarying features determine a match (Johnson, 1997). Violino reports that biometrics is likely to increase at an annual rate of around 30% due to the growth of electronic commerce and intranets.

## Functions

Smart cards have three broad functions: authentication, storing value and storing personalised information. Authentication is concerned with ensuring only authorised individuals gain access to systems and buildings. Smart card can be used as electronic purse to store units of value in different currency denominations as well as credit and other units of value such as bonus points or air miles. Values can be replenished on a smart card. The smart card can also be used as a portable storage device independent of some fixed location and with the capability of holding a large amount of data of different forms and for different purposes but usually of a personal nature.

The Supercard (Supernet, 1997) is an example of a generalised proprietary card available for a variety of applications. Various security measures are incorporated including PIN (Personal Identification Number), various security codes and digital signatures. It allows several functions to be incorporated:

- Cash purse sectors, allowing the card to be used to deliver electronic cash
- Charge accounts sectors, allowing the card to be used as a charge card or store card
- Membership sectors, allowing the card to be used to verify membership
- Points sectors, allowing the card to be used to record bonus points for consumer incentive schemes

# Smart Card Applications

In researching for this chapter, a number of sources were used. An email request was made over several relevant email lists for details of smart card example applications. The World Wide Web search engines were used to find reports particularly in the trade and popular press of smart card application. These were complimented by more traditional academic sources including conference and journal papers. The aim was to acquire an indication of the breadth and depth of current smart card application. From these varied sources, a total of 91 discrete applications were identified. These ranged from localised applications such as the use of smart cards in a road tolling project being undertaken by Leicester City Council in the United Kingdom to very wide applications such as the use of smart cards in mobile phones using the GSM standard which has been adopted by many countries. It was interesting to note that 41% of the identified applications were pilot schemes which were still being assessed as to their viability. It would appear that there continues to be much experimentation regarding smart card applications but there is evidence that transition to full implementation does not always follow. Indeed, Dorris (1997) suggests that while there are many smart card pilot schemes, very few evolve into long-term full applications due to political, cultural or privacy barriers. For example, of the 50 public sector smart card schemes in operation throughout the world, the majority are only small-scale pilots at the state or local government level (Honeywood, 1997).

Of the 91 identified applications, 27% were within banking, 18% within health and welfare, and 15% within transport. Other applications include telecommunications, identification, phone cards, retail loyalty schemes, metering, radio security, physical access and gambling. A smart patient data card is being tested in a region of the Czech Republic to replace the paper-based system that had limited capacity, was inaccurate, labour intensive to maintain and open to widespread abuse (Honeywood, 1997). There were several examples of multifunctional smart cards. Hilton International Hotels are investigating using a smart card that will take customer payments, handle customer loyalty schemes, and act as a door key. In Scotland, a super-loyalty card has been launched that holds status data for ten loyalty schemes as well as general customer marketing information. An unusual dual-function card is being piloted for the US Marines to store monetary value and to be used as tracking and identification purposes for weapon issuing (Caldwell, 1997). Two applications, the electronic purse and the benefit card, are now considered in more detail.

## *Electronic Purse*

There is an increasing use of smart cards for financial applications generally and electronic purses in particular. For example, Clarke (1996a) identified three smart card schemes, MasterCard, Visa and Mondex, being piloted in Australia as well as two further schemes, Digicash and CAFE that were relevant to the Australian context. Electronic purses such as Mondex link directly into existing banking procedures. They can handle very small purchases and so can be considered as a legitimate substitute for cash. Mondex is a technically mature scheme that has widespread international penetration. In a further publication, Clarke (1996b) undertakes a detailed investigation of the functionality and issues related to the Mondex scheme. He explains that the scheme comprises:

- Smart cards programmed to receive, store and issue value
- Cash-issuing devices capable of placing value onto the card

- Cash-receiving devices capable of accepting value transferred off the card
- Ancillary devices which can perform restricted functions

Cash transactions are anonymous, whereas Mondex transactions are pseudonymous. The retailer retains the card identification number with each transaction and this number is an indirect identifier of the account holder. A Mondex card has considerable functionality. It can directly transfer value from one card to another supporting person-to-person transactions as well as customer-to-retailer transactions. It can transfer value to and from the bank account linked to it. It can check value balances, report the last ten transactions made and lock the card using a PIN. The incentives that drive the implementation are summarised as follows:

- Reduces cash handling which is expensive
- Speeds up large cash transactions for retailers
- Reduces cheque transactions which are costly and cause delays at point of sale (POS)
- Improved customer service offers the opportunity to charge fees for smart card facilities

Clarke suggests that there are a number of consumer substantive and potential privacy issues related to Mondex.

*Substantive privacy impact*: The current Mondex implementation appears to have limited direct and substantive effects on individual consumer privacy. However, this is dependent on the assumptions that there are restrictions on retailers and telecommunications providers to collect transaction data into a database, and there is careful management of the existence, definition, and precision of card holder identification data held on the card and passed to other cards during transactions.

*Potential privacy impact:* The Mondex scheme has the potential for substantial privacy impact particularly as it involves a significant trail of pseudonymous transactions. Retailers may link the card identifier with the customer or gain access to at least some of the card issuer's data. A card issuer may gain access to at least some of the retailer's data. A third party may gain access to both the transactions trail gathered by one or more retailers and a card-issuer's index.

## Benefit Cards

Smart cards are being used in many countries to issue benefits. For example, in the United States, there exists the Electronic Benefit Transfer (EBT) system which uses smart cards to issue food and cash benefits. EBT card holders can access cash benefits via automated teller machines (ATMs) and food and cash benefits at POS terminals in authorised retailers (Department of Social Services for the State of Connecticut, 1996). Thirteen states have operational EBT systems, while the rest have started implementation.

In the United Kingdom, the Benefits Agency and the Post Office have embarked on the automation of benefits payments at the 20,000 post offices around the country to 20 million benefit recipients. The scheme replaces girocheques and order books with a benefits smart card that hold details of benefit types, amounts payable and payments received. The impetus for this scheme, which should be fully operational by the end of 1998, is to reduce internal costs and minimise benefit fraud. The overriding theme the overall service objectives reflect this and are as follows (ICL, 1995):

- A fraud-free method of paying benefits at post offices that is automated, with lower and continuously reducing costs
- Extending automation to the Post Office's other client transactions, its products and support processes to improve competitiveness, increase efficiency, and enable greater communication opportunities
- Full and speedy recalculation of benefit payments, with accounting arrangements consistent with recognised accountancy practices
- Improved service to the customer

The Economist (1996) reported an interesting use of smart cards in Mexico that is designed to improve the targeting of benefits towards those in real need of which about 66% live in the rural areas and yet 75% of benefits go to those living in urban areas. The smart card scheme will unify the 18 subsidy schemes which will greatly reduce administrative overheads and remove the opportunity of official discretion regarding benefit recipients. The aim is to link benefit payment with regular attendance at local health clinics for preventative care and with confirmation that parents are keeping their children at school.

# Social Benefits and Costs

Clearly, there are beneficial outcomes from the application of smart cards. Realising these benefits both for individuals and organisations may well profoundly change the relationship between clients or consumers and suppliers or government bodies. BP's European card service manager Mike Tunstall stated that "The smart card has a lot of potential as you can hold a lot of applications on it. The ultimate is your passport, driving licence, credit and debit card, access to your place of work and your card ignition key all on one piece of plastic." A multi-product card of this type will undoubtedly alter relationships due to potential uneasiness about what data is held, accessed and modified. Such cards are already being piloted. For example, in South Korea, a national citizen card is being introduced which is used as a driving licence, identity card, pension card and medical insurance card (Honeywood, 1997).

An attempt is now made to identify some of the key issues relating to social benefit and cost. Without any doubt, research undertaken for this chapter revealed that the overriding social issue both for reviewers and users of smart cards was privacy. The lists that follow privacy have been subdivided into different parts.

## *Social Benefits*

These are summarised in the following:

- Using smart cards is safer than carrying cash for an individual.
- Smart cards can improve access to services for the disabled and elderly.
- It is a secure means of authenticating one's own identity.
- It is a secure means of authenticating the identity of reader device.
- It is a portable and secure store of information available to all.
- Access can be made available in geographical locations where online communication is not possible.

- The opportunity of fraud is reduced using smart cards.
- Socially disadvantaged groups can gain access to facilities and resources without feeling stigmatised.
- Objective selection criteria can be upheld and the risk of bias or favouritism reduced.

## Social Costs

These are summarised in the following:

- Smart cards lead to a loss of anonymity.
- Pseudonymity can be mistaken for anonymity.
- Smart card schemes could lead to a reduction in the provision of non-smart card facilities and so affect freedom of choice.
- Smart cards can reduce access for the technology illiterate or technology wary.
- There are difficulties in viewing personal data.
- Smart cards can result in significant invasions of privacy.
- Profiling and tracking of individuals can occur.
- Increases in smart card use could lead to a de facto national and subsequently global identity card that has not been subjected to citizen consultation.
- Smart card functionality can be increased without proper consideration of the overall impact.

# Future Directions

As with all advances in information technology, it is difficult to forecast what might be achieved with smart cards. It is useful to consider some examples of beneficial applications as well as considering strategies that might promote sensitive and acceptable development, implementation and regulation.

## Public Transport

In response to the UK Government's consultation process on developing an integrated transport policy, the Centre for Computing and Social Responsibility suggested some innovative ways in which smart cards could be used in the future to revolutionise local ticketing. There could be a value card that held electronic money or tokens for the transport. An alternative would be to have a special debit or credit smart card. Incentive schemes could be put in place to encourage the use of public transport through a "public transport miles" scheme whereby the smart card kept a tally of total miles travelled and turned this into tokens that could be used to purchase "free" journeys.

The introduction of a single public transport smart card would enable a customer to purchase tickets from any operator, thus improving convenience and access. Smart card readers should be attached to public transport information points so that once a journey had been planned and availability confirmed then a ticket could be secured. The smart card could hold the ticket indeed a number of tickets so removing the need to issue paper tickets. All public transport would be fitted with readers to access, check and "clip" the smart ticket. Inspectors would have special readers to facilitate inspection. Customers would have to have some means of being able to read the information on their public transport smart cards.

However, as with all applications of smart cards, there are substantial privacy issues. Individuals have a legitimate interest in keeping their movements private unless there are subject to judicial processes. To maintain privacy, no information at all should be held about the route travelled once the journey is complete.

## The Disabled

According to comments made by a disabled person in recent conversations, the needs of the disabled can be summarised as access, independence and equality of opportunity. Smart card technology has the capability of addressing these needs through adaptive interfaces using its multimedia capabilities. For example, Star Micronics has developed a visual rewritable display into a smart card. This may prove useful for certain groups of disabled. It should be possible to incorporate sound in a smart card which has obvious applications for the visual impaired.

Gill (1997) suggests that individual requirements could be stored on the smart card so that the interface at the point of use would automatically adapt to the preferred customer verification method (e.g. hand geometry), input (e.g. voice activation and speech recognition), operation (e.g. reduced functionality), and output (e.g. large colour-specific characters). Gill also explains how contactless smart cards could be used to remove the necessity of card insertion into readers, unlock and open doors, activate location signals, increase road crossing times, and adjust heights of facilities.

## The Role of Government

For smart cards to realise their societal potential, an effective technology infrastructure needs to exist. This must promote innovation while at the same time create timely standardisation that empowers global application. Mechling (1997) suggests that government's role in this should be to encourage aggressive multi-institutional experimentation and to apply standardisation that enables effective electronic commerce to come on stream as quick as possible. He envisages that smart cards will be a key infrastructure in the information age and as such must not be viewed as simply an application tool for individual organisations.

## Guidance

This chapter has illustrated that there are many application policy issues that need to be addressed if smart cards are going to be accepted and welcomed by individuals within society. In a discussion paper on privacy, Foran (1997) suggests a number of principles that should be adhered to when considering if and how a smart card scheme should be implemented. A small selection of these principles is as follows:

- Smart cards must properly respect the legal and ethical rules pertaining to the rights of the card holder.
- Individuals should have the right to refuse cards.
- The card holder's prior consent is required for all uses of the card and disclosure of information it contains.
- Cards should not be used as tools for overt or covert surveillance.

Regarding detailed implementation, a subset of the design features identified by Clarke (1997) seems appropriate to all smart card schemes. These features are summarised as:

- Identified transaction trails should only be used where no acceptable alternative exists
- Identity should be safeguarded using pseudonymity
- Ensure integrity across applications on multi-purpose cards
- The design of smart card schemes must be transparent to the individual
- Biometric and encryption key data should be held on the card
- Two-way device authentication must be used

These two lists serve to illustrate the sorts of issues that need to be addressed. They are not put forward as being comprehensive. It is expected that application policy and design strategy will be the subject of much debate as more and more smart card schemes are proposed.

## Conclusions

This chapter has reviewed smart card technology and reported on a number of typical applications from different countries. Some general positive and negative social impact issues have been identified. The review and analysis have led to a discussion of the types of guidelines needed to promote the acceptable use of smart cards. Further research is necessary to inform those implementing smart card schemes of the broader implications of their proposals. The aim must be to achieve a redemptive technology and ensure ordinary people are involved in the technological decision-making process (Franklin, 1990) which precedes the application of smart card technology.

## References

Caldwell, B. (1997). Don't leave base without it. *Information Week*, 648, 15 September.
Clarke, R. (1996a) Privacy issues in smart card applications in the retail financial sector. In: *Smart Cards and the Future of Your Money*. Centre for Electronic Commerce, Monash University and the Australian Commission for the Future, pp. 157–184.
Clarke, R. (1996b) *Chip-Based Payment Schemes: Stored Value Cards and beyond*. Xamax Consultancy Pty Ltd.
Clarke, R. (1997). Chip-based ID: promise and peril. *International Conference on Privacy*, Montreal, 23–26 September.
Department of Social Services for the State of Connecticut (1996). *Electronic Benefit Transfer*. Available from http://www.dss.state.cs.us/ebt.htm (Accessed 1 September 1997).
Dorris, M. A. (1997). Worldwide trends in smart card applications. *Intergovernmental Solutions Newsletter*. Smart Card Edition, 1. Available from http://policyworks.gov/org/main/mg/intergov/oisnews.htm (Accessed 1 September 1997).
Economist (1996). Mexico – fighting poverty with a credit card. *The Economist*. 11 May. Available from http://www.economist,com/archive/buy.c...files/1996_out/11may96.hd/ecn.041.html (Accessed 1 September 1997).
Foran, B. (1997). *Privacy Framework for Smart Card Applications - A Discussion Paper*. Office of the Privacy Commissioner, Canada. Available from http://infoweb,magi.com/~privcan/pubs/priframe.html (Accessed 1 September 1997).
Franklin, U. (1990). *The Real World of Technology*. Anansi Press.

Gill, J. M. (1997). Design of smart card systems to meet the needs of disabled and elderly persons. Available from http://www.rnib.org.uk/wedo/research/sru/escart.htm (Accessed 1 September 1997).

Honeywood, A. (1997). Snapshots of smart card applications. *Intergovernmental Solutions Newsletter.* Smart Card Edition, 1. Available from http://policyworks.gov/org/main/mg/intergov/oisnews.htm (Accessed 1 September 1997).

ICL (1995). Post office counters and benefit payments. *Inform*, 84(September), 4–5. Available from http://www.icl.co.uk/news/inform/sept95/pg4-5.htm (Accessed 1 September 1997).

Johnson, R. C. (1997). Identity system eliminates the need for passwords - facelift recognition provides security alternative. *ETimes*, 961, 7 July.

Mechling, J. (1997). Smart cards as infrastructure: is government missing the big bets?. *Intergovernmental Solutions Newsletter*, Smart Card Edition, 1. Available from http://policyworks.gov/org/main/mg/intergov/oisnews.htm (Accessed 1 September 1997).

Message Factors Inc. (1996). *Qualitative Research Study on Visa Smart Card Usage.* Prepared for Home Financial Network. Available at http://www.homenetwork.com/news/smrtcrdr.htm (Accessed 1 September 1997).

Perri 6 (1996). *On the Cards: Privacy, Identity and Trust in the Age of Smart Technologies.* Demos.

Rogerson, S. & Bynum, T. W. (1995). Cyberspace the ethical frontier. *Multimedia, the Times Higher Education Supplement* (1179), 9 June, p. iv.

Supernet Ltd. (1997). *The Supercard.* Available from http://www.itl.net/business/supercard/thesupercard.html (Accessed 17 September 1997).

Violino, B. (1997). Biometrics. *Information Week*, 644, 18 August.

## Chapter 13

# A Moral Approach to Electronic Patient Records [2001]*

## Context

Healthcare computing (also called medical informatics) is one of the fastest growing areas of information and communication technology (ICT) application. ICTs have been applied in healthcare to performance indicators, financial (including insurance) systems, paramedical support, emergency services, electronic patient records (EPRs), computer-aided diagnosis, clinical governance, remote surgery, research support and hospital management. The implementation of information systems in healthcare is inevitably ethically charged and moving at a faster pace than ethical consideration of those developments. Developments in the exchange of EPRs are a particularly strong theme in the implementation of information systems in healthcare. Thus, in the United Kingdom, NHSnet, a national health information network, has been established for some years (Pouloudi & Whitley, 1996, p. 307), yet adequate security infrastructures for it are *still* some way off (Schneider, 1998; see also Gaunt, 2000, pp. 6–9).

All uses of ICT in healthcare should ideally promote, and must certainly not conflict with, the fundamental principles of medical ethics. There is a widespread consensus around the principles of beneficence, nonmaleficence, and respect for patient autonomy within medical ethics, and substantial acceptance of the principle of distributive justice (Beauchamp & Childress, 1994, p. 38). Beneficence can be taken as meaning a duty to promote good and to act in the best interest of the patient and the health of society.[1] Nonmaleficence indicates a duty to do no harm to patients. Respect for patient autonomy can be interpreted as a duty to protect and foster a patient's free, uncoerced choices. Finally, distributive justice implies ensuring that the costs and benefits of healthcare are fairly distributed, and according to some theories ensuring that the relationship between the distribution of costs and benefits is fair.

* This chapter was first published as: Fairweather, N. B. & Rogerson, S. (2001) A moral approach to electronic patient records. *Medical Informatics and the Internet in Medicine*, Vol. 26, No. 3, pp. 219–234. Copyright © Taylor and Francis Ltd. Reprinted by permission. DOI 10.1080/14639230110076412.

At a philosophical level, certain of the principles are more closely associated with particular positions in general ethics; thus, autonomy might be associated with deontologism and beneficence with consequentialism. Such an association is, however, simplistic. As Beauchamp and Childress (1994, p. 110) say, "Many different theories lead to similar action-guides and ... It is possible from several of these standpoints to defend roughly the same principles, obligations, rights, responsibilities, and virtues." Many plausible consequentialist theories, for example, would give rise to a deep concern for autonomy.

Whatever the level of agreement about these principles of medical ethics, there may at times be a tension between the duties implied by these various principles; and between them and other principles, either derived from them or with other strong moral support. It may appear inadequate to start from a basis of principles that at times are in tension, but since no claim to have identified the perfect moral theory has even come close to having been proven, there is, in our opinion, no better starting point available, and the questions at hand are too urgent to wait for a convincing proof of the perfect ethical theory to be discovered.

While this chapter is interested in principles, it is not attempting to develop the perfect principles no matter how impractical; our position, rather, is that practicality is one factor that needs to be considered, along with principles, perhaps through "The method of wide reflective equilibrium" (van den Hoven, 1996, p. 449), after Rawls and Griffin.

This chapter considers one aspect of healthcare computing: EPRs. It identifies a viable moral approach to EPRs taking into account the ethical principles discussed. EPRs enable some or all of the medical history of patients to be computerised. They offer new methods of storing, duplicating, manipulating and communicating medical and non-medical information of all kinds, including text, images and recordings of sound, video and tactile senses (Mauro, 1999, p. 2; Wagner et al., 1999, p. 4). Thus, they can be more powerful and flexible than paper-based systems. They allow providers, payers and patients to interact more efficiently, and in ways that improve health and can be life enhancing. Perhaps for these reasons, governments appear to favour national healthcare infrastructures with "longitudinal" patient records, which cover a patient's complete medical history (Schneider, 1997) from the womb (or perhaps even before conception) to the grave.

## Inappropriate Balances

The centrality of trust to the doctor-patient relationship can to some extent be gauged by the fact that ensuring patients will find medical professionals trustworthy provides a substantial part of the reasoning for regulation of medical professions (Beauchamp and Childress, 1994, p. 7). EPRs can facilitate doctor-patient relationships through the use of computerised notes, which the doctor and the patient can share and contribute to. However, at the same time, EPRs can harm the doctor-patient relationship and undermine trust. For example, in the United States, medical data clearinghouses sell patient data to a range of organisations including insurance companies, police departments, employers and drug companies (Alpert, 1998, p. 91). In doing so, they have the potential to reduce the cost of healthcare, and thus support the beneficent aim of medicine.[2] However, the knowledge that data may be widely distributed and sold means that patients are becoming increasingly reluctant to tell their own doctors everything about their symptoms and the possible causes of them (Alpert, 1998, p. 89; Mauro, 1999, p. 6; Utility Consumers' Action Network 1999).

The potential for severe damage to the relationship between doctors and patients if privacy is not adequately protected has been well known for some time (Annas, 1989, p. 177; Nevado

Llandres, 1998, p. 78). The relationship depends heavily on confidentiality, and patients withholding information about their symptoms and possible causes of them can damage the quality, and hence (paradoxically) the efficiency of care.

There has not been enough work on defining ethically appropriate procedures and criteria for disclosures to the vast array of potential secondary users of health data such as managed care evaluators, insurance companies, and drug companies. The locations of the boundaries of morally legitimate trade in medical information have not been sufficiently explored. More work is also needed on ensuring that data is completely anonymised when traded, even where patients have rare medical conditions and other unusual attributes (perhaps unusually high levels of educational qualification) that make them easy to identify when these facts are combined (Barber and Rogers, 2000, pp. 2–7). The aim of this chapter is to stimulate further debate about EPRs and to encourage others to participate in this essential work.

## Other Research into the Problem

The single most important answer to the problem that has been produced hitherto by other researchers is the Opinion of the European Group on Ethics, *Ethical Issues of Healthcare in the Information Society* (Wagner et al., 1999), which like this paper, "confines itself to the ethical [considerations] of the use of person identifiable personal health data" (Wagner et al., 1999, p. 3, emphasis removed). The "Opinion" identified a number of relevant "value conflicts in the provision of healthcare" including "effectiveness versus confidentiality," "privacy versus the collective good," and "efficiency versus beneficence" (Wagner et al., 1999, p. 9).

Since that "Opinion," further (less comprehensive) research has been published (Mauro, 1999; Cavanaugh, 1999; Vlug, 1999; Barroso Asenjo, 1999), providing further insights that have been taken into account in this paper. Alpert (1998) has made another substantial contribution on these issues. However, Alpert concentrates on the tension between privacy and needs to "maximise appropriate access to personal information" (p. 75), and in doing so reaches solutions that do not give enough weight to the influence of other moral principles.

The contribution of this paper differs from previous work by taking an interdisciplinary approach with insights from information systems and from moral philosophy, and by taking on board a wider range of sources, including material that has become available since previous work in this fast-moving field. It identifies and considers a larger number of relevant tensions between moral standards than previous work, but unlike Wagner et al. (1999, p. 10) it is not committed to the view that "Trust is a fundamental ethical value in itself," rather seeing strong grounding for trust in other, more fundamental, values. We further believe calls for closed networks that restrict access while operating globally (Wagner et al., 1999, p. 11) to be unsustainable. The failure of the "Opinion" of Wagner et al. to explicitly recognise the problems that can be caused by doctor-patient records being inappropriately widely available is an especially serious shortcoming that this paper seeks to rectify.

## Principles

As already stated, three of the most widely accepted principles of medical ethics are beneficence, nonmaleficence and respect for patient autonomy. Thus, there is a fiduciary responsibility on doctors towards patients "of acting only in the patient's best interests"

(Nevado Llandres, 1998, p. 79) which implies a duty normally to keep medical records private, as would be required by the Hippocratic oath, where it is still taken.

Others have argued that "Electronically based patient records ..., are ... patient analogues" (Kluge, 1998, p. 105), and because of this the promotion of autonomy requires allowing control for the patient over their analogue. We are not entirely convinced by this argument. Patients certainly have an interest[3] in what happens to their records after they are dead; yet their autonomy cannot be promoted once they are dead, even if their "analogue" persists as if they were alive. Concern for privacy derived from the promotion of autonomy as applied to a patient analogue appears to be too limited in scope.

Breaches of the duty of confidentiality can leave doctors subject to being disciplined by their professional body, and prosecution in many legal systems (Barroso Asenjo, 1999, p. 7). The fiduciary relationship extends to health information professionals (Kluge, 1998, p. 105) and thus, "The health care informatician should respect the privacy of individuals, groups or organisations and should know that any breach of their privacy through the utilisation of their data without their authorisation or consent constitutes a considerable threat to their person" (Gritzalis et al., 1990, p. 384). The principle that consent must be properly informed is well established in medical ethics (Beauchamp & Childress, 1994, pp. 142–157). However, this is not enough, because it must be remembered that there are times when individuals are required to give "consent" on pain of being excluded from significant benefits. It may even be that continued employment may on occasion be effectively dependent on giving such "consent" (Clagett, Povar and Morin, 1996), although it is more common for such benefits as gaining employment or securing life insurance to be conditional on releasing medical data in some jurisdictions. A requirement that access to private information be with "consent" would not be enough on its own to ensure that such access is morally correct.

Further, there are times when it is morally appropriate for access to be given without consent having been obtained from the data subject. These circumstances may arise when the patient is unconscious and cannot give permission, or when there is an overriding public interest (such as to prevent the spread of a communicable disease by tracing carriers; see also Barroso Asenjo, 1999, p. 8). When consent cannot be obtained from the data subject, access should only be with the consent "of a duly empowered legal authority acting with due process of the law" (Kluge, 1994, p. 336). This requirement for legal sanction is, like "consent," not enough on its own. In a regime that is corrupt, arbitrary, liable to prejudiced discrimination, totalitarian or otherwise acting beyond its moral authority; legal sanction may be given in circumstances where it should not, or denied when it should be given.

Privacy is not an all-or-nothing concept. A person never has either complete privacy (even the sole inhabitant of an abundantly fertile island will feel the impact of global climate change, which has been caused by other people), nor utter lack of privacy (even in the most humiliating imprisonment, some of the prisoner's thoughts remain private). Privacy can, as with those two extremes, relate either to the ability of others to make an impact on your life ("associative privacy": Decew, 1997), or to knowledge about you ("informational privacy": Spinello & Tavani, 2001, p. 340). Very often, but not always, both types of privacy are closely intertwined in practice (knowledge about my life would enable you to have impacts on it, while many of the impacts that you can make on my life leave you with the knowledge that my life has been affected in that way). This paper is more centrally concerned with privacy regarding knowledge about the subject.

The degree of privacy could, in principle, be different for each piece of knowledge about a person (insofar as it makes sense to talk in terms of discrete pieces of knowledge). For each piece of knowledge about an individual, x, the degree of privacy would be determined by how many, and which, other individuals and organisations had access to the knowledge at what effective cost ("cost" here should not be thought of solely in financial terms, but also in terms of time and effort, the risk of effective sanctions, whether from the law or others, etc.). Thus, for each piece of knowledge, greatest privacy is achieved when nobody but you knows it, and no amount of resources (not even the use of extensive torture facilities) could cause it to be revealed. Similarly, for each piece of knowledge, zero privacy would be when everybody who will ever live knows that about you; thus, zero privacy is not achievable in respect to any single item of knowledge, although near-zero privacy in respect of some items of knowledge is possible for such world-famous people as the late Diana, Princess of Wales.

According to Nevado Llandres (1998, p. 76), it is "quite clear to everyone that under no circumstances should the use of databases diminish the right of the patient to the privacy and confidentiality of his data." However, the use of databases is diminishing the practical extent of privacy and confidentiality. It may be that the *right* has not been diminished, but evidence suggests that the extent of *respect* of the right is declining. Violations of medical privacy may be easier than ever before because of the very efficiency of computerised systems so that we are now in an age when "Neither physicians nor patients can assume that rules regulating the use of patient information will effectively stop potential breaches of confidentiality" (Clagett, Povar and Morin, 1996). The extent and severity of damage to the privacy and broader well-being of a patient (Oram, 1999) whose confidentiality is violated may be proportionately greater because of the amount of data held within an EPR and the ease with which it can be replicated, distributed and data-matched.

Consideration of the principle of beneficence suggests that the best interests of patients are served (1) by improvements in care at reasonable and affordable cost; (2) by reductions in cost resulting in more care being provided for the same expenditure; and (3) by reductions in cost enabling the same care to be provided for less cost, freeing up resources to promote patient welfare in other fields.

Gritzalis et al. (1990, p. 385) argue that "The user of a medical computer system will not design systems that can come to originate considerable harm to the health of the patient or the reputation of the health care professional." However, the *potential* for considerable harm is virtually inevitable with medical computer systems, because even the best-designed system meeting all appropriate standards for safety-critical systems is liable to have the potential for being a contributory factor in considerable harm when in the hands of someone evil and technically proficient.

Distributive justice also plays an important role in medical ethics, and requires that the various outputs of healthcare (including medical wellbeing), and the costs to achieve them, be fairly distributed.

## The Fair Information Principles

According to Kluge (1994, p. 336), there has been "a remarkable convergence" in regulation of medical informatics "towards a uniform position centred in the so-called 'fair information principles.'" These principles are, in brief, openness, limitation of collection, limitation of disclosure, limitation of use, security and access. These six principles are re-worked into a more coherent, but less widely accepted, list of seven principles (Kluge, 2000, p. 90). Each of the original six principles is considered in turn.

- *Openness* is strongly associated with respect for patient autonomy, as without knowledge of "the existence of an electronic data-bank" or "the kind of information it contains" (Kluge, 1994, p. 336) it is simply impossible for the patient to make autonomous decisions on relevant questions (which may include whether to seek medical attention for an injury sustained in a particularly embarrassing way, for example). Respect for patient autonomy requires that patients be educated about the nature of EPRs and their rights (Wagner et al., 1999, p. 13), and be able to effectively articulate their views.

- The principle of *limitation of collection* is an aspect of the more general requirement to respect privacy, requiring that data only be collected and held if they are "necessary to achieve the legitimate aims" of the information system, and have been collected using "ethically defensible" procedures (Kluge, 1994, p. 336).

- *Limitation of disclosure* is essentially another way of expressing the privacy questions relating to consent for disclosure of data as discussed previously.

- *Limitation of use* relates to considerations both of privacy and autonomy, this time requiring that the uses to which data are put are limited to those which are "duly empowered legitimate purposes" of the information system (Kluge, 1994, p. 336). Clearly, any restriction on the extent of distribution and use of information about individuals promotes privacy. Autonomy is promoted by limitations of use because they enable the data subject (the patient, for medical data) to give (or decline to give) consent to the purposes to which the data actually will be put.

- *Security* is essential to privacy in practice. In a world in which a significant proportion of people seek information to which they are not entitled,[4] the only way to make sure that an item of knowledge is available to a limited number of people and organisations is to employ data security systems. These systems must be capable of withstanding sophisticated (and simple) attacks by those seeking to breach the security since there have been successful attempts to breach the security of EPR systems in the past (Barroso Asenjo, 1999, p. 11).

- *Access*, as a "fair information principle" is concerned with the right of the *data subject* to gain access to the data about them, and to correct it if it is inaccurate, incomplete, or contains irrelevant material (Kluge, 1994, p. 336). The Shipman murder case in the United Kingdom, however, suggests that correction of records should not be technically possible without the agreement of two doctors. Access to data about himself or herself would enable an individual to ensure that beneficence were maintained, at least in their respect as an individual (see also below on how "access" may at times be in tension with beneficence).

Kluge (1994, pp. 338–339) argues that EPRs are an analogue of the patient in a kind of nominal decision-space and as such should be treated according to ethical standards that mirror the standards that apply to treatment of the physical patient. In this light, Kluge (1994, p. 340) argues that the "fair information principles" are "Not the ultimate justification of an ethical course of action, but a heuristic move that is adopted for the sake of inferential brevity," when the right course of action is more correctly inferred from more basic moral principles. It is also clear, as Kluge (1994, p. 340) points out that, for all their usefulness, there are circumstances in which the right course of action may run counter to the "fair information principles."

## The Dead

There has been remarkably little consideration of moral obligations with respect to the dead (Floridi, 1998), but the issue is in practice inescapable when considering EPRs: a high proportion of the entries on an EPR are likely to relate to the period immediately before death.

In the only legal system with which we are sufficiently familiar (the English), the dead have no right to have their good name protected from defamation. It may be said that the dead no longer has rights because they can no longer make claims, when "the content of a system of rights is historically conditioned by the making of claims" (Golding, 1981, p. 64). However, we are interested in morality, not the law, when not all morality is rights-based; not all rights are claim-rights (Hofeld, 1920); and "there is a distinction to be made between *having* claims and *making* claims. The mere fact that someone claims something is not sufficient to establish it as his right" while "someone may have a claim relative to me whether or not he makes the claim or is even able to make a claim" (Golding, 1981, p. 64).

It may be argued that the dead "are no longer morally significant persons," and thus the only basis for respect towards the dead is the "psychological harm to the living relatives" (Fieser & Dowden, 1998). While we are not convinced that this is the only basis, this basis alone could give rise to substantial obligations with respect to the treatment of the dead. People do like to think well of the dead, and could be anxious, for example, that some aspects of a patient record remained confidential, rather than be allowed to tarnish a reputation.

Most of us do care about what happens to our body and our reputation after our death. This suggests that how we treat the dead may be morally important independent of the effect on relatives, at the very least because those who are alive are anxious not to be treated the same way. It is also worth remembering that the relationship of medicine to the dead is decidedly ambiguous: much medical knowledge (especially anatomy) has been derived from the treatment of corpses which in other contexts would be clearly unacceptable, while at times medicine appears to be working flat-out to prevent death at all costs.

Furthermore, the EPRs of the dead, like EPRs of the living, can have direct relevance to knowledge about the medical status of other family members. This gives rise to particular problems, however, with the dead, which are considered below.

## Tensions between and within Principles

In practice, there can be a need to provide timely access to as much relevant data as possible to allow the correct treatment of a patient, and especially in an emergency. "An accurate medical record helps the health care team avoid unintended complications by alerting them to a patient's condition and current treatment … [therapeutic] drugs … carry the risk of significant side effects and may interact negatively with other medications" (Clagett, Povar & Morin, 1996). EPRs can facilitate such timely access as is needed, but in an emergency access to the EPR may be needed (Barroso Asenjo, 1999, p. 7), possibly even by a paramedic who does not have "full" medical training, or by a doctor acting outside their field of medicine. Even more difficult cases arise when the only timely treatment available would be given by somebody who is not employed in any of the medical or related professions, and not subject to the associated enforcement of professional standards, but rather has received brief training in emergency life support. This need for access could apply when the patient has never met the person accessing his/her EPR, when the patient is unconscious and next of kin cannot be contacted sufficiently quickly. How can sufficient access to data be provided to such people without access to the EPR being open to all?

Although there is a need to provide timely access to as much relevant data as possible, patients should have the ability to allow selective access to their records. For example, a woman who has had an abortion may visit a doctor for treatment of an ailment that cannot possibly be related: she should have the right to withhold from the doctor such especially sensitive information that is not relevant to the matter at hand (Paul, 1999); contra (Wagner et al., 1999, p. 10). There are, of course, practical difficulties attached to patients making judgements about whether aspects of their history are relevant. However, EPRs can provide a greater potential for patient control in these matters, because a computer program can assess the likely relevance given other inputs (for example of current symptoms) before it even suggests to the patient that revealing a particular item of data may be beneficial.

The "fair information principle" of "access," while often being a useful way of maintaining beneficence (see above), can at times be in tension with other aspects of beneficence. Patients should also have the right to *not* be informed of some medical facts where, for example, the fact may undermine self-esteem and the way in which they live their lives (such as genetic data or information about terminal illness).[5] Where genetic data or data about infectious diseases is present that may be undermining in this way, family members also have the right to *not* be informed in the same way. While normally this would not be a problem (as EPRs are personally confidential among adults), there is particular cause for concern with the EPRs of minor children. Another possible cause for concern would be if relatives were to be allowed control of the EPRs of the deceased. It is appropriate for somebody to be appointed to uphold the interests of the deceased with respect to their EPRs. This cannot, however, normally be a relative of the deceased, because if it were, an exception would have to be made whenever the record contained data that could also be undermining to the family member. If such a procedure were followed, the making of such an exception would be tantamount to acknowledging the existence of the very data from which it was intended to protect the family member. A different procedure, outlined below, is needed.

There are further difficulties with genetic data and data about infectious diseases that are likely to be passed between family members. There is a mismatch between *individual* control over the collection and storage of EPRs and *individual* access to EPRs (on the one hand), and information that applies to a group of family members (on the other) (Cavanaugh, 1999, p. 1). One often cannot prevent such information about oneself being gathered, stored, or accessed as part of a family member's EPR. Worse, "in some cases," such as where a genetic condition only affects one gender, "the information has greater significance for others than it has for the one from whom it was gathered" (Cavanaugh, 1999, p. 2).

Electronic access to patient data can also be beneficial in a variety of settings where inaccurate interpretation of hand-written messages can have harmful effects. For example, electronic transmission of prescriptions with digital signatures can prevent some cases of potentially dangerous incorrect dispensing.

It is not in any way a matter of controversy that "notations of a psychiatric illness carry the risk of potential discrimination that could destroy the patient's current and future employment if the information is insufficiently protected." It would not, equally, be a matter of dispute that medical notes relating to a number of other types of symptoms or hinting at a number of other types of illness or medical procedures could cause similar harm if revealed to current or prospective employers. While this problem has not been entirely created by digitisation of patient records, the increases in ease of duplication, manipulation and communication of records that digitisation has enabled; make disclosure of more information and to more people than ever before very real prospects. The prospect of unauthorised access to records has also been increased by digitisation.

Epidemiology, public health surveillance and healthcare evaluation, each seek to promote the health of society. In the era of ICTs, each encourages the collation and comparison of many disparate facts about as large a proportion of the relevant population as practical (while the limits of the relevant population may not always be easy to discern, encouraging a wide interpretation). The databases so generated can be used, for example, "to trace long-term effects of certain drugs, trajectories of particular diseases, [and] outcomes of particular medical interventions" (Wagner et al., 1999, p. 5). They could also detect unusually high death rates, detecting some multiple murders (as in the Shipman murders), and flawed practice (as with the Bristol babies case in the UK). The large databases so used can give rise to a tension between the privacy of some individuals and the health of another group which may, or may not, overlap the group whose privacy is at stake. Clearly, principles relating to distributive justice are at stake here. There is also the possibility that data collected for epidemiological or scientific research might provide information relevant to the potential treatment of an individual, giving rise to a tension between the health of an individual and their own privacy (Gerardi, 1998, p. 231).

Due to considerations such as the principle of beneficence,[6] in healthcare there is a need to cut costs that are not inevitable costs of treatment where this can be done without harming treatment. Electronic transfer of patient records offers the potential to save money when compared to traditional methods (Pouloudi & Whitley, 1996, p. 308), freeing resources for "front-line" patient care. As all security and privacy technologies come with associated costs, there is a direct tension here between privacy and financial goals.

The categorisation and profiling of patients by managed care evaluators, insurance companies and the like also has the potential to enable cost savings, but may enable discriminatory or exclusionary effects that can run counter to the principle of nonmaleficence for some, even while promoting beneficence for others.[7] Thus, the principles of distributive justice could be violated at the same time as the principle of nonmaleficence.

It should be apparent that "the user of medical software assumes the social responsibility of utilizing it to promote the quality of the health care provided to the patient and the moral obligation to question whether or not its use is beneficial to the patient" (Gritzalis et al., 1990, p. 384). However, such concerns of immediate benefit to particular patients might be in tension with the potential benefits to other patients of more comprehensive testing, etc. The issues here are exactly the same as more typical medical trials.

## Striking a Balance

It is clear that a balance must be struck so that EPRs might realise their potential beneficial status, while ensuring the risk of harm is minimised. The main elements of this balance are discussed in this section. Further research may in due course disturb the current reflective equilibrium between the various principles which are in tension and between the principles and questions of practicality.

A patient's right to informed consent should be dominant, and in order to enable this, education about these issues should be available to patients (Wagner et al., 1999, pp. 10–13). All patients should, following the "fair information principle" of openness (Kluge, 1994, p. 336), have practical access to information about the existence of all databases with medically relevant information about themselves. There are rare exceptions. The first exception is where the knowledge about the very presence of a record in a particular database itself (regardless of content) may undermine self-esteem and the way in which the patient lives their life.[8]

The second exception is when knowledge about the existence of a record in a database may seriously jeopardise the health of others, seriously jeopardise an investigation into a serious crime, or have a similar impact.

A patient should have effective control over his/her data and the ability to prevent any casual distribution that might be harmful to himself or herself, ensuring EPRs maintain non-maleficence.[9] There may need to be exceptions again, for example, to combat contagion, but where the patient has at least an ordinary degree of rationality, strenuous efforts should be made at persuasion before release of the information is taken out of the individual's control.[10] Where a patient does not have the degree of rationality routinely present among adults, his/her representative (parent or guardian in the case of a young child) should have the control that the patient would normally have. We agree with Barroso (1999, p. 4), and certain jurisdictions, that "If a child is regarded as mature enough to make conscious decisions in relation to the confidentiality of personal information, the law should … recognise this and the child should have the right to make the decision."

Upon death, the executors of the estate should be able to exert control over the dead person's EPR (Karanja, 1995), except when the executors are family members, in which case a special "patient record executor" should be appointed in all cases: it should thus be standard practice for wills to appoint a "patient record executor" at the same time as the will is written if the executors are family members. The patient record executor (whether the same person as the general executor or not) should have most of the rights over the records that the deceased would have had (without any restrictions that may have been in place over records knowledge of which might have harmed the, now deceased, patient). Given that most patients never express any opinion about their records, and that when opinions are expressed, they are usually concerned for privacy or about "consent" to release records, it is not anticipated that the patient record executor would be called upon in any but the most exceptional cases. Further consideration is needed on whether they should have the right to correct records. On the one hand, an incorrect record can no longer harm the patient's health, and the possibility of introducing inaccuracies is much greater than when the patient can be consulted.[11] On the other hand, inaccurate data concerning the dead might harm living family members. Individualisation of data (see below) may ease this tension somewhat.

Given the existence in EPRs of genetic data and data about infectious diseases that also apply to other family members, we suggest that information gathered should be "as individualised as possible (e.g. not recording [the identity of] siblings, parents, offspring)" (Cavanaugh, 1999, p. 4). This will, however, reduce the amount of benefit that can be gained from some instances of genetic testing (thus inhibiting beneficence[12] to some extent). We have not, as yet, resolved all of the questions of how to reconcile this with the need to prevent the spread of infectious disease.

Where epidemiological data is required (including kinds that cannot be individualised while still maintaining their epidemiological relevance), anonymised data collection should be employed, employing suitable encryption and an anonymising gatekeeper (Vlug, 1999).

There needs to be safeguards to ensure that declining to give consent to access records (in employment and insurance contexts for instance) does not harm the patient unduly. This will have serious implications for employers who have been accustomed to health screening that enables them to decline to employ the disabled; and for insurers who have hitherto given cheaper or more comprehensive cover to those with a "clean bill of health."

Patients should have the ability to allow selective access to their records, being assisted to make informed choices about when it may be appropriate to reveal information they would normally prefer to remain confidential.

The appropriate scope for EPRs, and patients' rights with respect to their own medical information should be clearly defined. Prohibitions on certain sorts of uses of data and what principles should govern legitimate access to and use of personal health and medical data and information also need to be clearly enunciated in a way that ensures they are respected. In societies such as those that presently exist in the industrialised world, legislation is likely to be the most appropriate mechanism for such definition and enunciation. In societies where property is a dominant concern for the law, clarification of the ownership of patient data is vital. Mechanisms for the enforcement of applicable laws and oversight of use and access must be in place, adequately resourced and effective.

Harm to the doctor/patient relationship should not be taken lightly. While doctors have on occasion exaggerated the intimacy of the doctor/patient relationship; it is normally advantageous for such intimacy to be promoted,[13] if patients are to be appropriately treated. Healthcare providers and funders and other potential recipients of medical data should understand the impact of receipt of data on the doctor-patient relationship (Wagner et al., 1999, p. 13), and be aware that the knowledge that data is being collected may bias the data in ways that dramatically reduce its value.[14] Against this background, recipients of data should ensure (1) that whenever possible data is only collected in ways that are not individually identifiable (including by combining with other data sets); (2) that the data collected is the absolute minimum required for the purposes at hand, which are themselves morally scrupulous; and (3) that the advantages of use and further distribution of data are weighed against the potential for harm to individuals and to the data stream of such use.

## Implementation

While this paper does not focus on implementation, it must be explicitly recognised that there are serious issues in the implementation of EPRs. These are briefly discussed in this section.

The movement of EPRs over the Internet, intranets and extranets raises particular concerns. The further (in terms of logical steps rather than physical distance) data is from its original source, the greater the risks of duplication, falsification, inaccuracy, manipulation and unauthorised distribution. There has been little effective control over data use over computer networks, with high levels of security for dial-in and Internet links. While encryption of data in transmission, and in storage, can ease these problems (Hays, 1997; Wagner et al., 1999, p. 11) it is logically impossible for it to solve them: to be interpreted, data must be decrypted, yet "passwords are considered by many to be awkward and unnecessary" and "Re-establishing network connections can take so long that busy clinical staff avoid logging off between transactions" (Gaunt, 2000, p. 6). Another problem is that inappropriate "insider access to medical records" has led to violations of privacy for some years (Clagett, Povar, & Morin, 1996). While it may be possible to foster a good security culture, the first step is to recognise that purely technical "solutions" are insufficient.

There should be clearly defined limits of access for each type of authorised person. When implemented, systems should provide security alarms linked to all functions that involve an element of browsing, copying, or reporting (Hays, 1997), and record who has accessed sensitive information (Clagett, Povar, & Morin, 1996; Safran & Goldberg, 2000, p. 3).

While other issues are mentioned later, it is important to remember that manipulation, use, or abuse of healthcare information is not needed to cause harm. The mere suspicion that information might be, or might have been, leaked can cause harm (Clagett, Povar & Morin, 1996;

Schneider, 1997) whether by inhibiting the doctor/patient relationship or by meaning that records are incomplete.

Another issue is accuracy of the original data. Health care workers "may be highly capable and competent, but if they lack the training necessary to use the program correctly, they may cause irreparable harm; [thus] the ideal we seek is that the user introduce clinically accurate data into the computer" (Nevado Llandres, 1998, pp. 76). However, that ideal may well not be achieved, with the potential for serious detriment to the health and wider wellbeing of the patient.

## Inaccurate Data

According to Nevado Llandres (1998, p. 77) "if … erroneous or inadequate symptoms were introduced [i.e. input], then the responsible party is the physician." However, this leaves substantial problems. A requirement to guarantee adequate input of symptoms could lead to doctors conducting unnecessary duplicate tests with direct adverse consequences to patient welfare, and consequences through unnecessary expenditure. Further, it is quite possible for EPRs to be altered by someone (for example, a technician) who is not medically qualified: responsibility thus cannot fall entirely on medical professionals. Worse, it is possible for an inaccurate record to persist long after the person who was morally responsible for the introduction of the inaccuracy has ceased to practice: indeed, such inaccuracies could remain relevant to the (mis-)treatment of a patient long after the culpable person has died. While this was possible with paper records, the greater willingness to trust information that arrives in electronic form, the greater durability, the ease of reproduction, the ease of searching, and the greater distribution offered by electronic records all exacerbate the problem.

Another particular problem arises when there are suspicions about the privacy of the patient record. "Failure to record significant diagnoses and therapies … puts patients at risk" (Clagett, Povar & Morin, 1996), yet because of the fear that patients may be harmed if records do not remain private, "the practice of keeping 'double' records for patients [with psychiatric diagnoses] … has become widespread. Alternatively some clinicians … have created 'code language' to obscure the true content of clinical interactions" from those who were not present in the consulting room (Clagett, Povar & Morin, 1996). While there may be legal protection of the privacy of the patient record in many jurisdictions, such protections are not sufficient if there are still suspicions on the part of either the patient or their doctor that records will not remain sufficiently private for a long time. In both the United States and the United Kingdom, such suspicions would currently be well founded.

# Conclusions

This paper has focused on the ethical issues surrounding the growing existence and use of EPRs. The tensions between conflicting needs have been discussed. A morally defensible approach to EPRs has been suggested which can be summarised as follows:

- A patient's right to informed consent should be dominant: thus education about these issues should be available to patients, along with information about the existence of all databases with medically relevant information about the patient (with some minor exceptions).

- A patient should normally have effective control over his/her data and the ability to prevent any casual distribution that might be harmful, ensuring EPRs maintain nonmaleficence. There need to be safeguards to ensure that declining to give consent to access records does not harm the patient unduly.
- Patients should have the ability to allow selective access to their records.
- The EPRs of the dead should be treated with the same consideration as those of the living.
- In contemporary industrialised societies, legislation should clearly define the appropriate scope for EPRs, and ownership of patient data. It should clarify what principles should govern legitimate access to and use of personal health and medical data and information, and patients' rights with respect to their own medical information. There should be prohibitions on certain sorts of uses of data. Mechanisms for the adequate enforcement of applicable laws and oversight of use and access must be in place.
- Healthcare providers and funders and other potential recipients of medical data should understand the range of impacts of all sorts of medical data sharing, including on the requirement for openness in the doctor-patient relationship (both if patients are to be appropriately treated and if accurate data is to be collected) (Wagner et al., 1999, p. 13).

EPRs are indicative of a society that is increasingly dependent upon ICTs. The impact of this morally sensitive application of ICTs cannot and should not be ignored. We urge those involved in the creation, use, and promotion of EPRs to consider our suggestions.

## Notes

1 It should be recognised that "promoting good," "acting in the best interest of the patient," and "acting in the best interest of the health of society" give beneficence different senses in different contexts.
2 Potentially in either the individual or social senses of the principle of beneficence, depending how health care is paid for.
3 At minimum an anticipatory interest while they are still alive: we will not explore here the question of whether the dead still have interests.
4 In a recent survey, over 30% of the respondents agreed, or strongly agreed that "It is acceptable for me to use other employees' access codes with their permission to access data normally hidden from me" (Prior et al., 1999; pp. 28–29).
5 This right may appear paradoxical, in that if rights were only exercised at the request of the right-holder, this right could never be successfully exercised. However, as stated above, having such a claim does not require an individual to be in a position to actually make such a claim: a right can exist even if no individual is ever in a position to decide whether to exercise it. It is worth noting that beyond having a right to not be informed, R v Mid Glamorgan Family Health Services Authority and another, ex parte Martin (1951) holds that a patient does not have the right to access to medical records under such circumstances.
6 In the social sense, and in the individual sense if there is individual payment for treatment.
7 In the individual sense of the principle of beneficence, and in the social sense if the categorisation is widespread.
8 It is recognised that this exception could allow authorities with ill will to ignore the principle: there needs to be protection to ensure that this exception genuinely only applies when stated. Further, it may be worthwhile for there to be a procedure for routinely asking all citizens what their attitude would be to the knowledge of such sorts, and for recording such attitudes in advance of them becoming relevant.
9 In the case where a patient does not know the existence of data, due to the considerations in the preceding paragraph, the restrictions on the distribution of such data should be at least as strong as those on data that the patient does know about.
10 We will leave to one side the operational details of what would constitute sufficiently strenuous efforts, since this paper is not about operational details.

11 Further information might possibly be added as a result of a post-mortem, or as further knowledge is gained through other sources.

12 In the social sense, and in the individual sense for as yet unidentified individuals.

13 Although not by a reduction in the inhibitions and knowledge of the patient.

14 Both by inhibiting patients from revealing symptoms and other medically relevant information, and by inducing doctors to avoid recording, or disguise the recording, of especially sensitive information. Such biases would render any subsequent statistical analysis of the data unreliable.

# References

Alpert, S. A. (1998). Health care information: access, confidentiality, and good practice. In: Goodman, K. W. (ed.), *Ethics Computing and Medicine.* Cambridge, UK, Cambridge University Press, pp. 75–101.

Annas, G. J. (1989). *The Rights of Patients: the basic ACLU Guide to Patient Rights*, 2nd Edition. Carbondale, IL, Southern Illinois University Press.

Barber, B. & Rogers, R. (2000). *Response to Comments on First Working Document on 'Guidance for Handling Personal Health Data in International Applications in the Context of the EU Data Protection Directive.'* Available from http://forum.afnor.fr/afnor/WORK/AFNOR/GPN2/S95I/ PRIVATE/DOC/00033 ann.pdf (Accessed 14 June 2001).

Barroso Asenjo, P., 1999, Ethical problems generated by the use of informatics in medicine. In: D'Atri, A., Marturano, A., Rogerson, S. & Bynum, T. W. (eds.), *ETHICOMP99 Look to the Future of the Information Society: Proceedings of the 4th ETHICOMP International Conference on the Social and Ethical Impacts of Information and Communications Technologies.* Rome, Italy, Libera Universita` Internazionale degli Studi Sociali Guido Carli.

Beauchamp, T. & Childress, J., 1994, *Principles of biomedical ethics*, 4th edition, (New York, USA: Oxford University Press).

Cavanaugh, T. A. (1999). Genetics and the fair use of electronic information. In: D'Atri,A., Marturano, A., Rogerson, S. & Bynum, T. W. (eds.) *ETHICOMP99 Look to the Future of the Information Society: Proceedings of the 4th ETHICOMP International Conference on the Social and Ethical Impacts of Information and Communications Technologies.* Rome, Italy, Libera Universita` Internazionale degli Studi Sociali Guido Carli.

Clagett, C., Povar, G. & Morin, K. (1996). Documenting sensitive information poses dilemma for physicians. *ACP Observer* (December). Available from http://www.acponline.org/journals/news/ dec96/sensinfo.htm (Accessed 15 December 1999).

Decew, J. W. (1997). *In Pursuit of Privacy: Law, Ethics and the Rise of Technology.* Cornell University Press, p. 341. As quoted in Spinello & Tavani, 2001.

Fieser, J. & Dowden, B. (1998). Moral personhood. *The Internet Encyclopedia of Philosophy.* Available from http://www.utm.edu/research/iep/p/personho.htm. (Accessed 20 January 1999).

Floridi, L. (1998). *Information Ethics: On the Philosophical Foundation of Computer Ethics, ETHICOMP98.* Rotterdam, Netherlands. Available from http://www.wolfson.ox.ac.uk/~floridi/ie.htm (Accessed 20 January 2000).

Gaunt, P. N. (2000). Practical approaches to creating a security culture. Paper at *The 8th Working Conference of the IMIA WG4: Security of the Distributed Electronic Patient Record (EPR).* Victoria, BC, Canada, 21–24 June.

Gerardi, L. (1998). Data Medical Privacy Act: an Italian lacking, some remarks. In: van den Hoven, J., Rogerson, S., Bynum, T. W. & Gotterbarn, D. (eds.), *ETHICOMP98: The Fourth International Conference on Ethical Issues of Information Technology.* Rotterdam, Netherlands, Erasmus University, pp. 231–234.

Golding, M. P. (1981). Obligations to future generations. In: Partidge, E. (ed.), *Responsibilities to Future Generations: Environmental Ethics.* Buffalo, NY, Prometheus Books. Reprinted from *The Monist.* 56(Jan 1972).

Gritzalis, D., Tomaras, A., Katsikas, S. & Kekiloglou, J. (1990). Medical Data Protection: a proposal for a deontology code (HIDEC, Health Informaticians' Deontology Code). *Journal of Medical Systems*, 14(6), 375–386.

Hays, M. (1997). *A Model for Security*. Sidebar in: Schneider (1997) InSecurity: how safe are your data?.

Hofeld, W. N. (1920). *Fundamental Legal Conceptions as Applied in Judicial Reasoning, and Other Legal Essays*. Edited by Cook, W.W. New Haven, Yale University Press.

Karanja, S. K. (1995). *The Role of Legal Regulation in the Social Shaping of New Information Technologies: The Computerised Health Data Card (CHDC) as a Case Study*. Available from http://www.uio.no/~stephenk/thesis.htm (Accessed 24 January 2000).

Kluge, E. H. W. (1994). Health information, the fair information principles and ethics. *Methods of Information in Medicine*, 33(4), 336–345.

Kluge, E. H. W. (1998). Fostering a security culture: a model code of ethics for health information professionals. *International Journal of Medical Informatics*, 49(1), 105–110.

Kluge, E. H. W. (2000). Professional codes for electronic HC record protection: ethical, legal, economic and structural issues. *International Journal of Medical Informatics*, 60(2), 85–96.

Mauro, V. (1999). Patient privacy and economic interests: raising issues in health telematics. In: D'Atri, A., Marturano, A., Rogerson, S. & Bynum, T. W. (eds.), *ETHICOMP99 Look to the Future of the Information Society: Proceedings of the 4th ETHICOMP International Conference on the Social and Ethical Impacts of Information and Communications Technologies*. Rome, Italy, Libera Universita` Internazionale degli Studi Sociali Guido Carli.

Nevado Llandres, M. A. (1998). Ethical problems caused by the use of informatics in medicine. In: G.Collste, G. (ed.), *Ethics and Information Technology*. Delhi, India, New Academic Publishers, pp. 73–82.

Oram, A. (1999). A wronged individual. Message sent to email list med-privacy@essential.org. Available from http://lists.essential.org/1999/med-privacy/msg00010.html (Accessed 9 March 1999).

Paul, L. (1999). Europe: managed care principles gaining ground. *Healthcare Informatics*, 16(3), 24–26, 28. Available from http://www.healthcare-informatics.com/issues/1999/03_99/international.htm (Accessed 9 March 1999).

Pouloudi, A. & Whitley, E. A. (1996). Privacy of electronic medical records: understanding conflicting concerns in an interorganizational system. In: Barroso Asenjo, P., Bynum, T. W., Rogerson, S. & Joyanes, L. (eds.), *ETHICOMP96: III International Conference Values and Social Responsibilities of the Computer Science: Proceedings*, Vol. 1. Madrid, Spain, Pontifical University of Salamanca in Madrid, pp. 307–327.

Prior, M., Rogerson, S., Fairweather, N. B., Butler, L. & Dixon, S. (1999). *Is IT Ethical? 1998 ETHICOMP Survey of Professional Practice*. Sidcup, Institute for the Management of Information Systems.

R v Mid Glamorgan Family Health Services Authority and another, ex p Martin (1995). *Medical Law Review*, 2, 353–380.

Safran, C. & Goldberg, H. (2000). Electronic patient records and the impact of the Internet. Paper at *The 8th Working Conference of the IMIA WG4: Security of the Distributed Electronic Patient Record (EPR)*, Victoria, BC, Canada, 21–24 June 2000.

Schneider, P. (1997). InSecurity: how safe are your data?. *Healthcare Informatics*, 14(4), 76–78. Available from http://www.healthcare-informatics.com/issues/1997/04_97/safe.htm (Accessed 9 March 1999).

Schneider, P. (1998). Europeans ready for privacy law. *Healthcare Informatics*, 15(6), 137–144. Available from http://www.healthcare-informatics.com/issues/1998/06_98/interntl.htm (Accessed March 1999).

Spinello, R. A. & Tavani, H. T. (2001). Introduction to Chapter Four: privacy in cyberspace. In: Spinello, R. A. & Tavani, H. T. (eds.), *Readings in CyberEthics*. Sudbury, MA, Jones and Bartlett, pp. 339–348.

Utility Consumers' Action Network (1999). Fact Sheet # 8: how private is my medical information? Available from http://www.privacyrights.org/FS/fs8-med.htm (Accessed 18 January 2000).

van den Hoven, J. (1996). Computer ethics and moral methodology. In: Barroso Asenjo, P., Bynum, T. W., Rogerson, S. & Joyanes, L. (eds.), *ETHICOMP96: III International Conference Values and Social*

*Responsibilities of the Computer Science: Proceedings*, Vol. 1. Madrid, Spain, Pontifical University of Salamanca in Madrid, pp. 444–453.

Vlug, A. (1999). Double encryption of anonymized electronic data interchange. In: D'Atri,A., Marturano, A., Rogerson, S. & Bynum, T. W. (eds.), *ETHICOMP99 Look to the Future of the Information Society: Proceedings of the 4th ETHICOMP International Conference on the Social and Ethical Impacts of Information and Communications Technologies*. Rome, Italy, Libera Universita` Internazionale degli Studi Sociali Guido Carli.

Wagner, I. Lenoir, N., Quintana Trias, O., Martinho Da Silva, P., Mclaren, A., Sorda, M., Hermere, G., Hottois, G., Mieth, D., Rodota, S., Schroten, E. & Whittaker, P. (1999). *Ethical Issues of Healthcare in the Information Society*. Opinion of the European Group on Ethics in Science and New Technologies to the European Commission. Opinion 13, 30 July. Available from https://op.europa.eu/en/publication-detail/-/publication/ea106948-e6f5-11e8-b690-01aa75ed71a1/language-en (Accessed 21 November 2021).

## Chapter 14

# Internet Voting – Well at Least It's "Modern" [2003]*

## Introduction

The Government has set a target for all service delivery to be e-enabled by 2005, and while, technically, voting is not a service, as part of the same process it has been looking at electronic voting. Instinctively this seems to make sense, since a vote is, essentially, a piece of information, and the electronic sphere is precisely the sphere of information and communications technologies (ICTs). Similarly, the public is already used to voting by telephone and the internet for television shows. Thus, ministers such as Robin Cook have argued that voting by marking a cross in pencil on a piece of paper in a plywood polling booth is "astonishingly quaint" (Ashley, 2002). Since electronic delivery of services is being built around the use of the internet, it is hardly surprising that electronic voting is usually thought of as internet voting. As part of the Government's move to full implementation of electronic voting, internet voting was piloted at local elections in 2002, and will be in 2003, and the Government is committed to making the General Election after next "e-enabled" (Cabinet Office, 2002, section 4.3). This chapter explores some of the issues surrounding internet voting to assess how near internet voting (in particular) is to meeting that target.

## If You Can Bank on the Internet ...

If anyone suggests that it is difficult to run an election on the internet, a typical response is "What on earth is the problem? You can do business on the internet, you can bank on the internet. If you can do those, why can't you vote on the internet?"

A key issue here is anonymity: electronic voting "differs from the aforementioned applications due to the fact that, in addition to the requirements for accuracy and privacy, there is the

* This chapter was first published as: Fairweather, N. B. & Rogerson, S. (2003) Internet Voting – Well at least It's 'Modern'. *Representation*, Vol. 39, No. 3, pp. 182–196. Copyright © Taylor and Francis Ltd. Reprinted by permission.

mandated necessity to provide … anonymity. In other words, banking … applications can (in fact must) allow tracking back to the user of the system, but the [electronic voting system] must ensure that such tracking is impossible" (Mercuri, 2001b, pp. 8–9). It should not be possible to track who cast the vote for party X (at least without a court order), whereas an integral part of the banking transaction is knowing who made it. Achieving the degree of anonymity required means that key techniques to ensure banking security are not available.

This alone would provide an answer about why there might be big problems with internet voting that there are not with internet banking, but there are other reasons why banking is very different from voting. Banks can, and do, take a financial analysis of how much loss they can stand (typically as a percentage of turnover), and insure against such losses. Perhaps a political decision could be taken that the loss of a certain percentage of votes is acceptable, but it is hard to imagine a politician attempting to defend such a decision. Even if first-past-the-post makes a nonsense of the idea, the principles that every vote is equally important and that every vote is counted are still formally supported throughout the political system and could not easily be abandoned. In the absence of a decision that the loss of, say, 1% of votes is acceptable, security appropriate for banking cannot be considered sufficient for electronic voting.

Similarly, individuals can and do receive compensation for financial losses due to problems with online banking (whether caused by general disruption, by failures or by hacking). If votes were similarly affected, in many situations it is hard to see how anyone would know which individuals were affected (how do you tell which people were unable to connect to a website during a denial of service attack?). Anyway, what would be appropriate compensation for inability to vote? Equally, what would be appropriate compensation for the breach of your privacy of having the content of your vote revealed as a result of hacking (This is, of course, a type of case where the identity of the individual *will*, by definition, be known.)? Ensuring such a breach of privacy does not happen is vastly more important with electronic voting *precisely* because it is the sort of thing for which monetary compensation can never be appropriate.

Another factor that marks electronic voting as distinctive is that if there is disruption, an election delayed by a few days may well have a different result (particularly since the cause of the delay is likely to be a matter of political controversy). The situation can be rather different with substantial financial transactions, where often if an eCommerce application delays a deal between two willing partners, it may be possible to conduct it by other means, or a few days later, since such transactions are rarely conducted on a whim (There may be a change of a few percent in the price due to market movements in the interim, or similar effects.). Occasionally, after encountering difficulties of this sort such a transaction may encounter more serious problems due to the intervention by a third party, or penalty clauses taking effect, but this is still unlikely to have such a dramatic effect as a situation where a completely different Government is elected under our first-past-the post electoral system.

A further concern about thinking that the security for financial transactions would be good enough for internet voting is that banks are known to cover up losses through computer crime. While this sort of behaviour is unacceptable on the part of banks, if there were a successful attack on internet voting, a similar cover-up would strike at the core of our democratic system.

## The Pilots of May 2002

In May 2002, internet voting was piloted in Crewe, Liverpool, St Albans, Sheffieldand Swindon.

According to the Electoral Commission's (2002a, p. 4) strategic evaluation of the pilots, "The primary aim of the e-pilots was to establish the security and reliability of the voting mechanisms and to start to build public confidence; this was achieved."

However, of the eleven criteria for assessment of the pilots (Electoral Commission, 2002a, p. 12), the nearest to concern for security was judgement of "Whether the procedures provided for by the scheme led to any increase in personation or other electoral offences, or in any other malpractice in connection with elections." While this is related to security, many breaches of security would be possible that are not *electoral* offences or technically electoral malpractice.

Worse, the pilots were logically unsuitable to establish security and reliability of the voting mechanisms. The detailed evaluations of the pilots reveal that "No formal risk assessment process was undertaken" (Electoral Commission, 2002b, p. 6) for most, if not all, of the pilots. In the absence of such an assessment, it would have been impossible to design methods to detect security breaches systematically. In a subsequent response to the Government consultation on e-democracy (Cabinet Office, 2002), the Association of Electoral Administrators (2002) is quite clear that "A full risk analysis of voting systems is required."

Beyond this, however, detecting security breaches is a long way from establishing security, which according to Lorrie Cranor of AT&T research laboratories (2002) "is pretty much an impossible task." It is vastly easier to prove that nobody has broken into a bank vault than to prove it is impossible to break into such a vault. Even if somehow you were to make impossible all the routes of attack that you can think of, you cannot be sure that there is not some other method of attack that you have not thought of. It is thus logically impossible to draw a valid conclusion that the establishment of "the security and reliability of the voting mechanisms … was achieved" by the pilots (Electoral Commission, 2002a, p. 4).

Worse, the security of the 2002 pilots did not achieve anything even vaguely like making all known methods of attack impossible.

For example, all the internet voting pilots were designed to work with Microsoft Internet Explorer, yet according to computer consultant Joe Otten of Datator Ltd (2002), Internet Explorer "is designed to be extendable, and therefore to welcome *malware* [Malware is a generic term that includes all software that is intended to have an adverse effect, including viruses, 'trojan horses,' and worms. Thus, computers "might easily be infected by a virus that, for example, makes it appear to the voter that they are voting for one candidate when in fact their vote is being cast for another" (Cranor, 2002)] with open arms." It is not a question of security oversights that can be fixed." Similarly, computer security consultant Robert Logan (2002) states, "It [Internet Explorer] is insecure, has many holes, takes far too long to be updated, and updates cannot be verified to be secure."

There were many other security weaknesses of the 2002 pilots. There was no way for voters to reliably ensure that they were connected to the correct website, rather than a look-alike impostor (criminals have used such look-alikes of commercial sites for financial gain). Equally, "the Internet, … allows denial of service attacks from anywhere around the globe – and it is estimated that around 4,000 such attacks occur every year" (FIPR, 2002). More detail on these types of attack follows.

Similarly, there is a severe problem with the claim about another pilot of electronic voting and counting that "There is no evidence that the scheme lead [sic] to any increase in personation or other electoral offences, or other malpractice; the risk of personation was neither greater nor lesser than usual as the reliance on the electoral register was the same as in manual elections" (Electoral Commission, 2002c, p. 10). Such a claim logically cannot be true: it was possible for additional people (technical staff) to commit such offences using technical means. While the *probability* of them so doing is much lower than the probability of political activists or members of the public committing such offences, the potential *impact* could have been vastly higher. It is precisely this ability for technical staff to determine corruptly the outcome of an election without detection that has persuaded a number of commentators that electronic voting is only secure if accompanied by a paper audit trail [Such a paper audit trail precludes internet voting from unsupervised locations such as the home or office.] (Mercuri, 2001a). It is worrying that there was an assumption by the Electoral Commission that since the measures to protect against personation *by the public* were the same as in conventional elections for the pilot in question (which used electronic but non-internet voting), there were no further issues about risks of personation to consider. The very serious risks that were overlooked would similarly be present in internet voting.

While voter confidence in levels of security is important, it is deeply worrying that the Electoral Commission (2002a, p. 5) considers that "The key issues here relate to voter confidence." If, at some point in the future, substantial security breaches resulted in the wrong party being declared the winner, it would be inappropriate for public confidence in the electoral system to be maintained. Under those circumstances a massive loss of voter confidence in the system would be wholly appropriate, and any suspicion that the Electoral Commission thinks otherwise would undermine its credibility.

It is appropriate to welcome the recommendation of the Electoral Commission (2002a, p. 8) that "The Government should develop a high-level functional specification of what each type of voting or counting scheme should deliver, and determine formal security and control attributes against which each potential technical solution can be assessed." It is a shame that this recommendation only came *after* the pilots of 2002, since it meant that an opportunity to learn from the pilots was lost. A document, which presumably is intended to meet this need, has now been produced (CESG, 2002b). Although it does have a number of serious deficiencies (Fairweather, 2002), it *should* enable some key lessons to be learnt from the 2003 pilots.

# Vulnerabilities

Three vulnerabilities have already been mentioned briefly, but it is worth looking in more detail at how an internet election might be attacked.

## Denial of Service Attacks

It is almost guaranteed that if an internet General Election was held soon, hackers and publicity seekers would attempt to disrupt it using denial of service attacks. Such attacks usually work by placing such heavy demands on one part of the system (such as spurious requests to see a web page) that the particular part of the system is overloaded. Many such attacks are made every week on websites. It is also possible that people other than hackers may attempt to perform a denial of service attack, "yet this potential problem has not been sufficiently addressed by the manufacturers and purchasers of electronic vote tabulation systems" (Mercuri, 2001b, p. 98).

Denial of service attacks can only prevent the use of a system temporarily. However, they are still a very significant problem because elections are unusually time-critical. If voting was allowed over a range of dates, while the election campaign continued, then an attack that prevented people voting in the aftermath of a piece of particularly good news or publicity for one party (perhaps a key celebrity endorsement or a powerful speech by the leader reported on the news) might well affect the result of the election. Equally, a denial of service attack that prevented people voting immediately after some bad news for one of the parties in an election campaign could result in the detrimental effect of that bad news being minimised.

Similarly, an attack that prevented people from voting on the main polling day (or the last day of voting) could leave administrators with a choice of whether to leave voters disenfranchised or extend polling, when an election held over to a following day could well have a different result. "The time-critical nature of election day … makes this form of attack particularly likely" (Mercuri, 2001b, p. 98).

Attacks are not as likely for elections other than a General Election (such as local elections) since there is a lower level of interest in them. However, this lower level of interest itself may lead to dangers, since low turnout elections can be swung by relatively few votes being affected. This could result in such fringe parties as are prepared to use corrupt methods being overrepresented.

Even if there is no attempt to disrupt the election, there is always the possibility that general disruption to the internet, not specifically targeted at the election, could disrupt an election: few users of the internet in 2000–2001 will have forgotten the problems caused by "I love you," "Anna Kournikova," or "Homepage." While that spate of problems seems to have passed, there is nothing at the moment to guarantee that our defences will always keep up with the techniques of attackers. This fundamental unreliability with the internet makes it unsuitable for use for important elections until there is significant technological change, and the use of these new technologies becomes widespread.

## Virus and Malware Attacks

Another particularly likely and worrisome form of attack is that somebody wishing to disrupt or affect the outcome of the election may well attempt to distribute a virus, worm, or trojan horse that would sit largely inactive and undetected on the computers of voters, doing nothing more than spreading itself (slowly, so as to avoid attracting attention). When the voters attempt to cast their votes, everything appears absolutely normal to them. The problem is that the virus (or other malware), while telling them that they are casting a vote for candidate "x," actually sends a vote for candidate "y" (for a proportion of voters). To cope with this worry, voters asked "that a confirmation which stated that the vote had been received, and for which party it had been cast, was of critical importance. Having such a receipt was likely to reduce fears of reliability and inaccuracy" (BMRB, 2002, p. 27). But this does not solve the problem: a virus (or other malware) that tells the voter that they are casting a vote for candidate "x," while sending a vote for candidate "y" can just as easily display a message to tell the voter that a vote for candidate "x" has been received when it has not.

This sort of attack on the electoral system could be performed by hackers seeking publicity for themselves or some cause, but also there is a fair chance that it would be done by those who seek to influence the result of the election. The rewards for controlling or influencing the Government are seen as substantial. Large amounts of money are spent attempting to gain election as, or to achieve influence over, the UK Government. Given this, it is quite plausible that cheaper, illegal, methods will be used to achieve the same results. Much of this threat could come from the unauthorised actions of party sympathisers and activists.

There is a strong suspicion that illegal methods are already being used to influence the results of some elections in England, with Det. Chief Inspector Churchill of West Midlands Police Fraud Squad saying the police do not have enough powers to "either investigate or prosecute offenders" (as quoted in Warburton, 2002). Elsewhere, the former Deputy Leader of Oxford City Council,

Paul Ingram (2003) says, "I have no doubt that corruption of our voting system is rife, and getting worse." It seems unlikely that "mere" questions of legality will stop attempts to rig an internet General Election. Indeed, the transnational nature of the internet has always enabled people to make use of variabilities between national laws to get round restrictions on activities in their own countries (While child pornography has been successfully tracked across national borders, it is unusual because there has been an unusual degree of international determination and cooperation in combatting something about which there is also unusual unanimity in condemnation.). It seems most unlikely that a country such as China would pursue someone who had successfully used electronic means to rig a UK election unless put under severe pressure (and given that, in this scenario, the UK Government will be of the party that was the beneficiaries of the rigging, the chance of severe pressure being applied is minimal).

Attempts to rig local elections held on the internet are less likely, given that the rewards for success would be much lower and some of the risks higher, but the possibility still cannot be discounted.

Another theoretically possible type of attack comes from within the suppliers of web-browsers (such as Internet Explorer or Netscape) or computer operating systems (such as Windows). If they wish, those working within these software suppliers could hide within the program, instructions that would mean that it would change votes in just the same way as described above. There are so many millions of instructions within the program that nobody would find these particular instructions simply by examining the program if they did not know they were there. Even though Microsoft has a record of rigging online polls (Judge, 2002), such attacks are *not* likely. In theory, the attack could come from within the software house itself or from those who distribute the web-browsers and operating systems (most often with new computers). It seems less likely that the threat will come from the businesses themselves than from maverick individuals within the software suppliers. The simple question of the probability of this attack is not the issue, however. If we are to have confidence in our elections, we must be able to be sure that this attack has not taken place. The problem is that "verification that an arbitrary piece of software ... performs a certain task, is known to be intractable" (Mercuri, 2001b, p. 44). So, to have confidence in our election results, we cannot rely on software unless we know more about its properties. Yet the licences for the use of web-browsers and operating systems such as Windows prohibit attempts to examine them in the ways we would need, keeping the details closely guarded secrets. Unless they can be openly examined, an election needs to be insulated from them. On current technology, however, the methods to insulate would at best be extremely cumbersome (Fairweather & Rogerson, 2002, p. 38).

## Attacks on Websites

In principle, it is possible to defend against direct attacks on a website. Somebody attempting to breach security can be detected, and professional operators can be expected to keep the software on their computers sufficiently up to date to counter all known threats. However, according to security consultant Bruce Schneier (2000, p. 175), "One company that audits Web sites for application-level bugs ... has never found a Web site they could not hack. That's 100 percent vulnerability." There is no reason to believe that voting websites will fare any better, and there are enough people with enough motivation to attack them for this to be a serious concern. Depending on the attack mounted and the security employed such attacks could do anything from change thousands of people's votes through to "merely" preventing voters from accessing the website for a time as a type of denial of service attack.

As well as direct attacks on websites, there is a significant danger of attacks on the connection between the voter's computer and the website. One type of attack is on the domain name system (DNS) which used to convert the name of a website (e.g. www.election.gov.uk). Schneier (2000, p. 180) is clear that

> there's no security in the DNS system. So when a computer sends a query to a DNS server and gets a reply, it assumes that the reply is accurate and that the DNS server is honest. In fact, the DNS server does not have to be honest; it could have been hacked. And the reply that the computer gets from the DNS server might not have even come from the DNS server; it could have been a faked reply from somewhere else.

Another type of attack is on network routers, the switches that actually decide where the messages go (Lemos, 2002).

Whatever technique used, attacks on the connection between the voter's computer and the website could mean either that voters are unable to connect to the voting website (a denial of service attack), or are fooled into thinking they are connected to the voting website when they are in fact connected to a look-alike "spoof" site. Such a look-alike "spoof" site would appear to the voter to be the proper voting website and would appear to work in exactly the same way. The individual voter quite probably would have no way of knowing that they connected to the look-alike site rather than the proper one (indeed it might be impossible to tell). But if the voter connected to the look-alike site, it might be that the people running the look-alike site could "filter" votes so that votes for the "wrong" party did not get through to the real website, or even got changed to the "right" party, before being sent on to the real website along with all the votes that the people running the look-alike site approved of.

Another type of attack on the connection between the voter and the website is to intercept the messages that contain votes and change them. The fundamental design of the internet means that it is impossible to guarantee that they will not pass through the computer network of somebody untrustworthy. If they do, the corrupt operator of that network could, again, either filter out votes for the "wrong" party or change them. This is one type of attack that current technology *should* be able to defend against. Proper encryption of the vote, properly implemented, should make it impossible for the operator of the intercepting network to know who the vote is for, or to change it to a valid vote for the party of their choice. However, "Focus on issues such as the strength of encryption or the number of digits in a password/pin is misplaced. These should be the strongest links in a chain" (Otten, 2002). Our attention needs to be focussed elsewhere for the time being.

## *Conclusion on Vulnerabilities*

The opinion of the UK's National Technical Authority for Information Assurance (CESG, 2002a, p. 15) that "After consultation with the UK's threat authorities, it is clear that e-voting in a General Election would be a significant and attractive target" appears well-founded.

Pilots at local elections are highly unlikely to expose internet voting systems to anything like the same threats that they would face in a General Election, although it will be interesting to find out if the pilots of 2003 take security more seriously than previous pilots.

With the current state of technology, an internet General Election would be highly vulnerable to disruption and/or corruption.

## Current Proposals

As a way of insuring against "spoofing" attacks and enabling appropriate encryption without relying on the corruptible computational power of the voter's computer, there have been proposals for systems that distribute printed "ballot papers" with (pre-encrypted) combinations of code numbers to voters. One such system was proposed as part of the Government's e-democracy consultation (CESG, 2002a, p. 50; see also SureVote, 2001). The idea is that if voters input the code numbers that in combination identify the voter and who they wish to vote for (in a way that was meaningless if intercepted).

If they worked correctly, the methods suggested by such proposals would effectively thwart many of the possible attacks on websites and the network. They could also give voters their requested confirmation that their votes have been received correctly in the form of a unique code number that is also printed on the "ballot paper" alongside the name of their preferred candidate. A virus/malware attack or spoof website would find it impossible to give the correct confirmation codes (provided the codes were produced according to the right method).

It is, though, exceptionally easy to produce these "ballot papers" with the code numbers and confirmation numbers swapped between candidates, and individual voters would have no way of knowing if this has happened. Voters would simply have to take it on trust that this had not happened. To make sure this did not happen, high-security printing on high-security paper (banknotes use these techniques) would be needed, but this would not be enough. The computer processes used to produce the code numbers would have to be fully open to inspection (and, thus, could not use computer programs that were not themselves open to inspection in the way most commercial programs, and all the programs used by electronic voting suppliers are at present).

Worse, for this method to work, in most situations it requires the voter to type in a sequence of about twenty digits, yet when focus group members were asked to replicate this "inputting this number was found extremely difficult by many respondents" (BMRB, 2002, p. 28). The security of the system also depends vitally on voters actually checking the confirmation codes and reporting when they differ from those expected, but it is hard to believe that voters with no understanding of computer security will take them seriously. Moreover, voters falsely claiming that they have been sent the wrong confirmation codes could cause havoc, since there will be no way to tell if they are lying. Ironically, this could then constitute a form of analogue denial of service attack.

## Future Developments

There are plans to make the internet a more hostile place for hackers and virus writers. The Trusted Computing Platform Alliance (TCPA) initiative and Microsoft's implementation through "Palladium" software might move things significantly in that direction. If it works as planned, computers will only run programs that are approved, and viruses, worms and trojan horses will not be approved.

Under the initiative, "Microsoft claims that Palladium will stop spam, viruses and just about every other bad thing in cyberspace" (Anderson, 2002). If most computers have it installed it should make it more difficult for hackers to distribute viruses and malware that change votes or commandeer the computing power of other people's computers to mount denial of service attacks. However, since all the headline-grabbing virus and trojan-horse infections of recent years have exploited weaknesses in Microsoft software, there is scope for doubt about whether Palladium will be any different and thus have the advantages claimed.

Even if it works as claimed, there are serious concerns about TCPA and Palladium (Anderson, 2002), in part because of Microsoft's record of anti-competitive behaviour, but there are also particular concerns about internet voting under Palladium. As described above in the section on virus and malware attacks, the company, or less improbably maverick employees, could hide instructions in "approved" programs to change votes. In these circumstances, finding the hidden instructions that change votes may be even more intractable than at present, since TCPA and Palladium may be able to prevent computers from assisting in the independent examination of programs rather than them being assets in such examinations.

## The Digital Divide

Whatever the prospects for the security of internet voting, there are other serious problems with the prospect of internet elections. The proportion of the population with internet access has stabilised at between 40% and 50%. Internet voting will make it easier for this 40%–50% of the population to vote. This 40%–50% of the population correlates strongly with that part of the population which already is disproportionately influential in politics and which is already most likely to vote (Pratchett, 2002, pp. 32–33, 39–41).

Those who look to internet voting to increase turnout in elections may be disappointed if all it does is to make voting easier for those who were most likely to vote already. Rather than improving democracy, there is a significant danger that if electronic voting is based around the use of the internet (rather than other technologies which are more likely to be very widespread, such as Digital Television), it will entrench and reinforce inequalities of power (Pratchett, 2002, p. 34).

## Conclusions

There is a strong political impetus behind pursuing the implementation of internet voting at a General Election in the near future. However, even according to the technology suppliers, "Additional voting techniques should be piloted cautiously and on a one-by-one basis until security issues have been fully addressed" (CMG plc, 2002). In the case of internet voting, many of the security issues, by contrast, have hardly been addressed at all. Despite initial appearances, the many technologies that address the security issues of financial transactions on the internet are far from adequate for internet voting. Similarly, those pilots that have taken place thus far have been unsuitable for addressing the security issues with internet voting, and yet have been used to "justify" exaggerated claims about the levels of security achieved.

The time-critical nature of elections makes them unusually vulnerable to attacks on internet technologies, while the use of home and office computers leaves internet elections open to attacks that change the vote that is being sent in a way that voters cannot detect. The connection between voters' computers and an election website is especially vulnerable, either to denial of service attacks or to hijacking, so that voters think they are voting when in reality they are connected to a "spoof" website.

There are proposals for pre-encrypted voting codes to be distributed to voters which potentially could thwart many forms of attack on internet elections. A key cost of such a system is that voters are required to input long sequences of digits that many find excessively arduous.

While future developments may reduce some key problems, there are serious worries both about TCPA/Palladium itself, and also as applied to electronic voting.

Meanwhile, the digital divide suggests that internet voting is more likely to make voting easier for those who already have disproportionate influence, rather than those who do not currently vote.

All told, what can we say about internet voting? Certainly it can give politicians an opportunity to appear "with it", and to be doing something. It might not give accurate results, but well, at least it's "modern"!

# References

Anderson, R. (2002). *TCPA/Palladium Frequently Asked Questions: Version 1.0.* Available from http://www.cl.cam.ac.uk/~rja14/tcpa-faq.html (Accessed 24 January 2003).

Ashley, J. (2002). Intent on change, Radical Robin returns to the fray. *The Guardian.* 1 July. Available from http://www.guardian.co.uk/guardianpolitics/story/0,3605,628537,00.html (Accessed 24 December 2002).

Association of Electoral Administrators (2002). Response to 'in the service of democracy'. Available from http://www.edemocracy.gov.uk/feedback/responses/ASSOCIATION_OF_ELECTORAL_ADMINI-STRATORS.doc (Accessed 17 January 2003).

BMRB (2002). *Public Attitudes Towards the Implementation of Electronic Voting: Qualitative Research Report.* Available from http://www.local-regions.odpm.gov.uk/egov/e-voting/pdf/attitudes.pdf (Accessed 24 January 2003).

Cabinet Office (2002). *In the Service of Democracy: A Consultation Paper on a Policy for Electronic Democracy.* Available from http://www.edemocracy.gov.uk/downloads/e-Democracy-Policy.rtf (Accessed 17 January 2003).

CESG (Communications-Electronics Security Group, UK Government) (2002a). *e-Voting Security Study* (1.2). Available from http://www.edemocracy.gov.uk/library/papers/study.pdf (Accessed 21 January 2003).

CESG (Communications-Electronics Security Group, UK Government) (2002b). *e-Voting Technical Security Requirements* (1.0). Available from http://www.local-regions.odpm.gov.uk/elections/pdf/evoting.pdf (Accessed 17 January 2003).

CMG plc (2002). *CMG Response to the Consultation Paper: 'In the Service of Democracy'.* Available from http://www.edemocracy.gov.uk/feedback/responses/cmg.doc (Accessed 17 January 2003).

Cranor, L. (2002). Personal email. 23 October 2002.

Electoral Commission (2002a). *Modernising Elections: A Strategic Evaluation of the 2002 Pilot Electoral Schemes.* Available from http://www.electoralcommission.org.uk/files/dms/Modernising_elections_6574-6170__E__N__S__W__.pdf (Accessed 15 January 2003).

Electoral Commission (2002b). *Pilot Scheme Evaluation: Swindon Borough Council: 2 May 2002.* Available from http://www.electoralcommission.org.uk/files/dms/Swindon-final_6707-6259__E__N__S__W__.pdf (Accessed 22 January 2003).

Electoral Commission (2002c). *Pilot scheme evaluation: Chester City Council: 2 May 2002.* Available from: http://www.electoralcommission.org.uk/files/dms/Chester-final_6657-6218__E__N__S__W__.pdf (Accessed 15 January 2003).

Fairweather, N. B. (2002). *Response of the Centre for Computing and Social Responsibility, De Montfort University: CESG report on eVoting Security.* Available from http://www.edemocracy.gov.uk/feedback/responses/centre_for_computing_and_social_responsibility_cesg.doc (Accessed 27 January 2003).

Fairweather, N. B. & Rogerson, S. (2002). *Technical Options Report.* Available from http://www.local-regions.odpm.gov.uk/egov/e-voting/pdf/tech-report.pdf (Accessed 21 January 2003). Also at http://www.idea-infoage.gov.uk/services/laser/e-voting/Technical%20Options%20Report.doc; http://www.local-regions.odpm.gov.uk/egov/e-voting/02/index.htm; linked pages.

FIPR (Foundation for Information Policy Research) (2002). *Response to e-Democracy Consultation by FIPR.* Available from http://www.fipr.org/eDemocracy/FIPR.html (Accessed 7 January 2003).

Ingram, P. (2003). Personal email. 21 January 2003.

Judge, P. (2002). *Net Vote Rigging Illustrates Importance of Web Services.* Available from http://news.zdnet.co.uk/story/0,,t269-s2102244,00.html (Accessed 1 February 2002).

Lemos, R. (2002). *Flaws in Common Software Threaten Net.* Available from http://news.com.com/2100-1001-835602.html (Accessed 23 January 2003).

Logan, R. (2002). Personal email. 31 October 2002.

Mercuri, R. (2001a). *Rebecca Mercuri's Statement on Electronic Voting.* Available from http://www.notablesoftware.com/RMstatement.html (Accessed 15 January 2003)

Mercuri, R. (2001b). *Electronic Vote Tabulation: Checks and Balances.* Ph.D. thesis, University of Pennsylvania.

Otten, J. (2002). Personal email. 23 October 2002.

Pratchett, L. (2002). *The Implementation of Electronic Voting in the UK.* London, Local Government Association Publications. Available from http://www.local-regions.odpm.gov.uk/egov/e-voting/index.htm; linked pages (Accessed 27 January 2003).

Schneier, B. (2000). *Secrets and Lies.* Wiley.

SureVote, Inc (2001). Website/try it/web browser. Available from http://www.sure-vote.com/home.html (Accessed 19 December 2002).

Warburton, R. (2002). Time to tighten voting system. *Birmingham Post*, 29 October 2002. Available from http://icbirmingham.icnetwork.co.uk/0100news/0100localnews/page.cfm?objectid=12319998&method=full (Accessed 20 January 2003). See also www.stolenvotes.org.uk.

# Chapter 15

# Digital Existence – The Modern Way to Be [2018]*

## Introduction

The focus of this chapter is post 1990 which was the year the first web browser was developed and used by Tim Berners Lee. It is probably this single event which heralded the creation and resulting exploitation of the virtual world, first by pioneers and then more recently by nearly everyone. It was instrumental in promoting human technology intimacy as discussed by Tomasi (2008). He suggests that technology is not competing with humans but is there to enhance organic and mental shortcomings. Hence, an intimate relationship is established between human and technology. Taken one step further, this relationship could evolve into an amalgam as depicted by cyborgs and ultimately androids. This science-fiction style scenario, which is based on *intimacy* (Tomasi, 2008), might become a reality in the future. However, today such intimacy already exists in the virtual world.

### Approach

This chapter is an interpretative viewpoint which discusses a snapshot of the online world. It does not claim to be comprehensive but rather offers pointers for new avenues of research, and encourages rethinking by policy makers and regulators. The approach has been to blend a number of strands to form a composite view of digital existence which in turn highlights aspects worthy of further investigation. Thus, the chapter draws upon philosophy, sociology and linguistics to tease out some of the key issues.

According to Hine (2000), there are two ethnographic perspectives of the virtual world. The *cultural view* is of a virtual place where people form and reform practices and meanings, whereas the *cultural artefact view* is of technological product which is developed, marketed and used by people. Both perspectives are relevant to this discussion and together they support the idea of the existence of an online continuum which will be discussed in a later section.

---

* This chapter was first self-published as: Rogerson, S. (2018) Digital Existence – the Modern Way to Be. 16 June. Copyright © Simon Rogerson. DOI: 10.13140/RG.2.2.29522.25289.

The discussion commences by examining how technology has merged with humans and so in some sense humans have become more than their organic selves. In a virtual world, digital existence can be achieved through Daseinian avatars. The concept of self in this environment is explored. There then follows a broader consideration of the online world which in turn leads into a discussion as to how these new technologies become implicitly accepted by individuals and society. The influence of mass media is considered in this context. This is followed by a short analysis of the vocabulary used to describe the online world. The chapter concludes with a call to rethink how we all should view and react to this online world.

## The Virtual World

The virtual world seems more than simply an application area. Hendler et al. (2008) explain that it also acts as a social machine which enables different social processes to take place. In some sense, we can exist in this virtual world as Lessig (1999, 2006) already illustrated at a time the Internet was just at the beginning of its commercial development. Furthermore, in an early work, Panteli and Duncan (2004) describe the virtual world as a theatre where plays are enacted by actors who take on different roles and follow different scripts. Others direct or watch these plays. Together they define the nature of the virtual situation. ICT provides the tools, equipment, costumes and other facilities that enable plays to be performed. Panteli and Duncan use this concept to investigate the creation and operation of virtual teams but clearly it can be used for every activity in the virtual world. Previous work by Panteli and Dibben (2001) on virtual organisations implies that such organisations must be populated by virtual workers. It is interesting that Panteli and Dibben recognise that these virtual workers do other things than simply undertaking work tasks when they discuss the idea that virtual workers will exhibit not only work ethic characteristics but also playfulness characteristics. This is in line with Castells (1996), from a sociological point of view and Sunstein (2002), from a political scientist's position, who both explain that ICT changes human existence particularly regarding sociality and community. Such ideas establish a sense of people existing in a virtual space. In the intervening period, this sense of virtual existence has been strengthened as technology and its application spread have both advanced. Thus, digital existence is important since eventually many, if not all, of these services, products and interactions will only be available online, thus forcing us to live, work, learn and socialise in the virtual world. Technopedia (2016) defines a virtual world as an online community environment where individuals interact with each other using text-based, two-dimensional or three-dimensional graphical models called avatars. The virtual world is very similar to the physical world, with real-world rules and real-time actions and communications.

## Digital Beings

Balnaves and Luca (2005) suggest that operating in the virtual world occurs through a form of agency which simply acts as a mechanism by which information can be shared. Want (2008) discusses the mobile phone as an agent, arguing that it acts as a pervasive proxy mediating with services and other phones on behalf of the owner. Balnaves and Luca (2006) suggest that digital beings could therefore be at some point an electronic document, a digital signal or a data structure. Agency is discussed by Lanfranco (1995) but the implied meaning is different. The digital being is recognised as residing in the virtual workplace operating as an effective participant in both local and global activities. This suggests that Lanfranco's focus is more on digital being rather than agent as described by Balnaves and Luca (2005, 2008) and used by Want (2008).

The technological evolution leading to the creation of the virtual world has changed the way in which we should consider self. Self, as defined by Locke (1997 [1706]), is a conscious thinking thing regardless of substance. He postulates that self must be fixed in a body. However, in today's context, it is reasonable to acknowledge that this body is likely to have both physical and virtual components. Indeed, De Vries (2006, p. 70) recognises this is Ihde's embodiment (I-technology)→world relationship where technology and humans coalesce. Brey (2000) explains that Ihde's view is based upon the special relationships between human beings and artefacts which enable them to interact with the environment because such relationships become part of our embodiment. Brey (2000) further suggests that Merleau-Ponty's theory of embodiment relations extends Ihde's theory by considering how relationships are constituted and by defining experience not only as the experience of the artefact but also the experience of the location of the artefact.

The concept of self has been discussed at length by Kant (1983 [1781/1787]) particularly in *Critique of Pure Reason*. This includes the thesis of consciousness of self as a single, common subject of experience (KdRV, A350 translated into English in Kant, 1997). The individual may have a variety of experiences but it is the combination of these viewed as a whole which defines self. So, for example, an individual may have experiences both in the physical world and virtual world but the individual self is the totality of these experiences. This holistic view of self fits with Heidegger's (1979) concept of Dasein in "Being and Time" where the human being is a whole rather than a compound of mind and body (Crowell, 2001). However, Spencer-Scarr (2015) explains that Heidegger viewed time as being linear which is inappropriate in the virtual world. This is because humans as Daseins, "have the ability to be 'present,' albeit virtually, in a geographically boundless landscape in 'near instant' time for eternity within fluid space" (ibid, p. 6).

It is the Dasein which Kim (2001) uses to explore the phenomenology of digital beings. Just as in the physical world where humans have physical trappings such as paintings, keys and jewellery, in the virtual world, digital beings have digital trappings such as digital photographs, electronic papers and passwords. Kim (2001, p. 107) argues that as Daseins we can encounter others in the virtual world and that it "… will fundamentally change the ways in which human beings interact with one another and open up new horizons … ." It is this which Piliang (2015) refers to as an *imagined community* where space, location and body do not have a physical existence and so have to be imagined. Interaction is dominated by the digital screen which becomes of Dasein.

In this way, human beings are extended as they are both physical and digital which can raise new issues. For example, a teenager might be socialising happily in the school yard while at the same time being subjected to a vicious cyberbullying attack. What happens to the virtual element of self can have a catastrophic effect on the emotional and physical elements of self. The second example of cybermourning is discussed by Campbell and Smith (2015). They conclude that open Internet forums which enable the public expression of grief establish an ongoing relationship which in effect amounted to keeping the physically deceased person virtually alive.

It is time to recognise that in some sense we now live in two worlds, one physical and one virtual. If this is true then we need to reconsider how the virtual world should be perceived, used and regulated. Two elements, avatars and personal data, provide some ideas of what must be considered.

## Avatars

An avatar is a graphical representation of an individual. It can be a three-dimensional body in virtual worlds and two-dimensional icon in online communities. It appears from Kim's argument that avatars are Daseins in the virtual world. Jones (2010) suggests that a Dasein as an avatar is a digital-being-in-the-world-wide-web made up of binary digits there to be conveyed and processed through single electronic channels. This being of self-expression is formed by a combination of textual communication and graphical imagery which enables it to mimic physical world actions (Wolfendale, 2007). Avatars exhibit attributes and emotions which reflect both the physical and virtual existence with such attributes often being gender specific (Nagy & Koles, 2014). Furthermore, an avatar has presence in a shared environment where other avatars exist (Wolfendale, 2007). Together avatars collaborate in the pursuit of a civil society (Adrian, 2009). As such, there is an opportunity to break down social silos. However, as Tett (2015) points out, this will only happen if digital beings view this virtual civic society as a malleable, multidimensional community.

## Personal Data

It follows that, in this virtual world, we exist as Daseins through a myriad of personal data and electronic interaction. We are digital beings who live out our digital existence in data repositories and travel along the conduits of data communication, taking with us our digital trappings wherever we roam. These comprise identification, possessions, content, preferences and records (Follett, 2007). As we roam we leave behind us permanent data shadows. In order to live and prosper in the virtual world, an individual must be visible, credible and creditable. As digital beings, we each develop electronic persona across a range of digital media and through digital icons such as digital signatures, #tags, electronic profiles, electronic patient records and electronic purses. This data is our virtual anatomy. We come to exist electronically and our needs are addressed through having these digital icons. Without them, we cannot function and we become invisible. How these digital icons are addressed in national and international legislation and regulation will impact on the rights and constraints of citizens in the virtual world. However, our digital persona is not simply characterised by our digital icons. The sense of self is completed through the relationships with others (Prosser & Ward, 2001).

Data communication conduits and data repositories are owned by others but the claim that our personal data and associated electronic interactions are owned by others is tantamount to accepting that we, as digital beings, can be owned by others, albeit in some form of distributed cooperative. With ownership comes the right to use, trade and dispose. Existing legislation such as data protection is concerned with the legitimate use of data items. It does not consider data items to be the organs of a digital being within the virtual anatomy and so is not concerned with the wellbeing of digital beings protecting them against colonialism, servitude and slavery.

According to Osterhammel (1997), colonialism involves the domination of one set of people on an indigenous population. New groups of people arrive and inhabit new territory as permanent settlers while maintaining allegiance with the territory of origin. The virtual world is experiencing colonialism. New settlers such as electronic traders and service providers are establishing permanent presences. Their actions, demands and policies remain aligned to the physical organisations from which they came. The existing indigenous virtual population is being pressurised into conforming to the norms of the new settlers. Thus, indigenous Daseins are at risk of being subjected to servitude and slavery.

Two recent examples, which have gained much media attention, illustrate how these concepts are being recognised by society at large.

The first is a marketing campaign which commenced in March 2018 by Experian, a consumer credit reporting agency. In the campaign, people are portrayed as composite beings. One of the campaign messages states, "You may not know it yet but out there in the world exists a version of you that you may never meet. Your Data Self. … made up entirely of your financial data." In the online and televised advertisements, two images appear of the same person albeit looking slightly different to differentiate between Physical Self and Data Self. The emphasis is on the person being financial data which is of great commercial importance to Experian.

The second example is the Facebook–Cambridge Analytica scandal when 87 million data profiles were shared. Melrose (2018) explains that Data Selves were harvested by Cambridge Analytica using a digital personality quiz together with collecting personal data within their Facebook profiles and information about their friends on Facebook. It was people as data who were the priceless commodities there to be data mined and subsequently used for a disingenuous purpose.

## The Online World Continuum

The online world is more than the virtual world as defined by Technopedia. One way to consider the online world is as a continuum. At one end, it is a toolset comprising search engines, information sources, communication conduits and so on. At the other end, it is a location within which one can "exist" as a Dasein thereby socialising and undertaking activities. Along the continuum lie agents which act as a go-between for individuals to access online products and services. Such agents operate in the individual's workstation and/or elsewhere in the online world (Balnaves & Luca, 2006). Thus, human technology intimacy manifests itself in many different forms along this continuum.

This online world has become pervasive across the whole of society as illustrated by the ongoing technological take-up. According to www.internetsociety.org in September 2014, there were more smartphones than non-smartphones sold in the developing world; in May 2015, there were 3 billion Internet users and 4.2 billion by December 2017, and in October 2015 more tablets were sold than PCs. Over 45% of the world's population used the Internet which had risen to 54% by 31 December 2017. According to www.statista.com in November 2015, there were over 1.5 billion Facebook users rising to 2.19 billion in December 2017 (this dipped in 2018 because of the Cambridge Analytica scandal), 900 million WhatsApp users, 316 million (November 2015) and 336 million (January 2018) Twitter users, and 300 million Skype users. Statista forecast mobile phone users in the world will exceed 5 billion by 2019.

The technology of the online world is continually evolving across this continuum providing new tools and experiences. Currently, individuals can choose how much or how little of the online world they wish to engage with. However, such things as peer group pressure, social norms, mass media, government policy and commercial marketing all influence what is available and which choice is made. It is likely that as technology evolves eventually online engagement will be mandatory for all. This absorption of the online into everyday lives continues to be worthy of investigation. An essential part of studying any online phenomena is through the available Internet-based information (Oates, 2005). For this chapter, it has been addressed through access to an online newspaper archive and a leading search engine to ascertain the level of everyday absorption. The outcomes are discussed in the following sections.

### *The Role of Mass Media*

In general, mass media influences social norms and people's attitudes and behaviours (Hilt & Lipschultz, 2016). A sample newspaper was chosen to consider coverage of the online world.

The Daily Mail was chosen as it is a middle-market tabloid newspaper that has the second highest circulation in the United Kingdom. Additionally, its website has more than 100 million unique monthly visitors and as such it claims to be the most visited newspaper website in the world. The website contains a comprehensive archive dating back to April 1996 (see http://www.dailymail.co.uk/home/sitemaparchive/index.html). This archive was used to search for stories about the online world as well as occurrences of some key words.

The sample of stories selected (Table 15.1) illustrates how the popular press depicts the online world. The first story, *Happily Caught in a Wonderful Web*, opens with, "The Internet revolution is rolling. It is losing its nerdy image and becoming accessible and affordable to anyone with a personal computer." It is typical of stories which heralded the beginning of accessible technology which will change society. By 2001, the two sample stories are reporting the Internet as a tool of leisure but also reporting the need to maintain social order. The three chosen stories of 2007 illustrate the evolution of the online to include "existence" as mentioned previously. Political campaigning, bullying and lifestyle are everyday aspects of the real world yet in these stories they have virtual counterparts. The story of 2008 illustrates the inclusivity of the online world discussing the increase of Internet users in the older generations. Finally, the story chosen in 2015, *Facebook in Virtual Reality Move*, is a good example of how social networking is developing into a complete experience rather than one dominated by text.

Such stories influence people's perception of technology, how it is embedded into our lives and what is considered as societal norms. This mass media influence is further enhanced through the adoption of vocabulary by reporters. A search for chronological occurrences of some key words was undertaken on 13 January 2016. Only material written by Daily Mail journalists was searched. There were 560 items which included words beginning with "cyber." Such words include cyberart, cybercafé, cybercitizen, cybercrime, cybersecurity, cybersex, cyberspace, cybersquatting, cyberstalking, cybersurfer and cyberterrorist. It first occurred on 24 May 1999 in a story about Internet booths and most recently on 28 December 2015 in a story about online shopping. There were 1,341 items which included "Google." It first occurred on 3 May 2004 in a story about the growth of Google and most recently on 13 January 2016 in a story about content censorship. There were 275 items which included "Skype." It first occurred on 3 October 2008 in

**Table 15.1 Typical Newspaper Stories About the Online World (source: www.dailymail.co.uk/home/sitemaparchive/index.html)**

| Date | Headline |
| --- | --- |
| 13 December 1998 | Happily caught in a wonderful web |
| 18 April 2001 | Internet police force is launched |
| 20 May 2001 | Hit TV shows score in cyberspace |
| 13 March 2007 | Hillary's virtual campaign |
| 31 May 2007 | Warning over cyber-bullying in Second Life |
| 26 June 2007 | Virtual utopia where you only live twice |
| 24 March 2008 | Silver surfers' spending two hours a day on the Internet |
| 25 March 2015 | Facebook in virtual reality move |

a story about content censorship and most recently on 6 November 2015 in a story about group communication. There were 2,561 items which included "blog." It first occurred on 17 November 2005 in a story about content and most recently on 13 January 2016 in a story which quoted from a blog as a reliable source. The ongoing use of such vocabulary in the popular press promotes usage, leads to widespread adoption which in turn influences societal norms.

## A New Vocabulary

Technology has always spawned new vocabulary. Some of this vocabulary are transient reflecting technological trends while other parts are longer-lasting with some eventually entering the permanent vocabulary. This transition into permanency is an indicator of technology becoming part of the very fabric of society. A set of words and phrases, which described the online world, was chosen to search in Google. The set was subdivided into technology descriptions, people, locations, activities and problems. A set of everyday words was also used in order to place the occurrences of the technological words and phrases into the context of permanent vocabulary. Frequency of word occurrence is a legitimate method of analysing changes in vocabulary (Abele et al., 2008; Chen & Ge, 2007). This form of analysis was used to produce the results shown in Tables 15.2 and 15.3.

On this basis, it appears that words and phrases relating to technology descriptions are within the permanent vocabulary and only lag a little way behind everyday words. Those relating to activities are also well established in the permanent vocabulary. Those relating to location and

**Table 15.2   Occurrences of Words and Phrases Using a Google Search on 14 January 2016**

| Technology Descriptions (in Millions) | |
|---|---|
| Computer | 2,240 |
| Information society | 5.39 |
| Digital era | 0.760 |
| Internet | 4,140 |
| World Wide Web | 37.2 |
| www | 25,270 |
| Email | 7,280 |
| Internet of Things | 28.3 |
| Cyber | 307 |
| **People (in Millions)** | |
| Cybercitizen | 0.022 |
| Digital being | 0.112 |
| Digital persona | 0.357 |

*(Continued)*

**TABLE 15.2 (Continued) Occurrences of Words and Phrases Using a Google Search on 14 January 2016**

| Locations (in Millions) | |
|---|---|
| Virtual reality | 34.9 |
| Second life | 18.1 |
| Augmented reality | 14.5 |
| **Activities (in Millions)** | |
| Skype | 305 |
| Blog | 4,590 |
| Podcast | 242 |
| Wiki | 1,060 |
| Social network | 175 |
| Facebook | 14,870 |
| Hashtag | 262 |
| **Problems (in Millions)** | |
| Cyber crime | 5.1 |
| Data privacy | 5.11 |
| Spamming | 38.2 |
| **Everyday Words (in Millions)** | |
| Home | 14,940 |
| House | 4,540 |
| Road | 3,300 |
| People | 7,480 |
| Sport | 3,190 |
| Books | 2,890 |
| Love | 4,180 |

problems appear to be in a transitional state while those relating to people exhibit little permanency. This aligns with the idea that vocabulary remains only if it is useful and represents something that exists over the passage of time, thus filling a lexicon gap (Maxwell, 2009). The ranking of the chosen words and phrases is shown in Table 15.3. Unsurprisingly, all the everyday words rank highly. The highest ranking of all is "www" which is understandable as it fills a lexicon gap and is related to an ongoing technology which itself appears permanent. With around 25% of

**Table 15.3  Ranking of Words and Phrases**

| Rank | Word or Phrase | Occurrences (Millions) |
|---|---|---|
| 1 | www | 25,270 |
| 2 | Home | 14,940 |
| 3 | Facebook | 14,870 |
| 4 | People | 7,480 |
| 5 | Email | 7,280 |
| 6 | Blog | 4,590 |
| 7 | House | 4,540 |
| 8 | Love | 4,180 |
| 9 | Internet | 4,140 |
| 10 | Road | 3,300 |
| 11 | Sport | 3,190 |
| 12 | Books | 2,890 |
| 13 | Computer | 2,240 |
| 14 | Wiki | 1,060 |
| 15 | Cyber | 307 |
| 16 | Skype | 305 |
| 17 | Hashtag | 262 |
| 18 | Podcast | 242 |
| 19 | Social network | 175 |
| 20 | Spamming | 38.2 |
| 21 | World Wide Web | 37.2 |
| 22 | Virtual reality | 34.9 |
| 23 | Internet of Things | 28.3 |
| 24 | Second life | 18.1 |
| 25 | Augmented reality | 14.5 |
| 26 | Information society | 5.39 |
| 27 | Data privacy | 5.11 |
| 28 | Cyber crime | 5.1 |
| 29 | Digital era | 0.76 |

*(Continued)*

**TABLE 15.3 (Continued) Ranking of Words and Phrases**

| Rank | Word or Phrase | Occurrences (Millions) |
|---|---|---|
| 30 | Digital persona | 0.357 |
| 31 | Digital being | 0.112 |
| 32 | Cybercitizen | 0.022 |

the world's population using Facebook, its ranking is reasonable because so many people know what Facebook is. Activities which mimic established activities such as communicating, writing, searching all rank well. Technological concepts such as augmented reality and virtual reality rank less which suggests they are not so well understood by the wider population. Finally, those which relate to the extension of person (digital persona, digital being and cybercitizen) are ranked at the bottom. These represent a controversial complex concept which currently remains primarily with the realms of research.

The online world vocabulary is littered with both common and proper nouns which represent new products and services. Many of these have been transformed into verbs via antimeria which is the conversion of word use into a new use. This is not a new phenomenon. In the 1920s, the Hoover brand name would eventually transform into the verb "to hoover" meaning to clean something with a vacuum cleaner. It is a verb which is still in common use. In a similar vein *to google* has now come to mean to search for information about someone or something on the Internet using any search engine, although www.oxforddictionaries.com still defines it as a search using Google. Table 15.4 contains this verb together with some other online world verbs. All

**Table 15.4   Verbs Created from Nouns through Anthimeria (The Definitions Are from www.oxforddictionaries.com)**

| Verb | Definition | First Usage |
|---|---|---|
| Google | To search for information about someone or something on the Internet using the search engine Google. | 1990s |
| Skype | To have a spoken conversation with someone over the Internet using the software application. | 2000s |
| Tweet | To make a posting on the social media website Twitter. | 2000s |
| Email | To send an electronic mail to someone. | 1970s |
| Spam | To send the same message indiscriminately to large numbers of Internet users. | 1930s, then 1970s |
| Surf | To move from site to site on the Internet. | 1990s |
| Blog | To add new material to or regularly update a blog which is a regularly updated website or web page, typically one run by an individual or small group, that is written in an informal or conversational style. | 1990s |

these verbs fill a lexicon gap. Each is phonetic as well as being easy to say and spell. All are in common use and once again contribute to society's intimate engagement with this technology and further evidence that technology is part of the very fabric of life.

Finally, it is important to mention the use of metaphors in the online world vocabulary. It is through metaphors that guidance is provided about the technological capabilities to individuals and society at large (Jamet, 2010). The information superhighway is a phrase coined by Vice President Al Gore first in 1978. This metaphor suggests travel, the speedy transmission of large amounts of information and the ability to visit other places. Surprisingly, this metaphor is still in use. For example, Sabarra (2015) wrote about *Cyber Suitors. Shattered Illusions Along the Information Superhighway* in The Huffington Post, and Price and Norris (2014) wrote about *Connecting Cars to the* Information Superhighway in The Telegraph. Jamet (2010) identifies an interesting dichotomy in such metaphors when he writes, "... if internet metaphors have largely been motivated by the perception of internet users, there is also a reciprocal influence because internet metaphors also structure our very perception of it, which is in keeping with the mutual relationship between language and thought." This dichotomy seems to pervade all aspects of the online world vocabulary.

## Conclusion

There appears to be a range of online world experiences which has been described as being on a continuum. The more sophisticated technology becomes the experience is extended and intimacy increases. These experiences change our perception of self, place, action and belonging. Acceptance of the technological evolution is affected by the mass media and the vocabulary that is used to describe both in the press and by society in general.

A carpenter will have a favourite hammer, a cook will have a favourite pan, a painter will have a favourite brush and a cleaner will have a favourite mop. It is natural that any artisan will have a special affection for a favourite tool. Similarly, we all have our favourite search engine and web browser tools. Such tool affection is at one end of the online world continuum. At the other end, there is a much deeper intimacy in the virtual world where human and technology have integrated. Digital existence is played out through Daseins of which avatars are examples.

With this increase in the intimacy between humans and technology, thinking and concepts need to be revisited. Acknowledging that humans are becoming composite beings leads to the needs to think of us not as data subjects but data selves. Data, the virtual anatomy should not be owned by third parties. The physical building of trust relies on visual cues not accessible online and so an alternative effective way needs to be found to establish online trust as current establishment attempts seem to be ineffective yet the use of texting and emoticons by ordinary people seems to have substance. Social scaffolding such as the Universal Declaration of Human Rights needs to be reviewed and revised in the light of composite human beings. In the United Kingdom, there have been moves to establish a Digital Bill of Rights which aligns with this idea. The new data protection legislation across Europe has acknowledged that personal data is an important part of an individual and as such the individual must have much greater control over that data. There is an implied acceptance of Data Self in such legislation.

This chapter raises issues which impact on universal access. How we view the virtual world impacts on the manner in which we design associated systems which in turn impacts on how effective is access for all. Therefore, policy, regulation and social norms need to be revisited, modified, and enhanced so that the whole continuum from tool through agent to being is accommodated. This is because quite simply

Digital being, the modern way to be,
I am the data and the data is me.

# Acknowledgement

My thanks to Karsten Weber for his philosophical input some time ago.

# References

Abele, A. E., Uchronski, M., Suitner, C. & Wojciszke, B. (2008). Towards an operationalization of the fundamental dimensions of agency and communion: trait content ratings in five countries considering valence and frequency of word occurrence. *European Journal of Social Psychology*, 38(7), 1202–1217.

Adrian, A. (2009). Civil society in second life. *International Review of Law, Computers & Technology*, 23(3), 231–235.

Balnaves, M. & Luca, J. (2005). The impact of digital persona on the future of learning: a case study on digital repositories and the sharing of information about children at risk in Western Australia. 22nd Annual Conference of the Australasian Society for Computers in Learning in Tertiary Education "Balance, Fidelity, Mobility: Maintaining the momentum?", pp. 49–56. Brisbane.

Balnaves, M. & Luca, J. (2006). Protecting the digital citizen: the impact of digital personae on ideas of universal access to knowledge and community. In: Pearson, E. & Bohman, P. (eds.), *Proceedings of World Conference on Educational Multimedia, Hypermedia and Telecommunications 2006*. Chesapeake, VA, AACE, pp. 2918–2923.

Brey, P. (2000). Technology and embodiment in Ihde and Merleau-Ponty. In: Mitcham, C. (ed.), *Metaphysics, Epistemology, and Technology*, Research in Philosophy and Technology, Vol. 19. Emerald Group Publishing, pp. 45–58.

Campbell, K. & Smith, K. (2015). Cybermourning frames and collective memory: remembering comedian Robin Williams on Legacy.com. *Journal of New Media and Culture*, 10(1). Available from http://ibiblio.org/nmediac/summer2015/cybermourning.html (Accessed 10 May 2016).

Castells, M. (1996). *The Rise of the Network Society*. Oxford, Blackwell.

Castells, M. (2010). *Rise of the Network Society: The Information Age: Economy, Society and Culture*, 2nd Edition, Vol. 1. Blackwell Publishers.

Chen, Q. & Ge, G. C. (2007). A corpus-based lexical study on frequency and distribution of Coxhead's AWL word families in medical research articles (RAs). *English for Specific Purposes*, 26(4), 502–514.

Crowell, S. (2001). Subjectivity: locating the first-person in Being and Time. *Inquiry*, 44(4), 433–454.

De Vries, M. J. (2006). *Teaching about Technology. An Introduction to the Philosophy of Technology for Non-Philosophers*. Dordrecht, Springer.

Follett, J. (2007), Envisioning the whole digital person. *UXmatters*, 20 February. Available from http://www.uxmatters.com/mt/archives/2007/02/envisioning-the-whole-digital-person.php (Accessed 11 January 2016).

Hendler, J., Shadbolt, N., Hall, W., Berners-Lee, T. & Weitzner, D. (2008). Web science: an interdisciplinary approach to the Web. *Communications of the ACM*, 51(7), 60–69.

Hilt, M. L. & Lipschultz, J. H. (2016). *Mass Media, an Aging Population, and the Baby Boomers*. Routledge.

Hine, C. (2000) *Virtual Ethnography*. Sage.

Jamet, D. L. (2010), What do Internet metaphors reveal about the perception of the Internet?. *meta-phorik.de*, 18. Available from http://www.metaphorik.de/sites/www.metaphorik.de/files/journal-pdf/1 8_2010_jamet.pdf (Accessed 14 January 2016).

Jones, S. (2010), *Web 2.0's Response to Heidegger's Challenge of Technology*. Available from https://www.academia.edu/3172672/Web_2.0s_Response_to_Heideggers_Challenges_of_Technology (Accessed 18 January 2016).

Kant, I. (1983 [1781/1787]) Kritik der reinen Vernunft (Werke in zehn Bänden; Bd. 3 und 4). Darmstadt, Wissenschaftliche Buchgesellschaft = KdRV. English: Kant, I. (1997). *Critique of Pure Reason* (trans. P. Guyer and A. Wood). Cambridge, New York, Cambridge University Press.

Kim, J. (2001). Phenomenology of digital being. *Human Studies*, 24(1–2), 87–111.

Lanfranco, S. (1995). The citizen, the expert and wisdom in the virtual workspace. Knowledge tools for a sustainable civilisation. *Fourth Canadian Conference on Foundations and Applications of General Science Theory*, 8–10 June, pp. 303–311. IEEE. Date of Conference: 8–10 June 1995. Conference Location: Toronto, ON, Canada. DOI: 10.1109/KTSC.1995.569186

Lessig, L. (1999). *Code and Other Laws of Cyberspace*. New York, Basic Books.

Lessig, L. (2006). *Code Version 2.0*. New York, Basic Books.

Locke, J. (1997 [1706]). *An Essay Concerning Human Understanding* (ed. Woolhouse, R.). London, Penguin Books.

Maxwell, K. (2006). New word of the month. *MED Magazine*, 37(April). Available from http://www.macmillandictionaries.com/MED-Magazine/April2006/37-New-Word.htm (Accessed 17 January 2016).

Maxwell, K. (2009). Survival of the fittest – new words and longevity. *MED Magazine*, 55(November). Available from http://www.macmillandictionaries.com/MED-Magazine/November2009/55-Feature-New%20Words-Longevity-Print.htm (Accessed 17 January 2016).

Melrose, R. (2018). *Facing up to Responsibility*, 23 March. Available from http://elasticcreative.co.uk/2018/03/23/facing-up-to-responsibility/ (Accessed 16 June 2018).

Nagy, P. & Koles, B. (2014). "My avatar and her beloved possession": characteristics of attachment to virtual objects. *Psychology & Marketing*, 31(12), 1122–1135.

Oates, B. J. (2005). *Researching Information Systems and Computing*. Sage.

Osterhammel, J. (1997). *Colonialism: A Theoretical Overview* (trans. Frisch, S. J.). Princeton, Markus Wiener Publishers.

Panteli, N. & Dibben, M. R. (2001). Revisiting the nature of virtual organisations: reflections on mobile communication systems. *Futures*, 33(5), 379–391.

Panteli, N. & Duncan, E. (2004). Trust and temporary virtual teams: alternative explanations and dramaturgical relationships. *Information Technology and People*, 17(2), 423–441.

Piliang, Y. A. (2015). Redefining ethics and culture in the virtual world. *MELINTAS*, 31(3), 236–251.

Price, C. & Norris, A. (2014). Connecting cars to the information superhighway. *The Telegraph*, 29 August. Available from http://www.telegraph.co.uk/sponsored/technology/4g-mobile/machine-to-machine/11 059313/connected-cars-become-norm.html (Accessed 12 October 2015).

Prosser, B. T. & Ward, A. (2001). Fear and trembling on the Internet. *ETHICOMP 2001 Conference Proceedings*, Vol. 2, pp. 131–140.

Sabarra, J. (2015). Cyber suitors: shattered illusions along the information superhighway. *HuffPost*, 23 March 2015. Available from http://www.huffingtonpost.com/josh-sabarra/cyber-suitors-shattered-illusions-along-the-information-superhighway_b_6920138.html (Accessed 12 October 2015).

Spencer-Scarr, D. C. (2015). Digital engagement: personality is the context of the text. *Proceedings from the Document Academy*, 2(1), Article 13.

Sunstein, C. (2002). *Republic.com*. Princeton University Press.

Technopedia (2016). Definition - what does virtual world mean? Available from https://www.techopedia.com/definition/25604/virtual-world (Accessed 15 January 2016).

Tett, G. (2015). Beyond the bubble. *RSA Journal*, 161(5563), 30–35.

Tomasi, A. (2008). The role of intimacy in the evolution of technology. *Journal of Evolution and Technology*, 17(1), 1–12.

Want, R. (2008). You are your cell phone. *IEEE Pervasive Computing*, 2(April–June), 2–4.

Wolfendale, J. (2007). My avatar, my self: virtual harm and attachment. *Ethics and Information Technology*, 9(2), 111–119.

## Chapter 16

# Is Professional Practice at Risk Following the Volkswagen and Tesla Revelations? [2017]*

## Introduction

Each day society becomes more and more technologically dependent. Some argue that as a consequence society becomes more and more vulnerable to catastrophe. With the world in economic crisis, the headlong drive for efficiency and effectiveness (and resulting profit) is the watchword. Such pressure might have resulted in real gains but has also led to unscrupulous or reckless actions. The tempering of such drive with ethical consideration is often neglected until there is a detrimental event causing public outcry. Such an event will usually attract both media interest and social media posting which in turn places more and more pressure on the actors to account for the reasons why the event had occurred. This cause and effect map is commonplace. Consider, for example, transport which is a fundamental element of the fabric of society. In this area, there have been two recent events which illustrate the drive for efficiency and effectiveness without proper ethical consideration. The first example is the Volkswagen emissions scandal which came to light in September 2015. The company installed software into millions of vehicles with diesel engines so that impressive emission readings would be recorded in laboratory conditions even though the reality is that the diesel engines do not comply with current emission regulations. The second example concerns Tesla Motors and the public beta testing of the Autopilot software in their cars. In May 2016 there was a fatal accident when a Model S Tesla under the control of the Tesla Autopilot software drove at full speed under a trailer resulting in the driver of the Tesla being killed.

* This chapter was first published as: Rogerson, S. (2017) Is professional practice at risk following the Volkswagen and Tesla revelations? software engineering under scrutiny. ACM SIGCAS Computers and Society. Vol. 47 No 3, September. pp. 25–38. Copyright © Simon Rogerson. DOI 10.1145/3144592.3144596

Both examples centre on the use of software which is the focus of this paper. Both are pieces of safety-critical software which is defined as software that, if it fails or malfunctions, will cause death or serious injury to people, and/or result in loss or severe damage to property or equipment, and/or cause environmental harm. The development of application software does not occur in a vacuum. Within Volkswagen and Tesla there will have been a complex network of individuals involved in decision making at different levels resulting in the production of application software which achieved a particular goal. The software engineers who wrote the software may or may not have been privy to higher-level decisions and the associated reasons why such decisions were taken. But it is the software engineer who can ultimately be identified as the creator of the software and so rightly or wrongly can be held responsible for any un-favourable outcomes.

The aim of this paper is to undertake an ethical analysis of each case study using existing published accounts. Over 80 sources have been analysed but only some key sources are spe-cifically referenced in this chapter. This broad literature establishes confidence in the facts of each case described below. The ethical analysis is undertaken from a software engineering perspective through performing a *professional standards analysis* within the case analysis method as defined by Bynum (2004). The *Software Engineering Code of Ethics and Professional Practice* of the ACM (see http://www.acm.org/about/se-code) is used in this analysis as it is regarded as the most applicable set of principles for these cases. It is long-established; documenting the ethical and professional obligations of software engineers and identifying the standards society expects of them (Gotterbarn, Miller & Rogerson, 1999). The focus of the paper aligns with the following statement within the preamble to the Code, "These Principles should influence software engineers to consider broadly who is affected by their work; to examine if they and their colleagues are treating other human beings with due respect; to consider how the public, if reasonably well informed, would view their decisions; to analyse how the least empowered will be affected by their decisions; and to consider whether their acts would be judged worthy of the ideal professional working as a software engineer. In all these judgments concern for the health, safety and welfare of the public is primary; that is, the 'Public Interest' is central to this Code."

The two case analyses highlight a set of key issues which need to be addressed if professional integrity within software engineering is to be protected and promoted. The findings are compared with previously published analyses to ascertain common and conflicting outcomes. The paper concludes by identifying general issues which underpin guidance for future software engineering practice.

## The Volkswagen Case Study

Combustion engines are the source of pollution and therefore have been subjected to emission control. The formation of NOx (nitrogen oxides) through combustion is a significant contributor to ground-level ozone and fine particle pollution. In congested urban areas, motor vehicle traffic can result in dangerous levels of NOx emission. The inhalation of fine particles can damage lung tissue and cause or worsen respiratory conditions such as asthma, emphysema and bronchitis. It can aggravate existing heart disease. Children, the elderly and people with pre-existing respiratory disease are particularly at risk. The regulations in place aim to reduce pollution through NOx emission and thus reduce health risks.

The statement issued by the US Department of Justice (2017) details the facts of the Volkswagen emissions scandal. Two senior managers, Jens Hadler and Richard Dorenkamp appear to be at the centre of the so-called defeat software's ongoing design and implementation processes. It states, "… in 2006, Volkswagen engineers began to design a new diesel engine to meet stricter U.S. emissions standards that would take effect by the model year 2007. This new engine would be the cornerstone of a new project to sell diesel vehicles in the United States that would be marketed to buyers as 'clean diesel,' a project that was an important strategic goal for Volkswagen's management. When the co-conspirators realised that they could not design a diesel engine that would both meet the stricter NOx emissions standards and attract sufficient customer demand in the U.S. market, they decided they would use a software function to cheat standard U.S. emissions tests. … Volkswagen engineers working under Dorenkamp and Hadler designed and implemented a software to recognise whether a vehicle was undergoing standard U.S. emissions testing on a dynamometer or it was being driven on the road under normal driving conditions. The software accomplished this by recognising the standard published drive cycles. Based on these inputs, if the vehicle's software detected that it was being tested, the vehicle performed in one mode, which satisfied U.S. NOx emissions standards. If the software detected that the vehicle was not being tested, it operated in a different mode, in which the vehicle's emissions control systems were reduced substantially, causing the vehicle to emit NOx up to 40 times higher than U.S. standards. … Disagreements over the direction of the project were articulated at a meeting over which Hadler presided, and which Dorenkamp attended. Hadler authorised Dorenkamp to proceed with the project knowing that only the use of the defeat device software would enable VW diesel vehicles to pass U.S. emissions tests." Drawing upon the 'Statement of Facts,' Leggett (2017) reported that whilst there had been some concerns over the propriety of the defeat software all those involved in the discussions including engineers were instructed not to get caught and furthermore to destroy related documents.

According to Mansouri (2016) Volkswagen is an autocratic company with a reputation for avoiding dissent and discussion. It has a compliant business culture where employees are aware that underperformance can result in replacement and so management demands must be met to ensure job security. The Volkswagen Group Code of Conduct (2010) seems to promote this culture of compliance. Three statements align with the ongoing conduct encouraged during the emissions debacle.

*Promotion of Interests* (ibid., p15) "Each of our employees makes sure that their conduct and opinions expressed in public do not harm the reputation of the Volkswagen Group."

*Secrecy* (ibid., p16) "Each of our employees is obligated to maintain secrecy regarding the business or trade secrets with which they are entrusted within the scope of the performance of their duties or have otherwise become known. Silence must be maintained regarding work and matters within the Company that are significant to the Volkswagen Group or its business partners and that have not been made known publicly, such as, for example, product developments, plans and testing."

*Responsibility for Compliance* (ibid., p22) "Each of our employees who do not conduct themselves consistently with the Code must expect appropriate consequences within the scope of statutory regulations and company rules that can extend to termination of the employment relationship and claims for damages."

The use of defeat software was discovered by accident (Rufford & Tobin, 2016). In 2013 the EPA in the USA commissioned West Virginia University to check the emissions of three diesel cars. Two happened to be VWs. The laboratory results were compliant. However, during on-road tests both VWs were emitting up to 38 times the permitted levels of NOx. The results were reported to the EPA and subsequent further investigations led to the discovery of installed defeat software and the legal action which followed.

On 11 January 2017, the US Justice Department announced that "Volkswagen had agreed to plead guilty to three criminal felony counts, and pay a $2.8 billion criminal penalty, as a result of the company's long-running scheme to sell approximately 590,000 diesel vehicles in the U.S. by using a defeat device to cheat on emissions tests mandated by the Environmental Protection Agency (EPA) and the California Air Resources Board (CARB), and lying and obstructing justice to further the scheme"(US Department of Justice (2017)).

## Professional Standards Analysis

According to principle 1.03 of the Software Engineering Code of Ethics and Professional Practice, software engineers should "approve software only if they have a well-founded belief that it is safe, meets specifications, passes appropriate tests, and does not diminish the quality of life, diminish privacy or harm the environment. The ultimate effect of the work should be to the public good." The defeat software is clearly unsafe given NOx pollution damages both health and the environment. The public were under the misapprehension that VW cars were emitting low levels of NOx and therefore not a health risk. Software engineers installed the defeat software in violation of this principle.

According to principle 1.04 software engineers should "disclose to appropriate persons or authorities any actual or potential danger to the user, the public, or the environment, that they reasonably believe to be associated with software or related documents." There is no evidence that any software engineer disclosed. Given that there must have been a large number working on this project there appears to be a widespread violation of this principle.

According to principle 1.06 software engineers should "Be fair and avoid deception in all statements, particularly public ones, concerning software or related documents, methods and tools." The emissions software was heralded publicly as a success when internally there was widespread knowledge that this claim was fraudulent. Software engineers were likely to have been privy to this cover-up and so violated this principle.

According to principle 2.07 software engineers should "Identify, document and report significant issues of social concern, of which they are aware, in software or related documents, to the employer or the client." There is some evidence that there was concern raised about the efficacy of the defeat software but it seems those in dissent allowed themselves to be managed towards deception. Once again a principle was ultimately violated.

According to principle 3.03 software engineers should "Identify, define and address ethical, economic, cultural, legal and environmental issues related to work projects." The EPA regulations are explicit and are legally binding. From the evidence accessed it is unclear as to whether software engineers knew of the illegality of their actions. Nevertheless, ignorance cannot be and must not be a form of defence. Hence the principle was violated.

According to principle 6.06 software engineers should "Obey all laws governing their work, unless, in exceptional circumstances, such compliance is inconsistent with the public interest." This relates to the analysis under principle 3.03. Compliance to further the prosperity of Volkswagen was at the expense of legal compliance.

According to principle 6.07 software engineers should "Be accurate in stating the characteristics of software on which they work, avoiding not only false claims but also claims that might reasonably be supposed to be speculative, vacuous, deceptive, misleading, or doubtful." Software engineers could argue internally that the software indeed performed as it was designed to. However, the design was to achieve regulatory and public deception which is a violation of this principle.

According to principle 6.13 software engineers should "Report significant violations of this Code to appropriate authorities when it is clear that consultation with people involved in these significant violations is impossible, counter-productive or dangerous." Given the apparent corporate culture within Volkswagen there was little point in reporting concerns further up the line. In fact, the corporate code seems at odds with the professional code regarding this point. Software Engineers failed to report these breaches to appropriate authorities.

Much has been written about the Volkswagen emissions case. Many of the accounts focus on business ethics with only a few touching upon the role of the software engineers in this situation. These accounts at times are repetitive but intertwine to provide a rich view which is discussed here. There are two recurrent issues.

The first issue is whistleblowing. Software engineers are faced with a challenging landscape in which some issues are difficult to identify whilst others are easily identifiable. The Volkswagen case falls into the latter category because of the legal constraints established through EPA regulations. Plant (2015) suggests that in this situation the software engineers should have alerted external bodies since the internal lines of reporting were compromised. Merkel (2015) concurs citing the *Software Engineering Code of Ethics and Professional Practice* by way of justification, and adds that the lack of whistleblowers in such a large group is surprising. Both authors point to the potential personal cost of whistleblowing as the reason it did not happen. The second issue adds weight to this argument.

Rhodes (2016) argues that corporate business ethics is very much a *pro-business stance* which is implemented through corporate control and compliance systems, and instruments of managerial coordination. This can enable the pursuit of business self-interest through organised widespread conspiracies involving lying, cheating, fraud and lawlessness. This is what happened at Volkswagen. Queen (2015) concurs explaining that Volkswagen intentionally deceived those to whom it owed a duty of honesty. The pressure for continuous growth and the perception that failure was not an option (Ragatz, 2015) created a culture where corporate secrecy was paramount which in turn implicitly outlawed whistleblowing.

## The Tesla Case Study

The American Tesla Motors is currently the world's second-largest plug-in electric car manufacturer. According to the Tesla website (https://www.tesla.com/autopilot): 'All Tesla vehicles produced in our factory, including Model 3, have the hardware needed for full self-driving capability at a safety level substantially greater than that of a human driver'; 'Enhanced Autopilot adds these new capabilities to the Tesla Autopilot driving experience. Your Tesla will match speed to traffic conditions, keep within a lane, automatically change lanes without requiring driver input, transition from one freeway to another, exit the freeway when your destination is near, self-park when near a parking spot and be summoned to and from your garage.'; and 'Once on the freeway, your Tesla will determine which lane you need to be in and when. In addition to ensuring you reach your intended exit, Autopilot will watch for opportunities to move to a faster lane when you're caught behind slower traffic. When you reach your exit, your Tesla will depart the freeway, slow down and transition control back to you.'

In 2016 Tesla came under scrutiny following a fatal accident involving a Model S Tesla under the control of the Tesla Autopilot. According to Lambert (2016) the attending police officer reported "On May 7 at 3:40 p.m. on U.S. 27 near the BP Station west of Williston, a 45-year-old Ohio man was killed when he drove under the trailer of an 18-wheel semi. The top of Joshua Brown's 2015 Tesla Model S vehicle was torn off by the force of the collision. The truck driver, Frank Baressi, 62, Tampa was not injured in the crash." Tesla issued a statement that, "the vehicle was on a divided highway with Autopilot engaged when a tractor trailer drove across the highway perpendicular to the Model S. Neither Autopilot nor the driver noticed the white side of the tractor trailer against a brightly lit sky, so the brake was not applied. The high ride height of the trailer combined with its positioning across the road and the extremely rare circumstances of the impact caused the Model S to pass under the trailer, with the bottom of the trailer impacting the windshield of the Model S. Had the Model S impacted the front or rear of the trailer, even at high speed, its advanced crash safety system would likely have prevented serious injury as it has in numerous other similar incidents" (ibid.).

The Tesla statement (ibid.) addressed the issue of Autopilot software explaining, "It is important to note that Tesla disables Autopilot by default and requires explicit acknowledgement that the system is new technology and still in a public beta phase before it can be enabled. When drivers activate Autopilot, the acknowledgment box explains, among other things, that Autopilot '*is an assist feature that requires you to keep your hands on the steering wheel at all times,*' and that '*you need to maintain control and responsibility for your vehicle*' while using it. Additionally, every time that Autopilot is engaged, the car reminds the driver to '*Always keep your hands on the wheel. Be prepared to take over at any time.*' The system also makes frequent checks to ensure that the driver's hands remain on the wheel and provides visual and audible alerts if hands-on is not detected. It then gradually slows down the car until hands-on is detected again.

National Highway Traffic Safety Administration (NHTSA) investigated the incident. NHTSA (2017) has recently published its findings. It confirmed that Tesla car was being operated in Autopilot mode at the time of the collision; that the Automatic Emergency Braking (AEB) system did not provide any warning or automated braking for the collision event; and that the driver took no braking, steering, or other actions to avoid the collision. NHTSA found no defects in the design or performance of the AEB or Autopilot systems of the subject vehicles nor any incidents in which the systems did not perform as designed. The report states that Tesla Autopilot is an SAE Level 1 automated system and becomes Level 2 when Autosteer is activated. The SAE's 6 levels of driving automation for on-road vehicles are shown in Figure 16.1. As can be seen, Tesla Autopilot is not classified as an automated driving system which monitors the driving environment.

According to Jaynes (2016) even though Autopilot is classified as Level 2 in practice, to many, it feels like Level 4. In these circumstances, a driver can be lulled into a false sense of security and become distracted. The perception is further strengthened by the brand name *Autopilot* which implies a fully autonomous system, not the semi-autonomous system which it is in reality (Roberts, 2016). Furthermore, simply having a warning that Autopilot is a beta test version does not convey the seriousness of system failure to the driver (Jaynes, 2016). Indeed, Solon (2016) explains that this is contrary to traditional car manufacturers where public beta testing software which relates directly or indirectly to safety is never used. Tesla collects in real-time technical and personal data from its customers' vehicles using this data to test the effectiveness of new software which it then, often secretly, installs into the vehicle for road testing albeit without controlling the vehicle (Simonite, 2016). On the Tesla website within a subsection of the legal terms and

| SAE level | Name | Narrative Definition |
|---|---|---|
| \multicolumn{3}{c}{Human driver monitors the driving environment} | | |
| 0 | No Automation | the full-time performance by the human driver of all aspects of the dynamic driving task, even when enhanced by warning or intervention systems |
| 1 | Driver Assistance | the driving mode-specific execution by a driver assistance system of either steering or acceleration/deceleration using information about the driving environment and with the expectation that the human driver performs all remaining aspects of the dynamic driving task |
| 2 | Partial Automation | the driving mode-specific execution by one or more driver assistance systems of both steering and acceleration/deceleration using information about the driving environment and with the expectation that the human driver performs all remaining aspects of the dynamic driving task |
| \multicolumn{3}{c}{Automated driving system monitors the driving environment} | | |
| 3 | Conditional Automation | the driving mode-specific performance by an automated driving system of all aspects of the dynamic driving task with the expectation that the human driver will respond appropriately to a request to intervene |
| 4 | High Automation | the driving mode-specific performance by an automated driving system of all aspects of the dynamic driving task, even if a human driver does not respond appropriately to a request to intervene |
| 5 | Full Automation | the full-time performance by an automated driving system of all aspects of the dynamic driving task under all roadway and environmental conditions that can be managed by a human driver |

**Figure 16.1   Levels of driving automation for on-road vehicles. (Source: SAE International [2014])**

conditions there are statements confirming these practices (https://www.tesla.com/en_GB/about/legal#privacy-statement).

Tesla's corporate culture is manifest within its *Code of Business Conduct and Ethics* (Tesla, 2010). In stark contrast to the *Software Engineering Code of Ethics and Professional Practice*, there is no explicit reference to health, safety and welfare of the public. Rather the code's focus is explicitly the health, safety and welfare of Tesla. The implication appears to be that employees are expected to put Tesla first.

## Professional Standards Analysis

According to principle 1.03 of the Software Engineering Code of Ethics and Professional Practice, software engineers should "approve software only if they have a well-founded belief that it is safe, meets specifications, passes appropriate tests, and does not diminish the quality of life, diminish privacy, or harm the environment. The ultimate effect of the work should be to the public good." Autopilot software falls within the relatively new family of autonomous vehicle software. No evidence was found to suggest that stringent safety-critical software engineering standards were in place. If this is true it is a poor risk mitigation strategy. Safety, quality of life and privacy could all be compromised, and software engineers are in violation of this primary principle.

According to principle 1.06 software engineers should "Be fair and avoid deception in all statements, particularly public ones, concerning software or related documents, methods and tools." It appears that the use of moral algorithms and a public beta test regime is underplayed regarding potential dangers and overplayed regarding potential benefits. If this is the case it is unacceptable and software engineers are obligated to challenge this misconception.

According to principle 2.07 software engineers should "Identify, document, and report significant issues of social concern, of which they are aware, in software or related documents, to the employer or the client." It is unclear as to whether software engineers consider and subsequently report on issues of social concern in developing autonomous vehicle software. Given the potential social impact of such software the lack of transparency is surprising, disappointing and unacceptable.

According to principle 3.10 software engineers should "Ensure adequate testing, debugging, and review of software and related documents on which they work." Autopilot software is safety-critical software and yet beta testing was, and continues to be, undertaken in the operational environment i.e. the public highway. There is no evidence to suggest that Autopilot software is defined as safety-critical with Tesla. This leads to the question of the adequacy of the process. Software engineers need to be vigilant in ensuring adequacy bearing in mind public welfare is paramount. There is some doubt as to whether software engineers are adhering to this principle.

According to principle 3.12 software engineers should "Work to develop software and related documents that respect the privacy of those who will be affected by that software." By default Tesla collects a wide range of personal data on the basis that this might be useful in testing existing and future software. This approach is contrary to international data privacy conventions and hence software which enables such personal data capture is questionable. Therefore, software engineers may be contravening this principle.

According to principle 4.01 software engineers should "Temper all technical judgments by the need to support and maintain human values." Using utilitarian moral algorithms in autonomous vehicle software has been proven to be technically feasible. However, the moral justification is open to debate since other human values should be taken into account beyond simple calculus. Software engineers have an obligation to ensure this. Given such moral algorithms are in use, it follows that software engineers may well be contravening this principle.

According to principle 6.07 software engineers should "Be accurate in stating the characteristics of software on which they work, avoiding not only false claims but also claims that might reasonably be supposed to be speculative, vacuous, deceptive, misleading, or doubtful." The branding and marketing of Autopilot suggest to some members of the public that the software is greater than SAE Level 2. Such perceptions are dangerous. Tesla has an obligation to ensure realistic public perceptions pervade. As employees of Tesla software engineers must share this obligation.

## Other Analyses

There are many accounts about autonomous vehicles which relate to the cars manufactured by Tesla. Whilst many issues are identified, two appear prevalent; public beta testing of software and the use of moral algorithms in software. This broad body of literature has been drawn up in the discussion which follows.

Autonomous vehicles will almost certainly crash and the moral algorithm in the controlling software will affect the outcomes. Currently, these algorithms use utilitarian moral decision making. However, Goodall (2014) argues that there is no obvious way to encode effectively human morality in software. If so, moral algorithms are reliant upon an implied higher machine pseudo-intelligence. Bonnefon, Shariff and Rahwan (2016) found that moral algorithms create a social dilemma. Even though people seem to agree that everyone would be better off if autonomous vehicles were utilitarian (in the sense of minimising the number of casualties on the road), they all have a personal incentive to ride in autonomous vehicles that will protect them at all costs. McBride's analysis (2016) concludes that the real ethical worth is in how autonomous vehicles enable people to connect, interact and strengthens communities which might have been difficult or impossible before. If true, this adds a further complexity to the design of moral algorithms. Indeed Lin (2013) argues that utilitarian ethics is naïve and incomplete; rights, duties, conflicting values, and other factors should be taken into account. This is in line with the *Federal Automated Vehicles Policy* (2016, p26) which states that "Algorithms for resolving these conflict situations should be developed transparently using input from Federal and State regulators, drivers, passengers and vulnerable road users, and taking into account the consequences on others."

Public Beta testing requires the testers to report back their findings to the developers (ISTQB) which implies a dialogue between tester and developer. The Tesla approach is based on covert testing and so the testing public do not and cannot enter into a dialogue. The question which needs to be answered is, does the public beta testing regime of Tesla comply with the *System Safety Policy* (p20) which requires companies to, "follow a robust design and validation process based on a systems-engineering approach with the goal of designing autonomous vehicle systems free of unreasonable safety risks? Thorough and measurable software testing should complement a structured and documented software development process."

As discussed earlier there is concern about driver's perception as to the sophistication of Autopilot. This is addressed in the *Human Machine Interface Policy* (p22) which in part focuses on the boundary between Level 2 systems and Level 3 systems. It states, "Manufacturers and other entities should place significant emphasis on assessing the risk of driver complacency and misuse of Level 2 systems, and develop effective countermeasures to assist drivers in properly using the system as the manufacturer expects. Manufacturers and other entities should assume that the technical distinction between the levels of automation (e.g. between Level 2 and Level 3) may not be clear to all users or to the general public. Manufacturers and other entities should develop tests, validation, and verification methods to assess their systems for effective complacency and misuse countermeasures."

## Synthesis

The two cases highlight the dangers of an autocratic, hierarchical business structure which focuses on compliance rather than values. There is little opportunity to raise objections and share concerns about operational directions. Staff development regarding social values is likely to be limited. The nature of software impact is likely to be misunderstood and underestimated.

Addressing safety-critical software is problematic in these business structures. In the fluid environment of application software, practice and process rapidly change. For safety-critical software McDermid and Kelly (2006) recommend a range of approaches for software safety rather than applying dogmatically a standard prescriptive approach. This would promote a wider range of safety-critical software than the current traditional areas. In support of this, the autocratic hierarchical business structure would need to be replaced by a more democratic, flat business structure.

Public acceptance of safety-critical software is promoted through debate and transparency. In this way, the ethical issues which impact public acceptance can be analysed and addressed. For example, the *Federal Automated Vehicles Policy* (2016) recommends, "Manufacturers and other entities, working cooperatively with regulators and other stakeholders (e.g. drivers, passengers and vulnerable road users), should address these situations to ensure that such ethical judgments and decisions are made consciously and intentionally."

The ethical behaviour of those involved in software development greatly influences the nature of the end product. Moral courage is needed to raise concerns in the face of business pressure. Those involved include business managers, technical managers and software engineers. It is useful to describe systematically the underpinning individual ethical ideology because this helps in the understanding of judgement and action. Forsyth (1980) suggests a taxonomy of ethical ideologies which is summarised in Figure 16.2. There are two dimensions; the first being the degree an individual accepts universal moral rules and the second being the degree of idealism. It appears that there is a tendency for those, including software engineers, involved in the two case studies to lie within the subjectivist quadrant focusing on what is right for the company at the expense of everything else. This is problematic and a challenge to establishing professional integrity within software engineering.

| Idealism | Relativism | |
|---|---|---|
| | High | Low |
| High | Situationists<br><br>• Rejects moral rules<br>• Advocates individualistic analysisof each act in each situation<br>• Relativistic | Absolutists<br><br>• Assumes that the best possible outcomes can always be achieved by following moral rules |
| Low | Subjectivists<br><br>• Appraisals based on personal values and perspectives rather than universal moral principles<br>• Relativistic | Exceptionists<br><br>• Moral absolutes guide judgements but pragmatically open to exceptions to these standards<br>• Utilitarian |

**Figure 16.2   Taxonomy of ethical ideologies. (Source: Forsyth [1980, p. 176])**

# Conclusions

Of the two cases discussed in this chapter Volkswagen concerns illegal actions and Tesla concerns legal ones but both concern unethical actions. There are serious issues related to professional practice which need to be addressed. It is hoped such issues are exceptional but sadly it is likely they are commonplace. Unethical actions related to software engineering can be addressed from two sides of application software development. One side focuses on resisting the temptation to perform unethical practice whilst the other side focuses on reducing the opportunity of performing unethical practice. Recommendations are either reactive where the measure is in response to a particular event or circumstance or proactive where the measure is an attempt to promote desired future behaviour. This approach is illustrated in Figure 16.3 as a matrix containing some examples of typical measures.

In the proactive side-two quadrant, Plant (2015) suggests the US government should create a framework, an ombudsman role and safe harbor legislation in order to promote the ethically challenged software industry. In the proactive side-one quadrant new software engineering graduates should have the ethical tools, skills and confidence to challenge decisions made by and instructions from their seniors where such actions from these senior staff are ethically questionable. Such challenge should be capable without detrimental impact on these junior members of staff.

Bowen (2000) suggests a strategy across the complete matrix which is pertinent to base case studies. He states, "it is unethical to develop software for safety-related systems without following the best practice available. All software engineers and managers wishing to produce safety-critical systems in a professional manner should ensure they have the right training and skills for the task. They should be able to speak out without fear of undue repercussions if they feel a system is impossible or dangerous to develop. It is important that companies, universities, standards bodies, professional institutions, governments, and all those with an interest in the well-being of society at large ensure that appropriate mechanisms are in place to help achieve this aim."

So is professional practice at risk following the Volkswagen and Tesla Motors revelations? The short answer is definitely yes unless software engineers are capable and willing to identify the ethical challenges in software being developed, have the confidence to articulate identified ethical risks, and have the opportunity to influence key decision-makers about these ethical risks.

|  | SIDE ONE | SIDE TWO |
|---|---|---|
|  | Resist the temptation to perform unethical practice | Reduce the opportunity of performing unethical practice |
| REACTIVE | • Issue fines and other penalties for unethical practice<br>• Rewards and recognition for good practice | • Replacing senior decision makers who have line responsibility for those involved in unethical practice |
| PROACTIVE | • Education and Training programmes<br>• Mandatory ethics committees associated with operational actions | • Regulation and policies frameworks<br>• Public awareness programmes which generate public pressure |

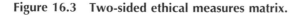

**Figure 16.3  Two-sided ethical measures matrix.**

# References

Bonnefon, J., Shariff, A. & Rahwan, I. (2016). The social dilemma of autonomous vehicles. *Science*, 35(24 June), 1573–1576.

Bowen, J. (2000). The ethics of safety-critical systems. *Communications of the ACM*, 43(4), 91–97.

Bynum, T. W. (2004). Ethical Decision-Making and Case Analysis in Computer Ethics. In: Bynum, T. W. & Rogerson, S. (eds.), *Computer Ethics and Professional Responsibility*. Blackwell Publishing, pp. 60–86.

Forsyth, D. R. (1980). A taxonomy of ethical ideologies. *Journal of Personality and Social Psychology*, 39(1), 175–184.

Goodall, N. J. (2014). Ethical Decision Making During Automated Vehicle Crashes. *Transportation Research Record*, 2424, 58–65.

Gotterbarn, D., Miller, K. & Rogerson, S., (1999). Software Engineering Code of Ethics is Approved. *Communications of the ACM*. 42(10), 102–107 and *Computer*. Oct, 84–89.

ISTQB. (2017). *What is beta testing?* Available from http://istqbexamcertification.com/what-is-beta-testing/ (Accessed 14 January 2017).

Jaynes, N. (2016). Tesla is the only carmaker beta testing 'autopilot' tech, and that's a problem. *MashableUK*. 9 July. Available from http://mashable.com/2016/07/09/tesla-beta-testing-autopilot-on-public/#dbKporN3uaqT. (Accessed 20 July 2016).

Lambert, F. (2016). *A fatal Tesla Autopilot accident prompts an evaluation by NHTSA. Electrek*. 30 June. Available from https://electrek.co/2016/06/30/tesla-autopilot-fata-crash-nhtsa-investigation/ (Accessed 20 July 2016).

Leggett, T. (2017). *VW papers shed light on emissions scandal*. BBC News, 12 January. Available from http://www.bbc.co.uk/news/business-38603723 (Accessed 17 January 2017).

Lin, P. (2013). The Ethics of Autonomous Cars. *The Atlantic*. 8 October. Available from https://www.theatlantic.com/technology/archive/2013/10/the-ethics-of-autonomous-cars/280360/ (Accessed 20 July 2016).

Mansouri, N. (2016). A Case Study of Volkswagen Unethical Practice in Diesel Emission Test. *International Journal of Science and Engineering Applications*, 5(4), 211–216.

McBride, N. K. (2016). The ethics of driverless cars. *ACM SIGCAS Computers and Society*, 45(3), 179–184.

McDermid, J. & Kelly, T. (2006). Software in safety critical systems: achievement and prediction. *Nuclear Future*, 2(3), 140–146.

Merkel, R. (2015). Where were the whistleblowers in the Volkswagen emissions scandal?. *The Conversation*. 30 September. Available from https://theconversation.com/where-were-the-whistleblowers-in-the-volkswagen-emissions-scandal-48249 (Accessed 14 September 2016).

NHTSA (2017). *The Automatic Emergency Braking (AEB) or Autopilot systems may not function as designed, increasing the risk of a crash*. Final Report, Investigation: PE 16-007.

Plant, R. (2015). A Software Engineer Reflects on the VW Scandal. *The Wall Street Journal*. 15 October. Available from http://blogs.wsj.com/experts/2015/10/16/a-software-engineer-reflects-on-the-vw-scandal/ (Accessed 15 January 2017).

Queen, E. L. (2015). How could VW be so dumb? Blame the unethical culture endemic in business. *The Conversation*. 26 September. Available from https://theconversation.com/how-could-vw-be-so-dumb-blame-the-unethical-culture-endemic-in-business-48137 (Accessed 15 September 2016).

Ragatz, J. A., (2015). What Can We Learn from the Volkswagen Scandal?. *Faculty Publications*. Paper 297. Available from http://digitalcommons.theamericancollege.edu/faculty/297 (Accessed 6 September 2016).

Rhodes, C. (2016). Democratic Business Ethics: Volkswagen's emissions scandal and the disruption of corporate sovereignty. *Organization Studies*, 37(10), 1501–1518.

Roberts, J. (2016). What is Tesla Autopilot? Tesla's driving assist feature explained. *Trusted Reviews*. 14 July. Available from http://www.trustedreviews.com/opinions/what-is-tesla-autopilot (Accessed 20 July 2016).

Rufford N. & Tobin, D. (2016). Who is to blame for dieselgate? Driving tracks down the engineers and asks, could the scandal really destroy VW?. *Sunday Times Driving*. 7 March. Available from https://www.driving.co.uk/news/who-is-to-blame-for-dieselgate-driving-tracks-down-the-engineers-and-asks-could-the-scandal-really-destroy-vw/ (Accessed 15 January 2017).

SAE International (2014). *Taxonomy and Definitions for Terms Related to On-Road Motor Vehicle Automated Driving Systems: Standard J3106.* issued 16 January.

Simonite, T. (2016). Tesla Tests Self-Driving Functions with Secret Updates to Its Customers' Cars. *MIT Technology Review*, 24 May. Available from https://www.technologyreview.com/s/601567/tesla-tests-self-driving-functions-with-secret-updates-to-its-customers-cars/?utm_campaign=add_this&utm_source=email&utm_medium=post (Accessed 21 January 2017).

Solon, O. (2016). Should Tesla be 'beta testing' autopilot if there is a chance someone might die?. *The Guardian*. 6 July. Available from https://www.theguardian.com/technology/2016/jul/06/tesla-autopilot-fatal-crash-public-beta-testing (Accessed 14 January 2017).

Tesla (2010) *Code of Business Conduct and Ethics.* Adopted by the Board of Directors on May 20, 2010.

US Department of Justice (2017). Volkswagen AG Agrees to Plead Guilty and Pay $4.3 Billion in Criminal and Civil Penalties and Six Volkswagen Executives and Employees Are Indicted in Connection with Conspiracy to Cheat U.S. Emissions Tests. *Justice News.* 11 January. Available from https://www.justice.gov/opa/pr/volkswagen-ag-agrees-plead-guilty-and-pay-43-billion-criminal-and-civil-penalties-six (Accessed 15 January 2017).

US Department of Transportation (2016). *Federal Automated Vehicles Policy: Accelerating the Next Revolution In Roadway Safety.* September, 12507–102616-v10a, DOT HS 812 329.

Volkswagen (2010). *The Volkswagen Group Code of Conduct.* Available from http://en.volkswagen.com/content/medialib/vwd4/de/Volkswagen/Nachhaltigkeit/service/download/corporate_governance/Code_of_Conduct/_jcr_content/renditions/rendition.file/the-volkswagen-group-code-of-conduct.pdf (Accessed 28 January 2017).

# Chapter 17

# The Dangers of Dual-Use Technology: A Thought Experiment Exposé [2019]*

## Introduction

According to the European Commission (see https://ec.europa.eu/trade/import-and-export-rules/ export-from-eu/dual-use-controls/index_en.htm), "Dual-use items are goods, software and technology that can be used for both civilian and military applications. The EU controls the export, transit and brokering of dual-use items so the EU can contribute to international peace and security and prevent the proliferation of Weapons of Mass Destruction (WMD)." However, the effectiveness of such controls has been questioned. The Editor-in-Chief of Communications of the ACM, Andrew Chien (2019) explains that because computing is now a dual-use technology with capability for direct aggression there needs to be a change in how such potential is identified, monitored and controlled. He writes that, "[we] must begin the difficult conversations of how to shape the development and use of technologies so that they can be a responsible and accountable force in society." What is even more problematic is the less obvious dual-use technology where alternative unacceptable use is discovered and exploited after the technology has become widely available. To illustrate this increasingly problematic situation, this chapter uses thought experiments to explore the potential dangers of dual-use technology and how these dangers increase as technology evolves in complexity, capability and reach.

Brown and Fehige (2014) explain that *thought experiments* are used to investigate the nature of things through one's imagination. Usually they are communicated through narratives and accompanying diagrams. Brown and Fehige state that, "Thought experiments should be distinguished from thinking about experiments, from merely imagining any experiments to be conducted outside the imagination, and from psychological experiments with thoughts. They should also be distinguished from counterfactual reasoning in general, …". This approach can be used to explore the possible dangers of dual-use of technological advances that could occur in

---

* This is an unpublished paper. Copyright © Simon Rogerson.

the absence of effective ethical scrutiny. In this chapter two thought experiments are used to acquire new knowledge about the dangers of Free and Open-Source Software (FOSS) components which could have dual usage in the context of a fictitious system, *Open Genocide*. It is an investigation which cannot use empirical data as this would require the actual and immoral construction of a system of annihilation.

## The Reality in Nazi Germany

These thought experiments are grounded in the Holocaust enacted by the Nazis. This is pertinent because over 75 years ago on 27 January 1945 the Nazi Concentration and Extermination Camp of Auschwitz-Birkenau was liberated. By the end of the war some six million Jews and many millions of Poles, gypsies, prisoners of war, homosexuals, mentally and physically handicapped individuals, and Jehovah's Witnesses had been murdered. The historical account of human suffering is sickeningly shocking but alongside this is the realisation of evil brilliance, not mindless thuggery, that orchestrated the *Final Solution* (a Nazi euphemism for the plan to exterminate the Jews of Europe).

The *Final Solution* had its foundations in medieval "Racist pseudo-scientific antisemitism …. which understood Jews as a biological infection to the social body." (Hirsh, 2007, p. 19). The Scientific Management Principles (Taylor, 1911) promote efficiency in an industrial process. Such principles appear central to the attempted extermination of a race using the abhorrent industrial processes at Auschwitz and Birkenau. For example, on 7 March 1946, testimony of engineer Fritz Sander (1946) states, "I decided to design and build a crematorium with a higher capacity. I completed this project of a new crematorium in November 1942 – a crematorium for mass incineration, and I submitted this project to a State Patent Commission in Berlin. This "Krema" [crematorium] was to be built on the conveyor belt principle. That is to say, the corpses must be brought to the incineration furnaces without interruption. When the corpses are pushed into the furnaces, they fall onto a grate, and then slide into the furnace and are incinerated. The corpses serve at the same time as fuel for heating of the furnaces. This patent could not yet be approved by the Main Patent Office in Berlin, because of its classification (as a state secret). I was a German engineer and key member of the [Ludwig] Topf works and I saw it as my duty to apply my specialist knowledge in this way to help Germany win the war, just as an aircraft construction engineer builds airplanes in wartime, which are also connected with the destruction of human beings." This is an engineer's dereliction of duty to society and humankind in order to satisfy the cynical aspirations of the fanatical few. It contravenes every subsequent Code of Ethics adopted by professional bodies associated with engineering of all types.

Edwin Black (2002) gave a detailed account of how IBM assisted Nazi Germany. At the time IBM's business was electromechanical tabulating machines designed to process information stored on punch cards. First used to process census data these machines were widely used for business applications. They heralded the dawn of the data processing industry and were the forerunner to computers. Without such automation it would have been impossible to identify all members of the Jewish population so they could all be "targeted for asset confiscation, ghettoisation, deportation, and ultimately extermination" (Black, 2012). Dehomag, IBM's German subsidiary developed a racial census-listing which recorded religious affiliation and ancestral bloodlines. On 17 May 1939, the quickest and most thorough population census took place. Within months a complete profile of Jewish existence in the Greater Reich had been compiled (Black, 2002, p. 217). Over time people registration, asset registration, food allocation, slave labour records, human transport consignments were all administered using tabulators and punch cards (Black, 2012). Every camp operated a Hollerith department with IBM sorters, tabulators and printers to input, process and output data. The applications included inmate profiles, new arrivals registers, death lists, slave labour "strength numbers," work allocations and transport schedules to the gas chambers (Black, 2002, pp. 45–48). "IBM had almost single-handedly brought modern warfare into the information age" (Black, 2002, p. 265).

Data coding was the foundation of the system. Those detained were not referred to by name but by a unique 5 or 6 digit number and an associated 3 digit camp identity (Black, 2002, p. 448). Each prisoner was classified, for example, 1 for political, 3 for homosexual and 8 for Jew (Black, 2002, p. 462). It was the 5 or 6 digit number which followed inmates to their death. In order to keep meticulous records of the journey to death the numbers were eventually tattooed on inmates' arms. Auschwitz inmate, Lale Sokolov became the head tattooist and, with his assistants, dispensed numbers to all inmates of Auschwitz and its sub-camps, Birkenau and Monowitz; the only camps where this practice took place (Prasad, 2018).

# First Thought Experiment 2006

On a bitterly cold day in February 2006, the author (Simon Rogerson) was quietly standing looking at the building which housed the gas chamber at Auschwitz. He reflected on the evil brilliance which had facilitated the *Final Solution.* He wondered what might have happened if the computer technology of 2006 had been available to the Nazis. It was a consideration which resonated with *Would you sell a computer to Hitler* by Nadel & Wiener (1977). On returning home he completed the first thought experiment which was subsequently published (Rogerson, 2006).

Technological Determinism argues that technology is the force which shapes society. Computing power would therefore be a major force in activating the *Final Solution.* Value Chain Analysis Porter (1985) is one way to consider the impact of this force. Indeed Porter and Millar (1985, p. 151) wrote, "Information technology is permeating the value chain at every point, transforming the way value activities are performed and the nature of the linkages among them …. information technology has acquired strategic significance and is different from the many other technologies businesses use." Here are just a few examples related to the *Final Solution.* These examples are based on computer application systems that existed in 2006 and which were proven and accepted. The narrative discusses some of the Value Chain components whilst the diagram in Figure 17.1 provides illustrative examples for all components.

## *Inbound Logistics: The Receiving and Warehousing of Raw Materials and Their Distribution to the Industrial Process as They are Required*

- Computerised transportation scheduling can minimise cost and ensure timely delivery to the points of industrial process. Humans are the raw material of this particular industrial process. Scheduling would enable enormous numbers of humans to be moved across occupied Europe in an efficient and timely manner. The effective flow of raw materials is a key factor in computerised industrial processes such as just-in-time manufacturing. The arrival of humans could be controlled by calculating transportation routes and speed so that there was a steady flow which did not overwhelm the camps or the industrial process. Rerouting and readjustment of speed could be triggered by "production data" being communicated electronically from the camps and associated industrial processes.

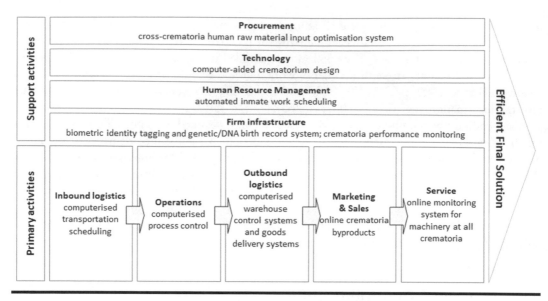

**Figure 17.1   Indicative examples across the *Final Solution* Value Chain.**

## Operations: The Processes of Transforming Inputs into Finished Products and Services

- Computerised process control is a method for maximising throughput, minimising disruption, and facilitating non-stop processing. The input flows of both human and chemical raw materials of the gas chambers could be fully automated to increase throughput. Once dead, humans need to be moved. The use of robotic devices would enable mounds of corpses to be loaded on to computerised conveyor belts which would route bodies to the next available furnace. This process would be endless. Automatically controlling the flow of corpses would open the possibility of secondary processes that are alternatives to cremation. For example, the element phosphorus is relatively rare in nature yet it is of vital importance to life. Bone meal is often used as a supplement for calcium and phosphorus through, for example, fertilisers. What would stop the *Final Solution* having two outcomes cremation and fertiliser manufacture?

## Outbound Logistics: The Warehousing and Distribution of Finished Goods

- The sorting of personal possessions, reuse of personal possessions and the recycling of materials could be facilitated by computerised warehouse control systems and goods delivery systems.

## The Infrastructure: Organisational Structure and Control Systems

- The annihilation of sectors of the population can only succeed if it is founded on meticulous record-keeping which identifies and tracks every member of a given sector. This is a manual impossibility but with computers is alarmingly easy. The linking of biometric identity tagging with genetic/DNA birth records provides the means to identify anyone. An individual's identification and location in computerised form enables inbound logistics and operations to identify and use all desired humans. Some could be redirected to slave labour camps before becoming the raw material of the *Final Solution* industrial process.

## Second Thought Experiment 2018

There has been a 12-year gap since the first thought experiment. Technology has evolved at a seemingly increasing pace. Indeed, "In the not-too-distant future with the cloud, big data, and maybe 80–90% of the world's population online and connected the scope for systems of oppression seems limitless. Consequently, we must consider and counter what oppressive regimes of tomorrow's world could and might do in their drive to subjugate humankind" (Rogerson, 2015, p. 4). The opportunity to harness this advance for *Open Genocide* exists. Imagine a world where all software is available as free open source. It might seem improbable, but it is possible. If it were so, the wherewithal to exploit every technological advance for any cause, albeit good or bad, would exist. The scene is set for *Open Genocide* brutally to further the cause of an extreme faction at the expense of the world at large and "destroy in whole or in part, a national, ethnical, racial or religious group" (United Nations, 1948). *Open Genocide* would comprise seven components:

1. Identify: Systematically review the whole geographic region to identify every person within the targeted group as well as every sympathiser of this group.
2. Detain: Organise the detention of all identified persons in distributed holding pounds. Each detainee is appropriately tagged.
3. Deport: Manage the distribution and redistribution of detainees to work compounds and prisons.
4. Use: Select detainees exhibiting work value for allocation to appropriate tasks.
5. Dispose: Remove to disposal units all valueless or dead detainees thereby freeing up space in prisons and work compounds.
6. Recycle: Collect, sort, recycle and market all seized assets. Produce and market detainee by-products.
7. Broadcast: Devise plausible propaganda for local and international audiences and communicate widely.

The pervasive nature of current computing technology facilitates all components of *Open Genocide*. This is illustrated in Figure 17.2 as three layers. The first level is the geographical boundary of the territory where the targeted population resides. The second level is the pervasive computing technology infrastructure stretching beyond the geographical boundary. Finally, the third level is the *Open Genocide* human activity system which integrates technological functionality with human endeavour in pursuit of a single mission.

Typical technological advances which could be used include the following:

- Microchip implants: an identifying integrated circuit placed under the skin of an animal using passive RFID which remains inert until powered by a scanner.
- CCTV, webcams and image recognition: electronic surveillance devices which monitor behaviour, activities, or other changing information for the purpose of influencing, managing, directing, or protecting people.

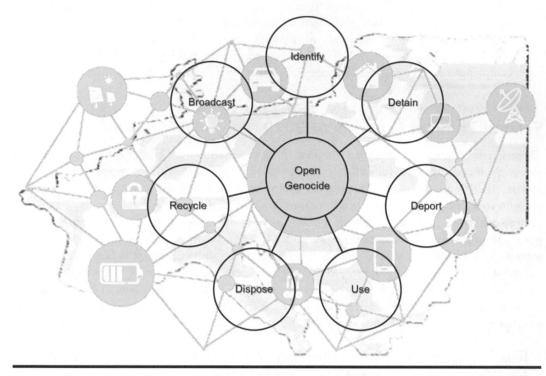

**Figure 17.2 Pervasive *Open Genocide* enabled through technology.**

- Industrial robots: an automatically controlled, reprogrammable, multipurpose manipulator capable of undertaking most manufacturing tasks on a continuous basis.
- Social Bots: automatic software posing as humans which is employed to generate messages or promote certain ideas, support campaigns and public relations.
- GPS location tracking technology: provides extremely accurate location information for mobile objects and people.
- Web crawler: automatic software browses the World Wide Web in a methodical, automated manner searching for particular information which can subsequently be sorted and indexed.
- Internet of Things: a network of physical objects which are embedded with electronics, software, sensors, actuators and connectivity that enables such objects to connect and exchange data.
- Big Data: extremely large data sets which can be analysed to reveal patterns, trends and associations, especially relating to human behaviour and interactions.
- Drone: a flying robot which can fly autonomously through software-controlled flight plans working in conjunction with embedded sensors and GPS.

A cursory inspection of two open source portals, *SourceForge* and *The Black Duck Open Hub* reveals many useful items for the construction of *Open Genocide*. Here are just a few examples of software which might prove useful. *Openbravo Business Suite* is a cloud-based technology platform which enables organisations to operate effectively and efficiently across geographically dispersed locations. It utilises ERP (Enterprise Resource Planning) which integrates and manages all financial, supply chain, manufacturing, operations, reporting, and human resources activities. *InnovaSPY* is a spy application which enables tracking of smartphones in real time.

*AI-TRIP* produces the quickest and cheapest optimal routes between given start and destination points using trains and buses. *Flyingros* is a fully-functional operating systems for drone applications. Finally, *Pösnatch* is a semantic web application for social networking, word-of-mouth analysis and person profiling, and includes a web crawler and an inference engine.

Open source portals can be used to host projects. This facilitates ongoing development, testing and sharing which could be exploited covertly for *Open Genocide* through the creation of three euphemistic, fictitious projects: pandemic emergency management, administration of residential care for the infirm and hazardous waste disposal. The open-source population would contribute to these seemingly legitimate projects. The dual-use principle enables a sinister alternate system, for once merged, the three projects would form the foundation of *Open Genocide.*

## Concluding Remarks

These thought experiments might be shocking to many readers. That is their intention. It seems that if the Holocaust had occurred in our technologically-advanced modern world there is a very good chance that it would have completely succeeded. If ever there was an example to convince computing professionals, as custodians of the most powerful technology yet devised, of their responsibilities and obligations to humankind, this is it. To the narrow-minded technologist, akin to Fritz Sander, who seems intent on viewing the world as a computer playground where anything is possible and everything is acceptable, it is time to act with professional responsibility.

There needs to be a radical change in how the ethical and social responsibility dimension of ICT is included in education of the whole population rather than focusing on the elitist computing professional community. It is against this backdrop that this chapter explores new avenues for widening education, both formal and informal, to all those who may become involved in computing. The discussion concludes by laying out a new pathway for ICT ethics education which embraces people of all ages and all walks of life.

Remember, "All that is necessary for the triumph of evil is that good [people] do nothing" (sometimes attributed to Edmund Burke), but the good need to be aware of the dangers of dual-use before they can act. It is therefore imperative that we "make every effort to improve public awareness, strengthen intellectual defences, in a word, educate – because people are not born anti-Semitic, people are not born racist, they become so" (Azoulay, 2020).

## References

Azoulay, A. (2020). Message from Ms Audrey Azoulay, Director-General of UNESCO, on the occasion of the International Day of Commemoration in Memory of the Victims of the Holocaust, 27 January 2020. Available from: https://unesdoc.unesco.org/ark:/48223/pf0000372570_eng (accessed July 2019).

Black, E. (2002). *IBM and the Holocaust*. London, Time Warner Paperbacks.

Black, E. (2012). *The Nazi Party: IBM & "Death's Calculator"*. Jewish Virtual Library. Available from: http://www.jewishvirtuallibrary.org/ibm-and-quot-death-s-calculator-quot-2, extracts from Black, E. (2012) IBM and the Holocaust: The Strategic Alliance between Nazi Germany and America's Most Powerful Corporation. Expanded Edition, Dialog Press, Washington, DC. (accessed July 2019).

Brown, J. R. & Fehige, Y. (2014). Thought Experiments. First published Sat Dec 28, 1996; substantive revision Tue Aug 12, 2014. In: Zalta, E. N. (ed.) (2017) *The Stanford Encyclopedia of Philosophy* (Summer 2017 Edition). Available from: https://plato.stanford.edu/archives/sum2017/entries/thought-experiment/ (accessed 20 December 2020).

Chien, A. A. (2019). Open collaboration in an age of distrust. *Communications of the ACM*. 62(1), 5.

Hirsh, D. (2007). Anti-Zionism and Antisemitism: Cosmopolitan Reflections. Working Paper. Yale Initiative for the Interdisciplinary Study of Antisemitism (YIISA) Occasional Papers, New Haven, CT.

Nadel, L. & Wiener, H. (1977). Would you sell a computer to Hitler?. *Computer Decisions*. 28, 22–27.

Porter, M. E. (1985). *Competitive Advantage: Creating and Sustaining Superior Performance*. New York, The Free Press.

Porter, M.E. & Millar, V. E. (1985). How information gives you competitive advantage. *Harvard Business Review*. 63(4), 149–160.

Prasad, R. (2018). The Tattooist of Auschwitz - and his secret love. 8 January. Available from: http://www.bbc.co.uk/news/stories-42568390 (accessed July 2019).

Rogerson, S. (2006). ETHIcol – a lesson from Auschwitz. *IMIS Journal*. 16(2), 29–30.

Rogerson, S. (2015). *The ETHICOMP Odyssey: 1995 to 2015*. Self-published on www.researchgate.net, 12 September. Available from: doi: 10.13140/RG.2.1.2660.1444. (accessed July 2019).

Sander, F. (1946). Quoted in: *Testimony of Crematorium Engineers*. Available from: https://fcit.usf.edu/holocaust/resource/document/DocTest1.htm (accessed July 2019).

Taylor, F. W. (1911). Principles and methods of scientific management. *Journal of Accountancy*. 12(2), 117–124.

United Nations (1948). *Convention on the Prevention and Punishment of the Crime of Genocide*. 9 December.

*Chapter 18*

# Grey Digital Outcasts and COVID-19 [2020]<sup>*</sup>

## Introduction

Much has been, is being and will be written about the ramifications of the COVID-19 pandemic. Within this body of knowledge will be many valuable insights and discoveries. This chapter aims to contribute to this resource by considering the relationship between the pandemic and digital technology with a specific focus on the elderly who are acknowledged as being the most vulnerable group in this global health emergency.

The world has changed. The social glue has come unstuck and we have turned to technology to allow us to live and keep us connected (Rogerson 2020b). Communication channels provide information about the latest developments, advice and restrictions. Social media keeps social groups and families emotionally together. Online outlets provide the products and services we need in our everyday lives. For digital natives, the move to the virtual is plausible and possibly pleasurable but for digital outcasts the move is fraught and frequently frightening.

Throughout history, there have always been social divides predicated upon, for example, poverty, education, gender and status. With increasing technological global dependency, the digital divide has become one of the most significant social divides of our time. This has been acknowledged for many years. For example, in 2000 the UK saw an increasing number of digital natives which, at the time, was forecasted to rise to 60% of the total population by 2003 but with only 20% of the elderly using the Internet (Booz Allen and Hamilton, 2000). "However, far from evening out the emerging inequalities, the wave of growth is likely to exacerbate them in relative terms, leaving an unconnected or excluded group of over 20 million citizens" (Ibid).

Today, technological advancement continues to accelerate and so the digital divide is likely to become more acute with every passing day (Rogerson 2020a). One reason for this is the fact that many in government and industry promote the myth that societal wellbeing and prosperity is achieved through the move to digital-technology-based information, services, and facilities with

---

<sup>*</sup> This chapter was first published as: Rogerson, S. (2020) Grey Digital Outcasts and COVID-19. Conditionally accepted for publication in American Behavioral Scientist Copyright © SAGE Publications. Reprinted by permission.

the imposition of these on the whole population without any opportunity of alternative choices. For example, a Pew Research report states, "Digital tools will continue to be integrated into daily life to help the most vulnerable and isolated who need services, care, and support."[1] As Thornham (2013) explains that there is political tendency to shift from "digital when appropriate" to "digital by default," which makes assumptions about digital literacy levels and puts safety and security at risk. The perceived over-reliance on digital technology has spawned the concept of digital detox. Syvertsen and Enli (2020) explain, "Digital detox is a reaction to the experience of being temporally overloaded and invaded, trapped in a superficial, narcissistic and fabricated space, needing strategies to improve health and mindful presence."

According to the World Health Organisation (WHO), "COVID-19 is the infectious disease caused by the most recently discovered coronavirus. This new virus and disease were unknown before the outbreak began in Wuhan, China, in December 2019. COVID-19 is now a pandemic affecting many countries globally. People can catch COVID-19 from others who have the virus. The disease spreads primarily from person to person through small droplets from the nose or mouth, which are expelled when a person with COVID-19 coughs, sneezes, or speaks. These droplets are relatively heavy, do not travel far and quickly sink to the ground. People can catch COVID-19 if they breathe in these droplets or touch objects or surfaces where these droplets are located and then touch their eyes, nose or mouth."[2] WHO's advice to the elderly states,[3] "Inform yourself of the special measures taken in your community as well as the services and the sources of reliable information that are available during the health emergency (e.g. home deliveries, psychosocial support, health ministry website, alternative access to your pension)." The implication is that online channels are the primary sources of information and support. There appears to be a huge assumption that the whole of the elderly population will have access to these online channels. Rapid access to information and support is vital in protecting people against this rampant pandemic. There is no acknowledgment of grey digital outcasts who cannot access online channels and thus become even more vulnerable.

This chapter continues by first explaining the heuristic approach taken in an attempt to capture and interpret data about the rapidly changing pandemic landscape. It then moves on to define the terminology used for the digital population culminating in a discussion about the elderly. A world view of the pandemic, together with the use and value of digital technology, is undertaken through snapshots of ten countries. These snapshots are used to tease out common themes, which in turn, provide pointers as to actions that might be undertaken to alleviate the grey digital divide. The chapter concludes with comments concerning the interrelationship between the pandemic and the grey digital divide.

## Approach

The heuristic approach has been adopted which aligns with the four rules laid out by Kleining and Witt (2000). This is because the dynamic nature of the pandemic meant that preconceptions were problematic, outcomes of the crisis kept changing, people's differing and contradictory views evolved. The overall aim of this study was to try to identify some commonalities.

The chapter draws upon significant existing literature that addresses the issue of the digital divide and the smaller subset that focuses on impacts on the elderly. However, given the dynamic nature of the pandemic, it was necessary to access new information as it became available. This was a challenge since later information sometimes contradicted previous information. It is recognised that both subjectivity and objectivity exist in this information and that it is hard to verify the integrity of some information. A range of sources has been used to gather relevant information. Newspaper and television reports were collected and analysed over the period of the pandemic up to the point of writing. Personal contacts in various countries have shared their observations on national situations as well as supplying relevant local information. A short qualitative questionnaire was used in Japan, the UK, and the USA to collect the views of a small sample of people, mainly over 65 years of age. The views expressed were divided into positive and negative opinions concerning the current situation as well as future ramifications.

The use or non-use of digital technology has been differentiated by a simple three-part classification: *no-tech* – print media, written letters and face to face dialogue; *low-tech* – television, radio and telephone; and *high-tech* – smartphone, social media and Internet.

Quantitative measures were gathered from a range of national and international sources. These measures provide an indication of the size and seriousness of the existence of a digital divide at the time of a pandemic.

# Digital Technology Players

In this study, the population is classified and grouped according to digital technology usage. It is, therefore, necessary to define the terms used. In this context, it should be noted that demographic profile includes age, gender, ethnicity, faith, literacy and economic status.

## *Digital Divide*

Norris (2001) explains that the digital divide comprises every disparity within the online community. Fuchs (2008) suggests this disparity relates the ability to access, usage capability, and gained benefit not only related to the online world but also to all information and communication technologies. Therefore, this chapter uses the term to describe the disparity in access, usage and benefit of any digital technology.

## *Digital Native*

Selwyn (2009) argues convincingly that the term digital native is problematic as it describes distinct technological cultures and lifestyles of emerging generations of young people. This chapter uses the term *Digital Native* to describe the digitally literate, regardless of demographic profile, who use, and are somewhat dependent upon, digital technology.

## *Digital Outcast*

Wagner (2011) suggests that digital outcasts have been granted overt access to digital technologies but are not equipped with the skills, the finance, or the critical acumen to access the transformative capacities of such technologies. Isaacs (2011) further suggests that these are people born in the information age and will suffer economic, political and social exclusion through being outcasts. This chapter uses the term *Digital Outcast* to describe those, regardless of demographic profile, who are unable, for whatever reason, to access the benefits offered through the use of digital technologies.

## The Elderly

It is commonly accepted that "the elderly" refers to those in the population who are 65 years and older (see, for example, Netuveli and Blane (2008) and Vaccaro et al. (2019)). However, there are alternative views. Muiser and Carrin (2007) explain that in sub-Saharan Africa, it is commonplace to consider old as greater than 50 years. In the developed world, subcategories of "younger," "older" and "oldest old" are sometimes used when considering the needs and capabilities of the elderly (Ibid). For this chapter, it is necessary to ground the term elderly in digital technology. The first computer in a British school was installed in 1965 (Fothergill, 1989). It took a further 15 years of technological advance and government funding before critical mass in school-based computers was achieved which, in turn, heralded the birth of educational computing (Gardner and McMullan, 1990). In the US, between 1966 and 1971 the use of computers in high schools quadrupled (Anon, 1971). In 1975, Apple started donating Apple 1 computers to schools. The combination of technological and educational evolution in the 1970s was pivotal.

Those leaving school before that time are likely to (and often do) have a very different view of digital technology to those exposed to digital technology in their formative years (Rogerson, 2008). Therefore, this chapter uses the term *Elderly* to mean anyone of 65 years and over. Older people are often referred to as *grey* to differentiate them as a population group; hence *grey digital divide* is now a commonly used term. Given the focus on the chapter is the relationship between COVID-19 and digital technology usage by the elderly, it is appropriate to use new terms *Grey Digital Native* and *Grey Digital Outcast* to describe the elderly positioned on either side of the grey digital divide.

The grey digital native concept is explored at length by Birkland (2019). A user typology of five types is proposed comprising Enthusiast, Practicalist, Socialiser, Traditionalist and Guardian. The first three types are accepting of modern digital technology whereas the latter two prefer older technologies and are wary of the modern ubiquitous advance. Birkland supports the observation of Van Dijk (2005) that the elderly move between native and outcast depending upon the mental, physical, financial and motivational circumstances.

## Global Perspective

The statistics used globally and for each country are taken from the WHO COVID-19 dashboard[4] unless otherwise stated. At the time of writing, globally, the total cumulative cases of COVID-19 were 15,785,641 and the total cumulative deaths were 640,016. In Europe, it has been found that 94% of fatalities are uniformly concentrated in the population over 60 years of age.[5] On 25 March it was reported by the BBC that one-quarter of the world's population was living under some form of lockdown. Armitage and Nellums (2020) explain that self-isolation will disproportionality affect the elderly because of increased risk of cardiovascular, autoimmune, neurocognitive, and mental health problems.

It is estimated that 9% of the global population of 7.8 billion people are over 65 years of age.[6] Current access to the Internet stands at 62% of the global population[7] and of this 7% (0.3385 billion) are over 65 years of age.[8] This means that only 48% of the global population over the age of 65 years of age can be classified as grey digital natives. Therefore, the grey digital divide comprises 363.5 million digital outcasts. The global distribution of these outcasts will likely mirror disparities between developed and developing regions, urban and rural, rich and poor, and literate and illiterate people. By way of illustration, out of the total global digital outcast population, 27% reside in Africa, 31% in Southern Asia, and 19% in Eastern Asia.[9]

The global Internet economy has been defined as comprising three components: access provision – how we connect; service infrastructure - how we build and sustain the Internet; and Internet Applications - how we communicate, share and innovate.[10] During the pandemic, the performance of these components has been mixed. For example, video conferencing through portals such as Zoom has provided excellent links for digital natives although "zoom burnout" has become a new phenomenon. However, broadband in rural areas has significantly reduced the ability for reaching out to the elderly in those areas.

## UK Perspective

At the time of writing, for the UK the total cumulative cases of COVID-19 was 299,426 and the total cumulative deaths were 45,752.[11] Of these reported cases, 30.28% (90,666 people) were over the age of 65. In March the total monthly deaths were 4,486 of which 3,843 or 85.7% were 65 years or over. In June the total monthly deaths had fallen to 2525 of which 2331 or 92.3% were 65 years or over.[12] The total population of the UK is 66.82 million, of which 12.54 million are over the age of 65 and 5.81 million are over the age of 75.[13] There are 29% (3.64 million) of the elderly who are grey digital outcasts and 53% (3.1 million) of those over 75 years rarely use the Internet.[14] This means that there are 3.64 million elderly people in the UK who are reliant upon newspapers, television broadcasts and the telephone (i.e. no-tech and low-tech) for current information about the pandemic.

The UK Government and the National Health Service (NHS) each have dedicated COVID-19 websites to provide comprehensives information to citizens. These are the primary official sources. Loveday and Wilson (2020) criticise the Government for assuming that everyone has access and is able to negotiate websites. In addition, from the onset of the pandemic, the UK Government held daily television broadcasts to keep the public informed. A member of the Government was usually accompanied by two scientific advisors. Television and print media provided excellent numerical and graphical information to support the public information campaign (Ibid). These briefings and supporting infographics were eventually halted at weekends and advisors became less frequent participants. On 23 June it was announced that regular briefings would end and now only take place for significant announcements. The importance of the two websites has therefore increased over time as being the only sources of official information. As a result, grey digital outcasts, numbering 3.64 million people, have become less aware of detailed government information although extensive, albeit filtered, media coverage still continues.

The NHS administers a database of people needing shielding and protecting because they are defined on medical grounds as extremely vulnerable from COVID-19. In England this Coronavirus shielded patient list (SPL) holds 4% of the total population and includes 1,156,115 people over 65 years of age which is 51.74% of the SPL.[15]

The guidance on shielding states "If you have been told that you're clinically extremely vulnerable, you should: follow the advice in this guidance, register online even if you do not need additional support now."[16] There is no mechanism for registering any other way. Letters have been sent to those shielding, but this has been inconsistent. Some shielded people have not received letters whilst others have received several communications which at times have been contradictory (this is based on the author's own domestic experience). Those grey digital outcasts who need shielding are at a huge disadvantage with the reliance on predominantly online links.

During the pandemic, there has been a huge global increase in television news viewing figures. In the middle of March, it was reported that the BBC News programmes viewing had increased by around 25%, the BBC News Channel had recorded its biggest weekly audience since 2015 and Channel 4 News' audience had doubled in 10 days[17] This low-tech information source is important to the grey digital outcasts and particularly those who are shielded. In the UK households have to pay a TV licence fee to access television, specifically the BBC. Since 2000, those over 75 years of age have been eligible for a free TV licence but this has been under review for some time. On 9 July the BBC announced that from 1 August 2020 this free licence would be scrapped. The only exceptions are those households, in which one person is over 75, receiving a low-income benefit called Pension Credit. There are currently 2.84 million households eligible for Pension Credit but only 1.69 million have taken this up.[18] This means that 1.15 million of the poorest pensioner households which include someone over 75 will be missing out on a free licence. As mentioned previously, 3.1 million pensioners who are over 75 rarely use the Internet and so are likely to be very reliant upon the television. Many of these will struggle to pay the licence regardless of whether they receive Pension Credit or not. This single act by Government and the BBC has created an information poverty trap for some of the most vulnerable grey digital outcasts.

On Thursday night, 31 July, Health Secretary Matt Hancock announced via Twitter that increased measures were being brought in across parts of northern England because of the dangerous increase in infection rates in the region. The public was given just a few hours' notice as the restrictions commenced at midnight. Tracy Brabin, Labour MP for Batley and Spen in West Yorkshire, said "To announce this sort of measure late at night on Twitter caused an awful lot of anxiety in my community." Full details were later posted on the Government website during the night which kept digital natives informed. It is unclear whether any no-tech and low-tech channels were used to convey this urgent message which affected a very large population including those who were about to celebrate Eid al-Adha in a communal, albeit restricted, manner.

The importance of affordable broadband connectivity for all is now acknowledged but turning this into practice is problematic. Allman (2020) discusses a community-led broadband initiative, B4RN (Broadband for the Rural North) which has succeeded in connecting 7000 homes in rural north-west England; it is one of the best internet connections in the UK. Community members undertake the complete installation from mapping routes to digging trenches and cabling through to connecting routers. B4RN runs a weekly computer club to help community members use these new facilities. The digital divide appears to be fading through community action. "The mutual understanding and genuine friendships fostered among local people during the building process last well beyond the installation itself. … the collaborative effort that went into B4RN contributed to a pre-existing rapport that helped in the face of the coronavirus lockdown." (Ibid)

The UK residents who contributed to this study were all over 65 years of age. There was a mixture of grey digital outcasts and grey digital natives. It is interesting that some grey digital natives preferred low-tech to access COVID information and so are classified as traditionalists and guardians in the user typology. So in this sample, there was a reliance on no-tech and low-tech to be kept informed of the current pandemic situation and the impact on people. Generally, people felt that there was a real sense of community flourishing during the pandemic with many acts of kindness. However, there was a feeling that the pandemic had highlighted what was problematic with modern society such as the wealth gap, environmental indifference and political chaos. Isolation and lack of physical social interaction with family and friends were major concerns. One respondent wrote, "I felt like I aged and suddenly became an old person who had to be looked after and not in control of my life anymore."

Overall, the evidence suggests that the elderly are the most vulnerable and are more likely to die from COVID-19. For this reason, it seems that the whole of this group should receive special attention in terms of being informed and being socially and emotionally supported. Currently, this is not the case as information and support tend to be technology-based. The grey digital outcasts have been and continue to be overlooked.

# Perspectives from Other Countries

In order to complete the global perspective, snapshots of nine additional countries have been developed using a variety of data sources. Each snapshot includes orders of magnitude of COVID-19 infections and related deaths together with digital technology usage figures. Many of the snapshots include examples of how communities are addressing the crisis. It is accepted that these nine countries plus the UK provide an indicative rather than a comprehensive view.

## Australia

At the time of writing, for Australia, the total cumulative cases of COVID-19 was 13,950 and the total cumulative deaths were 145. Of the total population of 25 million, 15.8% (3.95 million) are 65 years or over. Nicola Heath[19] reports that digital inclusion is influenced by income, age, education levels, employment and geography, with the indigenous Australians having the largest proportion of digital outcasts. It has been reported that the elderly, the group that is most at risk of COVID-19, are the most digitally excluded in the country. Many of the elderly are digitally illiterate and cannot function online without assistance, and it is at public libraries, which are all closed due to the pandemic, where they typically seek help. They are grey digital outcasts cut off from face-to-face and virtual interactions.

## China

At the time of writing, for China, the total cumulative cases of COVID-19 was 86,839 and the total cumulative deaths were 4,659.

Kummitha (2020) gives an account of how China adopted a techno-driven approach rather than the West's human-driven approach to control the transmission of COVID-19. He suggests that the techno-driven approach may be more productive in identifying, isolating, and quarantining those infected but it also facilitates suppression and censorship. It would also seem to imply that digital outcasts are likely to be invisible. Fumian (2020) provides an analysis of the Wuhan Diary, written by 65-year old author Fang, which provides an unofficial account of Wuhan's quarantine every day for two months. These entries were published as posts of her blog on Weibo. Although these posts were censored by the authorities such was her following that they were copied and posted elsewhere beforehand. This account was seen by digital natives across the globe but it is unclear how many digital outcasts, particularly in Wuhan, had access to the diary, which Fumian implies is an emotional crutch for Wuhan's citizens who appear to have been pilloried by the Chinese authorities and many compliant supporters of the authorities.

A different dimension of the plight of the grey digital outcast relates to an observation that has been made that many of the elderly are suffering due to their lack of access to smartphones and contactless payment. For example, in April, an elderly man was found walking along the hard shoulder on a motorway towards a city in Zhejiang where he had a seasonal job offer at a small company that was about to reopen for business. He had walked for 20 days on the only open road from his rural village which was 1,000 kilometres away. He had not been able to use public transport because he did not have access to nor could afford a smartphone. He needed this because he was not allowed to book or board any train or coach without an app showing that he is not infected with COVID-19. At the end of May, the Chinese premier commented in Beijing that there are about 100 million elderly rural farmers who were relying on taking causal urban jobs but they were not familiar with using smartphones to book tickets or paying for services that are exclusively available via contactless payment. These people are suffering silently and unnoticed in remote places where they are reliant upon the postal service and being able to pay for goods and services with cash.

## Hong Kong

At the time of writing, for Hong Kong, the total cumulative cases of COVID-19 was 2,779 and the total cumulative deaths were 20.[20] In 2016, personal computer usage for those aged 65 and over was only 31.8% and 44% for Internet usage.[21] Chan et al. (2020) have conducted a landline-based telephone survey to ascertain citizen perceptions of the pandemic. They found less than half of the participants (47.8%) reported that they had sufficient knowledge to manage the health risk and safety during the outbreak of COVID-19. How information is conveyed is important. The authors found that television, Internet and smartphone apps were the top three channels for obtaining infectious disease information, covering more than 90% of the population. In Hong Kong, the middle-aged and elderly prefer television, while the use of Internet and smartphone apps is more popular in the younger age group (Ibid).

Recently, it has been observed that there has been an increased use of digital technology enabling the government, the police and the health authority to send vitally important messages. However, the digital divide has become more extreme leading, for example, to significant numbers not able to acquire surgical face masks because these are only available online.

## India

At the time of writing, for India the total cumulative cases of COVID-19 was 1,385,522 and the total cumulative deaths were 32,063. 6.4% (1.23 million) of the total population are 65 years or over. Some interesting observations were recently published.[22] The focus of attention is observed as being on the impact of COVID-19 on the working population with little consideration for the mental and emotional health of the elderly. Through a telephone survey, it was found that many elderly people were feeling anxious or were finding it hard to sleep or even had had some form of mental breakdown. Interestingly it was found that the majority of those in the survey had turned to digital technology during the pandemic. Many of these elderly people are now using digital technology for a range of functions including reading e-books, playing games on smartphones, ordering through delivery apps, watching videos or listening to songs online, and using Skype/Zoom/Hangouts/WhatsApp video calls to connect with friends.

## Italy

At the time of writing, for Italy the total cumulative cases of COVID-19 was 245,864 and the total cumulative deaths were 35,102. In 2019, Italy was the European country with the largest percentage of elderly population with 22.8% (13.78 million) of the total population aged 65 years and older.[23] Only 34% of households made up exclusively of people over the age of 65 have broadband and only 41.9% of those over 65 use the Internet.[24] This suggests that Italy has approximately 8 million grey digital outcasts. It has been observed that these outcasts rely upon television news and chat shows together with the telephone to remain connected and informed. The BBC reported on 14 March[25] that in a nationwide flashmob event Italians were singing from their windows and balconies to boost morale. It was to be repeated regularly over the following weeks. This is an example of bottom-up community action to support others through being together during the pandemic crisis.

## Japan

At the time of writing, for Japan, the total cumulative cases of COVID-19 was 29,382 and the total cumulative deaths were 996. Out of a total population 126.18 million, 28.2% (35.58 million) are 65 years or over. Internet usage rate is 79.8 % but 76.6% for 60-69 year olds, 51% for 70-79-year-olds and 21.5% for those 80 years old and over.[26]

All respondents were grey digital natives and yet some still used no-tech and low-tech combined with high-tech to remain informed in a balanced way. There was a common positive theme of having time to reflect and rethink life's priorities. Lack of direct contact was problematic for some. One person commented, "many aspects of our values depend upon our interaction with other persons on the occasions of face-to-face talking and we used to believe that our personal selection and decision can change our future." Whether this is still true is open to debate.

## New Zealand

At the time of writing, for New Zealand, the total cumulative cases of COVID-19 was 1.206 and the total cumulative deaths were 22. Out of the total population of 4.97 million, 15.3% (0.76 million) are over the age of 65.

Kirkpatrick Mariner, the Government's principal adviser on digital inclusion was reported as admitting that COVID-19 had highlighted the digital divide which mirrors social and economic inequality, and has exposed how digitally unprepared the country is. "Without affordable connections and devices for those who are most in need, and without the required skills, a huge number of New Zealanders will miss out on a suddenly critical ability to connect."[27] Grey Power in Nelson is an advocacy organisation promoting the welfare and well-being of all those citizens in the 50 plus age group. Half of its members do not have Internet access and, therefore, cannot access the Government's four-level COVID-19 alert system. For this reason, it started to use written information and the telephone to keep its members up to date.[28]

## Singapore

At the time of writing, for Singapore, the total cumulative cases of COVID-19 was 49,888 and the total cumulative deaths were 27. There are 0.58 million people who are 65 years or over[29] which is 10.18% of the total population of 5.7 million.[30]

Several media articles have covered Singapore's grey digital divide which was observed as being particularly problematic for the low-income elderly. At the end of 2018, it was reported that 80% of the elderly owned a smartphone but only 33% did mobile banking and 22% did online shopping.[31] This suggests that the majority of grey digital natives are traditionalists or guardians and that there are around 160,000 grey digital outcasts. Junie Foo explained that more than half of Singapore residents aged 65 and above live alone or with their spouses only and that constant news updates and large amounts of information available online, was difficult for many of the elderly, who were digitally illiterate, to comprehend which made them susceptible to fake news and rumours and caused unnecessary fear and panic.[32] It has been suggested that the lack of social interaction and physical activity could have a negative impact on the mental and physical health of vulnerable elderly populations. Some try to reduce the impact of isolation through talking to friends over the telephone and watching television.[33]

## USA

At the time of writing, for the USA the total cumulative cases of COVID-19 was 4,009,808 and the total cumulative deaths were 143,663. 16% (52.51 million) of the population are 65 or over.[34] Seventy-three percent of the elderly use the Internet[35] which means there are 14.12 million grey digital outcasts.

A newspaper report in Florida focussed on the inability of many elderly people in the state to utilise online facilities in the crisis resulting in potential mental health impact from the subsequent imposed isolation.[36] Conger and Griffith (2020) wrote about an elderly American, "For more than a week, Linda Quinn, 81, has isolated herself inside her Bellevue, Washington, home to keep away from the coronavirus. Her only companion has been her goldendoodle, Lucy. To blunt the solitude, Quinn's daughter, son-in-law and two grandsons wanted to hold video chats with her through Zoom, a videoconferencing app. So they made plans to call and talk her through installing the app on her computer. But 5 minutes before the scheduled chat last week, Quinn realised there was a problem: She had not used her computer in about 4 months and could not remember the password. … As life has increasingly moved online during the pandemic, an older generation that grew up in an analog era is facing a digital divide. Often unfamiliar or uncomfortable with apps, gadgets, and the internet, many are struggling to keep up with friends and family through digital tools when some of them are craving those connections the most." It is interesting that on 19 June Florida Governor Ron DeSantis was reported to state that Florida needed to continue to function and promised not to enforce a lockdown, but to instead focus on protecting and informing the elderly.[37]

On a positive note, Brown, Ezike and Stern (2020) found that, since COVID-19, some US cities had expanded low-cost or free Internet access and equipment as well as digital literacy training for residents. In contrast, medical clinicians Ramsetty and Adams (2020) describe the dire problems incurred while trying to support patients at free health care clinics as medical support transitioned into telemedicine. For example, their patients could not access the online system set up to operate screening processes for COVID-19. This problem was widespread and those whose access was impeded were the most vulnerable to poor health outcomes related to COVID-19. Many of these were grey digital outcasts. "… diminished accessibility to technology … was being exposed at a critical time in a public health crisis. Frighteningly, there were no measures at the ready to address it." (Ibid)

In January 2015, President Obama stated that high-speed broadband is not a luxury it is a necessity.[38] However, broadband roll-out emphasis remains on the populated urban areas rather than rural regions. On 30 March 2020, Matt Dunne of the Center on Rural Innovation wrote in The Hill, "Elderly Americans are forced to travel long distances and risk infection at hospitals, or even go without care, because the lack of rural broadband prevents deployment of telehealth …. Broadband is a critical piece of the infrastructure needed for rural communities to thrive."[39] He explained how the Rural Innovation network of 20 rural communities has implemented high-speed broadband through local initiatives. Rural grey digital natives are thus supported but technology alone does not provide support for the rural grey digital outcasts.

Those responding to the survey were a mixture of elderly and non-elderly, native and outcast. Both no-tech and low-tech were used by most for keeping informed. One grey digital native, who was probably a practicalist on the user typology, only used high-tech to be informed. There were very few positive outcomes mentioned other than some felt community spirit had improved. Most found lack of freedom and isolation from friends and family a real problem. Economic disaster and government ineptness were mentioned by many. One respondent felt "life as we have known it will never be the same again and that jobs, education, worship will all be more difficult for everyone."

## Commonalities and the Way Forward

There are many grey digital natives whose lives are enriched by digital technology but there are many grey digital outcasts who will never be inclined or able to engage with digital technology. There should be a choice. The elderly should be encouraged and supported to use the Internet but those who do not should be able to access services and resources in other ways that suit them.[40] Caro (2020) explores the use of digital technology for communication with the elderly who are technologically challenged and may also have cognitive impairment. The included a checklist that illustrates the issues that need to be considered when encouraging grey digital outcasts to cross the digital divide. The checklist is summarised as:

- The digital technology must arrive ready to go. There should be not set up procedures.
- WiFi must be automatically connected or the digital technology has a built-in cellular connection.
- The interface needs to be very simple and not confusing.
- The use of digital technology should not be dependent on the kindness of another person to operate it.
- If the digital technology stops working there needs to be a way to troubleshoot and fix the problem.
- The old-fashioned telephone is the acceptability benchmark for digital technology.

In undertaking this study the author has been struck by the numerous community-led support initiatives (only some have been mentioned in this chapter) which helped vulnerable outcasts, in particular grey digital outcasts when official responses have been sadly lacking. These have addressed not only the installation of digital technology but also the encouragement, mentoring and training of these people. This bottom-up community action is exemplary.

Understandably, governments and health-related organisations are focusing on the operationally feasible urgent actions in their attempts to overcome the pandemic. The juxtaposition of COVID-19 and digital technology has brought to the fore existing shortcomings in the social responsibility commitment of governments and organisations. The vast majority of COVID-19-related deaths are within the elderly population. The vast majority of digital outcasts are within the elderly population. Strategies of containment and eradication have centred predominantly on the Internet to inform and support people. This is socially irresponsible as grey digital outcasts have been put at greater risk which has possibly led to fatalities.

Based on this study a set of guiding principles has emerged which lays the foundation for a global response to supporting grey digital outcasts particularly in times of crisis. These are as follows:

- There should be a practical demonstration of social, political and individual commitment to remove the digital divide.
- Respect, dignity, autonomy, privacy, choice, access, connectivity and duty of care should be taken into account when addressing the grey digital divide.
- Whilst reactive action is necessary, in a state of emergency it should not be at the expense of proactive action aimed at long-term wellbeing.
- Those who are grey digital outcasts should not be subjected to the information poverty trap.
- There should be support for no-tech low-tech and high-tech preferences in time of public emergency when public information and public action are paramount.
- Listen to the community and support community-led actions.
- Social isolation on medical grounds should not lead to social exclusion through narrowly focusing on digital native networking.
- Fast broadband infrastructure should be a utility available to all regardless of location.

## Conclusion

This chapter has been authored by a grey digital native who lives in England and has been shielded for 150 days. He has been physically isolated and yet connected with people across the globe, some of whom are long-standing colleagues and some are new contacts. Data repositories, newspaper and broadcasting media, and people's public diaries (blogs) have been accessed online. During the COVID-19 pandemic, these real-time feeds have created a new research experience for the author. Information alerts have been a constant reminder of the rapidly changing situation across the globe. Almost with each keystroke, there has been new information and the need to change observation and inference. The focus of this study has been on the plight of the grey digital outcast during a global health crisis. The irony is that the grey digital outcast is unlikely to read this account because it will only be available in the exclusive online world from which the grey digital outcast is excluded. This is a major global issue as there are an estimated 363.5 million grey digital outcasts. Things have to and must change because the digital divide "has created a new underclass, non-citizens with little hope of opportunities for success or of help in times of need" (Rogerson, 1997).

## Acknowledgements

The author wishes to thank the following individuals for providing a rich body of empirical information on which this chapter is based: Wanbil Lee, Antonio Marturano, Kiyoshi Murata, Anthea Indira Ong, Laura Robinson, Anne Rogerson, and X-jian Wu

## Notes

1 https://www.pewresearch.org/internet/2019/10/28/4-the-internet-will-continue-to-make-life-better/
2 https://www.who.int/emergencies/diseases/novel-coronavirus-2019/question-and-answers-hub
3 https://www.who.int/emergencies/diseases/novel-coronavirus-2019/question-and-answers-hub/q-a-detail/q-a-on-on-covid-19-for-older-people

4  WHO Coronavirus Disease (COVID-19) Dashboard Data last updated: 2020/7/26, 2:34pm CEST at https://covid19.who.int/table

5  https://ec.europa.eu/knowledge4policy/publication/covid-19-cases-case-fatality-rate-age_en. European Commission

6  statista at https://www.statista.com/statistics/265759/world-population-by-age-and-region/

7  World Internet Usage and Population Statistics 2020 Year-Q2 Estimates at 20 June 2020 at https://www.Internetworldstats.com/stats.htm

8  statista at https://www.statista.com/statistics/272365/age-distribution-of-Internet-users-worldwide/

9  https://thenextweb.com/growth quarters/2020/01/30/digital-trends-2020-every-single-stat-you-need-to-know-about-the-internet/

10  the Internet Society 2019 Global Internet Report: The Forces Shaping Our Digital Future at https://future.Internetsociety.org/2019/wp-content/uploads/sites/2/2019/04/InternetSociety-GlobalInternetReport-ConsolidationintheInternetEconomy.pdf

11  https://coronavirus.data.gov.uk/?_ga=2.108789634.141510788.1591083134-1496647197.1578569146

12  UK Office of National Statistics 17 July 2020.

13  https://www.ons.gov.uk/peoplepopulationandcommunity/populationandmigration/populationprojections/datasets/tablei21lowpopulationvariantukpopulationinagegroups

14  UK Office of National Statistics May 2019

15  https://digital.nhs.uk/dashboards/shielded-patient-list-open-data-set

16  https://www.gov.uk/government/publications/guidance-on-shielding-and-protecting-extremely-vulnerable-persons-from-covid-19

17  https://pressgazette.co.uk/coronavirus-leads-to-staggering-demand-for-trusted-tv-news/

18  https://www.pensionspolicyinstitute.org.uk/research/pension-facts/table-1/

19  https://www.eurekastreet.com.au/article/digital-divide-made-even-wider-in-covid-19-times

20  https://www.worldometers.info/coronavirus/country/china-hong-kong-sar/

21  Usage of Information Technology and the Internet by Hong Kong Residents, 2000 to 2016 Hong Kong Monthly Digest of Statistics November 2017.

22  https://www.linkedin.com/pulse/covid-elderly-swathy-g/?articleId=6676425680022052864

23  https://www.statista.com/statistics/1105835/share-of-elderly-population-in-europe-by-country/

24  Citizens and ICT 2019 Report, Institute of National Statistics, 18 Dec 2019, https://www.istat.it/it/files/2019/12/Cittadini-e-ICT-2019.pdf

25  https://www.bbc.co.uk/news/av/world-europe-51886547/coronavirus-italians-sing-from-their-windows-to-boost-morale

26  https://www.soumu.go.jp/johotsusintokei/statistics/data/190531_1.pdf

27  https://www.researchprofessionalnews.com/rr-news-new-zealand-2020-4-digital-divide-means-vulnerable-will-miss-covid-19-updates/

28  https://www.rnz.co.nz/news/national/412294/concerns-elderly-people-not-getting-covid-19-messages

29  https://www.statista.com/statistics/624913/singapore-population-by-age-group/

30  https://www.statista.com/statistics/713063/singapore-total-population/

31  https://www.aseantoday.com/2018/12/singaporean-elders-tryst-with-digital-inclusion/

32  https://www.todayonline.com/commentary/helping-singapores-seniors-cope-covid-19

33  https://www.channelnewsasia.com/news/singapore/covid-19-loneliness-isolation-among-elderly-safe-distancing-12611158

34  https://www.kff.org/other/state-indicator/distribution-by-age/?currentTimeframe=0&sortModel=%7B%22colId%22:%22Location%22,%22sort%22:%22asc%22%7D#note-1

35  https://www.statista.com/statistics/266587/percentage-of-Internet-users-by-age-groups-in-the-us/

36  First Coast News, Jacksonville, Florida, United States, 25 March 2020.

37  https://www.news.com.au/world/coronavirus/global/coronavirus-us-florida-to-be-new-epicentre-of-virus-as-cases-soar/news-story/84e7fdd3807f6bfb2d97d7558981c288

38  https://digitalpedagogy.mla.hcommons.org/keywords/digital-divides/

39  https://thehill.com/opinion/technology/490151-how-covid-19-is-proving-the-urgency-of-delivering-universal

40  https://www.ageuk.org.uk/globalassets/age-uk/documents/reports-and-publications/age_uk_digital_inclusion_evidence_review_2018.pdf

# References

Allmann, K. (2020). The remote British village that built one of the fastest internet networks in the UK. *The Conversation.* 2 July 2. Available from: https://theconversation.com/the-remote-british-village-that-built-one-of-the-fastest-internet-networks-in-the-uk-137946, reprinted as Digital divide, Saturday 11 July 2020, *The Independent.* (accessed August 2020).

1971. Anon (1971). Computers Employed as Teaching Aids. *Reading Eagle.* United Press International, 4 February, p. 28.

Armitage, R. & Nellums, L. B. (2020). COVID-19 and the consequences of isolating the elderly. *The Lancet Public Health.* 5(5), 256.

Birkland, J. (2019). *Gerontechnology: Understanding Older Adult Information and Communication Technology Use.* Emerald Publishing.

Booz Allen Hamilton (2000). *Achieving Universal Access.* Booz, Allen and Hamilton, 7 March.

Brown, M., Ezike, R. & Stern, A. (2020). How Cities Are Leveraging Technology to Meet Residents' Needs during a Pandemic. Urban Institute. June. Available from: https://www.urban.org/sites/default/files/publication/102355/how-cities-are-leveraging-technology-to-meet-residents-needs-during-a-pandemic_0_0.pdf. (accessed August 2020).

Caro, R. (2020). *Virtual connections to the "Tech-Challenged".* Tech-enhanced Life, 15 July. Available from: https://www.techenhancedlife.com/citizen-research/virtual-connections-tech-challenged. (accessed August 2020).

Chan, E. Y. Y., Huang, Z., Lo, E. S. K., Hung, K. K. C., Wong, E. L. Y. & Wong, S. Y. S. (2020). Sociodemographic predictors of health risk perception, attitude and behavior practices associated with health-emergency disaster risk management for biological hazards: the case of COVID-19 pandemic in Hong Kong, SAR China. *International Journal of Environmental Research and Public Health.* 17(11), 3869.

Conger, K. & Griffith, E. (2020). As life moves online, an older generation faces a digital divide. *The New York Times,* 27 March. Available from: https://www.nytimes.com/2020/03/27/technology/virus-older-generation-digital-divide.html. (accessed August 2020).

Fothergill, R. (1989). *Implications of new technology for the school curriculum.* London, Kogan Page.

Fuchs, C. (2008). *Internet and Society: Social Theory in the Information Age.* New York, Routledge.

Fumian, M. (2020). To Serve the People or the Party: Fang Fang's Wuhan Diary and Chinese Writers at the Time of Coronavirus. *MCLC Resource Center Publication,* The Ohio State University, April.

Gardner, J. & McMullan, T. (1990). Computer Literacy in UK Education--An Evolving Strategy. *EURIT '90 Conference on Technology and Education,* Herning, Denmark, 23–27 April.

Isaacs, S. (2011). Shift happens: A digital native perspective on policy practice. In: Shah, N. and Jansen, F. (eds.) Digital (Alter)Natives with a Cause? Book 1 – To Be. (1.2 Essay), pp. 24–33.

Kleining, G. & Witt, H. (2000). The qualitative heuristic approach: A methodology for discovery in psychology and the social sciences. Rediscovering the method of introspection as an example. In *Forum Qualitative Sozialforschung/Forum: Qualitative Social Research.* 1(1), Art. 13.

Kummitha, R. K. R. (2020). Smart technologies for fighting pandemics: The techno-and human-driven approaches in controlling the virus transmission. *Government Information Quarterly,* 37(3), 101481. ISSN 0740-624X,https://doi.org/10.1016/j.giq.2020.

Loveday, H. & Wilson, J. (2020). COVID-19: fear, explanation, action, unity and ingenuity and World Hand Hygiene Day. *Journal of Infection Prevention.* 21(3), 80–82.

Morris, A. (2007). E-literacy and the grey digital divide: a review with recommendations. *Journal of Information Literacy.* 1(3), 13–28.

Muiser, J. & Carrin, G. (2007). Financing long-term care programmes in health systems with a situation assessment in selected high, middle and low income countries. *Discussion Paper No. 6,* World Health Organisation. Available from: https://www.who.int/health_financing/documents/dp_e_07_6-longtermcare.pdf. (accessed August 2020).

Netuveli, G. & Blane, D. (2008). Quality of life in older ages. *British Medical Bulletin.* 85(1), 113–126.

Norris, P. (2001). *Digital Divide: Civic Engagement, Information Poverty, & the Internet Worldwide.* New York, Cambridge University Press.

Ramsetty, A. & Adams, C. (2020). Impact of the digital divide in the age of COVID-19. *Journal of the American Medical Informatics Association.* 27(7), 1147–1148.

Rogerson, S. (1997). Computers - the ethical frontier. *SET97.* De Montfort University, 28 April.

Rogerson, S. (2008). Prolonging Active Life Through Ethical Technology. keynote address, *11th EU Hitachi Sciences and Technology Forum, Ageing and Technology.* 26–27 April, Munich.

Rogerson, S. (2020a) Is the digital divide of the past, present or future?. *News & Blogs.* Emerald Publishing, 17 March. Available from: www.emeraldpublishing.com/news-and-blogs/is-the-digital-divide-of-the-past-present-or-future/. (accessed August 2020).

Rogerson, S. (2020b) Digital outcasts & COVID19. *News & Blogs.* Emerald Publishing, 24 March. Available from: https://www.emeraldpublishing.com/news-and-blogs/digital-outcasts-covid19/ (accessed August 2020) and https://www.emeraldgrouppublishing.com/topics/coronavirus/blog/digital-outcasts-covid19. (accessed August 2020).

Selwyn, N. (2009). The digital native-myth and reality. *Aslib Journal of Information Management.* 61(4), 364–379.

Syvertsen, T. & Enli, G. (2020). Digital detox: media resistance and the promise of authenticity. *Convergence.* 26(5–6), 1269–1283. Available from: https://doi.org/10.1177/1354856519847325 (accessed August 2020).

Thornham, H. (2013). Digital welfare only deepens the class divide. *The Conversation.* 8 July. Available from: https://theconversation.com/digital-welfare-only-deepens-the-class-divide-15828 (accessed August 2020).

Vaccaro, R., Zaccaria, D., Colombo, M., Abbondanza, S. & Guaita, A. (2019). Adverse effect of self-reported hearing disability in elderly Italians: results from the InveCe. Ab study. *Maturitas.* 121(March), 35–40.

Van Dijk, J. A. (2005). *The Deepening Divide: Inequality in the Information Society.* Sage Publications.

Wagner, B. (2011). Natives, Norms and Knowledge: How information and communications technologies recalibrate social and political power relations. In: Shah, N. & Jansen, F. (eds.) *Digital (Alter)Natives with a Cause? Book 4 – To Connect.* 4.3 Essay, pp. 21–30.

# FUTURE IV

*"The IT [digital technology] revolution is not merely technological it is fundamentally social and ethical."*

(Simon Rogerson, 1998, p. 33)

As mentioned earlier, almost everyone, albeit as developers or as users, is involved with digital technology. The impacts of digital technology, whether positive or negative, spread rapidly and are very difficult to reverse Societal dependency will continue to increase and those involved in development and provision will stretch far beyond the ranks of traditional professionals working under contract. It would seem reasonable that the global community should be the primary future focus for digital technology development. Consequently, a global digital technology charter would be appropriate which aligned to, for example, the Universal Declaration of Human Rights. Through adapting the work of Franklin (1999) and Barratt (2007), a simple charter has been devised (Rogerson, 2015) which encourages everyone to:

- Promote social justice and social care
- Restore reciprocity for everyone
- Benefit the many rather than the few
- Put people first rather than digital technology
- Limit economic gain to minimise potential social and environmental cost
- Favour the reversible over the irreversible
- Create a more inclusive society by reducing barriers and creating new opportunities

Part Four comprises three chapters written in 1998, 2004 and 2015 respectively. Together, they offer a vision of how ethical digital technology might be achieved and what challenges need to be addressed.

## References

Barratt, J. (2007). Design for an ageing society. *Gerontechnology*. 6(4), 188–189.
Franklin, U. M. (1999). *The real world of technology*. House of Anansi Press.
Rogerson, S. (1998). Ethical aspects of information technology: issues for senior executives. London, Institute of Business Ethics.
Rogerson S. (2015). *ICT Codes of Ethics*. Keynote Presentation, Ethics Conference 2015, Council of European Professional Informatics Societies (CEPIS), 7 April, The Hague, The Netherlands.

*Chapter 19*

# E.Society – Panacea or Apocalypse? [1998]*

## Introduction

The advances in information and communication technology (ICT) present many opportunities and threats to individuals, organisations and society as a whole. Computers can be
shaped to any activity that can be described in terms of inputs, transforming processes and
outputs. It is the nearest thing to a universal tool (Moor, 1985). Consequently, society and its
organisations are becoming more dependent upon ICT as the means of providing information,
the new lifeblood of society. There is an increasingly wider access to and application of this
powerful resource.

Inevitably there will be winners and losers, costs and benefits. Information empowers those
who have it but it also disenfranchises those who do not. Wealth and power flow to the
information-rich, those who create and use ICT successfully. They are primarily well-educated
citizens of industrialised nations. The information-poor, both in industrialised countries and in
the developing world, are falling further and further behind.

The world has changed. Once people had to go to a particular place in order to communicate.
This is no longer the case with the advent of pagers, mobile phones and laptop computers with
communication cards. Communication now comes to people. Indeed, the creation of the fax, the
mobile phone and the Internet has permanently changed the way people live and work
(Anon2, 1997).

This chapter considers some of the issues that surround the advancing information age. It
illustrates that perceptions of what is appropriate and beneficial may be very different to what
really is appropriate and beneficial.

---

# What Can Go Wrong

ICT is not without its problems and its disasters. Many of these issues tend to go unnoticed unless they result in some newsworthy story. Two examples are discussed here; the first concerns the important issue of information integrity whilst the second briefly covers a headline-grabbing problem – the millennium bug.

## *Information*

There are concerns about the accuracy of the information held within computer systems. The potential impact is exacerbated as the distribution and use of information has become global rather than the localised focus of older media. The inputting of raw data is prone to error with the natural error rate for an experienced keyboard operator being one keystroke in 100. It has been reported that inaccurate information in systems could be as high as 2%. Given each adult has about 200 computer files relating to them then there will probably be four errors person on these files (Anon1, 1997). If people were wary of these potential errors then maybe pressure would be brought to bear to minimise this danger but there is a tendency by the public to treat computer-generated information with a degree of blind faith. Consequently, integrity is assumed and possible errors go unquestioned.

## *The Millennium Bug*

The widespread concern over the millennium bug is indicative of a society becoming increasingly dependent on ICT. There are many estimates of how much it will cost the companies and governments of the world ranging from a conservative $52 billion by the British investment bank, BZW to a staggering $3.6 trillion by Software Productivity Research in Boston, USA (Anon4, 1997). Companies are undertaking corrective work on a large scale. For example, Centrica which trades as British Gas, stated in the 1997 annual review to shareholders that during 1997 £3 million was incurred in millennium compliance. It stated a further £43 million was required in 1998 and a further £15 million in 1999. There are indications that 30% of companies worldwide will suffer a critical software failure due to the date problem. Information systems running on mainframe computers, personal computers and embedded chips in appliances all have to be checked. It is clear the integrity of date-dependent information is at risk. The consequences may be very serious. For example, one manufacturer had to recall a heart defibrillator because its safety features only worked if a recent service had been undertaken. Not being millennium-compliant meant that service dates after 2000 would be interpreted as 1900 resulting in a machine mal-function (Anon4, 1997).

These two examples illustrate the risks associated with information dependency. Quite simply, unreliable information and unstable information systems will lead to information bankruptcy.

# People Matter

The Club of Rome has identified the information society as one of the eleven global issues that must be addressed if the new global society is to flourish. It states, "The globalisation of the economy, the fact that we live from now on in an information society, the complexity and the uncertainty which are the common trademarks of the present word lead us to take into consideration a number of these new factors. We have to understand these new data in order to have a better understanding of other cultures, other languages, other modes of reasoning." Clearly, it is important to consider the role of people in the information society as illustrated by the following three issues.

## Identity

There has been much speculation that people can play with their identities on the Internet and present different electronic persona. Such speculation is characterised in the famous cartoon entitled "In cyberspace nobody knows you're a dog." This might be possible in the short-term but such mimicry is likely to be spotted in the long-term as identity is more than simply learning and applying rules, it is about learning within a context and reacting intuitively to different situations as they arise (Whitley, 1997). In the information society, the impact of physical characteristics of those communicating has been minimised. This is potentially beneficial as removing the visual cues about gender, age, ethnicity and social status allow different lines of communication to open up, which might have been avoided in the physical world (Whitley, 1997).

## Culture

The information society crosses traditional boundaries and as such comprises individuals from many different cultures. This cultural variability means that the expectations of individual cybercitizens can differ considerably. Nance and Strohmaier (1994) suggest there are two important dimensions to consider regarding this variability. The first dimension is the continuum from individualism to collectivism. Individualism emphasises self-interest and promotes the self-realisation of talent and potential. Its demands are universal. Collectivism emphasises pursuit of common interests and belonging to a set of hierarchical groups where, for example, the family group might be placed above the job group. The demands on group members are different to those on non-group members. The second dimension concerns cultural differences in communication referred to as low-context communication and high- context communication. In the former, the majority of the information resides in the message itself whilst in the latter the communication is implicit. Nance and Strohmaier (1994) suggest that the USA utilises low-context communication whilst Japan uses high context. Given this cultural variability, it is clear that there are great difficulties in providing information in a form that is acceptable to all. This is certainly one of the great challenges of the information age. It involves establishing a set of common behavioural standards whilst ensuring that there is no dominant participant.

## Conversation

There is concern by psychologists that computers are having a detrimental effect on society in that the "social glue" of casual conversation is being eroded (Mihill, 1997). The increasing use of email at work, the elimination of bank tellers and shop assistants, and the use of telephones and laptops to telecommute from the home illustrate how the opportunity for small talk is decreasing. This phenomenon is thought to be one reason why shyness is increasing in the population. There is of course a counter-argument in that by utilising computer-based communication tools such as the Internet those who are naturally shy become more outgoing since the psychological pressure of face-to-face contact is removed.

# Demands of the Information Age

Information has quickly become the most valuable commodity of our society. Information in the future is likely to take many different forms. Taylor (1995) suggests that information will be domesticated as utility networks reach the home of most people and information appliances become cheaper, intuitive to use, and interactive. He suggests the types of services and products that might bring about this domestication. They include tele-healthcare, tele-education, entertainment and media, real-time information services, electronic publishing, digital imaging and photography, virtual zoos and wildlife experience, virtual reality experiences and tele-travel. In a short space of time, most of Taylor's list has become a reality. It is a total information experience. Indeed E.everything has arrived. And what of the cybercitizen? In order to live and prosper in the Information Age, the cybercitizen must be visible and creditable. This is recognised by the Government and consequently, it is considering creating an electronic curriculum vitae detailing the achievements of every person from the cradle to the grave. The benefits and costs of such electronic profiles are yet to be identified.

# What We Should Do

A recent Communication of the European Commission addresses the development of the information society (Anon3, 1997). This provides guidance as to how the information society should evolve so that it is all things to all cybercitizens. Three points are particularly relevant to this chapter:

- If the information society is to be to the benefit of all, it needs to develop with a strong social dimension, not only integrating social policy into the information society, but also using the information society as a tool to promote a more inclusive and learning society.
- Particular attention is needed to avoid the risk that the information society might exaggerate existing divisions within society. People are concerned about how it will affect their jobs and about the risks of creating a society of haves and havenots.
- While the move to the information society is essentially market-driven, public authorities have an important role to play in shaping this process, striking a balance between policies to enhance equality of opportunity and security and policies to promote flexibility and adaptability.

As the communication points out the key to benefiting from technological progress is access to the tools, resources and services that form the information society. Quite simply, information must be available, affordable and accessible on-demand, whilst people must be aware of the information services on offer. It is important that individual countries ensure policies are in place that promote this. In the UK, the government.direct initiative illustrates the stance governments might take regarding the information society. Government.direct is founded on five core principles: choice, confidence, accessibility, rationalisation and fraud. Concern was expressed about several of these principles (Rogerson, 1997), two of which are discussed here. The principle of choice may well become meaningless in a society dominated by electronic preference as this might place pressure, through feelings of alienation and being treated in a second-class manner, on those who prefer other means of information access. The principle of rationalisation was couched in terms of minimum legal compliance rather than promoting social responsibility. It was suggested that the principle be amended to read, "legally permissible, morally permissible and socially acceptable." There appears to be a flaw in the principles in that government.direct assumes a reasonable level of literacy, technological understanding, and technological acceptance. This may not be the case in practice and so an additional principle is needed which addresses learning and awareness of ICT.

## Conclusion

This chapter has illustrated that delivery of services in the information society might not always be what is required. The cybercitizen is subjected to e.junkmail, e.money, e.commerce, e.library, e.identity, e.education to mention but a few. Whether these are beneficial may depend on a number of factors. What is paramount is that cybercitizens deserve empowerment and social benefit, inclusion rather than exclusion, and the right to choose between the electronic and the non-electronic.

The title of this chapter questions whether an electronic society is a panacea or an apocalypse. Inequitable access to the priceless resource of information is at best unfair and at worst disastrous for the information society – that is apocalyptic. An information society that empowers the disabled and less fortunate members of society and sustains equality of opportunity regardless of race, colour or creed is achievable – that is panacea. Governments, policy makers, developers, and service providers of the information society have the wherewithal to create the panacea. They must have the commitment as well, else apocalypse beckons.

## Note

On 23 September 1998, De Montfort University conferred Professor of Computer Ethics on me. At the time I was Europe's first professor of computer ethics. The paper, which forms Chapter 19, was the foundation of my Inaugural Professorial Public Lecture, *E.Society – Panacea or apocalypse? The rights and wrongs of the Information Age*, delivered at De Montfort University, on 26 May 1999 at 5.30 pm. Professor Terrel Ward Bynum attended and gave me a gift of *The Human Use of Human Beings by Norbert Wiener*, published in 1950. Terry wrote "Simon, I thought long and hard about what to give to the first Computer Ethics Professor in Europe. The first printing of the first complete book in Computer Ethics seemed right. I feel very proud of you – as if my brother accomplished a stunning and historical achievement! Congratulations! Terry." It has been 70 years since Wiener's book was published. Some of the issues he raised have still not been addressed effectively.

## References

Anon1 (1997). Betrayal by the digital angel. *The Guardian Online*. 12 May, Available from http://online.guardian.co.uk/paper/archive/863436364-12digiang.html (Accessed 15 September 1997)

Anon2 (1997). A connected world. *The Economist*. 13 Sept. Available from http://www.economist.com/editorial/freeforall/21-9-97/tel1.html (Accessed 27 January 1998)

Anon3 (1997). People first - the next steps. *Communication 397*. European Commission. Available from http://europa.eu.int/ (Accessed 19 June 1998)

Anon4 (1997). The millennium bug - please panic early. *The Economist*. 4 Oct. Available from http://www.economist.com/editorial/freeforall/current/sf0951.html (Accessed 3 October 1997)

Mihill, C. (1997). Computers spawn social 'ice age'. *The Guardian Online.* 16 July. Available from http://online.guardian.co.uk/paper/archive/8607 2141-16shy.html (Accessed 15 September 1997)

Moor, J. H. (1985). What is computer ethics?. *Metaphilosophy,* 16(4), 266–279.

Nance, K. L. & Strohmaier, M. (1994). Ethical accountability in the cyberspace. In: *Proceedings of the conference on Ethics in the computer age.* pp. 115–118.

Rogerson, S. (1997). *Government.direct: a response from the Centre for Computing and Social Responsibility.* February. Available from http://www.ccsr.cms.dmu.ac.uk/resources/general/responses/gov_direct.html (Accessed 6 July 1998).

Taylor, J. (1997). The networked home: domestication of information. *RSA Journal,* 143(5458), 41–53.

Whitley, E. A. (1997). In cyberspace all they see is your words. *Information Technology and People,* 10(2), 147–163.

*Chapter 20*

# The Virtual World: A Tension between Global Reach and Local Sensitivity [2004]*

## Introduction

Computers can be shaped to any activity that can be described in terms of inputs, transforming processes and outputs. It is the nearest thing to a universal tool (Moor, 1985). This has become increasingly so with the growing convergence of computing, telecommunications and mass media. Consequently, society, its citizens and its organisations are becoming more dependent upon this technology and its global application as the means of providing information and obtaining services. There is an increasingly wider access to and application of this powerful resource. Many herald these advances as the arrival of the global village mapped out by the Internet. It is a village where every place is only a push-button away. Indeed Moor (1998) explains that "The prospects of a global village in which everyone on the planet is connected to everyone else with regard to computing power and communication is breathtaking. What is difficult to comprehend is what impact this will have on human life. Surely some of the effects will be quite positive and others quite negative."

The world has changed. Once people had to go to a particular place in order to communicate. This is no longer the case with the advent of pagers, mobile phones and laptop computers with communication cards; communication now comes to people. Indeed, the development of communication devices such as the fax, the mobile phone and the Internet has permanently changed the way people live, work and socialise. This chapter considers some of the issues surrounding a virtual world of global reach yet still having to be locally sensitive.

Wealth and power flow to the information-rich, those who create and use ICT successfully. They are primarily well-educated citizens of industrialised nations. The information poor, both in industrialised countries and in the developing world, are falling further and further behind.

---

* This chapter was first published as: Rogerson, S. (2004) The Virtual World: a tension between global reach and local sensitivity. International Journal of Information Ethics. Vol. 2, November. Proceedings of the symposium "Localizing the Internet. Ethical Issues in Intercultural Perspective". Copyright © Simon Rogerson.

Local implementation issues can dramatically affect the potential of the virtual world, restricting access and thus creating or exacerbating social exclusion. Pinto, Garcia and Ferraz (2004) suggest there are three issues that need to be addressed; investment in ICT infrastructure which enables universal access, investing in flexible and adaptive user interfaces which enable users to communicate as they please, developing systems with embedded intelligence in order to process information sent and ensure its timely and qualitative receipt. These social exclusion issues can be particularly problematic in rural areas and yet often go unheeded (Fiander, 2004). The three-point strategy would go a long way to addressing this rural deprivation.

The dominance of the developed world, particularly the USA, can negatively affect the Internet. It has been the prime reason why the majority of accessible and catalogued online content is in English. It is vital that more localised content is funded (Murphy and Scharl, 2004). This would promote cultural identity and improve access for the less able social excluded who for example are unlikely to speak and read English as a second language.

# Culture

There is increasingly a homogenisation of culture in the virtual world, yet individuals still come from distinctive cultures. The expectations of individual participants in the information society thus can differ significantly (Fairweather and Rogerson, 2003). These differences threaten the potential benefits of the virtual world. This can be countered by focusing on core values that we all share such as life, happiness, ability, freedom, knowledge, resources and protection (Moor, 1998). However, developing systems for the virtual world based on only core values can be problematic in that such systems might clash with the deeply held convictions of a culture or community. It is for this reason that the virtual world must also be tolerant of the global moral pluralism (Vedder, 2001).

The Internet-based community crosses traditional geographical and political boundaries and as such comprises individuals from many different cultures. Nance and Strohmaier (1994) suggest there are two important dimensions to consider regarding cultural variability. The first dimension is the continuum from individualism to collectivism. Individualism emphasises self-interest and promotes the self-realisation of talent and potential. Its demands are universal. Collectivism emphasises the pursuit of common interests and belonging to a set of hierarchical groups where, for example, the family group might be placed above the job group. The demands on group members are different from those on non-group members. The second dimension concerns cultural differences in the communication referred to as low-context communication and high-context communication. In the former, the majority of the information resides in the message itself whilst in the latter the communication is implicit. Nance and Strohmaier (1994) suggest that the USA utilises low-context communication whilst Japan uses high context.

"So while there is a cultural homogenisation, the variability that remains makes it very difficult to provide information or conduct a debate in a way that is acceptable to all. This is especially problematic because to a significant extent the processes of globalisation are now unstoppable" (Fairweather and Rogerson,2003).

This is certainly one of the great challenges presented by the Internet. It involves establishing a set of common behavioural standards whilst ensuring that there is no dominant participant. The current offerings of the Internet are a long distance from this position.

# Information

Information providers have taken on a significantly important role in the virtual world. For example, Time Warner AOL is the producer and distributor of much of the information in various forms that we consume. The emergence of such organisations raises many issues. In many ways they are uncontrollable by governments because of their global reach and operation. They wield great power and influence through deciding information content and format. Not that long ago it was reported that Time Warner AOL had a debt which amounted to the GNP of a sizeable nation. Society as a whole is extremely vulnerable if information moguls such as this should they get into financial difficulty. The pressure is on to support and to protect these information providers.

Information moguls are commercially oriented seeking to maximise profit. Costs are minimised through a policy of homogeneous information offering devoid of cultural context. This seems unacceptable and inappropriate. Yet given the power these moguls wiled in the global village it is very difficult to influence them to move to a more heterogeneous offering.

# Freedom and Assembly

Access to information as well as the generation and dissemination of information relate to the fundamental concept of freedom in the virtual world. Consider two articles of the Universal Declaration of Human Rights. Article 19 states that "Everyone has the right to freedom of opinion and expression; this right includes freedom to hold opinions without interference and to seek, receive and impart information and ideas through any media and regardless of frontiers." Whilst Article 5 states that "No one shall be subjected to torture or to cruel, inhuman or degrading treatment or punishment." The application of these articles to the new context of the digital universe raises some important issues. In the name of protecting some civil or human rights, some governments appear to reduce the value and freedom of other rights. For example, "Human Rights Watch reported that Chinese authorities have issued more than sixty sets of regulations to govern Internet content since the government began permitting commercial Internet accounts in 1995 .... describes recent Chinese efforts to police Internet cafes ... cases of several people put on trial or sentenced to prison for downloading or posting politically sensitive material on the web" Human Rights News (2001).

Blocking, filtering and labelling techniques can restrict freedom of expression and limit access to information. Government-mandated use of such systems violates rights regarding freedom of speech. Global rating or labelling systems reduce significantly the free flow of information. Efforts to force all Internet speech to be labelled or rated according to a single classification system distort the fundamental cultural diversity of the Internet and potentially lead to domination of one set of political or moral viewpoints. It does not seem right to employ such techniques in a universal manner.

Article 20, clause 1 of the Universal Declaration of Human Rights states that "Everyone has the right to freedom of peaceful assembly and association." This right has a new twist in the context of the virtual world. Assemblies are an example of the two-way many-to-many communication on which the Internet is based. Bulletin boards, discussion groups, email lists are all examples of new forms of assembly within the virtual world. Therefore, an individual under Article 20 has a right to participate in such assemblies assuming they are peaceful. This brings into question the regulation and restriction put on such activities by governments and private organisations. There is a need to revisit this issue from the perspective of assembly. As it stands it is a conceptual muddle and policy vacuum as described by Moor (1985).

## Data and Self

Conceptual muddles abound in the virtual world. Consider the relationship between data and self. Society has long recognised that taking or using the property without permission is wrong. This extends not only to physical property but also to intangibles such as ideas and data these being collectively recognised as intellectual property. The concept of ownership is culturally sensitive. Whilst there is a reasonable agreement in countries of the West that individuals or groups of individuals have intellectual property rights (IPR), interpretations in other countries and situations are sometimes different (Spinello 1995). For example, IPR safeguards in countries of the Far East are minimal mainly due to a different philosophy that tends to treat intellectual property as communal or social property. In the poorer developing countries the view often taken is that the right to livelihood takes precedence over other claims on which IPR are based. It is only when prosperity increases that there is a shift from a social well-being interpretation of IPR to one with more emphasis on the individual. Regardless of whether the emphasis is on individual ownership or community ownership, there is a big problem which the fundamental concept of data ownership when considering the virtual world of the Internet.

In order to live and prosper in the virtual world, an individual must be visible, credible and creditable. As we each develop electronic persona across a range of digital media and through digital icons such as digital signatures, electronic curriculum vitae, electronic patient records and electronic purses, we come to exist electronically and our needs are addressed through having these digital icons. Without them we cannot function and become invisible. It is how these dilemmas are resolved across national and international legislation and regulation that will establish clear rights of citizens in the virtual world. However, our digital persona is not simply characterised by our digital icons. The sense of self is completed through the relationships with others (Prosser and Ward, 2001). These are represented in the virtual world by such things as emails and chat room dialogues. It can be seen that the electronic persona comprises a complex array of digital data.

In the virtual world, it is a fundamental right of every person to have control over his or her electronic persona. However, this right challenges the traditional views of data ownership because data is the virtual manifestation of self. It is the electronic persona. It is clear therefore that we need to redefine the meaning of self to account for our virtual world existence. We must acknowledge that much of the data relating to an individual cannot be owned by a third party for if we do not we are subscribing to electronic slavery.

One further issue relating to data and self is that of identity. There has been much speculation that people can play with their identities on the Internet and present different electronic persona. Such speculation is characterised in the famous cartoon entitled "In cyberspace nobody knows you're a dog" (Steiner, 1993). This might be possible in the short term but such mimicry is likely to be spotted in the long term as identity is more than simply learning and applying rules, it is about learning within a context and reacting intuitively to different situations as they arise (Whitley, 1997). In the information society, the impact of physical characteristics of those communicating has been minimised. This is potentially beneficial as removing the visual cues about gender, age, ethnicity and social status allow different lines of communication to open up that might have been avoided in the physical world (Whitley, 1997).

## Conversation

In any community conversation is essential. There has been concern by psychologists that computers are having a detrimental effect on society in that the "social glue" of casual conversation is being eroded (Mihill, 1997). The increasing use of email at work, the elimination of bank tellers and shop assistants, and the use of telephones and laptops to telecommute from the home illustrate how the opportunity for small talk is decreasing. This phenomenon is thought to be one reason why shyness is increasing in the population. There is of course a counter argument in that by utilising computer-based communication tools such as the Internet those who are naturally shy become more outgoing since the psychological pressure of face-to-face contact is removed.

However, conversation is culturally founded and this influences the way technology is used. Consider the example of mobile phone take-up in Africa. In December 2001 there were 21 million mobile phones in Africa. This increased to 35 million in 2002 and again to 52 million in December 2003. This amazing growth should be tempered by the fact that only half of sub-Sahara Africa is covered by a mobile signal, many Africans are too poor to buy a mobile and only half of all Africans have ever made a phone call. However, this technology has proved to be fit for purpose socially, culturally and economically. The right consumer proposition has been adopted through offering pay-as-you-go phones, which account for over 80% of phones in Africa. Most African countries permit competition in mobile networks which has kept costs down and evidence shows this is beneficial to all. The socio-economic benefit of improved communication has increased business activity and economic wellbeing. However, the remarkable story relates to culture. Africans are great talkers. They entertain through conversation. Mobile phones simply reinforce these oral traditions. It has become a device for socialisation. For example, Africa has seen the rise of the single-owner multi-user. Friends become a communication centre for a community and enjoy a new social status. The clear message from mobile phones in Africa is that there is an adaptation of both the technology and its implementation which not only is sensitive to local culture but also promotes and enriches it. It is fit for purpose.

## Fit for Purpose Technology

The virtual world must be built upon fit-for-purpose technology. Technology should fit users' needs rather than users should fit technology's needs. Technological communication networks should align with human rights. Systems on the Internet should be culturally sensitive. Systems should be designed to minimise complexity and opaqueness thus promoting trust in the virtual world. Bucy (2000) argues that these systems are, in their current form, too complicated for many people to use and derive benefit. They require a certain level of cognitive ability to navigate successfully. For this reason, he argues that "there is reason to believe that the digital divide will not be completely remedied through universal physical access to computer technology alone." The need to simplify systems radically should form a major design principle for the virtual world.

## Law, Regulation and Ethics

The networks of the virtual world offer exceptional possibilities in communication for exchanging information and acquiring knowledge, and provide new opportunities for growth and job creation. However, at the same time, they conceal risks to human rights and alter the infrastructure of traditional public and private operations. Johnson (1997) explains that the potential benefit of the Internet is being devalued by antisocial behaviour including unauthorised access, theft of electronic property, launching of viruses, racism and harassment. These have raised new ethical, cultural, economic and legal questions which have led many to consider the feasibility and desirability of regulation in this area. Similarly, it is questionable whether technological counter measures will be very effective either. The absence of effective formal legal or technological controls presents grave dangers to society.

The international aspect of the Internet, the transient nature of the content, and the rapid evolution of the techniques and strategies raise specific difficulties for the application of penal and commercial law. It is extremely difficult to determine which laws apply, who is responsible, and what proof is required in the event of a transgression. It is probably unattainable to create international law that can provide legal guarantees for this global community. This would require agreement on universal rights and wrongs which may well be possible for obvious cases such as the dissemination of child pornography but is very difficult for debatable issues such as individual privacy and intellectual property. Where once very few people had substantial enough impacts on the lives of distant people to have significant moral obligations to people tens of miles (or kilometres) away, now for many of us they are routine. As increasingly we interact on a global basis, we find that we do have responsibility for each other regardless of location, yet the moral standards to be upheld are often unclear (Fairweather and Rogerson, 2003). Johnson (1997) suggests that there are three general ethical principles that promote acceptable behaviour in the virtual world:

- Know the rules of the online forums being used and adhere to them.
- Respect the privacy and property rights of others and if in doubt assume both are expected.
- Do not deceive, defame or harass others.

The outcome of not subscribing to such principles is likely to result in chaos overwhelming democratic dialogue, absolute freedom overwhelming responsibility and accountability, and emotions triumphing over reason (Badaracco and Useem, 1997).

Psychologists working online serve as a good illustration of how such themes are relevant for those working within a modern organisation in the information society. King and Poulos (1999) explain that "Psychologists 'apply and make public their knowledge of psychology in order to contribute to human welfare' (APA, 1992). Online psychologists who maintain a website advertising their services often include a wealth of information about psychological disorders and their treatment. This psycho-educational service is available to the public 24 hours a day, can be accessed to the advantage of anyone, not necessarily a client, and is generally provided free of charge. In situations where a recipient of services is in a geographically remote location, online therapy may be the only psychological therapy available to them." In this situation, the psychologist's traditional approach has been transcended with the advent of the Internet. In this new situation, public welfare, distributed benefit, and equality of access are all promoted through exploiting the temporal and geographic independence of the online world. It is a good example of socially responsible transformation based on fit for purpose technology.

This type of transformation is common across many types of work. To assist in promoting social responsibility within the virtual world such transformation should follow a set of strategic pointers as follows (Rogerson, 2004):

- Develop a socially responsible culture within the organisation which nurtures moral individual action.
- Consider and support the well-being of all stakeholders.
- Account for global common values and local cultural differences.
- Recognise social responsibility is beyond legal compliance and effective fiscal management.

- Ensure all business processes are considered from a social responsibility perspective.
- Be proactive rather than reactive.

## Conclusion

In the virtual world, individuals are subjected to e.junkmail, e.money, e.commerce, e.library, e.identity, e.education to mention but a few. Whether these are beneficial depends on a number of factors some of which have been discussed here. However, what is certain is that individuals deserve empowerment and social benefit, inclusion rather than exclusion, and the right to choose between the electronic and the non-electronic.

Inequitable access to and communication of the priceless resource of information is at best unfair and at worst disastrous for society as a whole. An information society that empowers the disabled and less fortunate members of society and sustains equality of opportunity regardless of race, colour or creed is achievable. Governments, policy makers, developers, and service providers of the information society have the wherewithal to create this panacea which balances global common values and local cultural differences. They must have the commitment as well else apocalypse beckons.

## References

American Psychological Association (APA) (1992). Ethical principles of psychologists and code of conduct. *American Psychologists*, 47, 1597–1611.

Badaracco, J. L. & Useem, J. V. (1997). The Internet, Intel and the vigilante stakeholder. *Business Ethics: A European Review*, 6(1), 18–29.

Bucy, E.P. (2000). Social Access to the Internet. *Harvard International Journal of Press/Politics*, 5(1), 50–61.

Fairweather, N. B. & Rogerson, S. (2003). The Problems of Global Cultural Homogenisation in a Technologically Dependant World. *Journal of Information, Communication & Ethics in Society*, 1(1), 7–12.

Fiander, L. (2004). Rural life and Internet accessibility a partnership of exclusion?, *e-Society 2004 conference proceedings*. IADIS, pp. 95–102.

Human Rights News (2001). China Tightens Internet Controls. September. Available from http://www.hrw.org/press/2001/08/china-0801.htm (Accessed 20 July 2003)

Johnson, D. G. (1997). Ethics online. *Communications of the ACM*, 40(1), 60–65.

King, S. A. & Poulos, S. T. (1999). Ethical guidelines for on-line therapy. In: Fink, J. (ed.), *How to Use Computers and Cyberspace in the Clinical Practice of Psychotherapy*. Northvale, NY, Jason Aronson Inc. Publishers, pp. 121–132.

Mihill, C. (1997). Computers spawn social 'ice age'. *The Guardian Online*. 16 July. Available from http://online.guardian.co.uk/paper/archive/86072141-16shy.html (Accessed 15 September 1997)

Moor, J. H. (1985). What is computer ethics?. *Metaphilosophy*, 16(4), 266–279.

Moor, J. H. (1998). Reason, Relativity, and Responsibility in Computer Ethics. *Computers and Society*, 28(1), 14–21.

Murphy, J. & Scharl, A. (2004). Web indicators for globalisation and the virtual divide. *e-Society 2004 conference proceedings*. IADIS, pp. 118–125.

Nance, K. L. & Strohmaier, M. (1994). Ethical accountability in the cyberspace. In: Proceedings of the *conference on Ethics in the computer age*. pp. 115–118.

Pinto, F., Garcia, A. C. B. & Ferraz, I. (2004). A New Model for Digital Inclusion in Brazilian Cities. *IADIS International Conference e-Society 2004*. pp. 79–86.

Prosser, B. T. & Ward, A. (2001). Fear and trembling on the Internet. *ETHICOMP 2001 conference proceedings*. 2, 131–140.

Rogerson (2004). Aspects of social responsibility in the information society. In: Doukidis, G., Mylonopoulos, N. & Pouloudi, N. (eds.), *Social and Economic Transformation in the Digital Era*. IGI Global, pp. 31–46.

Spinello R. A. (1995). *Ethical Aspects of Information Technology*. New York, Prentice-Hall.

Steiner, P. (1993). cartoon. *New Yorker*, 69(20), 5 July, 61. Available from: http://www.unc.edu/courses/jomc050/idog.html (Accessed 10 October 2002)

Vedder, A. (2001). Misinformation through the Internet. *ETHICOMP 2001 conference proceedings*. 2, 35–41.

Whitley, E. A. (1997). In cyberspace all they see is your words. *Information Technology and People*, 10(2), 147–163.

# Chapter 21

# Future Vision [2015]*

## Introduction

> Now social networks
> Before tea-room social chat –
> IT changes us

The Japanese Haiku is a way of looking at the world and seeing something deeper. In English, a haiku poem consists of three lines, with the first and last line having five syllables, and the middle line has seven syllables. The use of punctuation such as a dash divides the poem and prompts the reader to reflect on the relationship between the two parts. The inclusion of three Haiku poems in this chapter serves to illustrate the value of cross-disciplinarity in analysing situations. Readers of this chapter are encouraged to reflect on the deeper meaning of each haiku and use this in their *Future Vision*. Together the three Haikus form a poem entitled *Technological Dependency* (Rogerson 2015).

Founded in 1884, J. Lyons & Co. was a market leader in the UK for fine teas and cakes. In 1894 it opened a teashop in Piccadilly, London and developed this into a chain of over 200 teashops known as Lyon's Corner Houses. In 1951, it built and programmed its own computer, LEO 1 which was used to manage the daily restocking of the Lyon's Corner Houses (Ferry, 2003). It was the first company worldwide to use a digital computer in a commercial setting and heralded the start of business data processing. Similarly, this commercialisation of computing was the beginning of the IT profession which today spans the world in terms of application reach and social impact.

In 1972, I entered the IT profession as a newly qualified graduate. By that time IT was well established as a vital corporate resource supporting all aspects of the business. However, it was still a back-office function staffed by specialist technologists with little experience of business. Fast forward to 2015 and we find that IT (or commonly termed ICT in recent times) now pervades almost every human activity. It no longer is restricted to scientific or commercial endeavour that

---

* This chapter was first published as: Rogerson, S. (2015) Future Vision. Special Issue – 20 years of ETHICOMP. Journal of Information, Communication and Ethics in Society, Vol. 13, Nos 3 & 4. pp. 346–360. Copyright © Emerald Publishing Limited. Reprinted by permission. DOI 10.1108/JICES-05-2015-0011

typified the era of the 1970s. It is a very different world from 64 years ago and the age of LEO. Those entering the ICT profession today are faced with a plethora of application areas using a vast array of technological armoury. Not only that but ICT has been democratised to the extent that many applications are built by non-ICT professionals.

In common with most ICT practitioners, I worked on many systems, some of which failed. Failed ICT systems are still commonplace. Here are just three of the many headline-grabbing failures of recent years. In 2002, a project was launched to upgrade NHS computer systems in England with the aim of revolutionising the way technology is used in the health service through electronic records, digital scanning and integrated ICT systems across hospitals and community care. The project was scrapped in 2011 due to technical and contractual problems at a cost of around £10bn. In 2014, Royal Bank of Scotland was fined £56m by the UK's financial regulators for a system crash which left millions of customers unable to make or receive payments. In 2012, the collapse of an ICT system at a border agency office prevented the processing of thousands of visa applications for foreigners in the UK. The system was used to issue non-EU nationals with a mandatory biometric residence visa or permit.

It was the issue of system failure which led to my involvement in ICT ethics. My industrial career spanned programming, systems analysis, project management and IT services management. Sharing this experience with my students led me to realise that the current practice of the time was having little effect on reducing the risk of system failure. It seemed practitioners were too close to the technological problem. By moving further away, other issues started to become visible – social and ethical issues which at that time were not within the remit of the ICT professional. I discovered the work of Deborah Johnson, Jim Moor, Don Gotterbarn, Chuck Huff and Terry Bynum in the fledgling field of Computer Ethics. The opportunity of working with non-ICT disciplines to address the issue of system failure seemed to offer a solution to this problem which had dogged ICT from the onset of business data processing.

It was this change in my approach which eventually led to the creation of the Centre for Computing and Social Responsibility, ETHICOMP and the Journal of Information, Communication and Ethics in Society. All three have made significant contributions to the development of a thriving international ICT ethics community over the last 20 years. In 1995, when ETHICOMP was launched, the world had become ICT-dependent. The conference brought together a worldwide community of scholars from many disciplines and backgrounds, who were worried about the lack of understanding or concern of the impacts of Information and Communication Technologies (ICT) on individuals and the world at large. At the time the *Times Higher* reported that at ETHICOMP 95 (THES, 1995), "…Delegates from 14 countries agreed in principle to set up a global network of centres to develop the debate and provide information on socially responsible computing. … Besides core ethical issues such as privacy, fraud and obscenity, the researchers will examine broader issues of social responsibility, including the devaluing of jobs and the possible emergence of a gulf between information haves and have-nots."

Two decades later it is time to look forward once more. Have we learnt anything about the manner in which ICT is created, developed and applied? Have academia, industry and government come together to address effectively the wider implications of an increasingly technologically dependent world? Sadly, on balance the answer to both questions seems to be no. There has been much detailed observation and analysis but still the transformation of this into widespread practical positive action remains elusive. In this chapter, I delve beneath these two questions to try to understand why progress has been difficult. The chapter concludes with suggestions of a future approach.

# An Ethics Progress Litmus Test

BCS, the Chartered Institute for IT, ran a special edition of *ITNOW* in the autumn of 2014 which focused on Ethics in ICT. In many ways, it is a litmus test of ethics progress by academics and practitioners working in tandem. It is a disappointing read.

Runciman (2014) points out the "philosophical challenges of extraordinary complexity" in the US Navy's pursuit of embedding moral competence in computational architecture of warfare technology. This project smacks of arrogant technological determinism which is so dangerous. The discussion by Bennett (2014) on robot identity assurance concludes with a series of uninspiring recycled actions. For example, "debate about the use of RFID and NFC technologies which enable tracking of individuals without their knowledge or consent." was an action called for many years ago (for example, see Rogerson (2004)).

Southey (2014) discusses the every-increasing scope of ICT application. He concludes, "The ethical dilemma that faces us is therefore: can I justify unleashing this IT development, knowing that I do not know the extent of its safety? Have I even come close to imagining the worst that could happen? Of course, we can argue, the IT profession is not regulated like law or medicine; BCS has a voice but, unfortunately, no real clout. If we refused to work on robot soldiers, someone else will do it." Once again he simply restates observations of the past. The same is true of Dainow (2014) who discusses the ethics of emerging technology. He concludes, "The IT professional is moving to join the doctor at the centre of modern ethical concerns for society. Society's gaze is sure to follow. It is no longer viable for IT professionals to remain ethically neutral. The next generation of technology will inevitably generate more controversy and concern than anything seen so far. We have enough experience to anticipate many of the issues and avoid them through conscientious and ethically aware design."

Cultural diversity is explored by Freeland (2014). He concludes by highlighting gender discrimination as a key issue in ICT application. This has been known about and investigated for over 20 years. Freeland's article seems naïve and shallow. Holt (2014) focusses on the issue of ethically fit-for-purpose. Once again her conclusions are disappointingly lacking in new insight when she writes "... as IT professionals we have a duty to build a mindset of considering the wider consequences of the IT solutions our developers design... we need to contribute to the wider debate of how IT solutions are used, and how ethical decisions are made around IT-enabled concepts.... So finally, let's get our professional bodies involved in leading the way to develop policy and opinion pieces before our politicians enforce laws, or our judges pronounce life-changing judgments that result in even greater ethical issues." Twenty years ago I wrote (Rogerson, 1995), "... no longer can the profession seek absolution through focusing only on the technical agenda. Indeed, the first question any IS/IT professional should ask is 'Is the action ethical?' and be able to answer based on reasoned thought. - We all need to act and act now!" It is disheartening to find Holt writing similar statements in 2014.

Overall, it is a disappointing edition of *ITNOW*. The lack of ethical consideration in systems design and implementation is evident. The calls for action are neither new nor inspiring. There is virtually no evidence and no pragmatic action; the emphasis being on top-down political rhetoric. In many ways, this edition illustrates at best that we have stood still but probably we are moving backwards in the quest for ethically acceptable technological implementations. There is little evidence of drawing from more than 20 years of effort in developing ICT ethics thinking and practical approaches. Even more surprising is that there is no mention or use of past BCS efforts in addressing ethics (for example, see Harris et al. (2011)).

In 1995, Terry Bynum and I wrote (Rogerson and Bynum, 1995), "The brave new world of the information society - with its robots and global nets, telemedicine and teleworking, interactive multimedia and virtual reality - will inevitably generate a wide variety of social, political and ethical questions. What will happen to human relationships and the community when most human activities are carried on in cyberspace from one's home? Whose laws will apply in cyberspace when hundreds of countries are incorporated into the global network? Will the poor be disenfranchised - cut off from job opportunities, education, entertainment, medical care, shopping, voting - because they cannot afford a connection to the global information network? These and many more questions urgently need the attention of governments, businesses, educational institutions, public advocates and private individuals. We ignore ethics and computing at our peril." The evidence from the *ITNOW* special edition suggests our warnings are yet to be heeded.

## The Evolving Landscape

The evolving landscape is complex and diverse. Technological advances increase the pervasiveness of application to the point where ICT seeps into all aspects of our lives. That in turn causes social turmoil and even ethical questioning. It is this landscape which has been the centre of attention for the ETHICOMP conference series for twenty years. The nature of this changing landscape is vividly illustrated by the themes of the ETHICOMP conferences.

After the generic call for papers for the first conference, ETHICOMP 95 each succeeding conference had an overall theme which reflected current topics of concern. ETHICOMP 96 had the theme "The value of IT to society and the likely impacts upon society's values." It covered areas such as: organisation and society structure and the location of work; privacy and monitoring; value and accuracy of data and information; software and data as intellectual property; security and computer misuse; and developing information systems now and in the future. Many, if not all, of these topics remain of concern and form part of the current landscape.

The theme of ETHICOMP 98 was "Computing and the workplace; the potential tension between financial goals, politics and personal agendas; and social and professional responsibility." Whilst the perspective was different the detailed areas of concern were similar to ETHICOMP 96. By ETHICOMP 99 the concerns over pervasion were evident. The conference theme was "Look to the future of the Information Society." The aim was to focus on how achievements of the past could be built upon to ensure that the important issues impacting upon society, its citizens and its organisations would be effectively addressed and so help improve the quality of life.

The concept of the information society had firmly been established and ETHICOMP 2001 reflected this in its theme "Systems of the Information Society." The aim was to focus on the ethical and social impacts of systems on society, organisations and individuals. This was done from four perspectives: Software engineering and systems development; Teaching ethics to computing students; Ethics in virtual communities; and Ethics in the off-line world. Concerns for the individual increased and ETHICOMP 2004 focused on "Challenges for the Citizen of the Information Society." The aim was to consider the social and ethical impact of ICT on individuals as consumers, as employees and as citizens.

ETHICOMP 2007 had the overall theme of "Glocalisation: Bridging the Global Nature of Information and Communication Technology and the Local Nature of Human Beings." The aim was to explore the global nature of ICT and the associated local as well as global challenges. Such challenges existed. still exist, for example, in eDemocracy, assistive technology, nanotechnology,

technology-enhanced learning, and health informatics. This global focus homed in on social media at ETHICOMP 2011 with the theme "The social impact of social computing" covering applications, technological infrastructure and theoretical underpinnings. Wang et al. (2007 p79) explain, "With the advance of Internet and Web technologies, the increasing accessibility of computing resources and mobile devices, the prevalence of rich media contents, and the ensuing social, economic, and cultural changes, computing technology and applications have evolved quickly over the past decade. They now go beyond personal computing, facilitating collaboration and social interactions in general. As such, social computing, a new paradigm of computing and technology development, has become a central theme across a number of information and communication technology (ICT) fields. It has become a hot topic attracting broad interest from not only researchers but also technologists, software and online game vendors, Web entrepreneurs, business strategists, political analysts and digital government practitioners, to name a few." This illustrates the point made in the call for papers for ETHICOMP 2015 that "many of the concerns of 1995 have deepened and many new ones have arisen." Thus, the landscape continues to evolve dramatically.

# Drivers

This evolving landscape is formed by the interaction of a set of drivers. There are top-down drivers which are typically impositions by bodies of authority which dictate where resources should be placed to achieve some overall goal. Bottom-up drivers emanate typically from grassroots collective action resulting in a widespread change. Middle-out drivers involve all those within, for example, an organisation, who are empowered to initiate change, support it, propose new ideas, and innovate. Middle-out drivers do not exhibit the hierarchal characteristics which the top-down and bottom-up drivers do. Boyle (2009) suggests top-down drivers provide political direction, middle-out drivers are the focus of change teams and bottom-up drivers are the voice of citizens. Three key drivers are now considered.

## *Bottom-Up*

Millennials are those currently in their late teens to early 30s and within five years they will constitute half of the workforce (Frey & Berger, 2014; Ericsson ConsumerLab, 2013). They are a bottom-up driver because they, as citizens, have grown up with technology and consider change as ever-present. Three quotations typify millennial perception:

> "For Millennials, technology is a sixth sense. It's a way of knowing the world. There is no real cognitive processing like there is for other generations who learn it later in life."

> "They are very, very comfortable with change. They have a global awareness, they are very resilient, and they are technologically very savvy, creative and collaborative."

> "When Millennials become managers, I think there will be zero tolerance for inefficient systems in technology. They already don't understand the legacy systems."
> (Ericsson ConsumerLab, 2013, p.8,10,11)

Increasingly millennials will influence the way in which society looks at technology, what is acceptable technology and what is not. The demand for more flexible working and the blurring of traditional boundaries between home and work will increase. The millennial voice will be heard and will have to be taken into account.

## Middle-Out

The ICT Relationship trinity is a middle-out driver concerning the delivery of ICT. The identification, development and use of ICT occur within a set of interrelated entities. These entities are defined in three sets: vendors of both hardware and software; developers of both infrastructure and application; and direct and indirect recipients of ICT. Relationships exist between this trinity of entity sets. If the trinity operates effectively then the likelihood of acceptable ICT is increased (Rogerson, 2014). The ICT relationship trinity will both be affected by and affect organisational culture, business strategy and societal norms.

Trust across the trinity is paramount. Smith (2011) explains that trust is a social relationship where 'A' trusts 'B' to do 'C'. 'A' will only trust 'B' if 'A' believes 'B' to be trustworthy with respect to 'C' and for 'B' to be trustworthy requires that 'B' has both the competence and the motivation to satisfy the requirements of 'C'. Smith suggests that trust is relational in nature and this implies that trustworthiness is but one component of a larger social relationship of trust between actors in this case across the ICT relationship trinity.

Consider this example. In the delivery of a graphical user interface operating system (GUI-OS), an application software developer will only trust a vendor if the developer believes that the vendor is trustworthy with respect to GUI-OS and for the vendor to be trustworthy requires that the vendor has both the competence and the motivation to satisfy the requirements of providing a robust GUI-OS. Similarly, a user recipient will only trust a developer if the user recipient believes that the developer is trustworthy with respect to the application and for the developer to be trustworthy requires that the developer has both the competence and the motivation to specify and produce acceptable application software.

Paradoxically, in the larger social relationship of trust, a recipient may distrust a developer to deliver new software because either competence or motivation or both are lacking but at the same time might trust the same developer regarding ongoing maintenance of existing software because both competence and motivation are present. This example illustrates the complex and dynamic nature of the ICT relationship trinity and how its success drives acceptable ICT and its failure leads to unacceptable ICT.

## Top-Down

As mentioned earlier, top-down drivers provide political direction. Therefore, high-level policies are top-down drivers. Within the European Union the research and innovation frameworks direct enormous effort in, for example, ICT development and application. Horizon 2020 (H2020) is EU Research and Innovation programme with nearly €80 billion of funding available over 7 years (2014–2020). It aims to drive economic growth and create jobs. The claim is that "It promises more breakthroughs, discoveries and world-firsts by taking great ideas from the lab to the market." There are three perspectives in H2020: social challenges; creating industrial leadership and competitive frameworks; and excellence in the science base. ICT is pervasive within these perspectives (European Commission, 2013). The stated aims and objectives show the political steer of H2020.

In the following example, ICT-related activity is considered (European Commission, 2014). In practice, Responsible Research and Innovation (RRI) has five different aims:

- Engaging society more broadly with research and innovation activities (public engagement)
- Facilitating the access to scientific results (open access)
- Ensuring gender equality in both the research process and research content (gender dimension)
- Taking account of the ethical dimension (ethical issues)
- Promoting formal and informal science education (education)

In contrast, Social Sciences and Humanities (SSH) are expected to provide a rich contribution to research and innovation, in at least two ways:

- Monitor economic, legal and social issues related to technological developments. Furthermore, explore the potential impacts of envisaged technological developments in order to mitigate risks and inconveniences and optimise benefits as well as the chance of success/uptake of these technological developments.
- Reframe and update the concepts, meanings and expectations arising from the deployment of ICTs. In particular, explore the "rebound" of technologies in society and how societal uptake creates new grounds for innovation.

This top-down driver lays out the action paths through the RRI aims and separately considers the impacts through the SSH. There is a clear demarcation of types of activity within silos of traditional disciplinary groupings. There is a distinct lack of linking such activity to practice which seems to contradict the overall H2020 mission.

## *The Amalgam*

Drivers, such as the three key examples described here, have a direct impact on advances in ICT application. These drivers affect attitudes and societal norms. Indeed, the amalgam of top-down, middle-out and bottom-up drivers leads to a complex situation where the attitude and behaviour of individual professionals and professional collectives are highly influential in the delivery of socially acceptable ICT. Therefore, with each passing day ICT ethics becomes more important as it is that which steers all those involved in ICT in an ethical direction.

## Linking Research and Practice

Single views are flawed
Life is grey not black and white -
Harmony spawns hope

ICT is a practical subject and so it is reasonable to expect related research should have a strong link to practice. In Europe, the European Parliament's support for the ethical and social consideration of ICT has increased with each research framework. Cross-disciplinary projects are encouraged and in the latest framework improved links to practice are demanded. In June 2014, the U.S. House of Representatives approved *Frontiers in Innovation, Research, Science and Technology Act of 2014* otherwise known as *FIRST Act of 2014*. Funding for research at the National Science Foundation (NSF) is laid out by this Act. It drastically cut the funding for the social, behavioural and economic sciences areas. The previous year the Act banned NSF from supporting political science work that did not meet very narrow criteria. These moves seem to stifle cross-disciplinarity and send out a clear message that technologists including those in ICT should focus on technological issues rather than wider impacts. This is a retrograde step.

The reports of four EU-funded research projects which included an ICT ethics perspective have been briefly reviewed. The projects were completed successfully under FP7 which was the European Union's Research and Innovation funding programme for 2007–2013. The four projects were: EGAIS (The Ethical GovernAnce of emergIng technologieS - New Governance Perspectives for Integrating Ethics into Technical Development Projects and Applications); EIW3R (The ethics of information warfare: risks, rights and responsibilities); ETICA (Ethical Issues of Emerging ICT Applications); and PHM-ETHICS (Personalised health monitoring – Interdisciplinary research to analyse the relationship between ethics, law and psychosocial as well as medical sciences). ETICA and PHM-ETHICS had a strong interdisciplinary flavour. The following direct quotes from the end of project reports provide a sense of project achievement.

EGAIS (2012) states, "Within EGAIS, we defined guidelines that *could* inform policy makers and researchers in planning, implementing and assessing the ethical governance of research both within research projects and in a broader policy context."

EIW3R (2013) states, "These research findings provided the conceptual ground for the identification of normative theories that *could* generate ethical principles of decision-making within the context of IW."

ETICA (2013) states, "Implementing these [ETICA] recommendations *will* contribute to better and ethically more sensitive processes of technology development. … ETICA *has made* significant inroads in disseminating these findings and influencing policy and practice in ICT ethics, in particular on the European level."

PHM-ETHICS (2013) states, "The PHM-ETHICS project developed a methodology which *can* be used modularly for the assessment of various aspects regarding impact and features and impact of PHM technologies."

It appears that only ETICA has had some immediate impact beyond research through its involvement in policymaking. This is a top-down driver influence. The other three projects seemed to conclude with potential impact claims providing explanations of what outputs could be used for. Overall, there are some general points which come out of this brief review. Links with practitioners appear tentative as the focus of these projects is weighted towards concepts and theory. However, some would argue that it is unreasonable to expect pragmatic outcomes from projects of 2 to 3 years' duration. If so then the purpose of such projects needs to be explored. From the four projects reviewed there was little evidence that projects had drawn from previously funded projects of others. If this is commonplace then research effort seems sporadic rather than catalytic or progressive. The value of such research needs to be questioned. If the focus of research is simply research and a tool for spawning the next funded project then its impact on the practical world of ICT at best will be very limited. The volume of published output from funded research is phenomenal, it is the classic information overload which, if left to fester, will mutate into information pollution which Nielsen (2003) argues, "stops being a burden and becomes an impediment to your ability to get your work done," in this case research.

# Educating Future Generations

One way in which *ICT ethics* research can be linked to practice is through the education of future generations of ICT practitioners. Programmes, in terms of both curriculum and pedagogy, should be informed by research in such a way that the relevance of research is implicit and that education goes beyond the confines of the technology. This broadening of education is paramount in reducing the risk of unacceptable ICT. Denning (2001) argues that "The problem is that IT's way of looking at itself is lopsided toward the technology and is therefore self limiting. Approaching the design of software and services with customers at the center runs against the grain of our field. We need a major shift of worldview to cross that chasm." This lopsided view is epitomised by the concluding remarks of Meijer and Kapoor (2014), "Sooner than you think, every company will be a software company. The obvious way to run a software company is as a meta software application, recursively structured as a layer of commuting closed-loop feedback systems, using a strictly layered architecture modelled after the time-proven hierarchal structure of armies and applying software-inspired profiling and debugging techniques to optimise the profitability of the enterprise." To conclude an article with jargon-ridden phraseology is unimpressive. The stated view is steeped in technology, has little regard for the environment in which an enterprise exists and appears to have no moral concern for society and its citizens.

Professional bodies often demand that ethical and social issues be included in programmes in order for accreditation to be achieved. It is important to consider how meaningful the coverage of ethics and social impact issues is in programmes. It is unacceptable if inclusion is more about compliance rather than a desire to include ethics and social impact because it is essential and relevant. Superficial compliance to achieve accreditation is unethical and therefore unprofessional.

There is an expectation by ICT undergraduates that they will be instructed in the theories, methodologies and application of ICT. They are usually unaware and therefore have no expectation that their university education must include the ethical and societal context within which ICT exists. These technologically-oriented students have a resonance with experiential learning. Consequently, any attempt to expose them to ethical and societal perspectives of IT is more likely to succeed if a varied diet of experiential learning is provided (see, for example, Essendal and Rogerson, 2011). Academic philosophers delivering lectures about the nuances of ethical theory is inappropriate and indeed is likely to strengthen the barriers behind which purist technologists will defend their technological ideology.

The opportunity to participate in an active rather than passive manner leads to an experiential journey of maturity from tutor-led activities to student-led activities. Through this process, ICT professionals of the future are more likely to gain the necessary skills and knowledge to act in a socially responsible manner not on the basis of instinct and anecdote but on rigour and justification. It is important to provide tools to support this broader approach. Research activity has led to several tools which can be used in programmes and subsequently taken into practice on graduation. Three exemplars are DIODE, RCIT and SoDIS.

DIODE is a structured meta-methodology for the ethical assessment of new and emerging technologies (Harris et al., 2011). DIODE was designed by a mixture of academics, governmental people and commercial practitioners. It was designed to help diverse organisations and individuals conduct ethical assessments of new and emerging technologies.

The Framework for Responsible Research and Innovation in ICT (RICT, 2015) is a tool that helps those involved in research and innovation in ICT to do so responsibly. The Framework consists of a set of scaffolding questions that allow researchers, funders and other stakeholders to consider a range of aspects of ICT research.

The Software Development Impact Statement (SoDIS) process extends the concept of software risk in three ways: it moves beyond the limited approach of schedule, budget and function; it adds qualitative elements; and it recognises project stakeholders beyond those considered in typical risk analysis (Gotterbarn and Rogerson, 2005). SoDIS is a proactive feed-forward approach which enables the identification of risks in the manner in which ICT is developed and in ICT itself.

Based on my experience of the many students I have had the privilege to teach, I believe ICT professionals of the future do care about the impact they will have on society. There is the wherewithal to build fit-for-purpose ethically sound systems by design but it will still happen more by accident unless effective education underpinned by relevant research exists.

# Future Vision and Conclusions

> Computer jargon
> Academic rhetoric –
> Actions not words count

When I first engaged with this community over 20 years ago I was struck by the open-mindedness of its members. It was a far cry from the single-minded, hierarchical culture that existed and still exists in some areas of academia. The core principles on which the ETHICOMP conference series is founded reflect this inclusive community. These principles are:

- It is a broad-based conference series which address the social and ethical perspectives of ICT and converging technologies.
- It is inclusive providing a forum for those with diverse opinions to share and debate issues in a collegiate atmosphere. Dialogue is fundamental.
- It is multidisciplinary. This means that both single discipline and multidiscipline papers are presented at the conferences. The community is receptive to these differing perspectives
- It is culturally diverse. Delegates have come from all continents and presented papers from many cultural perspectives.
- It is supportive of academic growth. New scholars and researchers are encouraged to present papers, all of which are within the main programme rather than in a separate stream. This promotes inclusivity and collegiality.

Many of those in the community exhibit common cognitive traits which can be summarised by Gardner's (2007) *Five minds for the future* classification described as:

- Disciplinary Mind: The mastery of specific scholarly disciplines, crafts or professions.
- Synthesising Mind: The ability to integrate ideas from disparate sources into a coherent whole and to communicate that integration to others.
- Creating Mind: The capacity to break new ground through new ideas, unfamiliar questions and fresh ways of thinking.
- Respectful Mind: An awareness and appreciation of differences among human beings and human groups.
- Ethical Mind: The realisation of one's obligations as a worker and as a member of society.

This type of collective action and individual attitude should be cherished and nurtured for it holds the key to the future. Unfortunately, today within academia, there seems to be a growing trend to address the ethical and social implications in a single disciplinary manner. There is a dwindling dialogue between industry and academia about such matters. Within industry and government the compliance culture has taken a firm hold and so strangles the opportunity for dialogue and analysis of complex multi-faceted socio-ethical issues related to ICT. The gate-keepers of past generations who provided the glue between academia, industry and government are becoming increasingly inactive and a serious void now exists.

## Global Action Plan

The global action plan called *Future Vision* is proposed as an initiative to address the serious fragmentation of work in and between academia and industry related to so-called *ICT Ethics*. We need to identify what and where progress has been made, what problems or barriers exist and where is the future potential. A number of actions are suggested to address this issue. Existing activity could be accumulated under these actions. The actions are as follows:

- Review projects (funded through, for example, FP7 and H2020 in the European Union, NSF in the US, EPSRC and ESRC in the UK and ARC in Australia) with significant ethics-social impact content to ascertain:
  - The level of multi/inter/transdisciplinarity
  - The level of engagement with industry, government and public sector services
  - The post-project impact on the roll-out of acceptable ICT
  - The key active individuals in the area of pragmatic *ICT ethics*

- Identify professional bodies, businesses and public bodies which have proactive initiatives to promote and sustain the good practice. For example, in Europe, the Council of European Professional Informatics Societies (CEPIS) is currently strongly promoting ethical ICT practice.
- Identify other active individuals who fall outside professional bodies, businesses and public bodies but have potential contributions to make. These could offer rich alternative perspectives.
- From these surveys develop a new network of those in academia, industry, public sector, government who are active in the area. Such a network would be the catalyst in *Future Vision*.
- Creative effective communication channels which will enable dialogue and collaboration across the network and beyond.
- Develop a new vision for *ICT ethics* which is theoretically grounded but pragmatic so that industry and government will engage, accept and embrace. *ICT Ethics* can be defined as integrating ICT and human values in such a way that ICT advances human values, rather than doing damage to them which therefore must include the formulation and justification of policies for the ethical use of ICT, and carefully considered, transparent and justified action leading to ethically acceptable ICT products and services (Rogerson, 2011).
- Make a difference through challenging complacency, indifference and ambivalence regarding ethical ICT by those involved in any aspect of researching, developing, implementing and using ICT.

The aim of *Future Vision* is to regenerate the relationships across the wider community so that ICT will be developed and utilised in an ethical and socially acceptable manner. It is not simply an academic initiative but a whole-world initiative which will lead to an improvement in practice. I and my generation are not the ones to drive this through. *Future Vision* is in the hands of the Millennials.

## Note

The paper, which forms Chapter 21, is an extension of the keynote lecture I delivered at *ETHICOMP 2014, Liberty and Security in an Age of ICTs* held in Paris in June 2014.

## References

Bennett, L. (2014). Robot identity assurance. *ITNOW*, 56(3), 10–11.

Boyle, R. (2009). Public sector change management – looking back to look forward. Keynote address, *Association of Chief Executives of State Agencies (ACESA) Conference*. 1 October.

Dainow, B. (2014). Ethics in emerging technology. *ITNOW*, 56(3), 16–18.

Denning P. J. (2001). When IT becomes a profession. In: Denning, P.J. (ed.), *The Invisible Future: The Seamless Integration of Technology Into Everyday Life*. McGraw-Hill. pp. 295–325.

EGAIS (2012), *EGAIS Report Summary*. Publications Office of the European Union. Available from http://cordis.europa.eu/result/rcn/53898_en.html (Accessed 28 April2015).

EIW3R (2013). *EIW3R Report Summary*. Publications Office of the European Union. Available from http://cordis.europa.eu/result/rcn/59645_en.html (Accessed 28 April2015).

Ericsson ConsumerLab (2013). *Young professionals at work*. An Ericsson Consumer Insight Summary Report, April.

Essendal, T. & Rogerson, S. (2011). A holistic approach to software engineering education. In: Hussey, M., Wu, B. % Xu, X. (eds.), *Software Industry Oriented Education Practice and Curriculum Development: Experiences and Lessons*. IGI Global, pp. 83–97.

ETICA (2013), *ETICA Report Summary*. Publications Office of the European Union. Available from http://cordis.europa.eu/result/rcn/54085_en.html (Accessed 28 April2015).

European Commission (2013), *A guide to ICT-related activities in WP2014-15*. Available from https://ec.europa.eu/programmes/horizon2020/sites/horizon2020/files/ICT%20in%20H2020%20WP2014-15_0.pdf (Accessed 28 April2015).

European Commission (2014). *How to Go about RRI and SSH in ICT-related parts of H2020 WP14*. Available from http://ec.europa.eu/information_society/newsroom/cf/dae/document.cfm?action=display&doc_id=4160 (Accessed 29 May2014).

Ferry, G. (2003). *A Computer Called LEO: Lyons Teashops and the World's First Office Computer*. London, Fourth Estate.

Freeland, A. (2014). Cultural difference. *ITNOW*, 56(3), 24–25.

Frey, C. B. & Berger, T. (2104) Work in the digital age. *RSA Journal*, 160(5559), 16–19.

Gardner, H. (2007), *Five Minds for the Future*. Boston, MA, Harvard Business School Press.

Gotterbarn, D. & Rogerson, S. (2005). Next generation software development: responsible risk analysis using SoDIS, *Communications of the Association for Information Systems*. 15(article 40), 730–750. Available from http://aisel.aisnet.org/cgi/viewcontent.cgi?article=3162&context=cais

Harris, H., Jennings, R. C., Pullinger, D., Rogerson, S. & Duquenoy, P. (2011). Ethical assessment of new technologies: a meta-methodology. *Journal of Information, Communication & Ethics in Society*, 9(1), 49–64.

Holt, A. (2014). Flight control. *ITNOW*, 56(3), 26–27.

Meijer, E. & Kapoor, V. (2014). The responsive enterprise: embracing the hacker way. *Communications of the ACM*, 57(12), 38–43.

Nielsen, J. (2003). Quoted in: Twist, J. Web guru fights info pollution. *BBC News Online*. Available from http://news.bbc.co.uk/1/hi/technology/3171376.stm (Accessed 29 April2015).

PHM-ETHICS (2013). *PHM-ETHICS Report Summary*. Publications Office of the European Union. Available from http://cordis.europa.eu/result/rcn/56833_en.html (Accessed 28 April2015).

RICT (2015). *Framework for Responsible Research and Innovation in ICT*. Available from http://responsible-innovation.org.uk/torrii/content/framework (Accessed 30 April2015).

Rogerson, S. (1995). But IS IT ethical?. *IDPM Journal*, 5(1), 14–15.

Rogerson, S. (2004). ETHIcol - Tag Ethics. *IMIS Journal*, 14(5), 31–32.

Rogerson, S. (2011). Ethics and ICT. In: Galliers, R. & Currie, W. (eds.). *The Oxford Handbook on Management Information Systems: Critical Perspectives and New Directions*. Oxford University Press. pp. 601–622.

Rogerson, S. (2014). Preparing IT professionals of the future. *Mondo Digitale*. AICA - Associazione Italiana per l'Informatica ed il Calcolo Automatico, 50(2). Available from http://mondodigitale.aicanet.net/2 014-2/ (Accessed 28 April2015).

Rogerson, S. (2015). Technological dependency. *ACM SIGCAS Computers and Society*, 45(2), 4.

Rogerson, S. & Bynum, T. W. (1995). Cyberspace the ethical frontier. *Multimedia, The Times Higher Education Supplement*, No 1179, June 9, p. iv.

Runciman, B. (2014). Drones, robots, ethical decision dilemmas. *ITNOW*, 56(3), 6–9.

Smith, M. L. (2011). Limitations to building institutional trustworthiness through e-government: a comparative study of two e-services in Chile. *Journal of Information Technology*, 26(1), 78–93.

Southey, D. (2014). What could happen?. *ITNOW*, 56(3), 14–15.

THES (1995), Companies offered ethics advice. *Times Higher Education*. 10 April.

Wang, F. Y., Carley, K. M., Zeng, D. & Mao, W. (2007). Social Computing: From Social Informatics to Social Intelligence. *IEEE Intelligent Systems*, 22(2), 79–83.

# EDUCATION                                        V

*The adoption of a broader [educational] approach that addresses economic, technological, legal, social and ethical concerns will help to harness technology to people's benefit, rather than allowing it to enslave or debilitate them.*

(Simon Rogerson, 1998, p. 33)

Education and awareness programmes related to the positives and negatives of digital technology must be appropriate and effective because, "Tell me and I forget, show me and I remember, involve me and I understand" (quotation sometimes attributed to Benjamin Franklin and sometimes attributed to Xun Kuang). It is argued that the promotion of social responsibility should underpin such programmes. This underpinning can be summarised as follows (Rogerson, 2004):

- Develop a socially responsible culture within work, home and society which nurtures moral individual action.
- Consider and support the wellbeing of all stakeholders.
- Account for global common values and local cultural differences.
- Recognise social responsibility is beyond legal compliance and effective fiscal management.
- Ensure all processes are considered from a social responsibility perspective.
- Be proactive rather than reactive when addressing the development and use of digital technology.

Part 5 focuses on how to provide effective digital ethics education and awareness. This includes provision for students, professionals and the public. The five chapters offer novel approaches to education provision which cross the boundaries between the science and technology offerings and the arts and humanities offerings.

## References

Rogerson, S. (1998). *Ethical Aspects of Information Technology: Issues for Senior Executives.* London, Institute of Business Ethics.

Rogerson, S. (2004). Aspects of social responsibility in the information society. In: Doukidis, G., Mylonopoulos, N. & Pouloudi, N. (eds.), *Social and Economic Transformation in the Digital Era.* IGI Global, pp. 31–46.

*Chapter 22*

# Preparing to Handle Dilemmas in the Computing Profession [1996]*

Society in general and organisations in particular are becoming more dependent upon computer technology. Those responsible for the development and application of computer technology are faced with decisions of increasing complexity which are accompanied by many ethical dilemmas. It is imperative that future computer professionals are taught the meaning of responsible conduct. The inclusion of computer ethics in a professional development programme should foster within individuals, as Maner (1995) puts it, "A reasoned and principled process by which reflective moral judgements are made."

The term "ethical dilemma" can be misleading and over-restrictive. As the *Encyclopaedia Britannica* points out, it is not necessary that a dilemma should have an unwelcome conclusion; but from its traditional use in rhetoric, the word has come to mean a situation in which each of the alternative courses of action (presented as the only ones open) leads to some unsatisfactory consequence. A professional development programme does, of course, need to have wider boundaries within which this is just one type of situation examined. Consequently, Gotterbarn (1992) suggests that the pedagogical objectives of the professional development programme within computing should include:

- An introduction to the responsibilities for their profession
- An articulation of the standards and methods used to resolve non-technical ethics questions within their profession
- The development of some proactive skills to reduce the likelihood of future ethical problems

All computer professionals and policy makers need to have skills and knowledge in this very broad range of areas in order to do their jobs effectively and sensitively (Bynum, 1992).

---

* This chapter was first published as: Rogerson, S. (1996) Preparing to handle dilemmas in the computing profession. *Organisations and People*, Vol. 3, No. 2, May, pp. 25–26. Copyright © Simon Rogerson.

A programme should give participants experience identifying, clarifying, comparing and contrasting computer ethics cases, including the practical resolutions of dilemmas. Such formal training, while including some conceptual content, ideally should focus primarily upon experiential learning. The intention should be not only to provide education in ethical principles as an underpinning to truly professional work but also to train the participant in ethical case analysis.

In a paper which I gave to a London conference earlier this year (Rogerson, 1996), I suggested that there are eight ethical principles that the computer professional should subscribe to, relating to honour, honesty, bias, adequacy, due care, fairness, social cost and action. All should be addressed in a well-balanced programme.

As to case analysis, Liffick (1995) suggests there is a need to provide a framework which enhances critical analysis and overcomes shortcomings in the understanding of ethical theories. He proposes nine steps in analysing scenarios.

1. List all participants and their actions
2. Reduce list through simplifying assumptions
3. List any legal considerations
4. List possible options of the participants
5. List possible justifications for the participants' actions
6. List the key statements
7. List the questions raised
8. Consider other models and related issues
9. Compare to codes of ethics

This process decomposes the complex problem into its constituent parts which in turn enhances understanding and increases the chances of deriving a solution that is reasoned out and ethically sensitive.

While formal training is important, providing an essential foundation, it will be worthless without some form of ongoing development and support. Newly acquired enlightened attitudes need to be nurtured. Acting from an ethical standpoint can often lead to conflict both with peers and corporate objectives. Support and encouragement, together with a wider ownership of ethically sensitive decisions and actions, must be achieved. There are several commonly accepted work practices which could be adopted to affect this change. For example, consider the interesting parallels between quality assurance and applied ethics. In both cases, there is a need to encourage work practices and attitudes which promote the fundamental concepts; yet these "softer" concepts are often misconceived, by both management and the workforce, as being secondary to "harder" concepts such as finance.

In the late 1970s and throughout 1980s, quality became more central to organisation strategy. With the realisation that quality was a prerequisite to economic security many organisations in the western industrialised countries, notably the United States and the United Kingdom, turned towards Japan to gain new insights into quality assurance. Some of the initiatives succeeded; others did not. One of the most interesting ideas to be adopted was the Quality Circle. This is a small group of people who do similar work meeting voluntarily on a regular basis to identify problems, to analyse the causes, to recommend the solutions to management and, where possible, to implement those solutions themselves. Given the parallels between quality and ethics, the establishment of Ethics Circles to support the consideration of ethical issues in organisations has merit. These could be operated on similar lines to Quality Circles, thus providing support to individuals who are engaged in ethically sensitive decision making, raising general awareness of ethical issues and acting as informal staff development in this area.

The combination of formal training through, for example, case study analysis and informal support through, for example, Ethics Circles, should ensure that computer professionals within organisations are equipped to handle the ethical dilemmas which they will inevitably face daily. The chances of achieving a socially sensitive profession will be increased and IT may well realise its potential as the technology of empowerment and freedom.

# References

Bynum, T. W. (1992). Computer ethics in the computer science curriculum. In: Bynum, T. W., Maner, W. & Fodor, J. L. (eds.), *Teaching Computer Ethics*. Research Center on Computing and Society, Southern Connecticut State University, pp. 12–25.

Gotterbarn, D. (1992). The use and abuse of computer ethics. In: Bynum, T. W., Maner, W. & Fodor, J. L. (eds.), *Teaching Computer Ethics*. Research Center on Computing and Society, Southern Connecticut State University, pp. 73–83.

Liffick, B. W. (1995). Analysing ethical scenarios. *ETHICOMP95 Conference*. UK, De Montfort University.

Maner, W. (1995). Unique ethical problems in information technology. *ETHICOMP95 Conference*. UK, De Montfort University.

Rogerson, S. (1996). The ethics of software development project management. *PASE'96 Conference*. UK, University of Westminster.

# Chapter 23

# Preparing IT Professionals of the Future [2014]*

## Introduction

J. Lyons & Co. was renowned throughout the United Kingdom for its fine teas and cakes which were mainly sold through its chain of more than 200 high street cafés. In 1951, it built and programmed its own computer, LEO which was used to manage the daily restocking of the Lyons tea shops (Ferry, 2003). It was the first computer to be used for business data processing. In many respects, this commercialisation of computing heralded the beginning of the IT profession which today spans the world in terms of application reach and social impact.

As a young graduate, I entered the IT profession in 1972. It was well established as a vital corporate resource but it was still a back-office function. Fast forward to 2014 and we find that IT pervades almost every human activity. It no longer is restricted to scientific or commercial endeavour that typified the era in which I joined the profession. It is a far cry from 63 years ago and the age of LEO. Those entering the IT profession today are faced with a plethora of application areas using a vast array of technological armoury. Not only that but IT has been democratised to the extent that many applications are built by non-IT professionals. The responsibilities of young IT professionals and their obligations to society are onerous. Yet it is uncertain how well they are prepared for such challenges and whether they have been educated to understand that they are the custodians of the most powerful and flexible technology mankind has invented.

The commercialisation of IT is not without its problems. To see IT as a powerful corporate resource simply to facilitate the prosperity of the organisation is wrong. Unfortunately, this perspective is commonplace. For example, the *2012 Cost of Cyber Crime Study* published by the Ponemon Institute (2012, p. 24) uses two separate cost streams to measure the total cybercrime cost for each participating organisation. These streams relate to internal security-related activities and the external consequences experienced by organisations after suffering an attack. The report fails to recognise the societal cost of cybercrime in terms of society at large or individuals directly

---

* This chapter was first published as: Rogerson, S. (2014) Preparing IT professionals of the future. Mondo Digitale, AICA – Associazione Italiana per l'Informatica ed il Calcolo Automatico, Vol. 50, No 2, April. Copyright © Simon Rogerson.

or indirectly affected. A second example concerns SAS, a leader in business analytics software and services, and the largest independent vendor in the business intelligence market. On its website, SAS (2013) states, "and big data may be as important to business – and society – as the Internet has become. Why? More data may lead to more accurate analyses. More accurate analyses may lead to more confident decision making. And better decisions can mean greater operational efficiencies, cost reductions and reduced risk." Again, the focus is very much on commercial wellbeing with only a passing remark about society. These two examples are indicative of the sort of emphasis given to IT potential or worth. There appears to be imbalance in this emphasis.

However, there are some hopeful signs of a more balanced view being adopted by some. Here are just two examples. The winner of the 2012 Australian Government ICT Young Professional of the Year Award, Christopher Giffard from the Department of Education, Employment and Workplace Relations, was quoted as saying in his acceptance speech, "It is my hope that the award will draw attention to the importance of accessibility and standards on the web, both for multimedia and for general web content, and the obligation that our industry has to ensure equal access for all Australians to information services and technology" (ACS, 2012). In India, the Al-Ameen Movement helps in the education of the young in the socially and economically deprived sections of the society in the region of Bangalore. As part of this, the Al-Ameen Institute of Information Studies prepares the youth of today to become future IT professionals. Its Principal explains, "Students are entrusted to our care for integrated development which includes technical, moral, physical and spiritual development, besides imparting knowledge in their disciplines. We at Al-Ameen nurture them … to develop into confident, proactive and ethical young IT professionals ready to take up the corporate challenges in the international arena" (AISS, 2014).

This chapter discusses the type of challenge to be faced; the practical tools that might be used in addressing such challenges and the style of educational preparation that could be used. The aim is to provide the stimulus to rethink the manner in which we should prepare IT professionals of the future.

## Issues to Address

The underlying aim that should be instilled in future IT professionals is to deliver fit-for-purpose systems which accommodate recipients' needs rather than recipients having to adapt to systems. They should be encouraged to move away from the traditional view of "one solution fits all" to the view that "one solution is no solution." Rights, justice, care, and empathy should pervade practice. The IT environment should be considered through two lenses: relationships and timeframes. This will have an impact on the manner in which IT is developed and implemented as illustrated by the Big Data example at the end of this section.

### IT Relationship Trinity

The first lens is a high-level issue which focuses on the actual delivery of IT. The identification, development and use of IT occur within a set of interrelated entities. These entities can be categorised into vendor of both hardware and software; developer of both infrastructure and application; and recipients both direct and indirect. Direct recipients comprise clients and users while indirect recipients comprise individuals, the general public, and society as a whole. Relationships exist between these entities and are defined as a relationship trinity as shown in

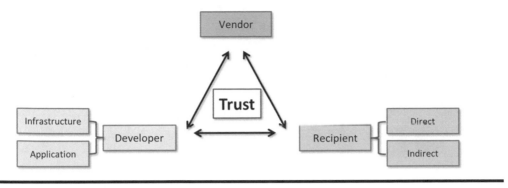

**Figure 23.1   The IT relationship trinity.**

Figure 23.1. If the trinity operates effectively then the likelihood of acceptable IT is increased. The IT relationship trinity will both be affected by and affect organisational culture, business strategy and societal norms. Relationships will be two-way between vendor and developer, developer and recipient, and recipient and vendor.

Trust across the IT relationship trinity is paramount. Smith (2011) explains that trust is a social relationship where "A" trusts "B" to do "C." "A" will only trust "B" if "A" believes "B" to be trustworthy with respect to "C" and for "B" to be trustworthy requires that "B" has both the competence and the motivation to satisfy the requirements of "C." Smith further suggests that trust is relational in nature and this implies that trustworthiness is but one component of a larger social relationship of trust between actors. For example, in the delivery of application software running under a graphical user interface operating system (GUI-OS), the user recipient will only trust a vendor if the recipient believes that the vendor is trustworthy with respect to GUI-OS and for the vendor to be trustworthy requires that the vendor has both the competence and the motivation to satisfy the requirements of providing a robust GUI-OS. Similarly, the recipient will only trust a developer if the recipient believes that the developer is trustworthy with respect to the application and for the developer to be trustworthy requires that the developer has both the competence and the motivation to specify and produce acceptable application software. Therefore, in the larger social relationship of trust, a recipient may distrust a vendor or developer because either competence or motivation or both are lacking to deliver this new software but at the same time might trust the same vendor or developer regarding ongoing maintenance of existing software because both competence and motivation are present.

It is important that future IT professionals understand the trustworthy nature of the IT relationship trinity. This becomes increasingly important the more pervasive IT becomes. It is simply wrong to instruct future IT professionals in technological subjects alone in isolation of the complex social structure in which systems design, development and operation exist.

## Timelines

The second lens is a high-level issue which concerns the respective timelines associated with evolving IT. This is illustrated in Figure 23.2. The horizontal axis represents time and the vertical axis has five separate, though interrelated, timelines.

In the beginning, there exist ethics and social norms which people subscribe to. These might change over time, but very slowly. There is existing law which provides a practical perspective of such ethics and social norms. A piece of IT is developed over a short period of time as shown in

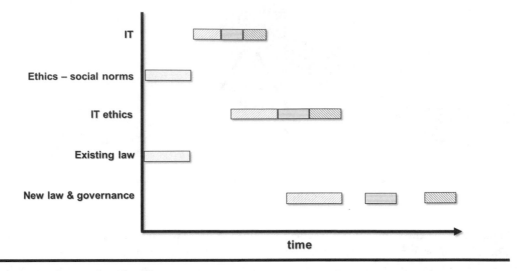

**Figure 23.2  Respective timelines.**

the IT timeline. This timeline has three elements representing the evolution of the piece of IT through three generations. Typically, the ethical implications of the piece of IT only come to light after the first generation is implemented. The ethical consideration continues but at slower pace than the technological evolution as illustrated in Figure 23.2. Indeed, it could be by the time that this consideration is concluded the IT has passed through 2 further generations. It may be that the IT requires a new or amended law or governance regulation. This legal consideration takes considerable time to bring new laws onto the statute book and for these to become operational as shown in Figure 23.2. By the time the law is in place, the third-generation IT may be well established operationally. From this discussion, it can be seen that there is a serious misalignment of timescales. As such, the piece of IT is operating for a considerable period in an IT policy vacuum. This will always be the case with evolving IT for ethical consideration will lag behind technological development and the provision of appropriate law or governance will lag even further behind. This is why there will always be a challenge for IT professionals in delivering acceptable IT. Furthermore, it is why the appropriate, balanced preparation of future IT professionals is paramount.

## *The Advent of Big Data*

Returning to 1951 and the first business data processing system, it is clear that the data collected and generated was localised, impersonal and unlikely to be shared with other systems, be they mechanised or manual. By 1972, the world had changed. Business data processing systems were commonplace. Data relating to people was being processed and generated. Systems were sharing data within single organisations. Transfer of data across organisations was limited but did exist. Concerns began to be voiced as personal data collection increased and relationships were established between data which was collected for very different purposes. These concerns grew as data was now accessible not only offline but also online. This prompted the Organisation for Economic Cooperation and Development (OECD) to publish its *Recommendations of the Council Concerning Guidelines Governing the Protection of Privacy and Trans-Border Flows of Personal Data* on 23 September 1980. Those concerned about the ethical issues surrounding the use of IT were similarly moved to publish. For example, Mason (1986) published his seminal paper in which he stated the four ethical issues of the information age: privacy, accuracy, property and accessibility (PAPA). It was not until 24 October 1995 that the European Parliament issued Directive 95/46/ EC *on the protection of individuals with regard to the processing of personal data and on the free movement of such data.* "The UK Government was required to implement this Directive which it did in the form of the Data Protection Act 1998. It came into force on 1 March 2000 although some provisions did not commence until October 2007" (The Data Protection Society, 2010).

This account illustrates the misalignment of timelines. The business data processing systems had evolved through many generations before growing ethical concerns eventually prompted legislation to be drawn up. It took many years for this legislation to be implemented in practice. During this period of concern which lasted in the region of 15–20 years, the only thing individuals had to rely on was the trustworthiness of the IT relationship trinity and there were many instances where the trinity was perceived as being untrustworthy.

There has been yet another technological shift in data processing in recent years. This is now known as Big Data. Big Data is data which is too large, complex and dynamic for any conventional data tools to capture, store, manage and analyse (WIPRO, 2013). According to Laney (2001), Big Data is defined by three attributes; volume in terms of the large amounts of data, velocity in terms of the need to analyse large amounts of data quickly and variety in terms of the vast range of structured and unstructured data types. To illustrate this it has been estimated (ASIGA, 2013) that everyday businesses and consumers together create 2.5 quintillion bytes of data. Each month 30 billion pieces of content are added to Facebook. Each day 2 billion videos are watched on YouTube. By 2015, 3 billion people will be online sharing 8 zettabytes (8 by $10^{21}$) of data. There have been growing ethical concerns about Big Data. For example, Matzner (2014) argues that the vast array and variety of data coupled with new data mining and knowledge discovery techniques create new types of privacy invasion and indeed challenges the very notion of privacy. If this is so then the current and proposed approaches to personal data protection are likely to be inappropriate.

On 25 January 2012, the European Commission unveiled a draft *European General Data Protection Regulation* that will supersede the Data Protection Directive. Will this address the ethical issues surrounding Big Data – probably not. Even if it does, how long will it take for this to be implemented – probably many years based on the previous data protection legislation track record and by that time technology will have morphed yet again. Alexander Solzhenitsyn (1969) wrote, "As every [wo]man goes through life, [s]he fills in a number of forms for the record, each containing a number of questions. There are thus hundreds of little threads radiating from each [wo]man, millions of threads in all. If these threads were suddenly to become visible, people would lose all ability to move." It would seem his words have come true with the advent of Big Data.

## Toolset for Practical IT Ethics

IT is a practical endeavour which is supported by many design and development tools. If the ethical dimension is to be taken into account through every step of design and development, and ultimately in implementation and operation then this consideration must either be embedded in existing tools or new tools produced which are compatible with existing technologically-oriented tools. For nearly 20 years, I have been involved in the development of a toolset for practitioners. In many instances, this has been in collaboration with professional bodies such as BCS and IMIS in the United Kingdom, ACM and IEEE-CS in the United States and ACS in Australia. A set of five tools are very briefly described here, of which three are then discussed in the next section as part of the experiential learning approach put forward as a way to prepare future IT professionals.

*Product-Process* (Rogerson, 2010): The decision-development-delivery cycle of IT is surrounded by complex interrelated ethical and social issues. These need to be addressed during the IT process and embedded within the IT product. Process concerns the activities of ICT professionals when undertaking research, development, and service/product delivery. The aim is for professionals to be virtuous in Aristotelian terms. In other words, a professional knows that an action is the right thing to do in the circumstances and does it for the right motive. Product concerns the outcome of professional ICT endeavour and the potential impact of these products on people, society and the environment. The ethics focus of the product perspective is technological integrity from, for example, a Kantian or utilitarian perspective. This can be addressed by embedding ethics within ICT products themselves. This tool provides a simple framework to consider issues from the two perspectives.

*DIODE* (Harris et al., 2011): DIODE is a structured meta-methodology for the ethical assessment of new and emerging technologies. There are two different angles for the ethical assessment of new technologies: a strategic/abstract angle and a project/application-specific angle. DIODE includes two channels to accommodate this distinction. DIODE comprises five components: Define questions; Issues analysis; Options evaluation; Decision determination; and Explanations dissemination. Without training and guidance, it is difficult for technologists to take ethical concerns into account during the development and deployment of new technologies. DIODE can provide that training and guidance through a practical meta-methodology which should help IT professionals, policymakers, and academics.

*SoDIS* (Gotterbarn & Rogerson, 2005): Limiting the focus of risk analysis to quantifiable factors and using a narrow understanding of the scope of a software project are major contributors to significant software failures. The Software Development Impact Statement (SoDIS) process extends the concept of software risk in three ways; it moves beyond the limited approach of schedule, budget, and function; it adds qualitative elements; and it recognises project stakeholders beyond those considered in typical risk analysis. It is a proactive feed-forward approach which enables the identification of risks in the manner in which IT is developed (Process) and IT itself (Product).

*Professional code of ethics* (http://www.acm.org/about/se-code): Every IT professional body has a code of conduct. The Software Engineering Code of Ethics and Professional Practice of ACM and IEEE-CS in partnership, has international standing having been translated in many languages and adopted by many professional bodies worldwide. It provides a practical perspective within its preamble and principles. The preamble states,

> These Principles should influence software engineers to consider broadly who is affected by their work; to examine if they and their colleagues are treating other human beings with due respect; to consider how the public, if reasonably well informed, would view their decisions; to analyse how the least empowered will be affected by their decisions; and to consider whether their acts would be judged worthy of the ideal professional working as a software engineer. In all these judgments concern for the health, safety and welfare of the public is primary; that is, the "Public Interest" is central to this Code.

*Dependencies mapping* (Rogerson, Wilford & Fairweather, 2013): This is a method comprising a lexicon, a diagramming tool, relationship tables, and structured commentaries. A dependencies map provides a structured way for knowledge of ethical issues to be identified and organised. Dependencies maps go beyond stakeholder relationships by covering multiple types of entities (such as processes and artefacts), and multiple types of relationships. Dependencies mapping is undertaken without the constraints of a pre-defined lens such a stakeholder, data or operation. A dependencies mapping tool can be utilised to raise awareness about the many external influences and impacts resulting from the development and use of IT.

# Experiential Learning for Computer Science and Software Engineering Undergraduates

There is an expectation by computer science and software engineering undergraduates that they will be instructed in the theories, methodologies and application of IT. They are usually unaware and therefore have no expectation that their university education must include the ethical and societal context within which IT exists. These technologically-oriented students have a resonance with experiential learning. Consequently, any attempt to expose them to ethical and societal perspectives of IT is more likely to succeed if a varied diet of experiential learning is provided (Essendal & Rogerson, 2011). As Benjamin Franklin once wrote, "Tell me and I forget, show me and I remember, involve me and I understand." Quite simply, academic philosophers delivering lectures about the nuances of ethical theory is inappropriate and indeed is likely to strengthen the barriers behind which purist technologists will defend their technological ideology. In this section, a series of experiential learning examples is discussed. These have been used and subsequently honed over many years to provide appropriate instruction for IT professionals of the future. The opportunity to participate in an active rather than passive manner leads to an experiential journey of maturity from tutor-led activities to student-led activities. Through this process, the IT professionals of the future are more likely to gain the necessary skills and knowledge to act in a socially responsible manner not on the basis of instinct and anecdote but on rigour and justification.

## *Exercise Using Product-Product*

In the public domain, there are many *Invitation to Tender* documents (ITT) relating to IT. This provides a rich resource of real-world requirements for IT solutions. Using the Product-Process approach, students, in small teams, are asked to analyse the specification of requirements included in a given ITT. The task is defined as:

- Read the specification in the ITTs
- In groups, discuss the potential ethical issues
- Split these issues into Process and Product
- Complete the Ethics Checklist form
- Present your findings to the cohort as an outline of the system followed by the identified Process and Product issues

This exercise gives students the opportunity to investigate current IT requirements which enables them to place their studies in the context of the real world. This consideration, through an ethical lens, encourages them to look beyond the technical. The requirement to present their small team's findings to the complete student cohort helps them to focus and firm up their thoughts on the identified ethical issues. This is a good way to experience for the first time an ethical analysis of an IT solution at its onset. The tutor can tease out general themes based on ethical theory out of the findings thereby providing the students with some insights of conceptual underpinnings.

## SoDIS Project Auditor Laboratory

SoDIS has been translated into a software decision support tool called SoDIS Project Auditor (SPA) (available at http://www.softimp.com.au/sodis/spa.html). Students use SPA in a computer laboratory over several weeks. For these laboratory sessions, a fictitious company called CHEMCO has been created. Chemco produces polyester and alkyd resins, gel coats and conventional and inverse water-based polymers from four manufacturing sites. It has decided to build a new manufacturing plant in Midtown and this will be operated using a new production control system called PRO-CHEM (http://www.ccsr.cse.dmu.ac.uk/staff/Srog/teaching/info3402/Chemco2/index.htm, accessed 5 March 2014).

SPA computer laboratories of up to 16 students split into teams of three or four are held to investigate PRO-CHEM. There are three phases to this extended activity as follows:

- Case Start-up Session where the objectives are: to review the CHEMCO company; to introduce the requirements of the new production control system; to identify the stakeholders of the system; and to initialise the SoDIS analysis.
- PRO-CHEM SoDIS Analysis Sessions where the objectives are: to undertake a SoDIS analysis for an allocated stakeholder subset of PRO-CHEM; and to produce a comprehensive data set in preparation for distillation.
- Case Outcome Preparation where the objectives are: to review the SoDIS analysis for an allocated stakeholder subset of PRO-CHEM; to identify the main concerns about PRO-CHEM; and to prepare a presentation of findings for the Board of Directors.

This extended activity gives students the opportunity to analyse thoroughly, from an ethics perspective, a system development project in its initial stage. Using a software tool in a computer laboratory to undertake, this work places students in a familiar setting albeit the task itself is very different. SPA structures their discussions and they experience a dichotomy of opinions as to what is acceptable and unacceptable in terms of the proposed system. The final output is a board-level report through which they experience the challenge of distilling a large amount of detailed analysis which combines ethics and technology into a succinct report that is accessible to a board of directors many of whom are likely to have little technical knowledge and experience.

## Exercise Using the Software Engineering Code of Ethics and Professional Practice

This exercise is undertaken in a large group setting on an individual basis. Students are given a case study of a system which has been developed and implemented. The case focuses on the ongoing operation of the system and provides details of the experience of users and the manner in which IT personnel respond to users, maintaining and modifying the system as a result. The case study has some obvious and some obscure issues within it. The student task is structured as follows:

- Use the Software Engineering Code of Ethics and Professional Practice to consider the case study.
- Did anyone violate any of the ethical principles in the code? If so, was the violation justified? Why do you say so?
- What "policy vacuum" does the case reveal that could be filled by adding a new principle to the code?
- How could that new principle be stated and justified?

The exercise concludes with a large group discussion of the students' findings. This is an opportunity for students to experience the value of a code of ethics if used proactively. The tutor summarises the session through offering a simple checklist in the form of five ethics-grounded questions (shown in parentheses) as follows:

- Who is affected by your work? (Utilitarian)
- Are others being treated with respect? (Kantian)
- How would the public view your decisions? (Publicity test)
- How will the least empowered be affected? (Rawlsian)
- Are your acts worthy of the model computing professional? (Virtue ethics)

Finally, the tutor points out that a code of ethics provides a practical justification for action and offers a framework within which to structure professional work.

## Student-Led Activities

Conventionally, student-led activities take place in small group sessions such as tutorials. The SPA computer laboratories and ethics analysis of case studies (Bynum & Rogerson, 2004, Chapter 3) are indicative of this. Large group student-led activities offer a different experience. A variety of approaches can be adopted such as break-out activities, periods of reflection, topic presentations and formal debates (Essendal & Rogerson, 2011), two of which are outlined here.

- Topic presentations: The culmination of a module on IT Ethics is a student-led seminar for which students organise, chair and present papers. A typical range of presentation topics taken from previous seminars is: How to prevent children from accessing unsuitable content; Engaging older, handicapped and other excluded people in ICT; Examples of real situations of professional responsibility; Software with Adware is ethical or unethical?; and New media – forms and reliability of the information.
- Formal debates: This provides students with the opportunity to develop their critical thinking, to increase their ability to defend ideas, to improve their communication skills, and to be tolerant of the arguments of others. Typical motions used in previous student-led debates are: "This house believes it is acceptable to force online services on those who prefer off-line interaction with government or who are technophobes" (Utilitarian focussed

debate); "This house supports the development of assistive technologies that exceed human abilities" (Aristotelian focussed debate); and "This house believes it is unnecessary to consider cultural diversity in generalised ICT products and services in order to promote ICT acceptance and effectiveness" (Kantian focussed debate).

## Conclusion

Based on my experience of the many students, I have had the privilege to teach, I believe IT professionals of the future do care about the impact they will have on society. I have had former students contact me about whistleblowing on unethical practice and about how the ethics element of their degree education has helped them to shape their professional lives.

However, there are problems that need to be addressed and resolved. Too many IT professionals hide in technological clouds seemingly indifferent to the ethically charged nature of IT. It is unclear whether this is through lack of awareness or a belief such issues are outside their scope of responsibility. Today we have the wherewithal to build fit-for-purpose ethically sound systems by design but I worry that it still happens more by accident.

In the past from the 1980s onwards, progress was made in ensuring the ethical dimension of IT was considered in education, research, government and industry. Sadly, today there is a sense of going backwards. It is important to find out why this is so. Perhaps it is because there are not so many headline-grabbing IT failures in the media these days. Perhaps it is because the excitement of IT ethics as a frontier has gone as ethics has moved more into the mainstream. Perhaps it is because of the sophistication of new technologies which increases transparency and makes it even harder to comprehend the potential issues. Perhaps it is because ethics has been politicised through target setting and the demand for tick-box compliance. Perhaps it is because public bodies, professional bodies and universities seem to place less emphasis on ethical issues. Perhaps it is because there is a growing silo-mentality in the delivery of ethics education at the expense of a transdisciplinary approach.

It is for these reasons that we need to educate our future generations of IT professionals in a way that gives them practical skills to address the complex ethical and societal issues which surround evolving and emerging IT. I firmly believe such education should be based on a varied diet of participative experiential learning delivered by those who have a practical understanding of the design, development and delivery of IT. It is for all in the IT profession to rise to this challenge and safeguard not only the IT profession but also society at large.

## References

ACS (2012). *Australian Government ICT Young Professional of the Year Award Winner.* Available at http://www.acs.org.au/news-and-media/news-and-media-releases/2012/2012-australian-government-ict-young-professional-of-the-year-award-winner (Accessed 3 March 2014).

AISS (2014). *Al-Ameen Institute of Information Sciences: Principal's Message.* Available at http://aiis99-edu.org/principal_message.htm (Accessed 2 March 2014).

ASIGA (2013). *What is Big Data?.* Available at http://www.prophet.com/theinspiratory/wp-content/uploads/2013/02/big-data-infographic.jpg (Accessed 14 October 2014).

Bynum, T. W. & Rogerson, S. (eds.) (2004). *Computer Ethics and Professional Responsibility.* Blackwell Publishing.

Essendal, T. & Rogerson, S. (2011). A holistic approach to software engineering education. In: Hussey, M., Wu, B. & Xu, X. (eds.), *Software Industry Oriented Education Practice and Curriculum Development: Experiences and Lessons*. IGI Global, pp. 83–97.

Ferry, G. (2003). *A Computer Called LEO: Lyons Teashops and the World's First Office Computer*. London, Fourth Estate.

Gotterbarn, D. & Rogerson, S. (2005). Next generation software development: responsible risk analysis using SoDIS. *Communications of the Association for Information Systems*, 15(article 40), 730–750. Available from http://aisel.aisnet.org/cgi/viewcontent.cgi?article=3162&context=cais

Harris, H., Jennings, R. C., Pullinger, D., Rogerson, S. & Duquenoy, P. (2011). Ethical assessment of new technologies: a meta-methodology. *Journal of Information, Communication & Ethics in Society*, 9(1), 49–64.

Laney, D. (2001). 3D data management: Controlling data volume, velocity and variety. *ETA group research note*, 6(70), 1.

Mason, R. O. (1986). Four ethical issues of information age. *MIS Quarterly*, 10(1), 5–11.

Matzner, T. (2014). Why Privacy Is not Enough Privacy in the Context of "Ubiquitous Computing" and "Big Data". *Journal of Information, Communication and Ethics in Society*, 12(2), 93–106.

Ponemon Institute (2012). *2012 Cost of Cyber Crime Study: United Kingdom Benchmark Study of UK Organisations*, October. Available at http://www.hpenterprisesecurity.com/collateral/report/HPESP_WP_PonemonCostofCyberCrimeStudy2012_UK.pdf (Accessed 23 April 2013).

Rogerson, S. (2010). A review of information ethics. *Journal of Information and Management, Japan Society for Information and Management*, 30(3), 6–18.

Rogerson, S., Wilford, S. & Fairweather, N. B. (2013). A dependencies mapping method for personal health monitoring. In: Schmidt, S. & Rienhoff, O (eds.), *Interdisciplinary Assessment of Personal Health Monitoring*. Vol. 187 of Studies in Health Technology and Informatics. IOS Press, pp. 79–93.

SAS (2013). *Big Data: What It Is and Why It Matters*. Available at http://www.sas.com/big-data/ (Accessed 11 October 2013).

Smith, M. L. (2011). Limitations to building institutional trustworthiness through e-government: a comparative study of two e-services in Chile. *Journal of Information Technology*, 26(1), 78–93.

Solzhenitsyn, A. I. (1969). *Cancer Ward*. Translated by Bethell N. & Burg D. New York, Farrar, Staus & Giroux.

The Data Protection Society (2010). *History of Data Protection*. Available at http://www.dataprotectionsociety.co.uk/history (Accessed 5 March 2014).

WIPRO (2013). *Big Data*. Available at http://www.prophet.com/theinspiratory/wp-content/uploads/2013/02/bigdata2_infographic.jpg (Accessed 5 March 2014).

## Chapter 24

# Using Technology to Incorporate Students' Work-Based Experiences into a Blended Learning Environment [2008]*

## Introduction

The Experiential Learning Via Industrial Stories (ELVIS) framework is the outcome of a Research Informed Teaching Award (RITA) funded project, to investigate how the industrial experiences of final-year computing students could be incorporated into their studies. As such, ELVIS is a student collaboration tool, as advocated by Christiansson (2004).

ELVIS currently exists as part of a compulsory final-year module, entitled *Software Quality, Professionalism and Ethics,* for students on computer science and software engineering sandwich courses. It is important to note the sandwich structure of these courses, where students spend two years at university, their third year in relevant industrial employment, and their final year back at university, because it is the experience gained during the industrial employment that forms the crucial core of the framework.

The *Software Quality, Professionalism and Ethics* module was designed to enhance the transformation of students from learners into mature and competent practitioners, as they move towards graduation. For this transformation to be successful, two issues had to be addressed:

* This chapter was first published as: Essendal, T. and Rogerson, S. (2008) Using Technology To Incorporate Students' Work-Based Experiences into a Blended Learning Environment. *ICICTE 2008*, Corfu, 10–12 July. Copyright © Simon Rogerson and Tugrul Essendal.

- An overlapping study of technology, application and ethics so that students understand the wider implications of and influences on computing technology in the real world.
- Student engagement in discussion and debate concerning a range of real-life professional issues within the three related topics mentioned earlier.

The module, which uses a blended learning approach, comprising weekly large-group interactive sessions, a virtual learning environment (VLE), and various technology clinics, does just that. The aim of ELVIS is to make the integrated study of these new and, to some, alien topics relevant to students' own experiences, in order to maximise their engagement with the module.

This approach is in accord with previous findings (Andresen, Boud & Cohen, 1999, p. 225), which advocate "the recognition and active use of the learner's relevant life experiences." The driving conviction behind this approach is the belief that "[if] new learning can be related to personal experiences, the meaning thus derived is likely to be more effectively integrated into the learner's values and understanding" (Andresen, Boud & Cohen, 1999, p. 225). In the case of ELVIS, learning is linked to industrial experiences.

A major component of ELVIS is reflection, leading to deep learning (Hinett, 2002a). Student reflection is accepted as a valuable tool that, according to Philip (2006, p. 37):

- Allows students to get the most from their education and other activities
- Sets the scene for and creates life-long learning
- Maximises personal and economic potential
- Enhances employability and enterprise skills

Indeed, Kolb (1984) suggests that reflection is key in cyclic experiential learning. McDermott, Göl and Nafalski (2002) reinterpret the Kolb cycle as an alternation between two groups of activities: experiential and reflective. In this case, we identify the experiential activities as the industrial placement year and the final year project. The reflective activities are the *Software Quality, Professionalism and Ethics* module and ELVIS as one of its components. There are, of course, barriers to students being able and willing to be reflective, which include the assessment-driven nature of students. "This is a natural strategic approach that is widespread amongst students, and maybe we should be more accepting of this and so ensure all desired learning outcomes are taken into account during the assessment process" (Philip, 2006, p. 37).

The type of deep learner that ELVIS seeks to promote was originally defined by Marton and Säljö (1984) and subsequently endorsed by Duignan (2002) who states, "The deep learner examines theoretical ideas in the light of his or her experience; evidence is gathered, organised and structured into a form that renders coherence to the information and to its relationships and cognitive consequences" (p. 218).

It was during a review of the module in its early days that the tutors became aware of the rich knowledge base of nearly 100 years of student industrial experience to be mined. The conclusion was that this was an invaluable source of knowledge that students would benefit from. Thus, the ELVIS research project was launched to address the question of how to capture and share this knowledge, and integrate it with the existing learning objectives of the module.

The key points that ELVIS is founded on are as follows:

- To promote deep learning rather than surface learning through reflection
- To share stories in order to support and enhance the relationship between students, thus creating new knowledge and learning from others

- To implement a reflection log (in the form of a student notebook) that facilitates purposeful learning
- To encourage students to learn from each other by way of complementing the traditional student-teacher learning relationship
- To overcome the barrier of assessment-driven pedagogy, replacing it with a learning-driven pedagogy
- To use storytelling as a means of encouraging reflection

# The Experiential Learning Pedagogy

The Experiential Learning Pedagogic model, which was adapted from Juwah (2002), is shown in Figure 24.1. While the original model supported problem-based learning, this model supports experiential learning, which is incorporated into various problem-based learning exercises carried out during interactive group sessions. In this respect, ELVIS begins by helping to develop reflection skills and story-telling capabilities on an individual basis, but as the year progresses and stories are released to the group domain, via a shared repository, ELVIS supports the collaborative learning that takes place in group sessions that leads to enhanced knowledge for all members.

# The ELVIS Framework

The ELVIS framework enables students to capture, communicate and consume workplace knowledge, experience and lessons learnt. The mechanism used is the production of short, work-based stories related to topics covered in the module. The framework comprises:

- A skills profiling tool, based on the industry-standard SFIA v3 (see http://www.sfia.org.uk/), so that (a) students appreciate the complete spectrum of skills used in IT and understand where their particular work fits into this scheme and (b) tutors can monitor the type of work their students were involved in
- A quiet period during the weekly large-group sessions to reflect on the topics covered, linked to ... A student notebook for capturing all reflections, ideas and story outlines, during and after the quiet period
- A repository of those stories, with summary of lessons learnt, that students have decided to release, to be shared among the cohort
- A student-led workshop
- An online evaluation using the current VLE

How these components fit together is shown in Figure 24.2.

The starting point is the skills profiling tool, followed by registration under ELVIS. Once students are fully familiar with the spread of skills in IT and their own place in it, they use that knowledge as part of their registration process. This is how the tutors are made aware of their students' experiential backgrounds.

Once the registration is complete, students take part in two parallel strands of work:

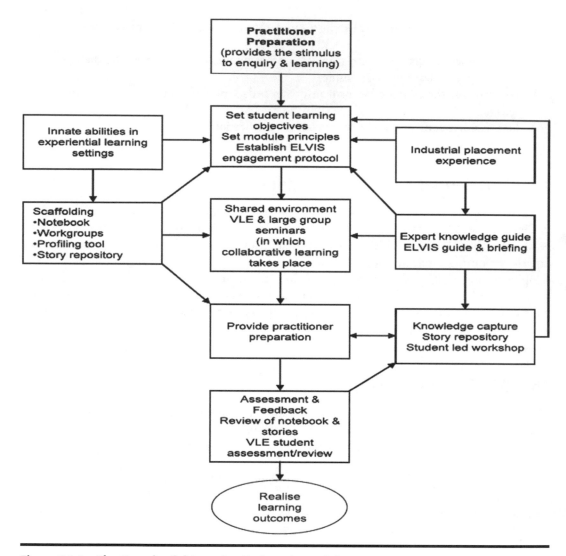

**Figure 24.1   The Experiential Learning Pedagogic model.**

- Producing their stories
- Preparing for the student-led workshop

The production of stories involves several phases:

- Reflection on the topics covered in weekly sessions and how these topics relate to their own experiences
- Participating in discussions during weekly sessions, to generate and fine-tune thoughts (i.e., moving their ideas forward)
- Making notes to identify potential stories
- Writing up and releasing a minimum of six selected stories to the group domain
- Commenting on the released stories of peers, as another way of moving ideas forward

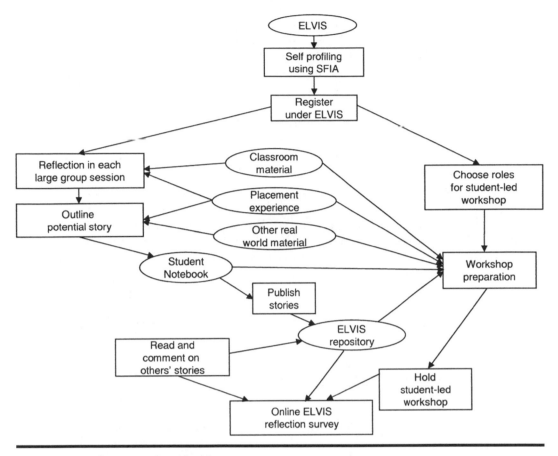

**Figure 24.2  The ELVIS framework.**

The culmination of ELVIS-related activities is the student-led workshop. The purpose of this workshop is for students to bring together their ideas and reflections, formulated during the year, and discuss these in an open forum.

For the workshop, the first thing students need to do is to choose the role they wish to play. There are several roles to choose from, these being coordinators, workshop chairs presenters, panel members, and researchers. Participation in the workshop is voluntary and, for those who chose to participate, the roles are allocated on a first-come-first-served basis. The incentive for undertaking a workshop role is the option to publish a minimum of three stories, instead of six. Students, acting as coordinators, oversee the forming of teams, their membership, and topics to present.

Once all required stories have been submitted and the workshop has been run, the last activity is the online reflection survey which provides students with one last opportunity to consider both the relationship between study and practice and the transformation from the former to the latter.

## Software Support

Every component of the ELVIS framework, except the quiet periods of reflection, is supported by software. Wherever possible, this support is via existing packages, like VLE for the online evaluation. However, the majority of activities are supported by custom software. There were two reasons for this: (a) to emphasise the novel nature of ELVIS, on the understanding that all university modules now use VLE, within which many activities use blogs, thus leading to a potentially boring and bland sameness of delivery, not helped by the rather unfriendly interfaces of many VLEs; and (b) the need for extra functionality that ready-made software could not provide.

Figure 24.3 shows the main storytelling screen, displaying a typical story. This screen is used for entering new stories and editing existing ones. It also enables students to set various defining characteristics of their stories, like, for example, relevance to quality, professionalism or ethics; impact on the storyteller; and involvement in the story.

The current version of ELVIS software is written in Visual Basic.NET and runs on the faculty intranet. The choice was taken on the basis of the expertise within the project team and the stability of the software environment. The executable files are made available to students via links on the VLE. However, because these executables are not, by nature, web-enabled, the drawback is that students cannot access the software when they are off-campus. The intranet manager imposes this restriction for reasons of access security.

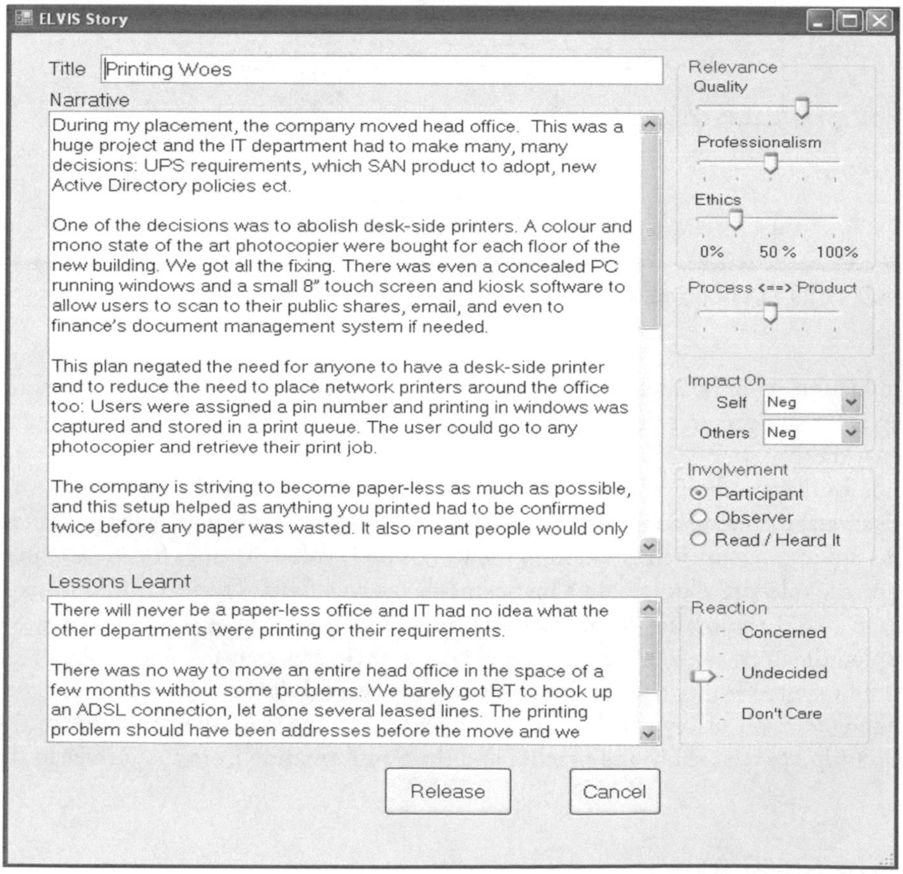

**Figure 24.3  Story screen.**

To solve this problem, the next version will be converted into ASP.NET to widen access. This will certainly remove one of the criticisms directed at ELVIS. Also, the RITA project remit is to widen the use of ELVIS, by making it available to all courses at the university and the wider academic community. This is only possible via the Internet.

## Student Engagement

Initial student response was mixed. The novelty of the storytelling aspect of the framework has been the biggest problem, hindering student engagement, simply for not knowing what to do and not appreciating the value of this learning style. Alterio (2003) suggests that some students may feel comfortable from the onset but others may need time and assistance to accept this type of learning. This is reiterated by Hinett (2002b) who states, "[students] often only appreciated [the value] some time after the process of reflection has begun." Storytelling is a significant learning tool (Clandinin & Connelly, 1998; McDrury & Alterio, 2002; McEwan & Egan, 1995; Pendelbury, 1995; Witherell & Nodding, 1991). It was, therefore, a disappointing start, given the many advantages of the story-telling approach, as suggested by Alterio (2003), such as:

- Encourage co-operative activity
- Encompass holistic perspectives
- Value emotional realities
- Link theory to practice
- Stimulate students' critical thinking skills
- Capture complexities of situations
- Reveal multiple perspectives
- Make sense of experience
- Encourage self-review
- Construct new knowledge

There is obviously a problem for those students who have not done placement or have not had previous employment and who, therefore, have no first-hand experience of the workplace. The advice to such students was to read the weekly IT publications, like Computing and Computer Weekly, as well as the IT sections of daily newspapers, like The Guardian. The expectation was that, over a period of time, they would pick out events that they could reflect on and write up as stories, in their own words.

For those students who have had placement experience or previous employment, the expectation was that they would reflect on the link between their classroom topics and their workplace experiences, in order to establish their observations and conclusions, which they would then write up as stories. Those observations and conclusions would also be used as contributions to classroom discussions and student-led workshop themes.

A large number of students seemed unable to carry out this task, without direct guidance and active help. They seemed reluctant to "read around" the topics or unable to establish a link between their academic activities and workplace experiences. One conclusion the tutors have reached is that neither their schooling nor the first two years of their studies prepare them for such activities.

Some students did not seem to understand reflection. They were confused about what to record in their notebooks. Also, they did not know how to take notes in lectures. To many, note taking seemed to mean copying down everything that was on the screen and everything the tutor said, instead of recording what was flagged as important. Even those who understood the concept had difficulty putting it into practice. This was thought to be the reason for their initial resistance to developing stories.

This problem became evident when the notebooks were evaluated in week 6 of the first semester (without prior warning) and too many were found wanting. This poor response to ELVIS alerted tutors to the mindset of students and the crucial role of tutors in terms of encouraging students into action. How far that encouragement should go and how often it should be applied is debatable.

Interestingly, the student-led workshop component seemed to be the most popular activity, judging by the rate and speed of participation. All roles were claimed quite quickly, indicating that students had taken ownership.

In summary, student unease was found to arise from:

- A different learning experience, the novelty of which prompted students to question its necessity.
- The removal of the traditional scaffolding of tightly specified requirements.
- A novel approach being taken in a 30-credit module (out of a total of 120 final-year credits) and its potential negative influence on degree classifications.
- An already challenging module, in terms of its topics, activities, and delivery style, the relevance of which is not immediately obvious.
- Predictable opposition to anything that threatens the safety derived from familiar requirements.
- The perception of ELVIS being a research tool for the tutors and, therefore, having little or no relevance to their learning.

## Lessons Learnt

At the start of the year, students were given time to find their feet and feel comfortable about interacting with ELVIS. It was left up to them to manage their time. As it turned out, the amount of freedom allowed was too much for many students and, instead of learning to adjust to ELVIS requirements, they simply did nothing. The conclusion was that students need:

- Encouragement, in terms of sample stories and support clinics
- Incentives, like "early birds get more marks"
- Milestones, like the first story in by the middle of November, three stories in by the end of the first semester, five stories by the end of the second semester, and all stories in by the time the workshop is held

Another conclusion was that we should do more to incorporate story-telling as a study mode into our courses from year 1 upwards, because not only will that prepare students for their final year activities but also because, "Dialogue is strengthened when it focuses on lived experiences, familiar contexts and real emotions. Storytelling accommodates the inclusion of these aspects and can assist students to view their experiences from different perspectives" (Alterio, 2003).

It appears that effort is needed by the tutors, in the initial stages of the academic year, to get students to take ownership of the framework, for it to become more student led. Therefore, an ongoing email/VLE-announcement campaign is recommended. Without such a campaign, given the daily pressures the students are under, ELVIS may become invisible.

It is our experience that ownership is certainly the best driver for active engagement and participation; but there is another dimension that cannot be ignored: "relevance," in that if students can see the relevance of their contribution, then they will participate actively. This is what was missing from the stories component. So, another recommendation is to demonstrate to students the relevance of their stories to the overall learning experiences of the cohort. This will happen in the next round when a library of stories will be available for use. This year being the first run, the students may not be seeing immediately how their stories are being used. Hence, they may have become distanced from ELVIS. After all, seeing the "big picture" motivates students.

It is also essential to provide examples of good and bad stories, derived from effective and ineffective note taking or recording of reflection. It is too much to expect students to run with an alien idea successfully, without first preparing them for it or, put another way, making up for the deficiencies of their early educational years. This was proven to be the case when early feedback indicated that many students were in the dark about the nature of storytelling; so, coaching and sample stories were provided, as a result of which participation rates went up.

In order to encourage students to read the recommended publications, they should be asked to record in the student notebook the name and date of what they read. Furthermore, it is important to monitor the use of ELVIS and emphasise the need for engagement whenever necessary, not unlike advertising campaigns in the media. Students need incentives that reflect current education policy focusing on assessment. Therefore, ELVIS participation is rewarded with a percentage of the overall module mark.

Finally, the period of quiet reflection needs:

- Structure, in terms of what students are required to do, within what time frame, and the expected outcome
- Stimulus, in terms of issues to consider, derived from the session topics, so that they have something to focus on, which may be reduced as time goes by

## Conclusion

ELVIS promotes a mixture of individual and shared learning environments, based on a single, shared repository. At the start of the academic year, the learning is on an individual basis, where students compose their stories and submit them to ELVIS. Later on, when the workshop teams are formed, the learning becomes shared among team members. It is the behaviour of students that defines the learning environment and not the behaviour of ELVIS. Even in the early stages, the tutors' perception is that the group discussions were enriched by ELVIS but, at the time of writing, there is no firm evidence of this.

ELVIS has contributed to the ethos of the module which is to create "an environment of learning activities and assessment from which it is very difficult for the student to escape without learning" (Houghton, 2004, p. 5). In spite of the initial problems encountered by many students, subsequent informal feedback is that ELVIS is a novel way of getting students involved in activities that they have not encountered before.

## References

Alterio, M. G. (2003). *Using Storytelling to Enhance Student Learning*. Higher Education Academy. Available from http://www.heacademy.ac.uk/resources/detail/id471_using_storytelling_to_enhance_learning (Accessed 25February2008).

Andresen, L., Boud, D. & Cohen, R. (1999). Experience-based learning: contemporary issues. In Foley G. (ed.), *Understanding Adult Education and Training*, 2nd Edition. Sydney, Allen & Unwin, pp. 225–239.

Christiansson, P. (2004). ICT supported learning prospects. *ITcon*, 9, 175–194.

Clandinin, D. & Connelly, F. (1998). Stories to live by: narrative understandings of school reform. *Curriculum Inquiry*, 28(2), 149–164.

Duignan, J. (2002). Undergraduate work placement and academic performance: failing by doing. *Proceedings of the 2002 Annual International Conference of the Higher Education Research and Development Society of Australasia (HERDSA)*, pp. 214–221.

Hinett, K. (2002a) *Improving Learning Through Reflection — Part One*. The Higher Education Academy. Available at http://www.heacademy.ac.uk/resources/detail/id485_improving_learning_part_one (Accessed 25 February2008).

Hinett, K. (2002b) *Improving Learning Through Reflection — Part Two*. The Higher Education Academy. Available at http://www.heacademy.ac.uk/resources/detail/id516_improving_learning_through_reflection_part2 (Accessed 25 February2008).

Houghton, W. (2004). *Engineering Subject Centre Guide: Learning and Teaching Theory for Engineering Academics*. Loughborough, HEA Engineering Subject Centre.

Juwah, C. (2002). *Using Communication and Information Technologies to Support Problem-based Learning*. Higher Education Academy. Available at http://www.heacademy.ac.uk/resources/detail/id449_using_it_to_support_problem-based_learning (Accessed 14 March2008).

Kolb, D. (1984). *Experiential Learning: Experience as the Source of Learning and Development*. New Jersey, Prentice-Hall.

Marton, F. & Säljö, R. (1984). Approaches to learning. In: Marton, F., Hounsell, D. J. & Entwistle N. J. (eds.), *The Experience of Learning*. Edinburgh, Scottish Academic Press.

McDermott, K. J., Göl, Ö. & Nafalski, A. (2002). Considerations on experience-based learning. *Global Journal of Engineering Education*, 6(1), 71–78.

McDrury, J., & Alterio, M. G. (2002). *Learning through Storytelling: Using Reflection and Experience in Higher Education Contexts*. Palmerston North, Dunmore Press.

McEwan, H., & Egan, K. (eds.) (1995). *Narrative in Teaching, Learning and Research*. New York, Teachers College, Columbia University.

Pendelbury, S. (1995). Reason and story in wise practice. In: McEwan, H. & Egan K. (eds.), *Narrative in Teaching, Learning and Research*. New York, Teachers College, Columbia University.

Philip, L. (2006). Encouraging reflective practice amongst students: a direct assessment approach. *Planet*, 17, 37–39.

Witherell, C., & Nodding, M. (eds.) (1991). *Stories Lives Tell: Narrative and Dialogue in Education*. New York, Teachers College Press.

## Chapter 25

# Poetical Potentials: The Value of Poems in Social Impact Education [2020]*

## Introduction

Over 500 years ago, Leonardo da Vinci wrote that poetry is painting that is felt rather than seen. Such sentiment is echoed in "We can never learn too much about a poem, but always we come back to the work itself, for it exists not only as an historical object and the product of a particular mind and vision, but also in its own right, as an enduring work of art" (Anon, 1980).

As such, poetry challenges us to think beyond the obvious and reflect on what has been, what is, and what might be. Poetry can reboot the way in which social impact education is delivered to technologists. According to Rule, Carnicelli and Kane (2004), incorporating poetry in science and technology teaching expands the curriculum beyond subject knowledge and process skills. They argue that images and metaphors in poems can clarify and intensify meaning. A poem has many layers and such richness can promote enlightenment and understanding. Poems can provide meaningful context. This is imperative in ICT education and awareness at all levels for all people as the social impact of technological advances is ever increasing. In partnership, computer science and liberal arts educators could offer an exciting new perspective through poetry as an instrument of presentation and discussion as well as in creative exercises for students.

For readers who are unfamiliar with haikus, Trumbull (2003) explains that a haiku takes a three-line format of 5-7-5 syllables known as a *kigo* and uses a cutting technique called *kire* to divide the verse into two parts for contrast or comparison. He argues that the more radical the verse the better the haiku. This is certainly the case when considering the broader issues surrounding the development and use of ICT. For example, in *Technological Dependency* (Rogerson, 2015), readers are encouraged to reflect on the deeper meaning of each haiku verse with regard to the

---

* This chapter was first published as: Rogerson, S. (2020) Poetical potentials: the value of poems in social impact education. *ACM Inroads*, Vol. 11, No. 1, pp. 30–32. Copyright © the Association for Computing Machinery Reprinted by permission. DOI 10.1145/3381025.

ethical and social issues surrounding ICT and how we might address such issues. This approach can also be seen in the haiku winners presented by Barr and Barr (2017).

## Information Integrity

An extract from a poem, *The Nature of Information* by Edward M. Housman (2000), who was the designer of the Panalog computer conferencing system in the 1970s, illustrates the richness and variety of information and, as such, implies that information integrity must be the watchword for any system designer.

### Extract from the Nature of Information

> Information occupies space.
> And time.
> It takes energy to move information.
> Information is necessary for life, for any organised activity.
> Information is form without substance, substance without form. Both.
> Information, like light, has weight; a gigabyte weighs less than a fingerprint.
> The same information can be expressed in different ways: a voice, a letter.
> Unlike matter, information can be in many places at once.
> A handshake is information. A nod. A look. A sigh.

## Societal Impact

Society is now computing dependent and anyone can develop computing systems which might be used by thousands, if not millions of people. Impacts, whether positive or negative, spread rapidly and are very difficult to reverse. Poetry can be effective in highlighting these challenges. It presents the issues from a literary perspective, helping to widen understanding and thereby reducing problems such as computer illiteracy. To illustrate this approach, three examples – *CTRL ALT DEL*, *Digi-me* and *Machine – The Final Chapter* – are now presented. Their titles should resonate with technologists and thus start to draw them in.

### CTRL ALT DEL

There is much to reflect upon in *CTRL ALT DEL*; including the title itself, the first letter of each line and the use of #tag to finish this short poem (Rogerson, 2019). Consider how all these elements fit into a compound view of the world we live in and the increasing irrelevance of the physical form.

> **Q**uickly technology pervades
> **W**e become subservient
> **E**arth's treasures plundered
> **R**eboot evolution
> **T**ype in your fate
> **Y**ou and me transformed into it
>
> **#Keys** of the modern world

### Digi-me

Rogerson concluded his invited presentation "Digital Being: the modern way to be" with *Dig-me*, which was simply a two-line poem warning of the dangers unleashed through digitisation (Rogerson, 2016).

Digital being, the modern way to be,
I am the data and the data is me.

### Machine – The Final Chapter

Such warning of technological advances without careful consideration beyond the technology is the focus of *Machine – The Final Chapter* (Rogerson, 2019). Lack of proper checks and balances means that advances in computer technology from its inception by pioneers such as Babbage and Lovelace, through to the forefronts of artificial intelligence giving rise to ensuing disaster, potentially moving towards Armageddon as laid out in these three haikus.

**Computer**
Bits, bytes, ones, zeros
So Charles and Ada conceive –
IT's Pandora's box
**Robot**
Man and beast replaced
Same task over and over –
Objective carnage
**AI**
Boolean bible
Artificial ignorance –
Logical ending
**Armageddon!**

## Humour

The examples discussed so far are poems with a solemn tone. This may seem appropriate given the serious topics being discussed. However, humour is a powerful tool which, when used effectively, can create change and avert disaster. Powell and Andresen (1985) found that humour can increase interest, and help to illustrate and reinforce messages. This is a useful instrument to use when teaching technology students about the broader non-technical issues surrounding their discipline. Torok, McMorris and Lin (2004) explain that humour has the potential to humanise, illustrate, encourage and keep people thinking. A good example of this is "The rime of the ancyent programmer." Thus, as Bakar and Kumar (2019) conclude, the role of humour is twofold: to facilitate understanding and to sustain engagement. The reader is asked to bear this in mind as he or she reads this final example, *Chimerical Algorithms*, a short story, which at first seems fanciful but underneath lie some serious messages (Rogerson, 2018). There is reference to the history of computing through Howard (Aiken) and Grace (Hopper), and Kates's eight plus two has translations of ten into binary, octal and hexadecimal in the title. Embedded within this story are two poems. The first is the algorithm *Thighs*, which is in fact a charter, in poetic format, for computing practitioners. The second is the concluding algorithmic poem that, on reflection, will encourage the reader to adopt lateral thinking in problem solving which is an important approach in computer systems development. This story sits comfortably as a contrast to the more serious take, "Expressing programming algorithms with poetic language" (Ebrahimi, 2014).

## Chimerical Algorithms

Ada grew up with computer technology. In fact, she was even named after one of its pioneers Ada Lovelace. Howard, her father had worked on some of the early computers. He had met her mother Grace while serving in the armed forces, working on the ADA programming language which was used in military defence applications. Grace was involved in computer programming too and had worked on developing COBOL – the **CO**mmercial **B**usiness-**O**riented **L**anguage.

So it was hardly surprising that Ada had always loved programming for it was in her blood. It was a world of logic, certainty and objectivity. Pouring over lines of code never failed to excite and motivate. She delighted in producing programs which included precisely defined rules to solve problems of all kinds. Back home, Ada relaxed, letting her unchecked imagination create a fantasy world which she shared with her fellow geeks through her Chimerical Algorithms Blog on the Seek Geek social network.

Ada's latest blog entry, *Kate's Eight Plus Two – 1010-12-A*, contained a group of carefully crafted items:

- Parrot – Nicknamed Pretty Polly, a method for painting the town red, and blue, and yellow, and green and any other colour you care to mention.
- Cherry – Method for cleaning dirty shoes with boot polish so that they blossom.
- Rhubarb – A political procrastination tactic similar to filibustering – rhubarb, rhubarb, rhubarb!
- Jealousy – A computer games algorithm used by programmers to incorporate green-eyed monsters into the characters.
- THIGHS – The procedural acronym, nicknamed Thighs of Relief, for sustaining a better society
  - be **T**ruthful
  - be **H**onest
  - exhibit **I**ntegrity
  - be **G**ood
  - act with **H**umility
  - be **S**ensitive
- Carousel – An iterative process for sorting items in a roundabout way.
- Addiction – A method of enunciating certain arithmetic operators.
- Champagne – An artificial intelligence algorithm for identifying personality traits, nicknamed Bubbly.
- Carrot – A process for providing psychological assistance for medics – euphemistically known as What's up doc?
- Pirate – A method for adding a small amount of tax to circular objects.

Ada finished her blog with a little algorithmic poem she thought would amuse her geek friends:

Start
Go home
Eat
Take feet off ground
Let mind wander
Capture imagination
Come back down to earth
Sleep
Waken
Go to work
End

## Conclusion

Poetry can be the key to unlock the door so the room can be explored. Therefore, why not heed Ada's advice take your feet off the ground and let your mind wander. Who knows what systems you might design, for remember:

With zeroes and ones
You can create infinite
Possibilities. (Kosa, 2017)

## References

Anon (1980). How to enjoy a poem. In: Cook, C. (ed.), *Pears Cyclopaedia*, 89th Edition. London, Book Club Associates, p. M3.

Bakar, F. & Kumar, V. (2019). The use of humour in teaching and learning in higher education classrooms: lecturers' perspectives. *Journal of English for Academic Purposes*, 40, 15–25.

Barr, J. and Barr, S. (2017). Haiku contest winners. *ACM Inroads*, 8(2), 80.

Ebrahimi, A. (2014). Expressing programming algorithms with poetic language. *ACM Inroads*, 5(2), 16–20.

Housman, E. M. (2000). The nature of information. *Bulletin of the American Society for Information Science*, 26(4).

Jenkins, S. B. (2007). The rime of the ancyent programmer. *Communications of the ACM*, 50(5), 17–20.

Kosa, M. (2017). Student choice in Barr, J. and Barr, S. Haiku Contest Winners. *ACM Inroads*, 8(2), 80-80.

Powell, J. P. & Andresen, L. W. (1985). Humour and teaching in higher education. *Studies in Higher Education*, 10(1), 79–90.

Rogerson, S. (2015). Technological dependency. *ACM SIGCAS Computers and Society*, 45(2), 4.

Rogerson, S. (2016). Digital being: the modern way to be. Presented at *12th IFIP TC9 Human Choice and Computers Conference*, 9 September, UK, University of Salford.

Rogerson, S. (2018). *Chimerical Algorithms*. 5 March.

Rogerson, S. (2019a) *CTRL ALT DEL*. 7 May.

Rogerson, S. (2019b) Machine - the final chapter. *PoetrySoup*. 2 October. Available at http://www.poetrysoup.com/poem/machine_the_final_chapter_1185554 (Accessed 5 October 2019).

Rule, A. C., Carnicelli, L. A. & Kane, S. S. (2004). Using poetry to teach about minerals in earth science class. *Journal of Geoscience Education*, 52(1), 10–14.

Torok, S. E., McMorris, R. F. & Lin, W.-C. (2004). Is humor an appreciated teaching tool? Perceptions of professors' teaching styles and use of humor. *College Teaching*, 52(1), 14–20.

Trumbull, C. (2003). An analysis of Haiku in 12-dimensional Space. *Paper for HAS Meeting*.

## *Chapter 26*

# Start a Revolution in Your Head! The Rebirth of ICT Ethics Education [2020]*

## Introduction

Computing is no longer the sole domain of professionals, educated and trained through traditional routes to service public and private sector organisations under paid contracts. Computing is now by everyone for everyone with the advent of economically accessible hardware, a multitude of software tools and the Internet (Rogerson, 2019a). The IDC survey of 2018 found that there were, worldwide, 18,000,000 professional software developers and 4,300,000 additional hobbyists. The combined membership of leading professional bodies, ACM, ACS, BCS and IFIP, represents only 3.09% of that global total. The youngest app developer at Apple's Worldwide Developers Conference in June 2019 was Ayush Kumar aged 10 who started coding when he was 4 years old (Graham, 2019). He is not alone, 15 years old Tanmay Bakshi, who is the world's youngest IBM Watson Developer, started software development when he was 5 years old (Param, 2018). These facts suggest that professional bodies, in their current role, have little influence on 97% of global software developers whose ethical code and attitude to social responsibility comes from elsewhere.

It is now over a year since the launch of the new code of ethics for the ACM. At the last ETHICOMP conference, much time was devoted to discussing the code and the part it would play in moving ICT ethics forward. The code has spawned the ACM Integrity Project: Promoting Ethics in the Profession (https://ethics.acm.org/integrity-project/). The aim of this 2-year project of the ACM Committee on Professional Ethics is to promote ethics in the profession through modern media: YouTube videos, podcasts, social media, and streaming video. The use of modern media

* This is a revision of the original paper to reflect the feedback provided by STEAM Education which is gratefully accepted. STEAM Education is a registered trademark. This chapter was first published as: Rogerson, S. (2020) Start a revolution in your head! The rebirth of ICT ethics education. In: Arias Oliva, M., Pelegrín Borondo, J., Murata, K. & Lara Palma, A. M. (eds.) Societal Challenges in the Smart Society. Proceedings of ETHICOMP 2020. pp. 153-164. Copyright © Simon Rogerson.

should certainly appeal to post-millennials and offers a new approach to engage with future generations of computer scientists. Unfortunately, there has been little exposure of this project in, for example, the ACM's flagship publication, the Communications of the ACM. However, that same publication ran as its cover story in the August 2019 edition "Embedded EthiCS: integrating ethics across CS education" (Grosz et al., 2019). This is a paper about Harvard reinventing the wheel of computer ethics education which has a long and comprehensive history stretching back to the 1980s (Aiken, 1983; Johnson, 1985; Miller, 1988). It offers little new insight, does not link to a 40-year history and experience (Pecorino & Maner, 1985; Martin et al., 1996; Bynum & Rogerson 2004), nor does it appear to connect with the Integrity Project.

Within industry and government, the compliance culture has taken a firm hold and so strangles the opportunity for dialogue and analysis of complex multi-faceted socio-ethical issues related to ICT. Superficial compliance is dangerously unethical and must be challenged vigorously in a technologically dependent world. The timeframes for ICT development and ICT regulation and governance are, and will always be, misaligned. By the time some control mechanism is agreed, the technology will have moved on several generations and thus what has been agreed is likely to be ineffective. Currently, this seems to be the case with the governance of Artificial Intelligence, as there are so many opinions and vested interests causing protracted debate while AI marches onwards. Thus, it is paramount to imbue strategists, developers, operators and users with practical ICT ethics. In this way, ethical computing has a chance of becoming the norm. Traditional approaches of professional bodies seem ineffective in a society which is moving rapidly towards complete dependency on technology

It is this landscape which makes the ETHICOMP 2020 theme, *Paradigm shifts in ICT* Ethics, so relevant. It is time to change. In the spirit of Kuhn (1962), we need a paradigm shift in ICT Ethics to address the societal challenges in the not-so-smart society of today. He suggests that scientific progress of any discipline has three phases: pre-paradigm phase, a normal phase and a revolution phase. Progress occurs when a revolution takes place after a dormant normal period and the community moves ahead to a paradigm shift. Given the ongoing frequent occurrence of ICT disasters, it seems ICT ethics education in its current dormant normal phase is in need of revolution. There needs to be a radical change in how the ethical and social responsibility dimension of ICT is included in education of the whole population rather than focusing on the elitist computing professional community. It is against this backdrop that this viewpoint explores four new avenues for widening education, both formal and informal, to all those who may become involved in computing. These avenues are science and technology museums, history, thought experiments, and poetry. Such avenues also offer greater awareness to the public at large and align with Burton, Goldsmith and Mattei (2018) who use science fiction to teach ICT ethics, rather than Harvard's unimaginative, traditional approach already discussed.

# Avenue 1: Science and Technology Museums

An innovative interactive facility, Ethical Technology, could be rolled out across the global network of science and technology museums and activity centres. It would be a programme for children and adults of all ages. It would be the catalyst for public awareness and public voice, schools' cross-curricular activities, higher education research, teaching and learning, and new meaningful purpose for professional bodies.

Ethical Technology comprises four elements: *If by chance*, *Story time*, *Worldwide watch* and *Out and about* which combine to form a compound view of the ethical dimension of computing technologies and the ramifications for general population.

The first element, *If by chance*, is an opportunity to see giants of computing and literature in a different light through a set of hypothetical conversations between contemporary pairs. The conversation is on an ethical technology topic which is relevant to the expertise, experience, and thinking of the pair of individuals. For example, Charles Babbage and Ada Lovelace discuss the increasing use of moral algorithms in everyday technology. The moral algorithm is used to embed ethical decision-making into, for example, driverless cars. In a second example, Isaac Asimov and an intelligent robot discuss the relationship between human and android. Global laws and legal frameworks provide the scaffolding for a civilised society. How do *The Three Laws of Robotics* and android rights impact on a human society?

The second element, *Story time*, is a series of case scenarios which contain at least one ethical dilemma. Every story is based on either a real event or created by combining existing technologies in a societally damaging manner. A typical example is this hypothetical story, *The Data Shadow*, about personal data which resides on the internet. It has its foundation in things which have happened (Rogerson, 2017). It raises serious questions about whether we should be more aware of the risks associated with data shadows and whether there are things organisations and individuals could do to reduce such risks. The person engaging with the story is given a range of options to choose from to resolve the dilemma. The likely outcome of a chosen option is displayed. An infograph displays the totals of each option chosen with a summary of the likely outcomes for each.

The third element, *Worldwide watch,* is a repository of ethical and unethical technology occurrences. This element is an interactive blog which tracks worldwide media to collect stories of unethical and ethical technology. People will be able to give their opinions via a simple Likert scale for ethics. This could be part of a web-based offering where people could also add comments. In this way, a rich dynamic record of ethical technology issues could be captured and retained. Again total opinions are captured using an infograph. This element offers an online link to be established across the participating community.

The fourth and final element, *Out and about*, is the outreach element of Ethical Technology. Much of the technology which pervades living space is ethically and socially sensitive. Such commonplace technology becomes invisible and unsurprising. *Out and about* aims to increase public awareness by providing multimedia information about technology and the associated ethical and societal sensitivity. Access could be, for example, through a QR reader on a smartphone. This element links people to Ethical Technology in their living space. Computer-based technology in everyday use in public spaces is used to illustrate the associated ethical and social issues. In this way, public awareness is increased resulting in greater community questioning and calls for justified accountability. The applications such as ATMs, CCTV, and contactless payment systems would be fitted with QR codes which provide links to multimedia information about the ethical and social dimensions. Using this element, virtual assistants, such as Alexa and Siri, which masquerade as pseudo-friends, could be ethically contextualised.

# Avenue 2: Learning from History

Deborah Johnson (1997, p. 61) wrote

> The ethical issues surrounding computers are new species of generic moral problems. This is as true when it comes to online communication as it is in any other area of computing. The generic problems involve privacy, property, drawing the line between individual freedom and (public and private) authority, respect, ascribing responsibility, and so on. When activities are mediated or implemented by computers, they have new features. The issues have a new twist that make them unusual, even though the core issue is not.

She has been proved correct and consequently there is much to be learnt from the history of computers through, for example, trade journal archives and the Communications of the ACM archive. However, in the context of ICT ethics, the annals of ETHICOMP provide a particularly rich resource from which to learn. These historical records are important because history forces both scholar and practitioner "to lift their heads beyond the lab bench or the clipboard and realize the greater social, economic, and racial contexts in which their [work] plays out. It gives them a sensitivity that only the humanities can teach" (Dubcovsky, 2014). The themes of the first conference, ETHICOMP 95, were *Ethical Development* (The use of development methodologies and the consideration of ethical dilemmas, user education and professionalism.); *Ethical Technology* (Advances in technologies and the ethical issues they are likely to raise when applied to business and social problems.); and *Ethical Applications* (Developing ethical strategies which allow technology to be exploited in an ethically acceptable way.). This remains a relevant landscape and so illustrates that reflecting on the past can help in addressing the ICT ethical challenges of today and the future.

In its 25 years history, ETHICOMP has evolved from a fledgling conference to become a multi-generational global community. Therefore, the value of ETHICOMP is not simply the conference themes and associated papers but it is its community of people and their thoughts and observations over the passage of time. Such narrative is often forgotten or overlooked. Oral history addresses this oversight because it is a way of gathering, recording, and preserving a diverse range of personal experiences that generally are not well documented in written sources (Dalton, 2017). It enhances reflective thinking in both typical and non-typical educational settings (Gazi & Nakou, 2015). For this reason, oral histories began being collected at ETHICOMP 2018. To date, 18 have been collected involving around 25 people belonging to the ETHICOMP community. Summaries are being prepared so that easy access can be facilitated.

Currently, there exists a comprehensive record of ETHICOMP (held by this author) which maps the complete history of the ETHICOMP conference series from the kernel of the idea through to the latest conference. However, this collection is inaccessible and the potential value for future generations of scholars, practitioners and observers is lost. This archive comprises conference themes and calls; programmes; abstracts, proceedings, posters and flyers; pictures; videos; oral histories; and spin-off activities and miscellaneous materials. This could be housed on a purpose-built website to establish an interactive repository which not only holds the archive but also had a blog and social media facility which enables visitors to add content and make comment. This interactive repository using a chronological taxonomy would offer practical ethical insight to all those involved in computing. The Chronological Taxonomy is novel and potentially valuable across all empirical research disciplines (Rogerson, 2018). It is a two-dimensional method of ordering: the first dimension is Chronology which focuses on time and the second dimension is Taxonomy which focuses on classification. A typical classification could be based on the structure of IFIP's technical committees and working groups. The Chronological Taxonomy is a powerful tool which can be used to structure and analyse the interactive repository through using concatenated keys to sort the data thus making issues, trends and patterns more visible. As the data set held in the repository expands and perhaps automatic feeds are established to harvest advances and issues, the use of Big Data analytics might be needed.

# Avenue 3: Thought Experiments (See Chapter 17)

Brown and Fehige (2014) explain that *thought experiments* are used to investigate the nature of things through one's imagination. Usually, they are communicated through narratives and accompanying diagrams. Brown and Fehige state that, "Thought experiments should be distinguished from thinking about experiments, from merely imagining any experiments to be conducted outside the imagination, and from psychological experiments with thoughts. They should also be distinguished from counterfactual reasoning in general …." This approach can be used to explore the possible dangers of dual use of technological advances that could occur in the absence of effective ethical scrutiny. Rogerson (2020a) uses two thought experiment instruments to acquire new knowledge about the dangers of Free and Open-Source Software (FOSS) components which could have dual usage in the context of a fictitious system, *Open Genocide*. It is an investigation which cannot use empirical data as this would require the actual and immoral construction of a system of annihilation.

These thought experiments are grounded in the Holocaust enacted by the Nazis. By the end of the war, some 6 million Jews and many millions of Poles, gypsies, prisoners of war, homosexuals, mentally and physically handicapped individuals, and Jehovah's Witnesses had been murdered. The historical account of human suffering is sickeningly shocking but alongside this is the realisation of evil brilliance, not mindless thuggery, that orchestrated the *Final Solution* (a Nazi euphemism for the plan to exterminate the Jews of Europe).

On a bitterly cold day in February 2006, the author (SR) was quietly standing looking at the building which housed the gas chamber at Auschwitz. He reflected on the evil brilliance which had facilitated the Final Solution. He wondered what might have happened if the computer technology of 2006 had been available to the Nazis. It was a consideration which resonated with *Would you sell a computer to Hitler* by Nadel and Wiener (1977). On returning home, he completed the first thought experiment which was subsequently published (Rogerson, 2006). Technological Determinism argues that technology is the force which shapes society. Computing power would therefore be a major force in activating the Final Solution. Value Chain Analysis (Porter, 1985) is one way to consider the impact of this force. Indeed, Porter and Miller (1985, p. 151) wrote, "Information technology is permeating the value chain at every point, transforming the way value activities are performed and the nature of the linkages among them. … information technology has acquired strategic significance and is different from the many other technologies businesses use." Many computer application systems that existed in 2006 and which were proven and accepted could have been used to realise the Final Solution. This is illustrated in Figure 26.1.

In 2018, 12 years later, the second thought experiment was undertaken. Technology has evolved at a seemingly increasing pace. Indeed, "In the not-too-distant future with the cloud, big data, and maybe 80%-90% of the world's population online and connected the scope for

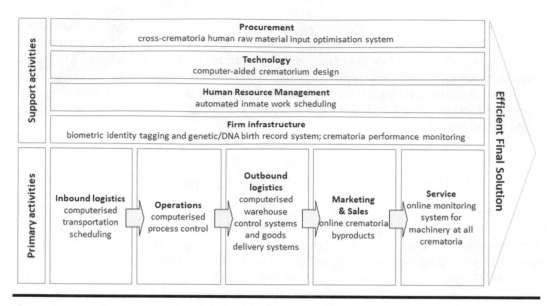

**Figure 26.1    Indicative examples across the *Final Solution* Value Chain.**

systems of oppression seems limitless. Consequently, we must consider and counter what oppressive regimes of tomorrow's world could and might do in their drive to subjugate humankind" (Rogerson, 2015, p. 4). Imagine a world where all software is available as free open source. It might seem improbable but it is possible. If it were so, the wherewithal to exploit every technological advance for any cause, albeit good or bad, would exist. The scene is set for an *Open Genocide* system brutally to further the cause of an extreme faction at the expense of the world at large and "destroy in whole or in part, a national, ethnical, racial or religious group" (United Nations, 1948, Article 2). *Open Genocide* would comprise seven components:

1. Identify: Systematically review the whole geographic region to identify every person within the targeted group as well as every sympathiser of this group.
2. Detain: Organise the detention of all identified persons in distributed holding pounds. Each detainee is appropriately tagged.
3. Deport: Manage the distribution and redistribution of detainees to work compounds and prisons.
4. Use: Select detainees exhibiting work value for allocation to appropriate tasks.
5. Dispose: Remove to disposal units all valueless or dead detainees thereby freeing up space in prisons and work compounds.
6. Recycle: Collect, sort, recycle and market all seized assets. Produce and market detainee by-products.
7. Broadcast: Devise plausible propaganda for local and international audiences and communicate widely.

The pervasive nature of current computing technology facilitates all components of *Open Genocide*. A cursory inspection of two open-source portals, SourceForge and The Black Duck Open Hub, reveals many useful items for the construction of *Open Genocide*.

These thought experiments might be shocking to many readers. That is their intention. It seems that if the Holocaust had occurred in our technologically advanced modern world there is a very good chance that it would have completely succeeded. If ever there was an example to convince computing professionals, as custodians of the most powerful technology yet devised, of their responsibilities and obligations to humankind, this is it.

## Avenue 4: Poetry (See Chapter 25)

There is value of linking the arts with the sciences in the delivery of ICT ethics education and poetry can serve as the vehicle (Rogerson, 2020b). Over 500 years ago, Leonardo da Vinci wrote that poetry is painting that is felt rather than seen. Such sentiment is echoed in "We can never learn too much about a poem, but always we come back to the work itself, for it exists not only as an historical object and the product of a particular mind and vision, but also in its own right, as an enduring work of art" (Anon, 1980). Poetry challenges us to think beyond the obvious and reflect on what has been, what is and what might be. Poetry can reboot the way in which social impact education is delivered to technologists. According to Rule, Carnicelli and Kane (2004), incorporating poetry in science and technology teaching expands the curriculum beyond subject knowledge and process skills. They argue that images and metaphors in poems can clarify and intensify meaning. A poem has many layers and such richness can promote enlightenment and understanding. Poems can provide meaningful context. This is imperative in ICT education and awareness at all levels for all people as the social impact of technological advances is ever increasing. In partnership, computer science and liberal arts educators could offer an exciting new perspective through poetry as an instrument of presentation and discussion as well as in creative exercises for students.

Consider this example of using haikus. For readers who are unfamiliar with haikus, Trumbull (2003) explains that a haiku takes a three-line format of 5-7-5 syllables known as a *kigo* and uses a cutting technique called *kire* to divide the verse into two parts for contrast or comparison. He argues that the more radical the verse is then the better the haiku becomes. This is certainly the case when considering the broader issues surrounding the development and use of ICT.

Warning of technological advances without careful consideration beyond the technology is the focus of *Machine – The Final Chapter* (Rogerson, 2019b). Lack of proper checks and balances means that advances in computer technology from its inception by pioneers such as Babbage and Lovelace, through to the forefronts of artificial intelligence giving rise to ensuing disaster, potentially moving towards Armageddon as laid out in these three haikus.

***Machine – The Final Chapter***
*Computer*
Bits, bytes, ones, zeros
So Charles and Ada conceive –
IT's Pandora's box
*Robot*
Man and beast replaced
Same task over and over –
Objective carnage
*AI*

Boolean bible
Artificial ignorance –
Logical ending
*Armageddon!*

Poetry can be the key to unlock the door so the room can be explored. In the ICT setting, this is important because often the most challenging ethical dilemmas are the least obvious. Different perspectives, for example, the poetical lens, can provide greater visibility.

## Beyond STEM Both Formally and Informally

ETHICOMP 2020s overarching theme of "Paradigm Shifts in ICT Ethics: Societal Challenges in the Smart Society" encourages its community to think beyond the obvious and traditional, and re-evaluate what should be done to ensure computing by everyone for everyone is ethically and societally acceptable. The four avenues discussed illustrate the way in which a paradigm shift might take place but for this to happen there needs to be an overarching framework to provide necessary scaffolding. A modification of the STEM model offers such a framework.

STEM has its roots in the US National Science Foundation and refers to teaching and learning in the fields of science, technology, engineering, and mathematics. It typically includes educational activities across all levels from pre-school to post-doctorate in both formal and informal settings. It requires the abandonment of top-down approaches with teachers willing to talk to each other and to believe that interactions between subjects will result in enhanced learning opportunities (Williams, 2011). However, the problem with STEM is that it sustains the principle that there are two separate fundamental cultures, the scientific and the humanistic. This can restrict reflection and innovation. As Yakman (2008, p. 19) states, "Trends have also shown many of the branches of the arts being more and more marginalized … this is a tragedy, as it eliminates many primary ways for students to obtain contextual understanding." Indeed members of the ICT ethics community often encounter opposition from those who subscribe to this principle thus hampering the quest for ethical technology by design rather than by accident.

In 2006, Yakman conceived a model which blends STEM and the arts in a way which addresses this shortcoming. The STEAM Pyramid, as it is named and shown in Figure 26.2, aims, "… to correlate the subject areas to one another and the business and social development worlds … [and] … to create a matrix by which researchers, professionals, and educators could share information to keep education as up to date as possible while still having a basis in methodologies" (STEAM Pyramid History at http://steamedu.com/pyramidhistory/). Watson and Watson (2013, p. 3) explain that "The arts contribute to STEM education by exposing students to a different way of seeing the world. Students learn through different pedagogical modalities engaging their other interests. By applying the STEM disciplines, combined with real-world experience, students become more comfortable in both worlds." In this holistic view, the single discipline silos are augmented by a blended approach which better reflects the real world.

STEAM is becoming increasingly important in ICT-related education and awareness. For example, recently published research discussed the combined use of robots and theatre for STEAM education across the science, art, and education communities (Barnes et al., 2020), whereas Song (2020) describes developing STEAM game content for infant learning. Finally, Ong et al. (2020)

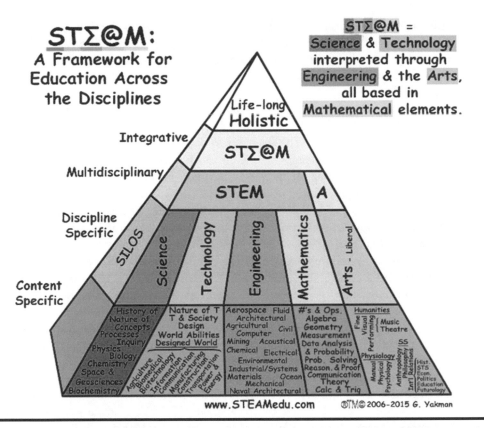

**Figure 26.2   The STEAM approach as conceived by G. Yakman of STEAM Education in 2006.**

investigate the effects of creative drama on situational interest, career interest, and science-related attitudes of science majors and non-science majors. It has been argued that computing is by everyone for everyone. Therefore, the ethical conduct of us all influences the acceptability of ICT and we all have the responsibility to challenge the unethical elements in ICT from inception through to implementation and use. Clearly, some more than others will have greater in-depth knowledge and experience of different facets. However, it is the population as a whole which has a complete view. This will include (by way of illustration) the hesitant user of a computerised public service who is the victim of poor system design as well as the junior software engineer who is bullied into unethical yet commercially valuable action. ICT ethics education and awareness must provide the tools and confidence to enable everyone to act responsibly and ethically.

The ICT ethics framework must cater for educational requirements of all. This is a paradigm shift. Yakman (2019) explains that "A" in STEAM represents the Liberal Arts which "include the ethics, ideals and emotional and physical expression grouped into overlapping categories of Humanities, Physiology and Social Studies (SS). In this way, STEAM formally adds in the subject area 'silos' of Language Arts, Social Studies, Music, Fine Arts, and PE." STEAM, therefore, appears to offer the basis of an ICT ethics framework. This author has been involved in ICT ethics education since 1994. This experience has led to the conclusion that for ICT ethics education programmes to succeed in making a difference there has to be persistent high visibility of these programmes and associated content. Ethics and

Responsibility are the keywords. If STEAM is to be used, it should be done so in an explicit ethics and responsibility landscape. Therefore, to ensure ongoing visibility, it could become STEAM-ER which would provide the fuel, impetus and environment to ensure that actions and outcomes in the technological world are more likely to be societally positive rather than societally negative.

Consider this example of how a STEAM-ER ICT ethics activity might work in practice. The example involves the poetry avenue discussed earlier. A cross-curricular project could be established for 11–18 years olds. The preparatory work, in various classes and activities, would focus on the uses and challenges of ICT in various settings. Poetry writing would also be covered both implicitly and explicitly. The culmination of this project would be a poetry writing exercise where pupils would be encouraged to consider the positive and negative effects of ICT, choosing a particular theme to be the subject of a poem. All poems would then be displayed in a public exhibition with pupils having the opportunity to engage with visitors to discuss their work. Those benefitting from this project would include staff through positive interdisciplinary work relating to ICT ethics; pupils through increased understanding of the social impact issues which surround ICT, as well as practising a range of communication skills; and the general public through increased implicit understanding of ICT ethics.

The STEAM-ER proposal parallels the Responsible Research and Innovation (RRI) advances in recent years. For example, Stahl and Coeckelbergh (2016) argue that traditional approaches to ethics and risk analysis need to be modified to include reflection, dialogue, and experiment which explicitly links to innovation practices and contexts of use. STEAM-ER offers a new approach to ICT ethics education which embraces a spectrum of disciplines in an integrated fashion. It could herald the rebirth of ICT ethics education and awareness which aligns more appropriately with a technologically dependent world of the present and the future.

## Conclusion

This chapter has discussed the current shortcoming in ICT ethics education because of the ongoing focus on ICT students who aspire to enter the profession. Four new avenues, by way of illustration, have been outlined which offer novel informal and formal educational experiences. The ICT ethics education framework has been outlined which embraces people of all ages and all walks of life. It is time to start a revolution in your head which will culminate in ethical computing by everyone for everyone. We have to accept and adjust to the fact that we are all technologist to a lesser or greater degree. How we educate our future generations must reflect this change to ensure ICT is societally beneficial. This chapter attempts to act as a catalyst for a much-needed paradigm shift in our thinking and application of ICT ethics education, one which heralds a rebirth.

## References

Aiken, R. M. (1983). Reflections on teaching computer ethics. *ACM SIGCSE Bulletin*, 15(3), 8–12.
Anon (1980). How to enjoy a poem. In: Cook, C. (ed.), *Pears Cyclopaedia*, 89th Edition. London, Book Club Associates, p. M3.

Barnes, J., FakhrHosseini, S. M., Vasey, E., Park, C. H. & Jeon, M. (2020). Child-robot theater: engaging elementary students in informal STEAM education using robots. *IEEE Pervasive Computing*, 19(1), 10–21.

Brown, J. R. & Fehige, Y. (2014). Thought experiments. First published Sat Dec 28, 1996; substantive revision Tue Aug 12, 2014. In: Zalta, E. N. (ed.), *The Stanford Encyclopedia of Philosophy*, Summer 2017 Edition. Available from https://plato.stanford.edu/archives/sum2017/entries/thought-experiment/ (Accessed 20 December 2020).

Burton, E., Goldsmith, J. & Mattei, N. (2018). How to teach computer ethics through science fiction. *Communications of the ACM*, 61(8), 54–64.

Bynum, T. W. & Rogerson, S. (eds.) (2004). *Computer Ethics and Professional Responsibility*. Blackwell Publishing.

Dalton, S. (2017). What are oral histories and why are they important? 9 August. Available from https://womenslibrary.org.uk/2017/08/09/what-are-oral-histories-and-why-are-they-important/ (Accessed 20 December 2020).

Dubcovsky, A. (2014). To understand science, study history. *Chronicle of Higher Education*, 60(24). Available from https://www.chronicle.com/article/To-Understand-Science-Study/144947 (Accessed 20 December 2020).

Gazi, A. & Nakou, I. (2015). Oral history in museums and education: where do we stand today. *Museumedu*, 2(November), 13–30.

Graham, J. (2019). WWDC 2019: meet Apple's youngest app developer, Ayush. *USA Today*, 5 June.

Grosz, B. J., Grant, D. G., Vredenburgh, K., Behrends, J., Hu, L., Simmons, A. & Waldo, J. (2019). Embedded EthiCS: integrating ethics across CS education. *Communications of the ACM*, 62(8), 54–61.

Johnson, D. G. (1985). *Computer Ethics*. Englewood Cliffs, NJ, Prentice-Hall.

Johnson, D. G. (1997). Ethics online. *Communications of the ACM*, 40(1), 60–65.

Kuhn, T. (1962). *The Structure of Scientific Revolutions*. Chicago, University of Chicago Press.

Martin, C. D., Huff, C., Gotterbarn, D. & Miller, K. (1996). Implementing a tenth strand in the CS curriculum. *Communications of the ACM*, 39(12), 75–84.

Miller, K. (1988). Integrating computer ethics into the computer science curriculum. *Computer Science Education*, 1(1), 37–52.

Nadel, L. & Wiener, H. (1977). Would you sell a computer to Hitler? *Computer Decisions*, 28, 22–27.

Ong, K. J., Chou, Y. C., Yang, D. Y. & Lin, C. C. (2020). Creative drama in science education: the effects on situational interest, career interest, and science-related attitudes of science majors and non-science majors. *EURASIA Journal of Mathematics, Science and Technology Education*, 16, 4–21.

Param, S. (2018). Tanmay Bakshi: the youngest IBM Watson developer in the world. *TechGig*, 5 June.

Pecorino, P. A. & Maner, W. (1985). A proposal for a course on computer ethics. *Metaphilosophy*, 16(4), 327–337.

Porter, M. E. (1985). *Competitive Advantage: Creating and Sustaining Superior Performance*. New York, The Free Press.

Porter, M. E. & Millar, V. E. (1985). How information gives you competitive advantage. *Harvard Business Review*, 63(4), 149–160.

Rogerson, S. (2006). ETHIcol – a lesson from Auschwitz. *IMIS Journal*, 16(2), 29–30.

Rogerson, S. (2015). *The ETHICOMP Odyssey: 1995 to 2015*, 12 September. Self-published on www.researchgate.net. doi: 10.13140/RG.2.1.2660.1444.

Rogerson, S. (2017). The data shadow. *ACM SIGCAS Computers and Society*, 47(1), 8–11.

Rogerson, S. (2018). Towards a Chronological Taxonomy of tourism technology: an ethical perspective. *ETHICOMP 2018*, Tricity, Poland 24–26 September 2018.

Rogerson, S. (2019a) Computing by everyone for everyone. *Journal of Information, Communication and Ethics in Society*, 17(4), 373–374. Translated into Japanese for inclusion in Murata, K. and Orito, Y. (eds.) *Introduction to information ethics*. Minerva Shobo, Kyoto, forthcoming.

Rogerson, S. (2019b) Machine - the final chapter. *PoetrySoup*, 2 October. Available from http://www.poetrysoup.com/poem/machine_the_final_chapter_1185554 (Accessed 20 December 2020).

Rogerson, S. (2020a) The dangers of dual use technology: a thought experiment exposé. In preparation.

Rogerson, S. (2020b) Poetical potentials: the value of poems in social impact education. *ACM Inroads*, 11(1), 30–32.

Rule, A. C., Carnicelli, L. A. & Kane, S. S. (2004). Using poetry to teach about minerals in earth science class. *Journal of Geoscience Education*, 52(1), 10–14.

Song, M. Y. (2020). Design and implementation of STEAM game contents for infant learning education using gyroscope sensor. *Journal of the Korea Society of Computer and Information*, 25(1), 93–99.

Stahl, B. C., & Coeckelbergh, M. (2016). Ethics of healthcare robotics: towards responsible research and innovation. *Robotics and Autonomous Systems*, 86, 152–161.

Trumbull, C. (2003). An analysis of Haiku in 12-dimensional space. Paper for HAS Meeting, Paper presented at the Annual Meeting of the Haiku Society of America, Evanston, Ill., Sept. 20, 2003. http://simplyhaiku.com/SHv2n5/features/Char les_Trumbull.html.

United Nations (1948). *Convention on the Prevention and Punishment of the Crime of Genocide*, 9 December.

Watson, A. D. & Watson, G. H. (2013). Transitioning STEM to STEAM: reformation of engineering education. *Journal for Quality and Participation*, 36(3), 1–5.

Williams, J. (2011). STEM education: proceed with caution. *Design and Technology Education: An International Journal*, 16(1), 26–35.

Yakman, G. (2008). STEAM education: an overview of creating a model of integrative education. February. Pupils' Attitudes Towards Technology (PATT-19) Conference: Research on Technology, Innovation, Design & Engineering Teaching Salt Lake City, Utah, USA

Yakman, G. (2019). STEAM – an educational framework to relate things to each other and reality. *K12Digest*, 12 December.

# CONCLUSION VI

*Technological Dependency*

Now social networks
Before tea-room social chat –
IT changes us

Single views are flawed
Life is grey not black and white –
Harmony spawns hope

Computer jargon
Academic rhetoric –
Actions not words count

*(This poem, which comprises three haikus, was first published in Rogerson, S. (2015) Technological Dependency. ACM SIGCAS Computers & Society, June, Vol. 45, No. 2, p. 4.)*

# Chapter 27

# Landscape for the Future

In December 2020, I was invited to participate in a webinar entitled, *Promoting Character Education as Part of a Holistic Approach to Re-Imagining the Digital Age*, which was organised by The Jubilee Centre for Character and Virtues at the University of Birmingham. Participation involved writing a position paper. I entitled my paper *Re-imagining the Digital Age through Digital Ethics*. This final chapter is based on a modified version of that paper which aligns perfectly with the evolving landscape discussed in this book.

The changing digital technology landscape has meant that the world has changed. In May 2020, Mobile App Daily published its 2020 technology trend forecast. It demonstrates the world is now digitised through, for example, 5G, clouds, AI, algorithms, augmentation, machine autonomy, data analytics, edge computing and the Internet of Things. This digitisation of everything requires a greater emphasis on, what we should now call, digital ethics. If not, then a very bleak, discriminatory world beckons. It would be a world of privileged digital natives and an underclass of digital outcasts, a world of danger, domination and despair.

There now exists global deep-seated dependency on digital technology. By way of illustration, look how the social glue has come unstuck during the pandemic and we have turned to digital technology to allow us to live and keep us connected (Rogerson, 2020). Communication channels provide information about the latest developments, advice and restrictions. Social media keeps social groups and families emotionally together. Online outlets provide the products and services we need in our everyday lives. For digital natives, the move to the virtual is plausible and possibly pleasurable but for digital outcasts the move is fraught and frequently frightening.

Everyone has moral obligations and responsibilities in ensuring that the digital age is inclusive and empowering rather than exclusive and constraining. Established rules may offer some guidance as to the correct path, but such rules can easily become the instruments of blatant superficial compliance which at best is problematic and at worst immoral. It is virtuous action that promotes an ethical digital age. A person is not virtuous because their actions comply, perhaps mindlessly, with established rules, the action is virtuous because of the virtuous nature of the person who performs it (Wyatt, 2008).

Virtuous action must occur in different ways, crossing traditional barriers and challenging established norms. Three drivers – top-down, middle-out and bottom-up – come into play (Chapter 21). As explained, top-down drivers are typically impositions by bodies of authority which dictate where resources should be placed to achieve some overall goal. Middle-out drivers involve all those within, for example, an organisation, who are empowered to initiate change, support it, propose new ideas, and innovate. Bottom-up drivers emanate typically from grassroots collective-action resulting in a widespread change. Boyle (2009) suggests top-down drivers provide political direction, middle-out drivers are the focus of change teams, and bottom-up drivers are the voices of citizens.

## Education and Learning

Churchland (1996) explains that the development of moral character in children takes time – "time to learn how to recognise a large variety of prototypical social situations, time to learn how to deal with those situations, time to learn how to balance or arbitrate conflicting perceptions and conflicting demands, and time to learn the sorts of patience and self-control that characterise mature skills in any domain of activity." The formality of school and the informality of home are equally important, particularly in the early stages of this journey to moral maturity. It is a journey which starts the moment a child is born, continues through childhood into adolescence and finally into adulthood.

The global population has a collective view of an acceptable digital age. This population will include those who have suffered directly from unethical situations. Examples include the hesitant user of a web-based public service who is the victim of poor system design; the junior software engineer who is pressurised into unethical, yet commercially valuable, action by an internet organisation; and the vulnerable young adult who is the victim of incessant cyberbullying. Digital ethics education and awareness must develop the individual's confidence and skills, through lifelong learning, and so provide the tools to enable everyone to act responsibly and ethically. Discussion, dialogue, storytelling, case study analysis, mentoring, and counselling are examples of techniques that can be used to nurture practical wisdom and insight which will lead to virtuous citizens of the digital age.

## The Digital Environment

The complex interrelated ethical and social issues within the digital environment must be addressed during the digital technology process and embedded within the digital technology product (Chapter 5). Process concerns the activities of digital technology professionals when undertaking planning, research, development and service/product delivery. The aim is for professionals to be virtuous in Aristotelian terms. In other words, a professional knows that an action is the right thing to do in the circumstances and does it for the right motive. Product concerns the outcome of professional endeavour and the potential impact of these products on people, society and the environment. The ethics focus of the product perspective is technological integrity from, for example, a Kantian or utilitarian perspective.

This can be addressed by embedding ethics within digital products themselves. For example, internet corporations could be proactive rather than reactive in promoting empowerment and safety for internet users. This virtuous action could lead to a new feature, information provenance, added to search engines. Information provenance would fix the origin and network of ownership, thus providing a measure of integrity, authenticity and trustworthiness. It would provide an audit trail showing where information originated, where it has been, and how it has been altered. In this way, people would be able to consider how much credence they would give to a piece of information before acting upon it. In the digital age, there is a moral obligation to address information integrity. Information provenance offers a normative instrument for turning the moral obligation of addressing information integrity into ethical practice.

While the imperative for organisations must be virtuous action, this, as Wyatt (2008) explains, must sit comfortably with other ethical analyses. This is likely to lead to ethically justifiable actions and outcomes. This approach can be summarised by four statements:

- Consider if your acts are worthy of the ideal digital technology professional (virtue ethics)
- Consider who is affected by your work (utilitarian)
- Analyse how the least empowered will be affected by your decision (Rawlsian)
- Examine if other humans are being treated with respect (Kantian)

One way to promote virtuous action would be to establish ethics circles. An ethics circle is a means of providing support to individuals who are engaged in ethically sensitive decision-making, raising general awareness of ethical issues and acting as informal staff development in this area (Chapter 22). The circle comprises a small group of people who do similar or complementary work meeting on a regular basis to identify problems, to analyse the causes, to recommend solutions and, where possible, to implement those solutions themselves.

## Governance

Governance must address both the process and product dimensions of digital technology development. It must promote a sense of obligation in professional developers, thus ensuring that digital technology products and services are fit-for-purpose. Governance implies a system in which all stakeholders have the necessary input into the decision-making process. A broader view needs to be taken in defining the stakeholders of the digital age. Stakeholders should include those:

- Whose behaviour/work process will be affected by the development or delivery of digital technology
- Whose circumstance/job will be affected by the development or delivery of digital technology
- Whose experiences will be affected by the development or delivery of digital technology.

Governance should have its foundation as delivering ethical, efficient and effective digital technology. These three factors must be multiplicative rather than summative.

## Virtually There

There is a need to develop a new vision for digital ethics which is theoretically grounded but pragmatic. It must exhibit phronesis and praxis so that industry and government will engage, accept and embrace this as a modus operandi. Digital ethics can be defined as integrating digital technology and human values in such a way that digital technology advances human values, rather than doing damage to them. It therefore must include the formulation and justification of policies for the ethical use of digital technology, and carefully considered, transparent and justified action leading to ethically acceptable digital technology products and services (Rogerson, 2011). This form of digital ethics is transdisciplinary, drawing upon many disciplines including ethics, computing, psychology and education. It is the grounding which enables us to focus on the long-term needs of everyone rather than the short-term interests of the few. Digital education from an early age should engender virtue, wisdom and humility as well as instrumental skill and technological prowess. There will then be a digital age created by everyone for everyone. We will make a difference through challenging complacency, indifference and ambivalence regarding ethical digital technology by those involved in any aspect of planning, funding, researching, developing, implementing and using digital technology. This is the landscape of the future. It is a landscape we should all nurture and cultivate so that humankind and the world at large will flourish in the digital age.

## And Finally …

In 1988, I wrote,

> The world of IT is a challenging world both for developers and for those who use IT products and services. Information technology is widely recognised as a competitive tool, crucial to the wellbeing of organisations. It is a technology which can have detrimental side effects on society. Those involved in IT development have the responsibility of optimising efficiency and effectiveness in satisfying user needs but also have a responsibility for ensuring that IT is used wisely for organisations and society as a whole. (Rogerson, 1988, p. 51)

Many years later, in 2015, I returned to this theme (Chapter 21). I explained that the gatekeepers of past generations, who enabled academia, industry and government to work collectively towards ethical digital technology, are becoming increasingly inactive. This void needs to be filled by millennials and post-millennials. Greenfield (2003, p. 9) explained that, "We must be proactive and set the agenda for what we want and need from such rapid technical advances; only then shall we, our children and our grandchildren come to have the best life possible. So first we need to evaluate the 21st-century technologies, and then unflinchingly open our minds to all possibilities."

For these reasons, it is fitting that a book about the evolving landscape of digital technology includes some thoughts of those in the next generations who are charged with ensuring digital technology is ethical. Five people from these next generations have very kindly agreed to share their views. The invited scholars were asked to consider what the future landscape of digital technology might possibly look like over the next 25 years. Alongside this, they were asked to suggest what the associated ethical hotspots might be. A 750-word limit was set. The resulting viewpoints offer a fascinating glimpse of the future. Katleen Gabriels takes an AI-human relationship perspective. A strong argument is made for joined-up, concerted effort on all fronts, so society can enjoy the positives of emerging technology. Stéphanie Gauttier considers the links between theory and practice in the pursuit of ethical digital technology. She argues that there is an urgent need to enrich political dialogue at all levels with digital ethics. Laura Robinson discusses the challenge of the increasingly serious paradox of digital elitism and digital empowerment. She explains that as digital technology evolves those in control become increasingly powerful, some of whom demonstrate social responsibility through philanthropy while, unfortunately, others ignore the social cost of the digital divide. Lachlan Urquhart analyses future challenges and foci for digital technology. It offers the foundation of strategic planning for future research funding which supports practice and application. Kirsten Wahlstrom takes a futurist stance and through this lays out the potential ethical challenges which lie ahead. She discusses increasing difficulty in differentiating between human and android. This aligns with the discussion in Chapter 15.

## Katleen Gabriels

What will the future landscape of digital technology look like over the next 25 years? Predicting the future is no easy matter. No one could have predicted what a strange year 2020 would turn out to be. The coronavirus crisis accelerated digital transitions in companies, schools, universities and other organisations. Meeting platforms such as Zoom faced serious security issues. Worldwide, there were concerns about privacy infringement because surveillance and AI-techniques were hastily implemented in the battle against the virus. China adopted thermal scans with facial recognition at an early stage, for instance at the entrances of public transport. This technology comes with many ethical concerns. Its accuracy can be questioned, since the temperature of the environment can affect the measures, leading to false positives. The thermal scanners are unable to identify people who are asymptomatic, that is, not showing typical and discernible symptoms, such as a fever. What if these technologies are here to stay and become standard at airports the world over? What happens with all these data, and how long will they be stored? There will be great differences between countries, with EU member states giving better privacy protection because of the GDPR.

AI-systems will increasingly become part of our daily lives, even on the toilet. The development of smart toilets is still in its infancy but already raises compelling ethical questions. If we introduce smart toilets to our homes in the future, it will be possible to detect disease markers in urine and stools more quickly. In order to trace data back to individuals, the smart toilet identifies people via fingerprints when they flush. The data could be sent immediately to healthcare providers and added to personal electronic health records. Of course, it would be easy to fool the technology, as another person could flush the toilet. To tackle this problem, researchers and developers at Stanford University have included other recognition systems: anal recognition. As it turns out, anal prints are just as unique and identifiable as fingerprints. What happens to the data? This question may seem far-fetched at this moment in time, but the smart toilet may one day become a part of standard bathroom equipment. Undoubtedly, technological developments will further increase existing privacy problems. AI-systems are getting better and better at de-anonymisation. A study in *Nature* (2019) showed that an AI-model would be able to correctly re-identify 99.98% of Americans in any dataset based on 15 demographic characteristics.

### A Plea for Interdisciplinarity

In the future, the collaboration between AI and humans will only increase. These innovations are accompanied by many challenges: not just technical, but also ethical, social, political and legal. This is going to require a combined effort.

The ethical aspects and consequences of AI have become something of a hot topic. Whether you call it Responsible AI, Accountable AI, Trustworthy AI or Beneficial AI, it largely boils down to the same thing, namely AI for which ethics are an inherent part of the design. This will have to come from humans: technology will not become ethical by itself. Ultimately, the key to ethical AI lies in interdisciplinarity. Different disciplines have to meet and talk to each other in order to understand one another's language and thinking processes. Some data scientists may think in a more binary way, whereas ethics is not binary.

More interdisciplinarity in policymaking is also needed, as few policy makers have a technical background. This might lead to situations in which the importance of regulation is under-estimated. Or that they do not look critically enough at the use of the word AI: several tech-nologies that start-ups or organisations claim to be AI do not even contain AI-techniques.

Anyone who designs makes choices: not just functional but also choices with ethical impact. This should be acknowledged in interdisciplinary education, by offering, amongst others, man-datory courses on ethics of technology to future engineers and data scientists. Fortunately, ethics of technology is not a new field and we are not starting from scratch, as this book has clearly shown. Ethics of technology has a positive role to play in the development of technologies that will fundamentally change society. For this to take place, we need a society that is well informed about the advantages and disadvantages of AI, a government that makes space for research into ethics of technology, and designers who are aware of the ethical aspects of their role. Designers, users, policy makers, and academics must lay down the ground rules for tomorrow's innovation, today.

*Dr. Katleen Gabriels is a moral philosopher, specialised in computer and machine ethics. She is an assistant professor at Maastricht University (Netherlands), where she is also the programme director of the BA Digital Society. She is an executive board member of INSEIT, a steering committee member and the deputy chair of ETHICOMP, and an affiliate member of 4TU Centre for Ethics and Technology. She is the author of Conscientious AI. Machines Learning Morals (VUBPRESS, 2020).*

## Stéphanie Gauttier

As the European Union multiplies ethical guidelines on artificial intelligence (Smuha, 2019) and legislation on privacy such as the GDPR, the main task ahead of information system ethics is to understand how ethical requirements affect individuals' practices of technology. This Herculean challenge requires abandoning a technological lens of analysis to the profit of a human perspective.

Stakeholders have been included in the development process for decades now. However, they lack tools to (1) question the ethics of technology; and (2) articulate their values and express them. Technological development often gives the impression that machines think on their own, by themselves, without any form of human agency. Coupled with firm faith in the accuracy and good of algorithms, this leads young generations, and potential future ones, to consider that the machine is "right" as it is.

Make a few students take the Moral Machine test (Awad et al., 2018), which requires users to indicate how self-driving cars should behave in case of dysfunction – and so who from passengers or pedestrians should be sacrificed, and you will see that a fair share considers that the car knows what to do. Confront these students to the trolley problem, assessing whether the human should pull the switch (Foot, 1967) or push a fat person over the footbridge (Thomson, 1976) to save others, and they will vigorously mention how impossible it is for a human to take action and decide.

Education on the role of human agency in programming is necessary so that future gen-erations, can identify what could be ethically problematic. If this can be achieved, individuals do not necessarily know how to question the ethical issue, even if they solve ethical dilemmas daily intuitively. Not proposing methodologies and frameworks, we risk seeing stakeholders surrender to utilitarian approaches, which are the most influential in popular ethics, and ignore other modes of ethical thinking. Nurturing ethical understanding in individuals, developing methodologies and frameworks for ethical problem solving (Van de Poel & Royakkers, 2007) and ethical deliberations to that end, is one of the tasks ahead of the field of information ethics.

Besides, there is a gap between how individuals declare they would solve ethical dilemmas, the values they hold as key, and how they act – the ethical paradox. For instance, an increasing number of individuals claim that technology should respect their privacy, yet they use technologies that compromise it for relatively small rewards (Kokolakis, 2017). Understanding why such paradoxes emerge is necessary to avoid the spread of practices that society does not see as ethical. However, it is a daunting task as it requires looking at the traditional triangle of technology-situation-individual and in the perspective of time. Indeed, as technology evolves, our societal and individual values change too, so that this paradox might be the result of time. The paradox could stem from practical considerations, linked to situations faced by individuals. It is also possible that individuals are not asked about their values adequately, leading to an impression of a paradox. Understanding whether there actually is a paradox, and how it comes to be, is necessary to assess the role of ethics in shaping technology usage. Taking on this challenge requires both conceptual and methodological understanding and demands collaboration between social scientists and ethicists.

Looking at this ethical paradox and integrating individuals' perception of what an acceptable technology is into design requires more than understanding what values are threatened and which are more important. The political and societal debates on artificial intelligence, on COVID-trackers, on social networks, often end in lists of values to be respected, principles to uphold (Jobin, Ienca, & Vayena, 2019). While this serves some legal and practical purpose, a key element to build ethical technologies is to understand what value conflicts can exist and which trade-offs between values might have to occur. Such decisions are essentially political. They put back responsibility onto the shoulders of individuals, stakeholders, society overall. As society has an appetite for ethics and the technological developments raise always more complex questions, a natural shift from a technology-driven analysis to an analysis of ethics in practice as politics will become necessary.

*Stéphanie Gauttier is an assistant professor of Information Systems at Grenoble Ecole de Management doing research on the role of ethics in technology acceptance. Stéphanie received her PhD from the University of Nantes for work on moral conditions of acceptance of human-enhancement technology. She received a Marie Curie fellowship in 2018 for work on ethics and organisational information systems.*

## Laura Robinson

The technologies meant to equalise and liberate society are now the shackles that increasingly bind us and subject us to a bold and ruthless new power elite. This is the digital paradox. Silicon Valley is the tip of the digital spear, the epicenter of the digital revolution, the frontier of the information society that exemplifies the growing disparities of the information age. Home to both the dizzying heights of innovation and the accelerating exclusion of the disadvantaged, Silicon Valley is radically and rapidly normalising a two-tiered society of the powerful and the powerless. This exponentially widening gap is at the heart of Silicon Valley that claims to be one of the most progressive communities in the United States but allows itself to be fueled by titanic marginalisation in which wealth and power are being ever more concentrated with every nanosecond that passes. Too many of the Valley's innovators are digital robber barons capitalising on a regulation vacuum that has allowed them to grow unchecked in a culture that all too often allows the almighty dollar to forgive too many sins and pushes everything else to the wall. This has been true before in American history; at first glance, the tech czars may seem to be the Vanderbilts or Rockefellers of our era. But there are important and ominous differences.

Historically, American culture has lauded innovators and given them incredible license in the pursuit of innovation that will ultimately benefit the public at large. In the words credited to Thomas A. Edison, "Hell there are no rules here – We're trying to accomplish something." Our history is marked by those who have harnessed our continent's crude strength and tied it to the seemingly boundless possibility that define American ingenuity at its irreverent best. In the words of Steve Jobs: "Why join the navy if you can be a pirate?" Yet our pirates have historically also been philanthropists supporting a social contract with two important dimensions. First, there has been a sense that, at its best, advancing frontiers through innovation should provide some kind of larger universal benefit to be shared by many within and beyond our borders. Second, there has been a strong sense of reciprocation to restore an ethical balance of power and benefit.

Historically, those who have reaped the fruit of success of American dynamism have given back to publics or entities far larger than themselves. Perhaps at some level recognising that the costs of their success were unequally paid by many others, American innovators founded institutions, charities, and other works in the public good at home and abroad. For all of their faults, one thing which has marked many American innovators was their willingness to give back to the greater public through institutions that foster larger universal ideals. This is exemplified by The Giving Pledge created by Bill and Melinda Gates and Warren Buffett. In 2010, twoscores of the richest American pledged to give away the majority of their money to philanthropic causes. As with many things "born in the USA" this has spread far beyond American borders and is no longer American. As described by Bill Gates, "This is about building on a wonderful tradition of philanthropy that will ultimately help the world become a much better place."

Yet this tradition of philanthropy is fading among all-too-many of the tech czars whose power is in ascendancy in Silicon Valley. The information age may have begun as a revolution with the potential to promote greater good but today the internet is increasingly being weaponised by digital elites and their allies to maintain their stranglehold on power. Instead of spreading the bounty of digital technologies, or at least some of the profits, to ameliorate human suffering, the Silicon Valley ethos of domination-above-all is ramping up the pursuit of privilege, power, and profit. As this indicates – whatever they might say to the contrary – the concept of innovation for the public good is fading at an alarming rate of speed. In pursuit of the almighty dollar, Silicon Valley is spewing forth endless technologies that undermine the idea of *in publica commoda*. In just a quarter of a century, digital technologies have become the great unequaliser by concentrating wealth and power in the hands of the increasingly few, the proud, the tech titans.

As we look to the future landscapes of digital technologies over the next quarter of a century, confronting the digital paradox will be our challenge. We must wrestle back digital power away from these profit-and-power driven models to restore the role of digital innovation *in publica commoda*.

*Laura Robinson is an associate professor at Santa Clara University and Faculty Associate at the Harvard Berkman Klein Center for Internet & Society. She earned her PhD from UCLA, where she held a Mellon Fellowship in Latin American Studies and received a Bourse d'Accueil at the École Normale Supérieure. In addition to holding a postdoctoral fellowship at USC Annenberg, Robinson has served as visiting assistant professor at Cornell University and the Chair of CITAMS.*

## Lachlan Urquhart

Emerging smart technologies are ethically and technically complex. They are delegated increasing degrees of agency, artificial intelligence and autonomy. Concurrently, they are becoming ubiquitous yet opaque in how they ambiently use personal data. Smart homes are enabling deeper inferences about daily life, for example, how we speak to smart speakers. Emotional AI is attempting to make internal human sentiment visible and actionable to external stakeholders, for example, tracking of facial micro-expressions in advertising. Smart cities are embedding sensors at scale in civic infrastructure e.g. smart street lights. While there can be benefits, these systems pose a plethora of ethical conflicts for privacy, surveillance, trustworthiness, identity, security and sustainability. I am particularly interested in challenges posed by affective computing, smart cities and homes as they become normalised in society. In response, I frame my commentary around four themes.

## The Complexity of Emerging Smart Technologies and the Future of Interdisciplinarity

Interdisciplinarity is key to engaging with value conflicts and hard problems posed by smart technologies. For example, understanding and addressing ethical risks posed by Emotional AI requires input from computer ethics, technology law, interaction design, psychology, science and technology studies, surveillance studies, computer vision, human computer interaction, and more. To date, there is an awareness that technologies pose multifaceted problems that need input by different communities. There has been progress in aligning communities through frameworks like responsible research and innovation, mediation theory, and value-sensitive design. However, the degree of autonomy and complexity of emerging artificial intelligence applications further complicate interdisciplinary endeavours. We need further work folding perspectives from different communities into addressing ethical problems. In part, this requires us to find common vocabularies, working practices and strategies that ultimately support building of more responsible smart technologies.

## Mundane Ethics and the Focus on Everyday Interactions

It will be increasingly important to critically look beyond the hype cycle and future visions for emerging smart technologies. Instead, focusing on everyday interactions with existing and new technologies can help anticipate the mundane ethical issues and value tensions that will arise. Ultimately, this will help inform better system design. Human-computer interaction can be instructive in situating ethical debates in the mundane relationships of daily life. Methodologies such as design ethnography, prototyping and participatory design can help put human-technology interactions in context, understand how a technology will be used in practice, and, importantly, appreciate the way it impacts the social order of a setting. This helps us to build an empirical picture of how they mediate and shape lives of users, providing a key site for unpacking ethical tensions and help us position our ethical and legal concerns more effectively.

With smart cities, for example, how might smart infrastructure mediate our lived experience of the built environment? How might it change our relationships with public space, other citizens and wider stakeholders (e.g. civic government)? There is a need here to make urban spaces we want to live with, and to ensure participation of citizens in designing and shaping that environment, to avoid systems that enable surveillance and challenge fundamental rights like privacy.

## Creating Responsible Technologies by Design

In law and policy, there is an increased focus on design-based strategies to governance, for example with privacy by design. Translating between normative frameworks of law/ethics, and design practice is key to this. We need to move beyond the call for technologies to be more ethical or legally compliant, towards formulating tools that support responsible design. As more complex systems emerge and become increasingly entangled in everyday life, the design, socio-technical and ethical challenges will increase too. In part, this requires an understanding of the working practices of technologists. For example, in my own research, I have been using card-based design tools that prompt reflection by designers on ethical aspects of their new technologies. Working with designers to understand how to utilise the affordances of new systems coupled with user centric design practices could enable creation of user experiences and technologies that they want to live with.

## Responsibility across the Technology Life Cycle

In addition to design-based approaches, mitigating ethical harms from smart technologies requires appreciation of how they are used over time. This involves unpacking the range of stakeholders involved, the nature of their responsibilities and how these are longitudinally shared across complex data supply chains. For example, as smart technologies become embedded into the fabric of buildings and homes, who manages the personal data flows as buildings are bought and sold? Who ensures security of the sensors in the walls in 5, 15, or 50 years' time? What new types of cyber-physical security vulnerabilities will emerge from unpatched smart technologies e.g. with compromised smart locks or actuating doors? Focusing on the life cycle from design to destruction is important for creating responsible smart technologies.

*Lachlan Urquhart is a lecturer in Technology Law at the University of Edinburgh and Visiting Researcher at Horizon, University of Nottingham. He has a multidisciplinary background in computer science (PhD) and law (LLB; LLM). His main research interests are in human-computer interaction, ubiquitous computing, data protection, computer ethics, and cybersecurity. He has been Co-I on funded projects totalling over £5m from EPSRC, ESRC, AHRC, Universitas 21, Impact Accelerator Funds, and Research Priority Funds.*

## Kirsten Wahlstrom

The day after Simon invited me to consider the future ethical hotspots of digital technology, Lisa Bailey (the Exhibition Manager at UniSA's Museum of Design) asked me via email, "Is it ethical to let people think you're a human if you're not?" My immediate response was to spend a moment wondering whether Lisa was not human because if so, she was taking a very sophisticated approach to refining her ethics!

Some thoughts that flowed from Lisa's entertaining question are now captured in this short section.

It seems likely that between now and 2046 various economic imperatives will have led to the development of digital technologies which are increasingly intelligent, ambient and transparent (IAT). IAT technologies will constitute a greater proportion of our immediate surroundings than at present and may, in some cases, be embodied. IAT technologies will mediate life in a multitude of subtle ways that will be imperceptible to many, providing seamless human-computer interaction. Artificial Intelligence will inform IAT technologies by almost instantly computing increasingly precise models of each individual person's needs and preferences. The possibility of IAT digital technology invites me to consider a problem that many before me have found compelling: what is a good life?

Understandings of the good life will deepen and take on previously unknown layers of complexity and nuance as IAT technology expands and more data is available to inform our perspectives. Will it be a life of consummate convenience? Will it be a life of rich intellectual engagement shaped in abstention from the digital? Or a life that economically coerces others to provide the cheapest possible labour? What do we value? What should we value? What should our future values be?

To explore these questions, imagine yourself in a hypothetical future in which IAT technologies know you better than you know yourself, are flexible, and source diverse data to support your own unique quest for a good life, whatever that might be:

- Your IAT technology is almost imperceptibly integrated with your life and it knows you well enough to support you in realising your potential. The technology provides art and music that leads you from negativity before you begin to feel it. It provides adversarial growth experiences tailor-made for you in that moment, boosting your confidence in yourself. You invest time in work suited to your preferences and aptitudes. Your free time is enriching, and you want for little. Your IAT suggests people you might like to give to or spend time with, and your deep confidence and happiness leads you to follow through on these suggestions, building the community around you and enabling both your giving and your gratitude.
- Life feels easier and more fulfilling each day. You are joyful and your sense of purpose is satisfied. You are fulfilled through doing what you love. You are living a good life.

While IAT technologies are likely to emerge, of course this is a utopian vision. Yet even so, it suggests a range of ethical puzzles: Where is the line between humans and digital technology, and how much does that line matter? Even though IAT enables a good life, ought we to engage in such a deeply mediated good life in the first place? By what utilitarian calculus do we keep each human's personal growth from impeding the growth of others? Are our experiences with IAT technologies homogenising and if so, how much does it matter? What new learnings will be possible when humans are optimally enabled? Assuming some will prefer a life of abstention, how will we pursue equity of access to the potential for a good life? What does this scenario mean for evil and those who are fulfilled by perpetuating evil? How do we develop standards and mechanisms against which the technologies can be audited? Here, I have not run out of questions, but word count.

Now take a moment to imagine the number and diversity of ethical puzzles that may emerge in a less utopian future of ambient technology.

My goal in articulating and responding to this vision is to suggest that we take the time to develop clear thinking, discourse, and analyses to support us in delineating human from IAT. With such capabilities, we are better equipped to make wise decisions in the teaching of children, in the setting of public policy, in the judiciary, and perhaps most importantly, in our personal choices.

And we won't need to consider whether the Lisa Baileys we encounter are human or not!

***Kirsten Wahlstrom*** *is a teaching and research academic at the University of South Australia. She completed her doctorate at the Centre for Computing and Social Responsibility at De Montfort University and she researches the social impacts of emerging technologies. She participates in organising the AiCE series of conferences. Kirsten is a certified professional member of the Australian Computer Society, Vice Chair of its Ethics Committee, and a member of its Profession Advisory Board.*

## *And So...*

Recently, I came across a handwritten outline of a method for ethics audit which I entitled ethics health check. This was dated 25 January 1996 with an update showing the draft schematic of the approach dated 6 February 1996. This was the year that the Centre for Computing and Social Responsibility launched its website – a world-class computer ethics portal. Patrick Foster became CCSR's first webmaster. He was a BSc Computer Science undergraduate on his placement year. I worked with Patrick on developing the ethics health check which he wrote up as his placement assignment. Figure 27.1 shows the final version of the schematic as it appeared in his assignment (Foster, 1996, p. 11).

The 8 meta-level guiding principles are discussed in Chapter 7. These, or indeed any other set of ethics principles, are used as the foundation to create a set of contextual metrics informed by

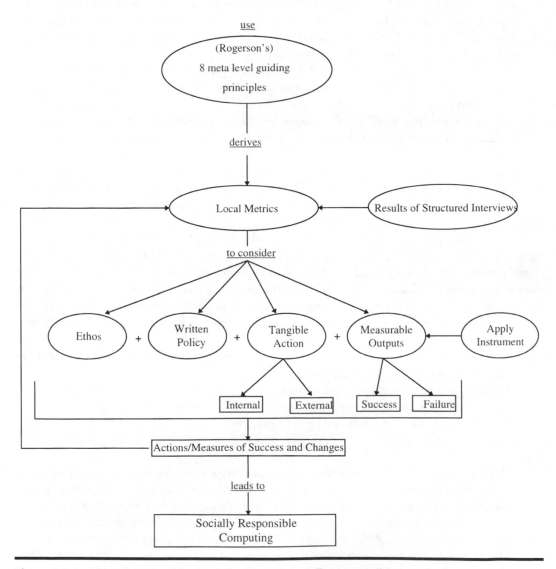

**Figure 27.1  The ethics health check leading to socially responsible computing (1996).**

interaction with the players in a particular setting. The local metrics are then used to undertake the ethics health check of the four perspectives: ethos, policies, actions and outputs. This audit leads to recommendations and commendations in support of socially responsible computing or, as it is now better termed, ethical digital technology.

This approach is similar to the global action plan, called *Future Vision* (2015, see Chapter 21) which addresses the serious fragmentation of work in and between academia and industry related to digital ethics. This ethics health check was designed to identify what and where progress has been made, what problems or barriers exist and where is the future potential for using digital ethics to realise ethical digital technology.

There is an obvious focus on people in both these approaches. Why should this be so? It is because in the digital age it is people who change things. It is people who make digital technology. It is people who use and abuse digital technology. The tension between use and abuse is where the ethical hotspots lie. Digital technology can add value to life, but it can also take value away from life. Some ethical hotspots may be obvious, while others may not. All must be addressed so that the digital age is good for everyone as well as the global environment.

# References

Awad, E., Dsouza, S., Kim, R., Schulz, J., Henrich, J., Shariff, A., Bonnefon, F. & Rahwan, I. (2018). The moral machine experiment. *Nature*, 563(7729), 59–64.

Boyle, R. (2009). *Public Sector Change Management – Looking Back to Look Forward*. Keynote address. Association of Chief Executives of State Agencies (ACESA) Conference, 1 October.

Churchland, P. M. (1996). The neural representation of the social world. In: May, L., Friedman, M. & Clark, A. (eds.), *Mind and Morals: Essays on Cognitive Science and Ethics*. The MIT Press, pp. 91–108.

Foot, P. (1967). The problem of abortion and the doctrine of the double effect. *Oxford Review*, 5, 5–15.

Foster, P. W. (1996). *Ethical Reviews in the IT Workplace: Assuring the Responsible Application of Information Technology and Information Systems*. BSc Computer Science Third Year Placement Assignment. De Montfort University.

Greenfield, S. (2003). *Tomorrow's People: How 21st-Century Technology Is Changing the Way We Think and Feel*. UK, Penguin.

Jobin, A., Ienca, M. & Vayena, E. (2019). The global landscape of AI ethics guidelines. *Nature Machine Intelligence*, 1(9), 389–399.

Kokolakis, S. (2017). Privacy attitudes and privacy behaviour: a review of current research on the privacy paradox phenomenon. *Computers & Security*, 64, 122–134.

Rogerson, S. (1988). The world of information technology. *Graduate Science and Engineer*, 9(6), 50–51.

Rogerson, S. (2011). Ethics and ICT. In: Galliers, R. & Currie, W. (eds.), *The Oxford Handbook on Management Information Systems: Critical Perspectives and New Directions*. Oxford University Press, pp. 601–622.

Rogerson, S. (2020). Digital outcasts & COVID19. *News & Blogs*. Emerald Publishing, 24 March. Available from https://www.emeraldpublishing.com/news-and-blogs/digital-outcasts-covid19/; https://www.emeraldgrouppublishing.com/topics/coronavirus/blog/digital-outcasts-covid19 (Accessed 20 December 2020).

Smuha, N. A. (2019). The EU approach to ethics guidelines for trustworthy artificial intelligence. *CRi-Computer Law Review International*, 20(4), 97–106.

Thomson, J. J. (1976). Killing, letting die, and the trolley problem. *The Monist*, 59(2), 204–217.

Van de Poel, I. & Royakkers, L. (2007). The ethical cycle. *Journal of Business Ethics*, 71(1), 1–13.

Wyatt, W. N. (2008). Being Aristotelian: using virtue ethics in an applied media ethics course. *Journal of Mass Media Ethics*, 23(4), 296–307.

# Index

Note: Page numbers in *italics* indicate figures, **bold** indicate tables.